Kate Binder

Sams **Teach Yourself**

Adobe®
Photoshop® Elements 6

in **24** Hours

800 East 96th Street, Indianapolis, Indiana, 46240 USA

Sams Teach Yourself Adobe® Photoshop® Elements 6 in 24 Hours

Copyright © 2008 by Pearson Education, Inc.

ISBN-13: 978-0-672-33017-9
ISBN-10: 0-672-33017-2

Library of Congress Cataloging-in-Publication Data

Binder, Kate.
  Sams teach yourself Adobe Photoshop Elements 6 in 24 hours / Kate Binder. – 1st ed.
     p. cm.
  Includes index.
  ISBN 978-0-672-33017-9 (pbk.)
  1. Adobe Photoshop elements. 2. Photography–Digital techniques. 3. Computer graphics.
I. Title. II. Title: Adobe Photoshop Elements 6 in 24 hours.
  TR267.5.A33B568 2008
  006.6–dc22

                                            2008017660

Printed in the United States of America
First Printing May 2008

Trademarks

Warning and Disclaimer

Bulk Sales

Sams Publishing offers excellent discounts on this book when ordered in quantity for bulk purchases or special sales. For more information, please contact

  U.S. Corporate and Government Sales

  1-800-382-3419

  corpsales@pearsontechgroup.com

For sales outside of the U.S., please contact

  International Sales

  international@pearson.com

Associate Publisher
Greg Wiegand

Acquisitions Editor
Laura Norman

Senior Development Editor
Laura Norman

Managing Editor
Patrick Kanouse

Project Editor
Mandie Frank

Copy Editor
Krista Hansing

Indexer
Publishing Works

Proofreader
Paula Lowell

Technical Editor
Lisa Sihvonen-Binder

Publishing Coordinator
Cindy Teeters

Designer
Gary Adair

Composition
Bronkella Publishing

This Book Is Safari Enabled

Safari BOOKS ONLINE ENABLED

The Safari® Enabled icon on the cover of your favorite technology book means the book is available through Safari Bookshelf. When you buy this book, you get free access to the online edition for 45 days.

Safari Bookshelf is an electronic reference library that lets you easily search thousands of technical books, find code samples, download chapters, and access technical information whenever and wherever you need it.

To gain 45-day Safari Enabled access to this book:

▶ Go to http://www.informit.com/onlineedition
▶ Complete the brief registration form
▶ Enter the coupon code EXQB-3GBQ-LFIT-73P5-79D6

If you have difficulty registering on Safari Bookshelf or accessing the online edition, please email customer-service@safaribooksonline.com.

Contents at a Glance

Part IV: Going Creative

Table of Contents

Part II: Simple Corrections

About the Author

Kate Binder has mastered Photoshop and several other graphics programs over the past 20 years, and is starting to feel quite old. She still enjoys tinkering with photos and does so at every opportunity. (It's much more entertaining than doing actual work.) When she can be found working, Kate is most likely to be doing magazine or book production, creating e-books for major publishers, or writing books like this one. Books Kate has written or co-written include *Easy Mac OS X Leopard* (Que, 2007, ISBN 9780789737717), *Sams Teach Yourself Adobe Photoshop CS3 in 24 Hours* (Sams, 2007, ISBN 9780672329357), *Easy Adobe Photoshop Elements 4* (Que, 2005, ISBN 9780789734679), *Get Creative!: The Digital Photo Idea Book* (McGraw-Hill, 2003, ISBN 9780072227215), *SVG for Designers* (McGraw-Hill, 2002, ISBN 9780072225297), *Microsoft Office v. X for Mac Inside Out* (Microsoft Press, 2002, ISBN 9780735616288), *The Complete Idiot's Guide to Mac OS X* (Alpha, 2001, ISBN 9780789725288), *Photoshop 6 Cookbook* (Silver Pixel Press, 2001, ISBN 9781883403836), *PhotoImpact Solutions* (Muska and Lipman Publishing, 2000, ISBN 9781929685127), and *Sams Teach Yourself QuarkXPress 4 in 14 Days* (Hayden Books, 1997, ISBN 9780756302771). Kate lives in an old house in New Hampshire with her husband, journalist Don Fluckinger, accompanied by assorted children, greyhounds, cats, and (she's pretty sure) a mouse under the dryer.

Dedication

For my mother, Barbara Hauck Binder, who was kind enough to share with me her patience, persistence, and logical mind, which have enabled me to do the work I love. Now if I could only convince her that playing around with Photoshop Elements qualifies as real work....

Acknowledgments

This book will always, in a way, belong to Carla Rose, who wrote the first edition six years ago. I also owe a great deal to Laura Norman and the rest of the crew at Sams; Lisa Sihvonen-Binder, my tech editor and the best possible sister-in-law; and Mark Dahm at Adobe for supplying review copies of the software. Then, of course, there are all the family members and friends who had to put up with me in my cranky book-writing mode once again. Thanks, everyone.

We Want to Hear from You

As the reader of this book, *you* are our most important critic and commentator. We value your opinion and want to know what we're doing right, what we could do better, what areas you'd like to see us publish in, and any other words of wisdom you're willing to pass our way.

You can email or write me directly to let me know what you did or didn't like about this book—as well as what we can do to make our books stronger.

Please note that I cannot help you with technical problems related to the topic of this book, and that due to the high volume of mail I receive, I might not be able to reply to every message.

When you write, please be sure to include this book's title and author as well as your name and phone or email address. I will carefully review your comments and share them with the author and editors who worked on the book.

Email: graphics@samspublishing.com

Mail: Greg Wiegand
            Associate Publisher
            Sams Publishing
            800 East 96th Street
            Indianapolis, IN 46240 USA

Reader Services

Visit our website and register this book at informit.com/register for convenient access to any updates, downloads, or errata that might be available for this book.

Introduction

I love Photoshop Elements, I really do. Now, I'm a graphics geek, so I'm a Photoshop user from way back—version 2. When I got my first good look at Photoshop Elements 1, I was thrilled that Adobe had managed to roll much of the power of Photoshop into such a simple, clean package. Now that we're up to version 6, I like the program even better.

Photoshop Elements is easy to use, but it still has a lot of great features brought over from Big Mama Photoshop, such as batch processing and my favorite Photoshop command, Shadow/Highlights. To sweeten the pot, there's a built-in photo catalog, called the Organizer, and easy ways to create fun projects using your photos, from hardbound books to slideshows that will really wow the boss or the grandparents.

You can get Photoshop Elements 6 for Mac OS X or for Windows, and it works almost identically on the two platforms. You'll find a few differences—for example, on the Mac, the Organizer is called Bridge—but for the most part, you can use either version with this book (which was written using the Windows version). If you are using a Mac, you'll need to translate keyboard shortcuts a bit; instead of using Ctrl, use the Command key, and instead of using Alt, use the Option key.

You've probably noticed that *Sams Teach Yourself Adobe Photoshop Elements 6 in 24 Hours* is divided into hours rather than chapters. Not surprisingly, there are 24 hours in the book. Don't view this as a challenge, however; I don't expect you to work through the book in 24 *consecutive* hours. Instead, complete each hour at your own pace. Feel free to skip around. If you're already familiar with Photoshop or with older versions of Photoshop Elements, don't skip the Workshop sections. I know they look like homework (and they are!), but I've tried to keep them fun, useful, and short—and even experienced users will find them valuable.

I've posted a bunch of the photos used in this book on the Sams website. You can find them by going to www.informit.com/title/0672330172. Now, you won't see all the book's photos in this downloadable collection; I've indicated in the text when a photo is included so that you can work along with me on the Try It Yourself sections. But the real point of all this is for you to learn to work with *your* photos, those special images of your family, the things you're interested in, the places you travel, and whatever else you snap pictures of. So jump on in using your own photos, and—whatever else you do—have fun!

PART I

Working with Elements

Welcome to Photoshop Elements

What You'll Learn in This Hour:

▶ How to use Photoshop Elements tool tips

▶ How Elements can walk you through projects step by step

▶ How to use Elements' built-in Help system

Okay, you have this digital camera, maybe a scanner, definitely a computer—now what? The answer to that question is an easy three words: Adobe Photoshop Elements. Using this one simple but incredibly powerful program, you can transfer pictures from your camera to your hard drive; control a scanner; organize your photos in a zillion different ways; clean up any messy bits they contain; crop, rotate, and resize them; adjust their lighting and color; and share them with the world online, as prints, or plastered on any number of cool gift items. Photoshop Elements gives you complete control over how your digital images look, without requiring you to become a photo editing expert to accomplish your goals. If your digital pictures are starting to pile up and you just don't know how to deal with them, I think you'll find that Photoshop Elements is exactly what you need.

If you hang around with graphics geeks, you've probably heard of Adobe Photoshop. This is the photo-editing program that has become such a standard that its name is now a verb: "Oh, that tree was messing up the image's composition, so I Photoshopped it out." Yes, *that* Photoshop. Now, Photoshop Elements is descended from Photoshop, with all the power that implies. If I had to guess, I'd say that probably 95% of the work done in Photoshop around the world every day could just as easily be done in Photoshop Elements; the Photoshop features that you *won't* find in Photoshop Elements are ones you're extremely unlikely to miss. Along with a good chunk of Photoshop's feature set,

Photoshop Elements has several features that Photoshop doesn't: a built-in image cataloger, auto-everything for days when you don't feel like doing the work yourself, and tons of templates for cool projects that you can make with your images. (And, of course, you don't need a graduate degree to use it.) For all this, you pay a fraction of the price of Photoshop: $99, as opposed to $649. Cool, huh? On top of that, every time Photoshop gets new features, some of them trickle down to Photoshop Elements, so it just keeps getting better. In fact, if you've used Photoshop Elements before, you'll be amazed at the new features you'll find in version 6.

But enough rhapsodizing about the wonders of Photoshop Elements. If you're reading this book, you've probably already decided that you want to learn how to use the program, so let's move on to some practical information. This hour starts you off with a few places to find help when you get stuck. What kind of help you need depends on what you're trying to accomplish.

Getting Help

Cropping photos? Adjusting lighting? Publishing web galleries? All of this might sound rather complicated, but there's no need to worry. Photoshop Elements can help you figure out what to do, whether you can tell a pixel from a pixie stick or not.

Tool Tips

If you know what you want to do, and you have a pretty good idea of how to accomplish it but you haven't used Photoshop Elements before, tool tips are for you. These look just like the little boxes that pop up over web links, but instead of telling you where a link goes, they tell you what you're looking at. If you place your cursor over a tool in the toolbox, the tool tip displays its name and its shortcut key. If you stop and hover over an image effect button, you'll see its name (see Figure 1.1).

Be sure to move your cursor around the whole screen; many more parts of the Photoshop Elements work area have tool tips than you might expect. Check palette tabs, buttons, pop-up menus, and anything else you're curious about.

If you don't like tool tips—they can be irritating if you don't need the information they supply—you can turn them off by choosing Edit, Preferences, General. Click the Show Tool Tips check box; click it again to turn tool tips back on.

In some cases, the name displayed in a tool tip is a link to the appropriate Photoshop Elements Help section. (We talk more about the built-in help shortly.) You'll recognize these because the text is blue instead of black. Just click the text of the ToolTip to learn more.

FIGURE 1.1
The tool tip shown here gives the name of the special effect I've just applied to this photo.

Guided Edit

When you know what you want to do, but you have no idea how to accomplish it in Photoshop Elements, turn to Guided Edit. This feature, which is new to version 6, presents you with step-by-step instructions and recommendations for a variety of standard editing tasks. The tasks in Guided Edit are divided into the following categories:

- ▶ **Basic Photo Edits**—Cropping, rotating, sharpening, and straightening photos

- ▶ **Lighting and Exposure**—Lightening and darkening photos and improving their contrast

- ▶ **Color Correction**—Making colors clearer, brighter, and more accurate

- ▶ **Guided Activities**—Fixing blotches or rips in a scanned image and performing a complete series of edits in a logical sequence to produce the best possible image

- ▶ **Photomerge**—Replacing part of a photo with the corresponding area in a similar photo to produce the best group photos

When you enter Guided Edit mode, the first thing you'll see is this list of tasks. Clicking one brings up instructions for completing it, with all the controls placed right there in the Guided Edit tab (see Figure 1.2). These are the same tool buttons you'll find in the toolbox, and the same sliders you'll find in a variety of dialog boxes if you're using Full Edit mode—but in Guided Edit mode, you don't have to go looking for them.

FIGURE 1.2
Guided Edit tells you how to accomplish your goal, but you still have to choose the settings yourself.

For each Guided Edit task, you can click Tell Me More below the instructions to view help information about the specific topic at hand.

Photoshop Elements Help

By now, you've probably noticed the Help menu at the top of the Photoshop Elements window. Not surprisingly, it provides access to Photoshop Elements' built-in Help. Choose Help, Photoshop Elements Help, or press F1 if you prefer keyboard shortcuts. The Help system displays in your web browser, offering you a choice of three ways to navigate: Find your topic in the table of contents, check the index for the keyword you have in mind, or search for relevant terms (see Figure 1.3).

The Help system provides what Adobe calls "abbreviated" information on just about every tool and feature of Photoshop Elements. If you want greater detail on any topic in Help, click This Page on the Web at the bottom of that topic's page to open the corresponding LiveDocs page on the Adobe website. These pages are constantly updated, so they provide the most complete and up-to-date help Adobe has to offer. And they look very much like the built-in help, so you might not even notice that you've switched to the Web. Of course, if you don't have an Internet connection when you click on a LiveDocs link, you won't go anywhere.

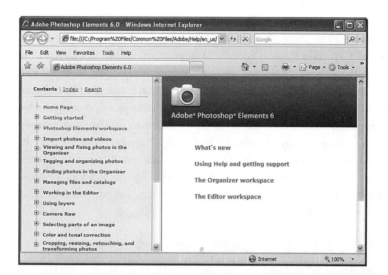

FIGURE 1.3
Click Contents to see this table of contents, click Index to view an alphabetical list of topics, and click Search to enter the words you want to find.

If you prefer to read useful information on paper, you can print any topic from the built-in help or LiveDocs using your web browser's Print command. Better yet, you can download the Photoshop Elements Help PDF (www.adobe.com/go/learn_pse_printpdf) and print the sections you want to read, or take the PDF with you on your PDA or e-book reader.

The Photoshop Help PDF is what we used to call a user manual, before software companies decided it was too expensive to bother printing them anymore. It's more than 450 pages of solid, comprehensive information, so although it's great to have around, you probably don't want to print the whole thing.

By the Way

Don't Know Much About History?

For those fortunate readers who have used Photoshop Elements before, some catching up might be in order. As I mentioned earlier, this program just keeps getting easier to use and more powerful with each upgrade. To give you an idea of where Photoshop Elements is as of version 6, here's a rundown on the new features and capabilities added in each new version of the program.

On the other hand, if you're new to Photoshop Elements and none of this means anything to you, that's fine—just skip ahead to the Summary at the end of this hour.

The first change experienced users will notice in version 6 is a new, streamlined, tab-based interface that draws a very sharp line between the Organizer and the Editor (see Figure 1.4). Then there's Guided Edit (mentioned earlier in this hour), which walks you through image-editing tasks without actually doing them for you. The Magic Selection tool has been renamed the Quick Selection tool, like its counterpart in Photoshop, and the Refine Edge dialog box enables you to modify the tool's selection parameters while keeping it active. Smart Albums, in the Organizer, update themselves automatically whenever a new image shows up that fits the criteria you've defined. You'll also find more Create options and a centralized Sharing center. And … but we should save some of the fun stuff for later hours. Don't worry, there's a lot more to learn about Photoshop Elements 6 as we travel through these 24 hours, and I think you're really going to enjoy the ride.

FIGURE 1.4
In Photoshop Elements 6, you choose the photo you want to edit in Organizer and then switch to the Editor to modify the image.

Summary

You learned about several ways—in addition to reading this book—to get help using Photoshop Elements. Tool tips and built-in help tell you most of what you want to know. If you have web access, you can also check out the great information on the Adobe website, in the form of both LiveDocs (expanded help) and a PDF version of a traditional user manual.

Q&A

Q. *All this talk about needing help is making me nervous. Isn't Photoshop Elements supposed to be easy to use?*

A. Don't worry—Photoshop Elements really *is* easy to use. You might not ever need to use any of the resources we've looked at in this hour, but wouldn't you rather know how to get to them if you ever *do* want them?

Q. *Can I find help in any other places?*

A. Oh, sure, especially on the Web. A couple of my favorite Photoshop Elements websites are Easy Elements (www.easyelements.com) and the About.com Photoshop Elements subsite (http://graphicssoft.about.com/od/pselements/). For print lovers, the *Adobe Photoshop Elements Techniques* newsletter comes out eight times a year and has tons of great tips, as well as a lot of extra content on the associated website (www.photoshopelementsuser.com).

Q. *What if I decide Photoshop Elements just doesn't have the power I really need?*

A. If and when you decide to make the move to the big leagues, you can upgrade from Photoshop Elements to Photoshop itself for about $100 less than it would cost to buy Photoshop outright. So you have nothing whatsoever to lose by starting with Elements and later moving on up.

Workshop

Quiz

1. Which Photoshop Elements feature is *not* found in Photoshop?

   A. CMYK color mode

   B. Color management

   C. Guided Edit

   D. The Quick Selection tool

2. Tool tips appear only when you place the mouse cursor over a tool in the tool-box.

   A. True

   B. False

Quiz Answers

1. C. You can think of Photoshop as the deep end of the swimming pool and Photoshop Elements as the warm, cozy Jacuzzi. Elements can walk you through tasks so you learn as you work, whereas Photoshop expects you to already know exactly what you're doing.

2. B. Tool tips pop up in all kinds of places throughout the Photoshop Elements interface, including palettes and the Options bar. You'll learn more about the Elements interface in the next hour.

Activity

Let's start things off easy. Choose Display, Date View to switch to viewing your photos in the framework of a calendar. Click the Month button at the bottom of the window, and then use the arrow buttons to move from month to month so you can check out the pictures on the calendar. Click a day to display its photo at the right side of the screen then use the arrows below the picture to see more photos from that day. Enter recurring events, such as birthdays and anniversaries, in the calendar by clicking the New Event button at the right edge of the window. You can even use this calendar as a journal by adding text notes to the days. Have fun!

HOUR 2

A Tour of the Desktop

What You'll Learn in This Hour:

▶ Take a tour of Photoshop Elements

▶ Learn about the toolbox and the tools it contains

▶ Learn how to switch among different work modes

▶ Find out where Elements keeps its program preferences and how to change them

One of the nicest things about a digital workspace is that nothing ever gets lost, torn, or messed up. Everything is right where you left it, ready to be used, instead of hiding under a pile of other stuff or missing because your neighbor borrowed it. Before you can use any of your nice, shiny digital tools, however, you have to learn your way around the workspace so you know where to find what you want. Photoshop Elements makes this job easier with its context-sensitive workspace. The visible tools and controls change depending on what you're doing, so you're never distracted by tools you don't need at the moment.

Using the Organizer and the Editor

You might be surprised to learn that Photoshop Elements is really two programs rolled into one package. Those two are the Organizer and the Editor, and each has its own functions. Which one you see depends on what you are doing at the time: whether you're in Organize, Fix, Create, or Share mode. You can always switch to another mode by clicking one of the colorful tabs in the top-right corner of the window.

Organize

The first thing you'll probably want to do with Photoshop Elements is add some pictures to it so you can start working—or playing, depending on how you look at things. You do this in the Organizer, which is like a very big, very smart photo album (see Figure 2.1).

FIGURE 2.1
In Photoshop Elements, you use the Organizer to locate, group, and organize your photos.

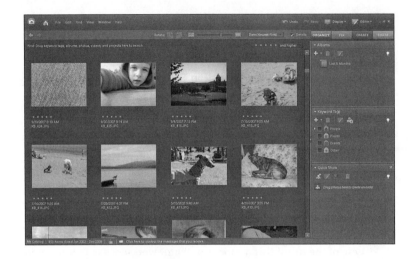

The Organizer is where you store your photos. Unlike a real-life photo album, it can tell when and where each photo was taken, find people's faces and ask you who they are, sort photos by how much you like them, remind you what camera you were using to take each picture, and much more. Within the Organizer, you can collect photos into albums that you can then convert to scrapbook pages, professionally bound books, or pretty much whatever else you can dream up. Each project begins in the Organizer because you have to start with a picture before you do anything in Photoshop Elements, and all your pictures live in the Organizer. Or, at least, that's the plan that Photoshop Elements has in mind.

Fix

When you want to modify a photo, click the photo's thumbnail in the Organizer and then click the Fix tab. Photoshop Elements asks you exactly how you want to fix the photo, using one of several autofixes right in the Organizer or using Quick Fix, Full Edit, or Guided Edit mode in the Editor. If you choose one of the latter three options, clicking that button starts up the Editor in a separate window (see Figure 2.2).

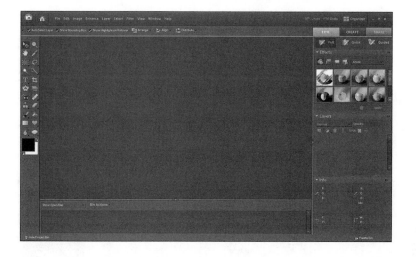

FIGURE 2.2
The Editor looks
very much like
Photoshop
itself.

Exactly what you see in the Editor window depends on which mode you're using. In Guided Edit mode, for example, the toolbox contains only two tools: the Zoom tool and the Hand tool, for zooming in and out and moving the image within the window. Full Edit mode, on the other hand, gives you access to a complete selection of 45 tools, from the Custom Shape tool to the Magnetic Lasso tool. Falling smack in the middle is Quick Fix mode, with just five tools; only one tool actually changes the image (the Red Eye Removal tool). We'll look at all the Editor's tools, modes, palettes, and menus later in this hour.

Create

When you have your pictures looking the way you want them—nice, sharp images with great color, and perfectly cropped—you'll want to *do* something with them. That's where the Create tab enters the picture (if you'll pardon the pun). This tab appears in both the Organizer and the Editor. If you click Create while in the Organizer, your new project starts with any selected photos; if you click Create in the Editor, the project begins with photos that are already open in the Editor.

You can print some of the Create projects yourself at home, such as CD and DVD labels; others are products that will be shipped to you from the company that prints them, such as photo books and calendars (see Figure 2.3). Still others are online galleries and slide shows; for the former, you need access to a website, but you don't need any special equipment or services to produce your own slide shows. Of course, if all you want to do is order drugstore-style prints of your photos, you can do that, too. These, along with the special products such as photo books, are offered by Kodak, but you can order them from within Photoshop Elements.

FIGURE 2.3
Display your
photos in style
by creating pro-
fessionally
designed and
printed photo
books.

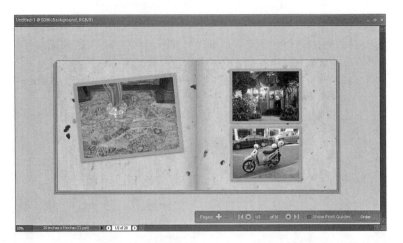

Having begun a project, you can modify it by adding or removing photos, rearrang-
ing photos on the pages, changing themes, adding text, and adding "extras" such
as clip art or page transitions from the Content, Favorites, and Effects palettes.

Share

Creating professional-looking projects with your photos is easy with Photoshop
Elements, but simply sharing your photos with friends and family is even easier. In
the Share tab (visible in both the Editor and the Organizer), you'll find lots of ways
to get your images in front of those who want to see them:

▶ Emailing photos, either as plain attachments or with fancy templates

▶ Burning them to a CD or DVD

▶ Creating a slide show from them

▶ Posting them on free photo-sharing websites

▶ Sending them to a digital picture frame

The Create options of Online Gallery and Order Prints are also available from the
Share tab. Each Share task has step-by-step instructions just like the Create projects
(see Figure 2.4).

FIGURE 2.4
You have a lot of options for sharing your photos, from plain prints to digital picture frames.

Finding Your Way Around the Organizer

Now that you understand the basic differences between the Organizer and the Editor, let's take a look around the Organizer's workspace to see exactly what the Organizer can do and how it does it.

The Menu Bar

To start, the menu bar at the top of the Organizer's window has six menus: File, Edit, Find, View, Window, and Help. You can do much of the work in Photoshop Elements by clicking buttons and dragging items around in palettes, but some of the more complicated functions take place in dialog boxes summoned by menu commands, such as printing and settings preferences. (For more on this topic, turn to "Setting Preferences," later in this hour.)

The first thing you see in the menu bar, at its left end, is a button that takes you to the Photoshop Elements Welcome screen at any time. If you ever get lost between the Editor and the Organizer or forget what mode you need to do what you have in mind, click this button—you'll start fresh with a clear view of your options (see Figure 2.5).

FIGURE 2.5
The Welcome
screen is a
good central
location to head
if you get lost.

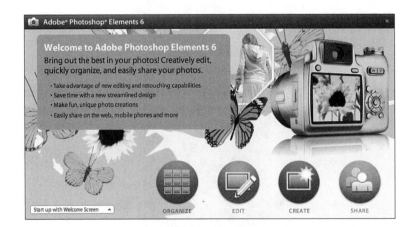

After the Welcome screen button, you'll see the following menus:

▶ **File**—Enables you to bring in images, create new images, manage the file that
contains your catalog information, copy and back up your files, rearrange
and manage the photos in your catalog, export images to different file formats, print, and quit Photoshop Elements.

▶ **Edit**—Contains commands for copying and pasting data, selecting images,
rotating thumbnails, editing image info, and setting preferences.

▶ **Find**—Offers different ways to search for images—by date, caption, filename,
history of changes, or visual similarity to another photo. This is also where the
Find Faces command is located.

▶ **View**—Determines what types of files are visible in the Photo Organizer and
what information is displayed about each one.

▶ **Window**—Displays and hides various panes, palettes, and windows.

▶ **Help**—Enables you to access the Help functions you learned about in Hour 1,
"Welcome to Photoshop Elements."

At the right side of the menu bar are a few other useful items, including the Undo
button, which allows you to quickly remove the effects of any edit you decide you
don't like, and the Redo button, which enables you to undo your Undos. A Display
menu enables you to set the way your photos are displayed in the Photo Browser
(the Organizer's main workspace). An Editor menu also lets you jump directly to Full
Edit, Quick Fix, or Guided Edit mode in the Editor.

Toolbar

Now let's go back to our exploration of the Organizer. Moving down from the menu bar, the next thing you'll see is the toolbar, which contains buttons for a few functions you'll need to access frequently (see Figure 2.6). Here's a list:

▶ **Back to Previous View and Forward to Next View**—As you change view options in the Photo Browser, Photoshop Elements keeps track of the various combinations of settings you use each time you start up the program, including the thumbnail size, whether you're displaying file details, and even if you're using Date View. You can click the Back button in the toolbar to go back to a view you used a few minutes ago, and then click Forward to go back to the view you were using before.

▶ **Rotate Left and Rotate Right**—Use these buttons to rotate image thumbnails in the Photo Browser. When you open a photo in the Editor, Photoshop Elements matches the rotation you choose in the Organizer.

▶ **Adjust Size of Thumbnail**—This slider is flanked by two buttons, Small Thumbnail Size and Single Photo View, that represent the smallest thumbnail view in the Photo Browser and the largest. Use the slider to choose a thumbnail size anywhere in between.

▶ **Date pop-up menu**—Choose Date (Newest First) or Date (oldest First) to determine whether the newest or the oldest pictures appear at the top of the Photo Browser.

▶ **Details**—Click this check box to show or hide image details, such as date and filename, in the Photo Browser. You can choose which details the View menu displays.

FIGURE 2.6
The most common functions in the Organizer, such as rotating thumbnails, can be performed using the toolbar.

Photo Browser

Here's where stuff really happens in the Organizer, because this is where the photos live. The main work area, called the Photo Browser, takes up most of the screen and displays all the photos in your catalog, along with the projects you've created with them (see Figure 2.7). You can set the size of the thumbnail images in the toolbar and check the Details box to show or hide image data. You can also assign your own star ratings and keyword tags (such as Kids or Holidays or Vacation) to images in the Photo Browser; if you do so, your ratings and tags become part of the Details information you can display.

FIGURE 2.7
Zoom out to see all your photos in the Photo Browser; zoom in to see just a few.

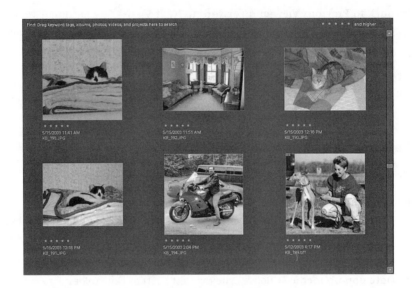

To select a photo to work on, just click it, or click and drag to select several photos next to each other. If you want to select multiple photos that *aren't* next to each other, Ctrl+click each one.

Did you Know?

Photoshop Elements offers you a lot of ways to filter your photos so that only certain images appear in the Photo Browser. One of the most intuitive is the Timeline. Choose Window, Timeline to display a bar graph of all your photos through the months or years at the top of the Photo Browser window. Click a bar in the graph to jump directly to the photos you took at that time; use the time range sliders at each end of the graph to set a beginning and ending time for the range of photos you want to display.

After you select your images, you can organize them by modifying their data, assigning ratings and tags, and grouping them into albums and stacks. If you're ready to work with the images, you can choose a Fix, Create, or Share option from the Task pane. (We'll talk about this area shortly.) First, let's look at the organizational magic of Photoshop Elements.

The point of being organized is to be able to find what you want, when you want it, with no digging or guessing required. That's the function of the Photo Browser's Find bar, where you can restrict the photos shown in the Photo Browser to ones that match your search criteria: star rating, keyword tags, or visual similarity. To get started, drag a keyword (to search for other images with that tag) or a photo (to search for similar images) to the Find bar at the top of the Photo Browser window. Click a star in the Find bar to find pictures that have at least that many stars, that many stars or fewer, or exactly that number of stars, depending on your choice from the pop-up menu next to the stars.

For all this to work, however, you have to assign keyword tags and star ratings. The latter provide a good way to mark the photos you think are really something special, the ones you'd consider sending in to a calendar contest or using on your holiday cards. Creating and assigning keyword tags is only a bit more complicated.

The Keyword Tags palette is located in the Task pane on the right side of your screen. If you don't see it, click the disclosure triangle next to Keyword Tags to open it (see Figure 2.8). You'll see a list of keyword categories (People, Places, Events, and Other) and subcategories (Family and Friends). The next step is to customize these by adding your own keyword tags within these categories, and perhaps even your own categories. We talk about how to do that in Hour 5, "Organizing Your Photos."

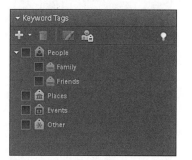

FIGURE 2.8
The more you use the Keyword Tags palette, the better organized your photos will be.

Task Pane

The area on the right side of the screen below the Organize, Fix, Create, and Share tabs is called the Task pane. Its contents vary depending on which tab you select. When you click Create or Share, the Task pane lists the projects you can do in each of those categories, such as Online Gallery, Photo Collage, or Order Prints. If you click the Fix tab, the Task pane lists several autofixes and each of the three edit modes: Full Edit, Quick Fix, and Guided Edit. At the bottom of the tab, you'll see a More Options pop-up menu that contains rarely used options for each of these three tabs, such as Edit with External Editor in the Fix tab.

An external editor is a program other than Photoshop Elements. If you prefer, you can use Photoshop Elements to do your photo organizing and minor edits, and make more complex edits in another program, such as Photoshop or PhotoImpact. You can choose the program you want to use in Photoshop Elements preferences. Then select an image and choose Edit with External Editor to open the image in the other program.

In Organize mode, the Task pane shows the Albums, Keyword Tags, and Quick Share palettes (see Figure 2.9). We've already looked at the Keyword Tags palette, so let's examine the other two now.

FIGURE 2.9
Most of the time, you'll want these three palettes visible in the Organizer. If you need more space for photos, you can drag the left side of the Task pane to the right to hide the palettes.

At the bottom of the Task pane is the Quick Share palette. This is a handy place to store information about people to whom you frequently have photos shipped. When the Quick Share palette contains the right names, you can order photos to be mailed to them with just a few clicks, starting by dragging the selected photos from the Photo Browser onto the recipient's name in the palette.

The Albums palette can contain collections of photos called albums. For example, you might create an album of the pictures from your grandma's birthday. This makes it easy to find those photos when you want to work with them or just look at them. You can also create smart albums that update their contents automatically based on the criteria you set. You'll set up a couple of albums in Hour 5.

Status Bar

This bar at the bottom of the window displays the number of selected photos or projects and the total number of items in the Browser view, as currently filtered. You'll also see the date range that those items encompass. If you agreed during program setup to receive messages about new services you can access via Photoshop Elements, this is where you'll find them. A mailbox icon displays a red flag when you have new messages to read.

Finding Your Way Around the Editor

Now that you know the Organizer inside out and backward (right?), it's time to take a look at what you'll find in the Editor. Its interface looks a lot like the Organizer's, but some of the same areas have different functions—for example, the Organizer's Task pane turns into the Palette Bin in the Editor. We start with a careful look at the Editor's Full Edit mode (see Figure 2.10) and then point out the differences between that and the Quick Fix and Guided Edit modes, which have fewer controls.

FIGURE 2.10
Full Edit mode offers myriad options for editing photos. With this image, my best bet is probably to start by cropping myself out.

The Menu Bar

When you first glance at the menu bar in the Editor, you'll see most of the familiar menus from the Organizer. But don't get too complacent; they have some different commands when you're working in the Editor. Here's a rundown of the Editor's menus:

▶ **File**—These commands enable you to create new image files; open, close, and save existing ones; import and export files in various formats; and print your work. You'll also see a Process Multiple Files command that enables you to rename, resize, and apply quick fixes to a whole batch of images at once.

▶ **Edit**—The first several commands here are pretty standard: Undo and Redo, Copy and Paste, and so on. You'll also find commands for applying color fills and borders to selected areas within an image, for making custom paintbrush tips, and for setting preferences.

▶ **Image**—Here's where you go to rotate, transform, crop, and resize photos, as well as change their color mode or delete their backgrounds using the Magic Extractor. Divide Scanned Photos enables you to scan multiple photos at one time and then break them up into separate image files.

▶ **Enhance**—Want to fix your photo's color, brightness, or sharpness? Here's where you'll find the commands to let you do all that.

▶ **Layer**—Using layers, you can stack picture elements on top of each other to form more complex (but easily editable) images. These commands enable you to create, delete, and modify layers; apply decorative styles to them; and rearrange them with respect to each other.

▶ **Select**—By selecting part of an image before you begin work, you restrict your edits to that area, leaving the rest of the image unchanged. With the Select commands, you can make hard- or soft-edged selections, combine selections in different ways, and save selections for future use.

▶ **Filter**—Want to make your picture look like a watercolor or oil painting? How about a mosaic or a patchwork quilt? All of Photoshop's image filters—dozens of them—are present in Photoshop Elements. Go crazy!

▶ **View**—These commands let you show nonprinting guides, rulers, and a non-printing alignment grid, as well as change the size of the image on your screen (not the photo's actual size).

▶ **Window**—In Full Edit mode, you can end up using a *lot* of windows and palettes. Use the Window commands to show and hide windows as you work, keeping your workspace as uncluttered as possible.

▶ **Help**—You'll find only one command in the Editor's Help menu that's not in the Organizer's Help menu: About Plug-In. This menu choice shows you copyright info on the plug-in modules Photoshop Elements uses, most of which provide the Filter commands.

You'll encounter the commands in these menus throughout the book, so don't feel that you need to memorize or understand them all at this point.

Options Bar

Instead of a toolbar, the Editor has the Options bar. Its primary function is to control settings for the tools you'll use when working in the Editor. Its buttons and menus change depending on the active tool. For example, when you're using one of the Type tools, the Options bar contains font, size, style, and alignment controls, among others. If you switch to the Eyedropper tool (with which you can "pick up" a color from anywhere in an image), the only thing you'll see on the Options bar is a pop-up menu that determines the size of the area the Eyedropper samples to choose the new color (see Figure 2.11).

FIGURE 2.11
The Options bar is vital to using the Text tool and less so to using the Eyedropper tool.

Toolbox

Here's something you won't see in the Organizer: The toolbox contains all the tools of the digital artist's trade, from the paintbrush to various tools that enable you to work on only a specified part of an image. The toolbox is roughly divided into sections of similar tools (see Figure 2.12).

Some toolbox buttons are marked with a tiny triangle in the lower-right corner; these function as pop-up menus holding yet more tools. Behind the Lasso tool, for instance, are the Magnetic Lasso tool and the Polygonal Lasso tool. To switch to a visible tool, just click its toolbox button; if you want to switch to a hidden tool, right-click the button where it's hiding and choose your tool from the pop-up menu.

FIGURE 2.12
Horizontal bars
in the toolbox
group together
related tools.

You'll learn how to use all the Photoshop Elements tools as you work through this book. For now, let's take a quick look at each tool group, just so you have a sense of what's available to you.

Navigation and Measuring Tools

These tools enable you to move around your image so that you can view all of it at once or concentrate on just the tiny details. Click and drag with the Hand tool to slide the image around within its window, and click with the Zoom tool to increase your viewing percentage. Alt+click with the Zoom tool to decrease the viewing percentage—in other words, make the image smaller within its window. Or click and drag to zoom in on the selected area (see Figure 12.13).

FIGURE 2.13
Zooming in on
the selected
area in the left
photo gives you
the close-up
view on the
right.

The Move tool is for dragging parts of the image to a new location; it works on objects located on layers, or active selections. (You'll learn more about making selections in the next section.) Finally, you can click with the Eyedropper tool to "pick up" the color at the location of your click and make it the Foreground color, which is applied to shapes and type that you create.

Selection Tools

When you paint things in the real world, you mask off stuff you don't want to paint, right? That's the principle behind Photoshop Elements selections. Using these tools, you can mask off everything in an image that you don't want to modify, and then you paint, adjust, and apply all kinds of filters without worrying about your edits "spilling over" into other parts of the image. And believe me, making selections is a lot easier—and more effective—than messing around with masking tape.

The simplest way to create a selection is to choose either the Rectangular Marquee tool or the Elliptical Marquee tool, and then click and drag in your photo to select a rectangular or elliptical (surprise!) area. Press Shift as you drag to make your selection square or circular. When you release the mouse button, the selection is created; now you can click and drag it to a new location, if you want.

If you prefer to freehand your selections, switch to the Lasso tool. Just click in the image and drag the mouse to draw a selection around the area you want to edit. The Lasso tool is backed up by the hidden Magnetic Lasso and Polygonal Lasso tools, which offer variations on its function. The Magnetic Lasso tool detects object edges within your image and tries to "stick" to them as you draw your selection. The Polygonal Lasso tool enables you to draw a selection by clicking at the corners; Photoshop Elements fills in straight lines between your clicks to form the selection.

Now, here's where that Photoshop Elements magic really starts to show up. If you click in an image with the Magic Wand tool, everything that touches the place you clicked and is a similar color gets added to your selection (see Figure 2.14).

The two remaining selection tools are the Quick Selection Brush tool and the Selection Brush tool. With the latter, you "paint" over the area you want to select. The Quick Selection Brush tool, on the other hand, is a combination of the Selection Brush and the Magic Wand. You can select an object by painting quickly over it—there's no need to worry about precision because Photoshop Elements analyzes the parts of the image under your cursor and uses its magic to select all the matching adjacent area (see Figure 2.15).

FIGURE 2.14
A single click in the middle of the field selects the whole thing. Now you're ready to make it purple (or not).

FIGURE 2.15
Using the Quick Selection Brush to paint squiggles over the bleachers results in the selection of the entire stadium, minus the sky and field.

Type Tools

With the Horizontal and Vertical Type tools, you create type—big surprise there, hmm? The Type Mask tools are a bit different; you use them to create type-shaped selections that you can then use in a number of ways. As with the Horizontal Type tool, the Horizontal Type Mask tool creates type selections that run from left to right. The Vertical Type Mask tool creates vertical type selections. One of the many fun things you can do with the Type Mask tools is fill type with a photo (see Figure 2.16).

FIGURE 2.16
I used the Type Mask tool to create a selection in the shape of the word *Evergreen*; then I cut that shape out of my picture to produce evergreen-filled type.

Crop Tools

The Crop tool enables you to trim an image to its best advantage. Using it, you can crop out peripheral objects that distract from the photo's subject, and you can change the image's proportions.

Similarly, the Cookie Cutter tool enables you to delete all of a photo that falls outside the bounds you set, but there are two huge differences. First, the Cookie Cutter tool comes in a variety of shapes other than rectangular; an Options bar menu enables you to choose the one you want. Second, instead of cutting off the sides of the image, it simply erases the image outside the cookie cutter area (see Figure 2.17).

FIGURE 2.17
Clicking the check mark deletes everything outside the tree shape, without changing the size of the image.

The final Crop tool is actually the Straighten tool, which you can use to straighten crooked photos.

Retouching Tools

A lot of tools have been thrown into this section, and the only attribute they have in common is that they're all used to modify an image rather than create new art. You can apply these tools to your pictures to hide what you don't want to show and emphasize what you do want to show. Here's a look at the tools you'll find in the group:

▶ The Red Eye Removal tool, the Spot Healing Brush, and the Healing Brush handle what I think of as cosmetic retouching. It's pretty obvious what the Red Eye Removal tool does. The Healing Brushes are for fixing small blemishes, such as a zit on someone's face or a crack in the wall behind your subject.

▶ The Clone Stamp is often referred to as the rubber stamp tool because that's what its icon looks like. Using this tool, you can paint an exact copy of part of an image somewhere else in the image. For example, you might clone bits of sidewalk and street to cover up a car that's sitting in the middle of your cityscape masterpiece. Its sibling, the Pattern Stamp tool, paints with a pattern (such as wood grain, paper, or flowers) instead of a color.

▶ Photoshop Elements offers you a choice of three different erasers, starting with the plain old Eraser, which just erases whatever you drag it over. The Background Eraser detects the edges of objects and erases only the parts of the image outside those objects. The Magic Eraser erases only the colors you tell it to erase.

▶ The Blur, Sharpen, and Smudge tools do exactly what their names indicate. You can use them to de-emphasize a background, direct attention to a fore-ground element, and smooth edges of pasted-in or painted images areas.

▶ Finally, three traditional photography tools close out this group: the Sponge, Dodge, and Burn tools. You can paint over image areas with the Sponge to remove or intensify color. The Dodge and Burn tools enable you to brighten and darken specific spots within an image; for example, you might use the Dodge tool to lighten the shadow falling across a person's face in a photo.

Painting and Drawing Tools

It's time for your inner artist to shine using tools that simulate several different tra-ditional artist's tools. The Brush is a paintbrush, with a selection of narrow and wide, soft and hard brush tips. The Pencil draws a hard, fine line. For special effects, try the Impressionist Brush, which adds soft, blurry Impressionist brushstrokes to an existing image (see Figure 2.18); or the Color Replacement Brush, which enables you to paint a blue sky pink without messing up the white clouds.

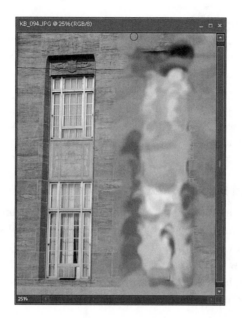

FIGURE 2.18
I went to town with the Impressionist Brush on the right window.

The Paint Bucket and Gradient tools work best in conjunction with selections; select the area you want to color, choose a Foreground color, and click the Paint Bucket in the selected area to fill the selection with color. Or, click and drag in the selected area with the Gradient tool to fill the selection with multiple colors shading into each other. You can control the colors used for gradients via menus on the Options bar, and you can save your favorite settings for future use.

Shape Tools

Can't draw a straight line? No problem. When you want to draw in Photoshop Elements, you can use the following Shape tools to make perfectly symmetrical shapes:

- ▶ Rectangle
- ▶ Rounded Rectangle
- ▶ Ellipse
- ▶ Polygon
- ▶ Line
- ▶ Custom Shape

The Custom Shape tool enables you to choose from a wide (*really* wide) variety of shapes, such as paw prints, musical notes, speech balloons, and much more, all accessible via a menu in the Options bar. And with the Shape Selection tool, you can adjust a shape's size and proportions after you've created it.

Did you Know?

> Press Shift as you draw with the Rectangle, Rounded Rectangle, Ellipse, and Polygon tools to make your shapes the same width and height—for example, square, circular, or, in the case of polygons, completely symmetrical.

Foreground and Background Swatches

The two colored squares at the bottom of the toolbox are the Foreground and Background color swatches; they let you know what color you'll see if you paint or erase, respectively, in an image. You can swap the two colors by clicking the double-headed curved arrow in the upper-right corner of the swatches. You can set them to the default colors of black foreground, white background by clicking the mini-swatch in the lower-left corner of the swatches.

▼   **Try It Yourself**

Creating a New Image

When you begin to explore the Photoshop Elements toolbox, you'll want a "scratch pad" to try out all the tools. Take a minute to create an empty image that you can draw all over so you can really give the tools a workout.

1. Choose File, New, Blank File, or press Ctrl+N.

2. From the Preset pop-up menu, choose Default Photoshop Elements Size (see Figure 2.19).

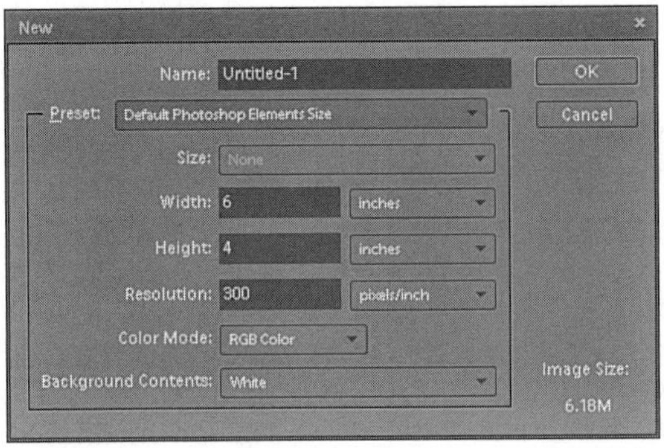

FIGURE 2.19
In the New dialog box, you choose a document size, color mode, resolution, and background color.

![New dialog box. Name: Untitled-1. Preset: Default Photoshop Elements Size. Size: None. Width: 6 inches. Height: 4 inches. Resolution: 300 pixels/inch. Color Mode: RGB Color. Background Contents: White. Image Size: 6.18M. OK and Cancel buttons.]

▼

3. From the Background Contents menu, choose White.

4. Click OK or press Enter to create the new, blank image file.

Workspace

As with the empty file you just created, each image or project has its own window that sits in the same area occupied by the Photo Browser in the Organizer. Click and drag a window's title bar to move it out of the way, or drag a window into the Image Bin at the bottom of your screen to hide it until you're ready to work with it.

Palette Bin

Found in the same location as the Organizer's Task pane, at the right edge of the screen, the Palette Bin is a handy place to store things such as the Effects palette and the Color Swatches palette. You can drag any palette into or out of the Palette Bin, and you can hide the bin by clicking the Palette Bin button at the bottom of the bin. Especially if you use Full Edit mode much, you'll find this innovation a vital way to regain the screen area that palettes tend to gobble up as they proliferate.

Status Bar

Unlike the status bar in the Organizer, the Editor's status bar appears at the bottom of each image window currently displayed in the Editor's work area and provides information about just that image. You'll always see the current magnification level—how large or small the image is onscreen in relation to its actual size—and you can choose what other information you want to see by clicking the triangle next to the zoom level. Here are your choices:

- ▶ **Document Sizes**—The size range of the current file, depending on whether you save it with or without its layers

- ▶ **Document Profile**—The selected color-management profile

- ▶ **Document Dimensions**—The physical size of the image

- ▶ **Scratch Sizes**—The amount of disk space Photoshop Elements is using to temporarily store information as it's running

- ▶ **Efficiency**—The percentage of time that Photoshop Elements is spending actually working on your image, as opposed to writing or reading image data from the disk

▶ **Timing**—How long it took for Photoshop Elements to accomplish the last task

▶ **Current Tool**—The name of the active tool

Most of the time, I leave my status bar set to display either Document Sizes or Document Dimensions. Settings such as Timing are interesting, but they're not particularly useful most of the time.

Image Bin

At the bottom of the screen, where you'd find the status bar in the Organizer, you'll see the Project Bin, where you'll see a thumbnail of each image currently open in the Editor. You can switch from one image to another by clicking thumbnails in the Project Bin. If you begin a Create project from the Editor that allows multiple images, such as a photo book, you can choose from the photos in the Image Bin.

What Changes in Quick Fix and Guided Edit Modes

The first thing you're likely to notice when switching from Full Edit mode to Quick Fix mode is that most of the tools go away. In Quick Fix mode (see Figure 2.20), you have access to only the Zoom, Hand, Quick Selection Brush, Crop, and Red Eye Removal tools. If you switch to Guided Edit mode, you're left with only the Zoom and Hand tools. However, remember that Guided Edit mode presents you with the tools you need over in the Task pane, so you don't need to look for them in the toolbox. For the most part, Options bar settings are the same throughout each editing mode.

The second big change you'll notice when moving from Full Edit mode to Quick Fix or Guided Edit mode (see Figure 2.21) is that the palettes in the Palette Bin disappear, replaced by Quick Fixes or Guided Edit topics. Finally, you'll notice that Quick Fix mode includes controls above the Image Bin for your preview; you can see a "before" version of each photo, an "after" version, or both.

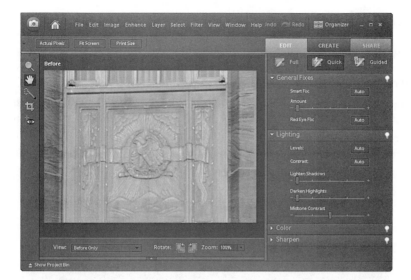

FIGURE 2.20
Quick Fix mode doesn't offer you much in the way of tools because you don't need them to make quick fixes.

FIGURE 2.21
In Guided Edit mode, the tools and dialog boxes you need appear in the Task pane so you don't need to search the toolbox and menus for them.

Setting Preferences

Whether you're using the Organizer or the Editor, and no matter which editing mode you're in, you open the Preferences dialog box (see Figure 2.22) by choosing Edit, Preferences, General, or by pressing Ctrl+K. Here you'll find several preference panes that enable you to control almost every aspect of how Photoshop Elements operates. We look at preferences that you need to change from their default settings as we progress through the book. For now, it's enough to know how to get to the Preferences dialog box. You might want to spend a few minutes poking around in it without changing settings, just to see what's there.

FIGURE 2.22
You might go your entire life without ever changing any Photoshop Elements preferences, but it's a good idea to check out your options.

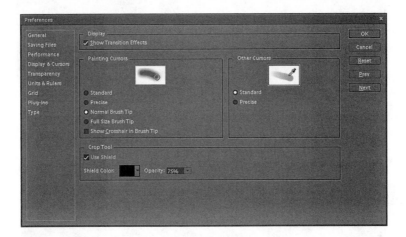

Summary

In this hour, we took a look at the different functions of the Photoshop Elements Organizer and Editor. We examined their respective interfaces, menus, and palettes; took a look at the Options bar; and learned the basics of the Editor's toolbox. We also talked about the four basic task types that you perform in Photoshop Elements (Organize, Fix, Create, and Share), as well as the three different editing modes (Full Edit, Quick Fix, and Guided Edit). Finally, we opened the Preferences dialog box and poked around a bit there. In the next hour, we move on to creating and saving new image files in a variety of formats.

Q&A

Q. *What should I do if I get confused about what part of the program I'm in and want to start fresh?*

A. Click the little house in the upper-left corner of the screen, next to the Photoshop Elements camera icon. This displays the Welcome screen, where you can pick a basic task such as Share and be taken to the right place for what you want to do.

Q. *Is it possible to do any editing tasks in the Organizer?*

A. Sure. If you're not into messing around with photos, you can spend all your time in the Organizer, making use of the autofixes you'll find on the Fix tab of the Task pane. With these, you can adjust color, brightness, contrast, and sharpness, as well as crop pictures and fix red eye.

Workshop

Before moving on to the next hour, go through the quiz and activities to be sure you're clear on everything we've done in this hour.

Quiz

1. The Clone Stamp is a _____ tool.

    A. Selection

    B. Retouching

    C. Filter

    D. Painting

2. The large colored squares at the bottom of the toolbox show the _____ colors.

    A. Most efficient

    B. Complementary and coordinating

    C. Default

    D. Foreground and background

3. What information *can't* you display in the status bar while working in the Editor?

    A. Efficiency

    B. Document dimensions

    C. Carbon footprint

    D. Current tool

Quiz Answers

1. B. Because it works with existing image data, instead of adding new data to a picture, the Clone Stamp is considered a Retouching tool instead of a Painting tool.

2. D. However, the default colors of black and white are also shown below and to the left of the Foreground and Background color swatches.

3. C. But wouldn't it be cool?

Activities

1. Find the dates of the oldest and newest pictures in your photo catalog. Then choose Window, Timeline, and locate the time period during which you've taken the most photos in the last year.

2. Create a new, empty image file and go to town! Using all your artistic talents, make a picture that includes type, at least one shape, and a painted border.

HOUR 3

Creating and Saving Image Files

What You'll Learn in This Hour:

▶ How to open existing images and create new ones
▶ How to save image files in different formats
▶ Ways to save images that are optimized for the World Wide Web
▶ How to go back and undo your mistakes

Any time you want to create artwork from scratch—a new logo for your business, signs for your garage sale, or whatever—you need to create a new file in which to save that artwork. In the last hour, you created an empty file so that you could experiment with the Editor's tools. Now we'll take you back to that process and examine your options more closely. We'll also look at formats in which you might want to save files if you're planning to use them outside of Photoshop Elements, such as on a website or in the newspaper.

Creating a New Image File

When you make a new file in which to create your artwork, you have to make a few choices about the image's size, colors, and ultimate purpose. It's sort of like choosing the right paper or canvas for a real-world art project. If you want to paint a tiny portrait to put in a locket, you don't start with a sheet of poster board. The best way to understand your choices is to work through them one by one.

▼   **Try it Yourself**

Create a New Image File from Scratch

Feeling a touch of déjà vu? Yes, you have done this before, but this time I'm not driving—you are. First, think of a project you want to do, such as creating a new logo or designing a greeting card. When you have that firmly in mind, give these steps a try:

1. In the Editor's Full Edit mode, choose File, New, Blank File (see Figure 3.1).

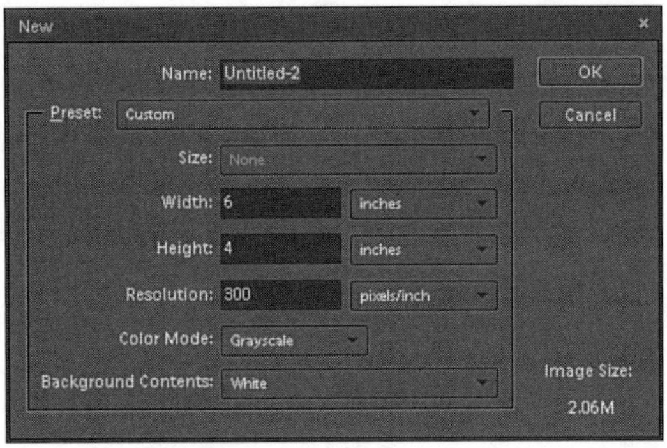

FIGURE 3.1
You can fill out the settings in the New dialog box by using the presets or by making your own choices.

New

Name: Untitled-2   OK

Preset: Custom   Cancel

Size: None

Width: 6   inches

Height: 4   inches

Resolution: 300   pixels/inch

Color Mode: Grayscale

Background Contents: White

Image Size:
2.06M

2. This time, give the file a name. This name automatically is entered in the Save As dialog box the first time you use the Save feature.

3. From the Preset pop-up menu, choose Custom. Now choose a unit of measurement for the Width and Height fields, and enter the values you want to use. For a greeting card, you'll probably want to use 8.5"×11" so you'll be able to print your card correctly on letter-size paper. If you're working on a logo or image that will end up being part of other projects, you might not be able to predict the final size you'll need. In this case, larger is better—you don't want to risk making the image jagged or blurry by having to enlarge it.

By the
Way

> Remember, the Width and Height values you enter in the New dialog determine the size of the canvas in your new image file. You can always create artwork that doesn't fill the entire canvas, and you can also reduce or enlarge the canvas as you work.

4. Enter a value in the Resolution field. For images that will be shown only onscreen, use 72 pixels per inch (ppi). For images that will be printed, start with 300ppi. Then check the Image Size in the lower-right corner of the New

▼

dialog; does it look manageable, or is it in the hundreds of megabytes? If the image size is getting out of hand, lower the resolution until the size is within a more reasonable range.

5. Choose an option from the Color Mode menu: Bitmap, Grayscale, or RGB Color. Use Bitmap only if you don't want any shades of gray in your image; for what we normally think of as "black and white" artwork, you want Grayscale (see Figure 3.2).

FIGURE 3.2
The left half of this photo shows what you get if you use only black and white; the right half is a grayscale image.

6. From the Background Contents menu, choose White, Background Color, or Transparent. You can see the results of the Background Color option by looking at the color swatches in the toolbox. If you think you'll want to use layers (layers enable you to rearrange overlapping artwork), choose Transparent. This starts your file with a transparent layer, called Layer 1, instead of an opaque background.

To learn more about creating layered images, turn to Hour 7, "Making Selections and Using Layers."

By the Way

7. Click OK or press Enter to create the new, blank image file.

Using Document Presets

Now that you've set up a document with custom settings, let's look at the built-in presets so you'll know when using one of them is appropriate. Here's a list of what you get:

▶ The first section in the Presets menu includes choices for the Clipboard, which sets the document size and color mode to match whatever image you have on the Clipboard, assuming you've just copied an image; and Default Photoshop Size, which is 6"×4", 300ppi, and RGB Color. The latter is a reasonable group of settings for messing around when you don't have a particular image size or resolution in mind.

▶ U.S. Paper includes standard paper sizes in the United States; International Paper has the equivalent paper sizes used in other countries. Photo presets encompass standard photo print sizes, such as 5"×7". All these presets set the Resolution to 300ppi and the Color Mode to RGB Color.

▶ Finally, the menu contains groups of presets for web images (primarily common monitor sizes); screen sizes for mobile devices, including cell phones; and standard TV screen sizes, both international and U.S., for regular and HD televisions. These presets are all measured in pixels and use 72ppi for their resolution, and they're all RGB Color.

As you can see, these preset combinations of settings are useful for many kinds of projects—but not all. You need to know how to choose your own custom settings when the presets don't fit the situation.

Opening an Existing File

Most of the time, you'll work with pictures that are stored in the Organizer. Sometimes, however, you'll need to open an image that's not in the Organizer—for instance, when you're working with a photo CD that someone else has given you.

As you know, you can add files to the Organizer by choosing File, Get Photos and Videos, From Files and Folders (or pressing Ctrl+Shift+G). If you just want to open a file to work on it, however, and you're not interested in adding it to your catalog, switch to the Editor and choose File, Open (or press Ctrl+O).

In the Open dialog (see Figure 3.3), first choose Thumbnails from the View menu so you can see the pictures in each folder. Then navigate to the disk or folder where your photo is stored and double-click it to open it.

FIGURE 3.3
The Open dialog's View menu offers you several ways to look at the files on a disk.

Photoshop Elements can open files saved in more than a dozen formats. Some of these you'll see often; others you'll probably never encounter. We'll go over the formats Photoshop Elements can use later in this hour when we look at how to save files.

> You can use the Open dialog's Files of Type pop-up menu to filter the files displayed in the Open dialog by format. This way, when you're looking for, say, a JPEG file, you don't have to sort through piles of TIFF and PCX files to find it. The menu lists all the formats you've just read about; just choose the one you want, and files in any other format magically disappear from the list. To remove the filter and again see the entire list, choose Files of Type, All Formats.

Did you Know?

You can open a file from Photoshop Elements in two other ways. The last several files you've opened are easily accessible by choosing File, Open Recently Edited File and then picking the file you want.

Of course, you can also open images in Photoshop Elements by double-clicking their icons in Windows—but for that to work, you must have the appropriate file types associated with Photoshop Elements instead of with another program. In Windows, this is easy to accomplish. First, find a file of the type you want to associate with Photoshop Elements (such as JPEG or TIFF). Right-click the file and choose Open

With, Choose Program from the contextual menu. In the Open With dialog (see Figure 3.4), first choose Adobe Photoshop Elements 6.0 (Editor), and then check the box below the list marked Always Use the Selected Program to Open This Kind of File. Click OK, and you're done—from now on, you can open this file type in Photoshop Elements with a simple double-click on the file.

FIGURE 3.4
You can choose a program to open the file this time or every time.

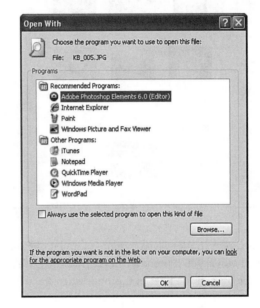

By the Way

Mac users must follow a slightly different procedure to change file associations. If you need to brush up on this or other Mac OS niceties, check out *Easy Mac OS X Leopard* (Que, 2007). *Full disclosure:* I wrote it, so I know the instructions work.

If you're opening a file to combine it with another file that you're already working on, you'll be pleased to know that there's an easy way to do just this. Choose File, Place; locate the file you want to open; and double-click it. This command inserts the new file into the existing image (on a new layer so that it doesn't interfere with anything you've already done) and puts it in Transform mode so that you can resize and position it to your liking (see Figure 3.5). When you get the new picture where you want it, just press Enter or click the check mark at the bottom-right corner of the image, and you're all set.

KB_055.JPG @ 33.3%(KB_053, RGB/8)

33.33%   2048 pixels x 1536 pixels (72 ppi)

FIGURE 3.5
You have all the time in the world to size and position a placed file before finalizing it by clicking the check mark.

Adjusting Resolution

Ah, pixels! These little beasties make up every single image you work with in Photoshop Elements, so it's important to understand what they are and how many of them you need to make a good-looking picture.

Let's start with what they are. The word *pixel* comes from the term "picture element." Pixels are, in fact, the building blocks of an image, like the tiles that make up a mosaic. Each one is a square area filled with a single color and laid out on a grid.

Video displays (in other words, computer monitors and TVs) also use pixels, but, in those cases, the term refers to a physical part of the display. To see your display's pixels, lean in close to the screen until you can see the squares. You might need a magnifying glass to see them on a computer, but they're much easier to spot on the screen of your cell phone or PDA.

At any rate, when you display one image pixel on one monitor pixel (also known as a zoom level of 100%), you won't see the individual pixels that make up the picture. But if you keep zooming in (see Figure 3.6), they become apparent. You'll see that all the curves and color gradations in your picture are actually illusory because the entire thing is really made up of a grid of colored squares. The more pixels you're working with to create the image, the more detailed it can be and the larger you can print or display it without noticing the individual pixels.

FIGURE 3.6
The window on the right shows the individual pixels that make up the blue sticky note.

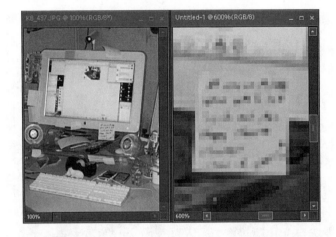

To get your head around this, think about the mosaic I mentioned a little bit ago. If you have only, say, nine tiles that you have to arrange on a 3×3 grid, you're not going to be able to create a very detailed picture. But if you use more tiles, you can construct a big, complex image with lots of details.

The same thing goes for pixels, with an added twist. A computer screen has 72 pixels per inch, for a total of 5,184 pixels in a square inch. However, photo printers can produce many, many more pixels per inch—ranging from 300ppi to 1200ppi, or even more. To produce a good printout that doesn't show the individual pixels, your image needs to be at least 300ppi. You can accomplish this in two ways.

First, you can resize the image without changing any of the pixels. For example, a 2"-square onscreen image (at 72ppi), when switched to 300ppi, will be less than half an inch square. Conversely, a 3"×5" photo print, scanned at 300ppi, will be 12.5" by almost 21" when viewed onscreen at 100%.

> To see how big an image will be when printed at its current resolution, choose View, Print Size.

Your second choice is to use a technique called *resampling*. This is what happens when you actually change the number of pixels in an image, whether downward or upward. Photoshop Elements has to create a new grid of pixels, each with its assigned color, that will produce an image that looks the same as the original—and that requires the program to guess what color some of those new pixels should be. Because of this, you should always avoid resampling, if possible. That said, it's better to decrease an image's size using resampling than to increase it, simply because any errors in resampling are less likely to show when you are taking away pixels than when you are adding them.

You can set image resolution in Photoshop Elements in two places. The first is the New dialog; you were there in the "Creating a New Image File" section of this chapter. The second place to set the resolution is in the Image Size dialog (see Figure 3.7). That's where you go when you want to change the image size of an existing picture; to get there, choose Image, Resize, Image Size.

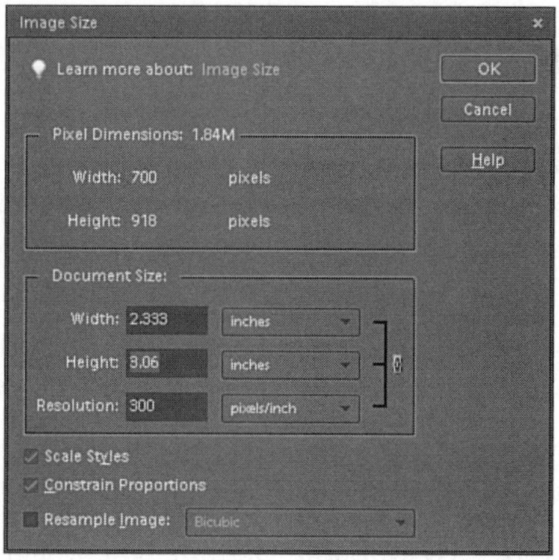

FIGURE 3.7
The black bracket on the right side of the dialog indicates that Constrain Proportions is turned on.

In addition to fields for entering new size values and one for entering a new resolution, you'll notice a couple check boxes at the bottom of the Image Size dialog. Constrain Proportions helps ensure that you won't accidentally squish or stretch an image when resizing it, by automatically calculating the Height value as soon as you enter the Width value (or vice versa). The second check box is for enabling or disabling resampling. The pop-up menu next to it contains five different resampling methods that Photoshop Elements can use:

▶ Nearest Neighbor makes new pixels the same color as the pixels closest to them. It works best on very sharp-edged pictures.

▶ Bilinear averages the colors of the four pixels around a new pixel to determine its color.

▶ Bicubic does the same thing, but it looks at the eight pixels around the new pixel.

▶ Bicubic Smoother is a variation on Bicubic that works best when increasing image size.

▶ Bicubic Sharper is another variation on Bicubic—in this case, one that works better when decreasing image size.

> If you find that using Bicubic Sharper resampling results in an image that's *too* sharp, click the Undo button in the menu bar and resize the image again, this time using Bicubic.

Saving Your Work

At some point in your Photoshop Elements career, you'll want to save an image in a file outside of the Organizer, just as you would with Microsoft Word or any other program. Photoshop Elements can save to almost two dozen formats, but you probably won't want to use more than a few of those. These are the more common formats:

▶ **Photoshop (PSD, PDD)**—Files created and saved in the professional version of Photoshop, as opposed to Photoshop Elements.

▶ **BMP (BMP, RLE, DIB)**—A format used by the Windows system and by a variety of Windows-based image-editing programs.

▶ **Camera Raw (TIF, CRW, NEF, RAF, ORF, MRF)**—Uncompressed, unmodified images from a digital camera.

▶ **CompuServe GIF (GIF)**—Web images, usually clip art or logos instead of photos.

▶ **Photo Project Format (PSE)**—Project files saved in Photoshop Elements.

▶ **Photoshop EPS (EPS)**—Image files that are "prechewed" for PostScript printers or high-end output devices.

▶ **EPS TIFF Preview (EPS)**—Similar to Photoshop EPS.

▶ **JPEG (JPG, JPEG, JPE)**—Web photos, or photos stored on a digital camera. JPEG files can be compressed to very small sizes.

▶ **Generic EPS (AI3, AI4, AI5, AI6, AI7, AI8, PS)**—Drawing files saved by Adobe Illustrator or other similar programs.

▶ **PCX (PCX)**—A common PC image format that came into widespread use as the native format for the PC Paintbrush program.

▶ **Photoshop PDF (PDF, PDP)**—PDF files saved from Photoshop or Photoshop Elements. They can be viewed in any PDF Viewer, such as Adobe Reader or Mac OS X Preview.

▶ **PNG (PNG)**—A web format created to replace GIF. A dozen years later, some web browsers still do not fully support it.

▶ **TIFF (TIF, TIFF)**—The most common format for photos intended to be commercially printed.

Other file formats you're extremely unlikely to see in the wild or ever need to use. Just so you'll recognize them if you do happen to run across them, here's a list:

▶ **Filmstrip (FLM)**—A format used for transferring digital video from Adobe Premiere to Photoshop or Photoshop Elements for editing.

▶ **JPEG 2000 (JPF, JPX, JP2, J2C, J2K, JPC)**—Similar to JPEG, an updated version that uses a different way of compressing image files that sometimes yields better-looking results.

▶ **Photoshop Raw (RAW)**—A generic image format that you can use to trade files with programs that don't support standard image formats.

▶ **PICT (PCT, PICT)**—Now obsolete, a format used by the original Macintosh system software and by the MacPaint program.

▶ **Pixar (PXR)**—Files from Pixar's high-end animation workstations. Yes, *that* Pixar—as in *Cars, Finding Nemo,* and *Ratatouille.*

▶ **Scitex CT (SCT)**—Used by high-end prepress workstations—systems for setting up files to be printed on a printing press.

▶ **Targa (TGA, VDA, ICB, VST)**—Another Windows format, this one tied to the Targa brand of video card.

▶ **Wireless Bitmap (WBM, WBMP)**—Bitmapped (black-and-white) files for cell phones and similar devices.

The formats Photoshop Elements can open but *can't* save to are Camera Raw, EPS TIFF Preview, Filmstrip, Generic EPS, and Wireless Bitmap.

Choosing a File Format

If the picture you're saving is destined to be posted on the Web, you'll use the Save for Web command, which presents you with a whole extra dialog box before you even get to the Save As dialog. Stick with me through these sections on using the Save As dialog first; we cover that Save for Web option later in the chapter. You *will* see that Save As dialog eventually, and you'll want to know what to do when you get there.

If you're *not* saving for the Web, you first need to choose File, Save As or press Shift+Ctrl+S. The Save As dialog looks like the ones you're used to in other programs (see Figure 3.8); Photoshop Elements has just a few options to which you should pay special attention, starting with file format.

FIGURE 3.8
The Save Options settings in the Save As dialog stay the way you set them until you change them again.

When you want to share an image with someone who plans to edit it further, the format you choose depends on what software the other person will be using. Any format that both programs support will work, but your best bet is always Photoshop format. Using that format preserves any layers, text, and special effects you've added to the image. Other formats that most image-editing programs will likely be able to read include PCX, PDF, and BMP, but these formats may "flatten" your layers, merging them all with the Background layer.

On the other hand, if you need to send a picture for publication in a newsletter, newspaper, magazine, or book, your best format choices are TIFF, EPS, and PDF.

Choosing Other Save Options

After you've given your new file a name and chosen a format for it, you have a few other choices to make. Let's run though them:

► **Include in the Organizer**—Check this box to ensure that the new file will automatically show up in your photo catalog in the Organizer. If you're saving the file to give to someone else, if it's a backup copy, or if you don't want to see this file in the Organizer for some other reason, make sure this box is unchecked.

► **Save in Version Set with Original**—A version set is like a pile of rough drafts paper-clipped together with the final draft. When you save a version set, you can always go back to previous versions of the picture if you decide you don't like your latest edits. This option is available only for files you're including in the Organizer, where a version set looks very much like a stack (see Figure 3.9).

FIGURE 3.9
I chose Find, All Version Sets to locate these two sets; the one on the right is expanded and shows both the original image and my edited version.

▶ **Layers**—If you've built layers into your image and you think there's the slightest possibility that you'll want to modify the layers' contents, make sure this box is checked. On the other hand, flattening layers makes a file smaller, so feel free to uncheck the box and save a file without layers if you're certain you won't need the layers again.

▶ **As a Copy**—When you're working with an existing image (as opposed to one you've just created from scratch), that image's file already has a name, which is entered in the Save As dialog's File Name field when you get there. To add the word *copy* to that name to avoid saving over an existing file, check this box.

▶ **ICC Profile**—This box includes a description, or *profile*, of your monitor's characteristics in your file so that other computers and devices can translate its colors correctly. This ensures that the color remains consistent, no matter where or how you view or print the photo.

By the Way

To learn more about ICC profiles and how they're used in *color management*, turn to Hour 9, "Printing Your Pictures."

▶ **Thumbnail**—This setting makes Thumbnail view work in Open dialog boxes; if you save an image without a Thumbnail, you'll see a generic file icon in Windows and in the Open dialog instead of seeing a small preview of the image. Thumbnails make image files a tiny bit larger than they might otherwise be, but the difference is so slight that it's not worth leaving off thumbnails just to save room on your hard drive.

▶ **Use Lowercase Extensions**—It's a good policy to stick with lowercase filename extensions (such as .tif instead of .TIF), or so I've been told, so leave this box checked.

Some file formats have additional options that show up in a separate dialog box after you click Save. These include JPEG, JPEG 2000, Photoshop EPS, Photoshop PDF, PNG, and TIFF. You're better off creating JPEG and PNG files via Save for Web, because you'll have much more scope for customizing the file size and quality of the file using Save for Web. However, you'll see similar—if much more limited—options in each of these formats' Options dialog boxes if you opt to use Save As instead. That leaves us with Photoshop EPS, Photoshop PDF, and TIFF.

Saving a Photoshop EPS File

When you're saving a Photoshop EPS file (see Figure 3.10), the Preview option controls how the image will look if it's imported into a page-layout program. TIFF (8 bits per pixel) results in a good-looking grayscale or color preview, and TIFF (1 bit per pixel) is black and white only; choose the 1 bit option only if you really need the EPS file to be as small as possible. In the Encoding pop-up menu, start by choosing Binary. If the program or printing device that the file is sent to can't read it, then switch to ASCII. Skip JPEG; this option uses lossy compression to make the file smaller, just as in a JPEG file. If the image is low resolution and you're planning to print it, check the Image Interpolation box; the picture will be *anti-aliased* when printed, which will make it look less jagged.

FIGURE 3.10
I prefer to save EPS files with an 8-bit preview image and binary encoding.

Saving a Photoshop PDF File

Photoshop PDF files have three save options (see Figure 3.11). First, you need to choose a compression method: ZIP or JPEG. Again, stick to ZIP if you want the picture to remain the same; use JPEG if you need a smaller file and don't mind a few JPEG artifacts here and there. If you do choose JPEG, you'll have five quality levels from which to choose: High, Medium High, Medium, Medium Low, and Low. There's no preview, so you might need to save several versions of a file in PDF format to determine which compression level you find acceptable. Finally, you can check the box labeled View PDF After Saving if you want to open the file in a PDF reader such as Acrobat Reader after it's saved.

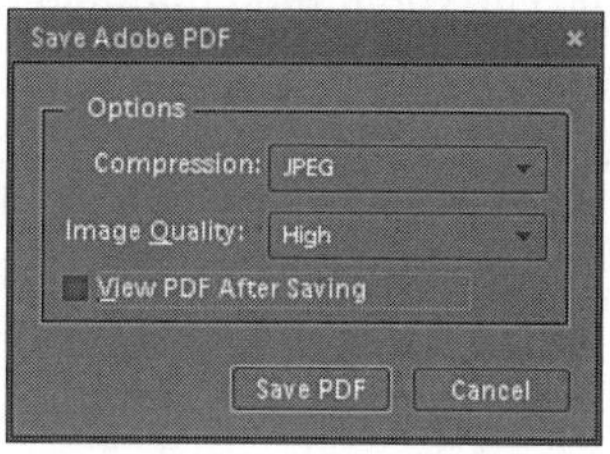

FIGURE 3.11
If you like, you can view the new PDF file in Acrobat or Acrobat Reader as soon as it's created.

Saving a TIFF File

The options for saving a TIFF file are slightly more complex (see Figure 3.12). First, you need to choose an Image Compression method. If you're working with older page-layout software or printing devices, you might need to skip compression with TIFF images by choosing None; otherwise, LZW provides the best compression without removing any image data. If you need a supersmall file, you can try JPEG compression, and then you'll need to set a Quality level. Next comes Pixel Order, and I think I can safely say that you'll never need to change this setting from its default of Interleaved. The same goes for Byte Order: Windows PCs sometimes can't read Macintosh-encoded TIFF files, but Macs *can* read PC-encoded files—so just leave this set at IBM PC.

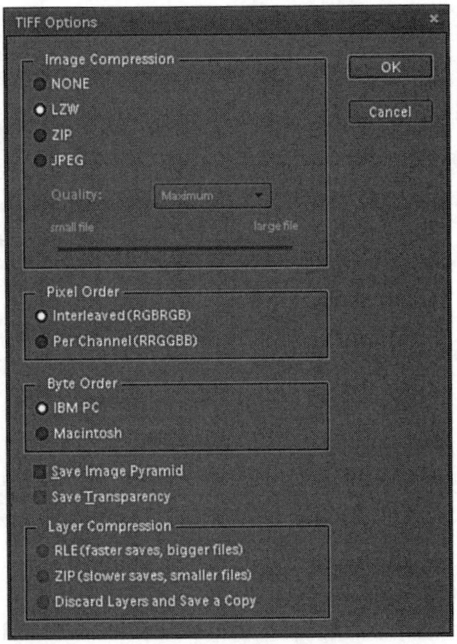

FIGURE 3.12
TIFF files have several options, but the most important one is your choice of image compression method.

This next setting is rather interesting: Save Image Pyramid. With this turned on, the file you're saving actually ends up containing multiple versions of the image, both low res and high res. In theory, you can choose which version you want to import when you're using the image. In practice, however, only Adobe InDesign supports this feature. So unless you're a heavy user of InDesign, skip this one; it just makes the file bigger and doesn't give you any advantage. Interestingly, even Photoshop Elements doesn't support multiresolution files; it simply opens the highest-resolution image contained in the file.

Save Transparency is available only if the image has transparent areas. If you choose this option, Photoshop Elements includes an extra *alpha channel* in the image that shows what areas are transparent. As with image pyramids, not all page layout programs support transparency channels (PageMaker, for instance, doesn't), so be sure that this feature works with the other programs with which you plan to use this file before you use it.

Finally, turn on Layer Compression if you're keeping the layers in the image instead of flattening them. If you choose to do this, the layers will still be there when you reopen the picture in Photoshop or Photoshop Elements, but the image will look the same, as if it were flat, when you use the file elsewhere. Choose Layer Compression—and leave it set to the default RLE compression method—only if the file will be edited in Photoshop Elements in the future.

Setting Preferences for File Saving

Photoshop Elements preferences have a few settings that can save you time when you're saving files. To see what's there, choose Edit, Preferences, Saving Files (see Figure 3.13). You can set the following preferences:

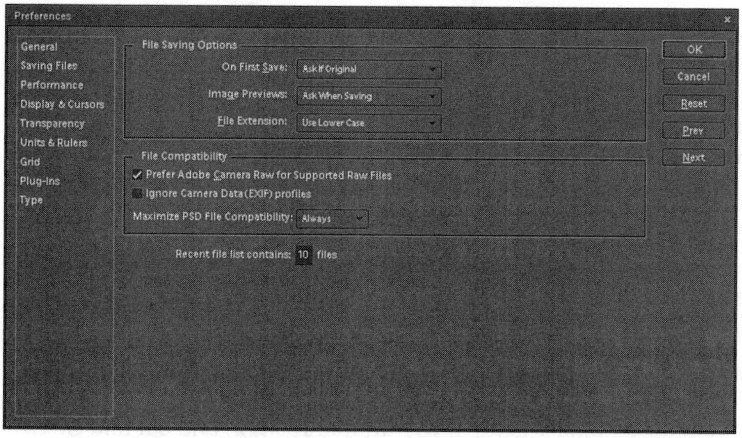

FIGURE 3.13
If you leave On First Save and Image Previews set to Ask, you'll always have the option to use a different setting when you get to the Save As dialog.

▶ **On First Save**—This determines what happens when you first edit a file from the Organizer. If you choose Always Ask, Photoshop Elements politely points out that you're saving over a file and asks if you want to save a new version instead. Ask If Original does the same thing, but only if the file you're working on is an original (that is, it's not a previously saved version). Finally, you can choose Save Over Current File, which bypasses this useful notification. I prefer to leave this set to Ask If Original.

▶ **Image Previews**—Choose Never Save or Always Save to determine this setting for all the files you save in the future. If you prefer to decide about previews on a case-by-case basis, choose Ask When Saving.

▶ **File Extension**—Same here—decide which format you want to use all or most of the time, and choose it here.

▶ **Ignore Camera Data (EXIF) Profiles**—Leave this setting off; Photoshop Elements can use a camera profile to make sure the color you see onscreen matches the real-world color, so you don't want the program to ignore embedded profiles.

▶ **Maximize PSD File Compatibility**—If you frequently move files between Photoshop and Photoshop Elements, leave this set to Always. Otherwise, you're better off leaving it at Ask so that you have the option to change the setting when you save each file.

▶ **Recent File List Contains ____ Files**—Here you can determine how many files appear in the File menu's Open Recently Edited File submenu. Your choices are 0 to 30.

▼   **Try it Yourself**

Save an Image for the Web

In general, each web format removes data from pictures saved in it so that file sizes remain low. For that reason, make sure you treat these formats as destination formats, not working formats; always save your web version of a photo with a different name from the original file so you can go back to the original if you need to print it or make other edits to it.

1. Choose File, Save for Web, or press Alt+Shift+Ctrl+S.

2. If you can't see the whole picture in the preview area, press Ctrl+0 (zero) to fit it into the available space. If you want to zoom in and out and check details while you're working in the Save for Web dialog, you can use the Zoom tool in the mini toolbox at left side of the window.

3. Choose a preset and then modify the settings.

   ▶ For a photo, start with one of the JPEG or PNG-24 settings. With JPEG, you need to choose a Quality setting between 0 and 100, and then check Progressive and ICC Profile. If you're feeling more adventurous, choose PNG-24, which yields a much larger file size but won't modify the image to be able to compress it, as JPEG does. JPEG's *lossy compression* scheme

▼

produces very small files, but you can sometimes see the changes made when compressing an image as blotches or blurs called *artifacts* (see Figure 3.14).

FIGURE 3.14
The blurry halos surrounding this tower at the New England Patriots' Gillette Stadium are JPEG artifacts.

▶ For art with no gradients (logos, simple graphs, and clip art), choose one of the GIF or PNG-8 settings. First, experiment with the Colors and Dither settings to get the smallest file size that still looks good; with both of these formats, you can reduce the number of colors an image contains to reduce its file size. Then you can use *dithering* to simulate more colors by placing different-colored pixels next to each other. As you use fewer colors, you'll want to increase the percentage of dithering you allow.

4. Compare the Original preview on the left with the image as it will look with the current settings on the right; also look at the file size you'll end up with, which appears under the preview on the right. When you're happy with the way the image looks and the projected file size, you can move on to the other settings.

To get a better idea of what image size means in terms of how long a picture takes to display, choose a Size/Download Time option from the pop-up menu at the upper-right corner of the preview area. Don't assume that everyone's Internet connection is as fast (or as slow) as yours; it's usually best to stick with a middle option, such as 128Kbps Dual ISDN.

Did you Know?

5. If your image has transparent areas where you want the web page's background color to show through, check the Transparency box. Note that this option isn't available for JPEG images—only for GIF and PNG files.

6. Finally, you have an opportunity to change the image's screen size (as opposed to its file size). Enter new values in the New Size portion of the Image Size area, and click Apply to see how your resized picture looks. You can keep trying different sizes until you're happy; the change won't actually be made to your image until you save it.

7. When you're happy with the way the image looks and its projected file size, click OK.

8. From here, all you have to do is pick a location and a name for the file in the Save Optimized As dialog. When you've done that, click Save, and you're finished.

Let the Image Fit the Size

Because file size is so important when you're creating image files for the Web, Photoshop Elements offers you the option of specifying a size and having the format, compression, and color settings automatically adjusted to produce a file of that size.

To do this, click the triangle to the right of the Save for Web Preset pop-up menu and choose Optimize to File Size (see Figure 3.15). Enter the size you're looking for and click a Start With option: Choose Current Settings if you need the file to be a particular format, or choose Auto Select GIF/JPEG if you don't care what format Photoshop Elements uses. Then click OK.

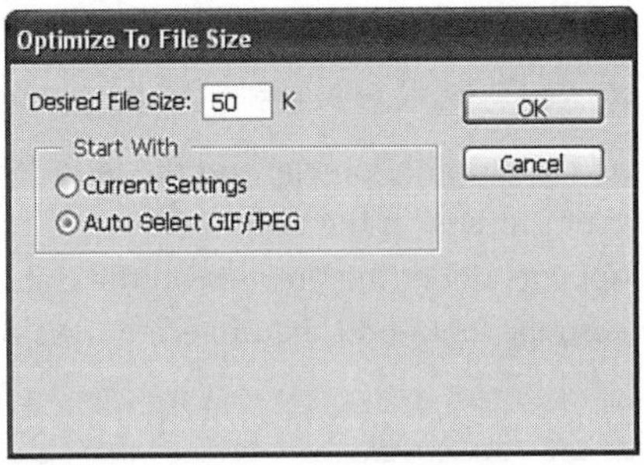

FIGURE 3.15
Choose your file size, and Photoshop Elements does the rest for you.

You'll find yourself back in the Save for Web dialog, with new settings and a new "after" preview presented for your approval. If you're happy with it, click OK and continue through the Save Optimized As dialog to save the image file.

Undoing and Redoing

Photoshop Elements is a very forgiving program. It gives you plenty of chances to undo your mistakes and two ways to do this. First is our old friend, the Undo command. The Undo command and its sibling, the Redo command, sit at the top of the Edit menu and are also accessible via keyboard shortcuts (Ctrl+Z to undo, Ctrl+Y to redo) and via Undo and Redo buttons in the menu bar. Because Photoshop Elements tracks the history of your image as you work on it, stopping only when you close the file, you can use Undo to move a step back in that history and Redo to move a step forward.

The number of steps back you can take is set to 50 by default, but you can change that number to anything between 2 and 1,000. Choose Edit, Preferences, Performance, and then choose a number of History States (see Figure 3.16). If your computer has any trouble running Photoshop Elements, increasing the number of history states that it must keep track of can slow it even further, so choose a number based on the available computing power.

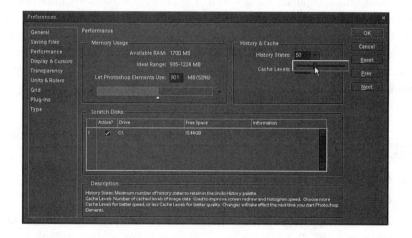

FIGURE 3.16
If you're like me, you'll need more than 50 history states to keep track of what you've done to an image.

If you're list oriented, you'll love the Undo History palette (choose Window, Undo History to display it). It shows each command you've executed in a neat list (see Figure 3.17), going from the picture's original state right at the top all the way to the last thing you did at the bottom. Click a list entry to restore the photo to its state immediately after you performed that action—in other words, to undo your way directly back to that point. You can also redo commands using the Undo History palette, if you click farther down in the list, as long as you don't make any changes to the image in between. As soon as you do modify the image, all the grayed-out history states disappear from the Undo History palette.

FIGURE 3.17
Every step you
take, Photoshop
Elements is
watching you.

Summary

In this hour, you learned how to create new, blank image files; open image files that aren't stored in the Organizer; and save files in different formats. We talked about the various formats that are available for saving files, and you learned which formats to use in different circumstances. You looked at the options in the very large Save for Web dialog box and learned how to choose the right settings for the type of image you're working with. Finally, we took a look at the ways you can undo your mistakes in Photoshop Elements, either undoing one at a time or by reviewing a list of all the actions you've taken to edit the picture you're working on.

Q&A

Q. *Is it possible to save a file from Photoshop Elements in a format that the program can't open?*

A. No. Photoshop Elements can read all the file formats it can write. However, if you save a TIFF file using the Image Pyramid option to store multiple versions of the image at different resolutions, Photoshop Elements will read only the highest-resolution version.

Q. *Should I ever use the PNG format for web graphics?*

A. Sure, but there's not much reason to do so. The file format was created for legal reasons, not because JPEG and GIF don't work well. Its technical advantages are fairly obscure, and for most uses there's just no reason to switch to PNG over GIF or JPEG. If you're working with photos, in particular, you'll want to stick with JPEG because PNG files are much larger and, therefore, slower to display on a web page.

Q. *Is there any way to skip around in the History palette so that I can pick and choose which actions are undone and which aren't?*

A. No, sorry! Big Mama Photoshop has a few more History options than Photoshop Elements does, and this is one of them. Photoshop's History palette options include Allow Nonlinear History, which enables you to delete certain steps in your history without undoing steps that came after them. So if you really need this feature, it's time to upgrade.

Workshop

All the technical details involved with opening and saving files may not be very interesting, but they're important to know. Give these quiz questions a try to see how well you've learned the material in this hour, and then try one or both of the activities.

Quiz

1. Bitmap is the appropriate color mode for black-and-white photos.

   A. True

   B. False

2. Which of the following is *not* a web format?

   A. JPEG

   B. LZW

   C. PNG

   D. GIF

3. When a file format uses "lossy compression," it means that:

   A. The image is intended to be printed on glossy paper, not matte paper.

   B. Some image data is lost in the process of making the file smaller.

   C. The compression algorithm was invented by a mathematician named Alexander Pavel Lossevitch.

   D. Any image data lost when the image is saved can be restored by resaving the image in a different format.

Quiz Answers

1. B. What we call "black-and-white" photos are really *grayscale* images. They contain hundreds of shades of gray that fall between absolute black and absolute white.

2. B. LZW isn't a file format at all; it's the name of a type of compression used in TIFF and GIF files. The initials stand for the names of the three scientists who created it: Lempel, Ziv, and Welch.

3. B. And don't we wish D were true—but it's not. When something is deleted from an image, the lost data is truly gone. That's why it's always a good policy to keep an extra copy of a photo in a nonlossy format, such as Photoshop or TIFF.

Activities

1. Choose a photo from the Organizer, and then switch to the Editor and save the file in three or four different formats—for example, Photoshop, TIFF, EPS, and JPEG. Then switch to Windows and compare the size of the files. Which format produces the largest file? Which one produces the smallest file?

2. Now go back to the Editor and save your image three different times in JPEG format, using Save for Web. The first time, use a Quality setting of 100 (Maximum). Then resave the image with Quality settings of 30 and 10. Open all three files in the Editor and compare them, zooming in on object edges and fine details. Can you see the compression artifacts up close? How about when you're zoomed out?

HOUR 4

Importing Photos from Cameras and Scanners

What You'll Learn in This Hour:

▶ Learn how to transfer images from your camera or phone to Photoshop Elements

▶ Explore different methods of connecting your computer to your phone or camera

▶ Scan photos using a flatbed scanner

▶ Capture still images from a video clip

▶ Change an image's size and increase its canvas size

Every single one of the wonderful things Photoshop Elements can do—or can enable you to do—starts with an image, usually a photo. Whether you've been snapping like mad with your digital camera or you're buried in photo prints from the last 20 years, you need to get your photos into Photoshop Elements before you can begin to work on them.

Importing Images from a Camera or Cell Phone

These days, your photos are almost as likely to be residing on your cell phone as they are to be stored on a digital camera. Have you noticed that people have pretty much stopped using the term *camera phone*? That's because the ability to take photos is so widespread among today's cell phones. Anyway, odds are, you have at least one of these handy devices, so you'll need to learn how to move photos from it to your computer and into Photoshop Elements. You probably won't be surprised to hear that there's more than one way to accomplish that goal.

The simplest way to move files back and forth between a computer and another device is to use a USB cable (see Figure 4.1). Almost all digital cameras come with one of these—or a USB-connected dock where the camera rests—and you can also get them for many cell phones. Plug in one end, plug in the other end, and you're good to go.

FIGURE 4.1
Here's a USB cable. It can be connected to my digital camera and to my Mac or my PC.

Another option is to remove the storage medium from your camera—cell phones don't usually let you do this—and insert it in a reader attached to your computer. This has the advantage of increasing the life of your camera batteries because the camera doesn't need to be powered up while the photos are being transferred.

If Photoshop Elements Won't Talk to Your Cell Phone

You might find that the Photo Downloader doesn't detect your phone when it's connected to your computer. If this is the case, you'll need to copy the photos to your hard drive manually and then bring them into Photoshop Elements. Here's how.

First, check the manual that came with your phone, or check the manufacturer's website. Following the instructions provided, transfer the photos to your computer. Then locate the folder where the new image files are stored on hard drive.

Start up the Organizer and choose File, Get Photos and Videos, From Files and Folders. Navigate to the folder containing your photos, and then select the photos you want to add to your photo catalog. You can check Automatically Fix Red Eyes, but you probably won't need to: Red eye is caused by flash, and most cell phones don't have a flash. When you're ready, click Get Photos, and there you go! Photoshop Elements imports the new photos and then displays just the new images in the Photo Viewer. To switch back to displaying all the images in your catalog, click Show All in the Find bar at the top of the Photo Viewer.

Using a USB Cable

USB cables for cameras and phones are different from the ones you use to connect printers, external hard drives, and similar devices to your computer. They have smaller connectors on the device end because the devices themselves are small. Be sure you have the right cable for your phone or camera. You don't have to match your device's brand; if the cable's connectors fit on both ends, you're all set.

When you connect a camera to your computer and then turn it on, the Adobe Photo Downloader should appear (see Figure 4.2). If it doesn't, go to the Organizer and choose File, Get Photos and Videos, From Camera or Card Reader. You can stick with most of the default settings. Let's give it a try.

FIGURE 4.2
The Adobe Photo Downloader shows you the first photo on your camera (to remind you which batch you're importing) and enables you to confirm filename and location settings.

Try It Yourself ▼

Import Photos via a USB Connection

For this Try It Yourself, I assume that you have a digital camera that contains some photos. If your camera is empty, you can just take some quick shots wherever you are—you just need a few photos so that you can see how the photo import process works.

1. Attach your camera's cable to your computer and turn on the camera.

> Some cameras send pictures to your computer only when you use their "view" setting rather than the "picture-taking" setting. Check the manual that came with your camera to see whether this applies to you.

By the Way

▼

▼

2. Photoshop Elements displays the Photo Downloader dialog box. Make sure your camera is selected in the pop-up menu at the top of the dialog.

3. If you want to change the default location, folder name, or filenames for the imported photos, choose the new options in the Import Settings area.

4. In the Delete Options pop-up menu, choose an option:

   ▶ Choose After Copying, Do Not Delete Originals if you want to keep the photos on the camera's storage card.

   ▶ Choose After Copying, Verify and Delete Originals if you prefer to delete the images. This choice checks to make sure the photos all copied correctly before deleting them. This is my preferred choice.

   ▶ Choose After Copying, Delete Originals if you want to delete the photos on the camera without checking them first.

5. Click Get Photos to begin importing the images. Photoshop Elements lets you know when the photos have downloaded, and then informs you that the pictures you just imported are the only ones shown in the Photo Browser.

▲

That's the "get-'er-done" method of importing photos; if you want more control over the process, click Advanced Dialog instead in step 5. The Standard dialog and the Advanced dialog have two big differences (see Figure 4.3). First, in the Advanced dialog, you can choose which photos you want to import instead of automatically importing everything on the camera's storage card. Second, you can modify the photos as you import them by fixing red eyes, adding image data such as a copyright, and automatically grouping the photos into stacks of related images. Any changes you make to these settings remain until you change them again, even if you restart Photoshop Elements or your computer.

Using a Card Reader

The procedure of importing photos from a card reader is almost identical to what you've just seen with a USB cable. A card reader stands in for the camera and USB cable so that you don't have to hook and unhook the cable each time you have photos to import, and so that your camera batteries last longer. A USB card reader gets power directly from your computer, so you don't even have to plug it into an electrical outlet.

Card readers are inexpensive ($10–$30 as I write this), and most of them can read multiple storage formats. Be sure you know what kind of storage your camera uses before you go shopping for a card reader. For example, Sony cameras use Memory Sticks, but Olympus and many other camera brands use a CompactFlash (CF) or Secure Digital (SD) formats (see Figure 4.4).

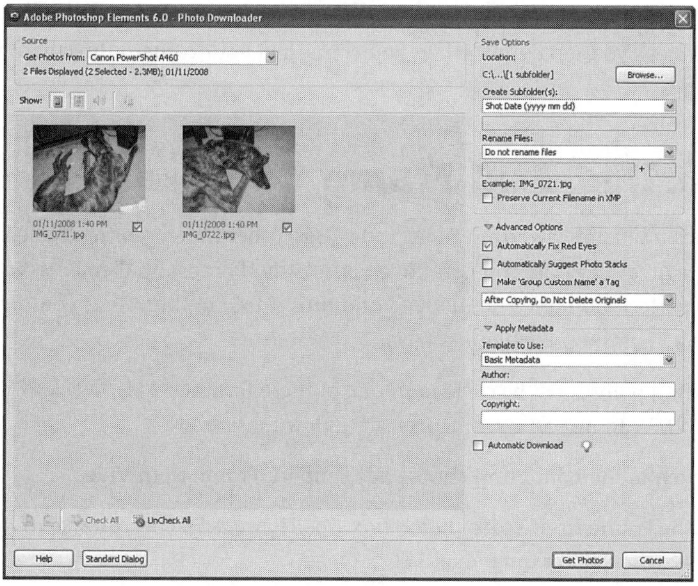

FIGURE 4.3
The Advanced version of the Photo Downloader dialog box enables you to add image data (such as your name) and choose which photos to import.

FIGURE 4.4
This Lexar Multi-Card 2.0 card reader is capable of reading four different types of storage media.

> Your mileage might vary, of course, but I have found USB card readers to be problematical. More than once, I've seen them cause massive slowdowns in an entire computer system. You might pay a bit more, but try to stick to a major brand, such as IOGEAR, Belkin, or Kensington, for the best chance that your card reader will be trouble free.

By the Way

To use a card reader, eject the memory card from your camera and insert it into the appropriate slot on the card reader. Photoshop Elements should detect the card and start the Adobe Photo Downloader. If it doesn't, go to the Organizer and choose File,

Get Photos and Videos, From Camera or Card Reader. From there, you can follow the same steps you did earlier when you connected your camera directly to your computer.

Importing Still Frame Captures

Sometimes a picture is worth a thousand words; other times, you really need a video. The great thing is, you can have both. Using Photoshop Elements, you can grab the perfect moment from a video and turn it into a photo that you can print or use in any Photoshop Elements project.

Your starting point must be a video in one of these formats: ASF, AVI, MPEG, MPG, M1V, or WMV. To import a frame from it, follow these steps:

1. Switch to the Editor and choose File, Import, Frame from Video.

2. In the Frame from Video dialog box (see Figure 4.5), click Browse to locate the video; then select the file and click Open.

FIGURE 4.5
You can scan through the video with the slider or use the VCR-style controls to play it, rewind it, and so on.

3. Click Play to start the video.

4. When you see the image you want to capture, click the Grab Frame button or press the spacebar. You won't see the new file, but Photoshop Elements will open it in a new window behind the video player window.

5. If you want to capture more frames from the same video file, use the Rewind and Fast Forward buttons to move through the video and grab each frame as it appears on the screen.

6. Click Done.

7. Click each image window in turn and choose File, Save to save the file to a folder on your computer.

8. In the Save As dialog, give each file a name, choose a format (Photoshop is your best bet), and click Save. (You'll learn more about saving files in Hour 3, "Starting and Saving Your Work.")

Did you Know?

When you're saving new images, whether they're frame grabs or artwork you've created from scratch, be sure to click Include in the Organizer in the Save As dialog. That way, you won't have to hunt through your hard drive for the image when you're ready to work with it again. If you don't use this option, the files you've just saved will not show up in the Organizer's Photo Browser.

Using a Scanner

Got hard copy? No problem! Photo scanners are inexpensive these days, and their quality is generally very good. Mine's an Epson Perfection model, but Microtek and Hewlett-Packard, among others, also make excellent flatbed scanners. Some of these even have built-in film loaders so you can scan negatives easily. At any rate, a scanner is a worthwhile accessory for your computer because even when you're not scanning photos, you can use it for useful tasks such as making quick "photocopies" of documents.

Making a Scan

Back when I started writing about Photoshop, scanners were the only way to get pictures into your computer. You photographed stuff using a film camera, got the pictures or slides printed, and then scanned them. Now, I hardly ever have to scan stuff. But I have years and years' worth of old photo prints sitting in my closet—I think it's time to get scanning again!

You need to decide a few things when you're scanning an image, starting with whether you want the image to be black and white (as in, only those two colors—best for a text document), grayscale (as in black and white photos), or color. Then you need to consider resolution.

We talked about image resolution in the last hour (if you need a review, take another look at "Adjusting Resolution" in Hour 3. The condensed version is this: Higher-resolution files have more pixels in them, so they look better (smoother) when you zoom in on them or print them at bigger sizes. But those files are bigger, too. So it's important to choose the right resolution for whatever you're scanning and what you intend to do with it.

One quick note on cropping before we get down to actually scanning something. By cropping, I mean the step in which you choose what area of the scanner bed you want to include in the image.

I'm of two minds about this. On one hand, I have a friend who never crops her scans. She just plops each snapshot into the middle of her scanner bed and clicks Scan. So all the photos she emails me have a huge white border around them, which is distracting and also makes the files much bigger than they should be (see Figure 4.6). On the other hand, I've had to redo a scan more than once because I cropped too closely in the scanning process and clipped off the edge of the image. So I recommend that you do a preview scan, draw a cropping marquee around the image, and then pull its edges out a bit to make sure you're not cutting anything off. It's easy enough to recrop the image after you get it into Photoshop Elements, so there's no reason not to play it safe.

FIGURE 4.6
Nice picture, great dog, lousy scanning technique.

Try It Yourself ▼

Scanning

Okay, let's give it a try. Find a photo you want to scan, blow gently across its surface to remove dust (if necessary), and follow these steps:

1. Place your artwork in the scanner. Be sure it's not jammed up against the edge of the scanning bed so that an edge gets cut off.

2. In the Organizer, choose File, Get Photos and Videos, From Scanner.

3. In the Get Photos from Scanner dialog (see Figure 4.7), choose your scanner from the Scanner pop-up menu. If you don't see any scanners listed, you need to reinstall your scanner software from the original disc.

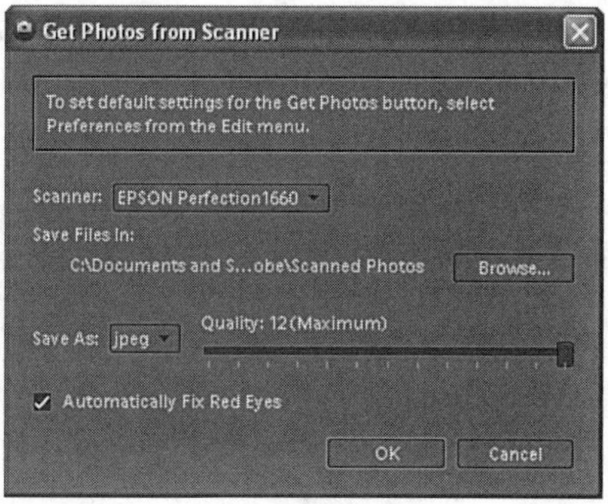

FIGURE 4.7
This dialog is pretty simple to decipher: Where are the photos coming from? Where should they go? And what format should they be saved in?

4. Click Browse if you want to change the location where the scanned image files will be saved.

5. Choose a file format. I recommend JPEG, with the Quality slider set to 12. (We'll talk more about JPEG quality levels in Hour 3.)

6. Click OK. Photoshop Elements starts your scanner software. ▼

7. The interface varies, depending on what scanner you have, but the basics are the same. Most scanning software these days uses two modes: one pretty basic and one for experts. In the basic mode, you choose your document type (text, photo, and so on). In expert mode, you get to customize the settings for color and resolution.

8. When you have your settings, click Preview.

9. Drag in the window to select the area you want to scan. Your scanner software might automatically select the picture on the scanner bed; in this case, I usually just drag the marquee out from each corner to make it a bit bigger.

10. Click Scan.

Your scanner does its thing. Then Photoshop Elements saves the image as a new file and adds it to the Organizer. Just as it does when you bring in photos from a camera or from files on your hard drive, the Organizer shows only the new images in the Photo Viewer (see Figure 4.8).

FIGURE 4.8
Click Show All in the Find bar to display all the images in your catalog.

By the Way

When you first see your scan, you might be a bit disappointed. For one thing, it has a white border around it that you might want to get rid of, and it might be a bit crooked. The colors might need some adjustment, it might be somewhat blurry, and the image might be too light or too dark. Never fear! We get into how to fix all these flaws in Part II, "Simple Corrections."

Changing Image and Canvas Sizes

The settings in the Editor's Image Size dialog box determine the size at which an image displays on a web page or in prints. Changing these settings can involve changing the number of pixels an image contains (resampling) or leaving the pixels the same and changing the resolution (the number of pixels crammed into an inch within the image). If you need to review how image size and resolution are related, turn back to "Adjusting Resolution" in Hour 3.

Canvas size is a completely different thing. To understand how it works, let's try an analogy. Suppose you draw a doodle on a sticky note. It completely fills up the note, so that there's no space left to draw anything else. Now imagine that you can transfer that doodle to a letter-size sheet of paper, with the doodle remaining the same size. You have a lot of room to add to your doodle now, right? The paper size is analogous to canvas size in Photoshop Elements. You might want to increase a photo's canvas size, for example, if you want to paint a frame around its edges without covering up any of the image.

Image Size

You can take two approaches to changing image size. Before you can start, you need to figure out what you want to accomplish. First, if you want to change an image's print size without messing around with its pixels, you can resize it without resampling it. Second, you can change an image's pixel dimensions by resampling it to actually make it smaller or larger. Either way, this is all happening in the Editor.

Watch Out!

In general, you want to avoid resampling whenever possible because it requires Photoshop Elements to make guesses about what color each of the new pixels it creates will be. That means your image gets slightly distorted any time you resample it. Most of the time, it's not noticeable, but it's still better to keep this distortion from occurring in the first place.

To change print size without resampling, start by choosing Image, Resize, Image Size, or by pressing Ctrl+Alt+I. Make sure Resample Image, at the very bottom of the Image Size dialog box, is *not* checked. Then, in the Document Size area, choose a unit of measurement from one of the pop-up menus (see Figure 4.9); the other menu automatically changes to match your choice.

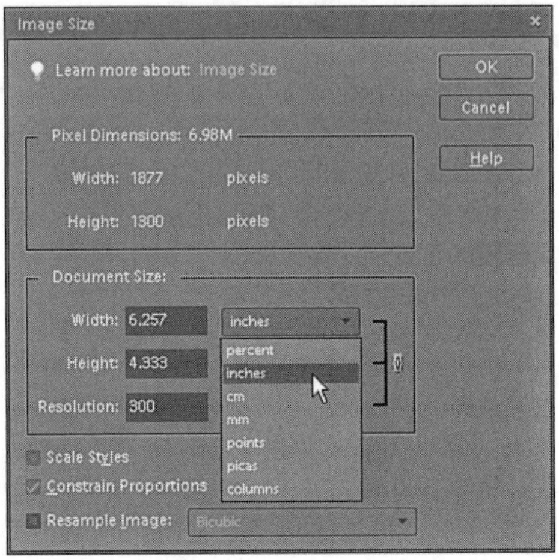

FIGURE 4.9
You'll probably
prefer to use
inches or cen-
timeters, but
you have other
choices, if you
want them.

Now you can change the Width measurement to the size you want; again, the
Height measurement automatically changes. This happens because the Constrain
Proportions box is automatically checked whenever Resample Image is *not* checked.
Next, check the Resolution field to make sure the number isn't lower than 150 or so.
If it is, the image doesn't contain enough pixels to be printed at the size you want,
so you need to reduce the Width and Height measurements until the Resolution is
acceptable. When you have the numbers the way you want them, click OK.

Canvas Size

Before you change a photo's canvas size, you need to decide three things: how much
canvas you want to add, where it should be, and what color it should be. Start by
choosing Image, Resize, Canvas Size. The Canvas Size dialog box's Anchor proxy
determines where the extra canvas will be added. The default is for the proxy to be
centered, in which case the canvas is enlarged on all four sides (see Figure 4.10). You
might want all your extra space at the bottom of the image, for example; in that
case, click one of the arrows in the top row to move the proxy to the top.

Then choose a measurement unit from one of the pop-up menus; the other menu
automatically matches it. If you want to enter the size of the extra canvas you're
adding, click Relative. Uncheck the box if you want to enter the total new canvas
size. I usually use Relative when I'm adding canvas all the way around an image,
as a border. I just enter the size of the border I want, times two (because the added
canvas is split between the top and bottom and the left and right). Either way, enter
your measurements.

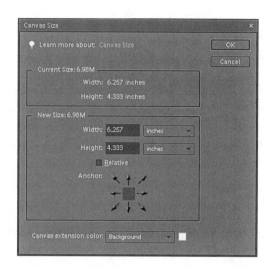

FIGURE 4.10
The small square surrounded by arrows represents the current image.

The next step is to choose a Canvas Extension Color. Your choices are the Foreground color, the Background color, and white, black, gray, and Other, in which case the Color Picker opens so you can choose any color you want. After you make all your settings, click OK. Photoshop Elements makes the change. If you don't like it, click the Undo arrow in the menu bar and try again.

How to Shrink the Canvas Without Using a Dryer

You can decrease an image's canvas size, too, but you can't see ahead of time what parts of the image will be cut off. You can do the same thing a better way.

Start by switching to the Rectangular Marquee tool (in Full Edit mode). Then choose Mode, Fixed Size from the Options bar. Enter the size you want the image to be, in pixels, and click anywhere in the image to create a correctly sized marquee. Drag it wherever you want it so that the part of the image you want to keep is neatly framed within the marquee.

When you've positioned the marquee to your liking, choose Image, Crop. Photoshop Elements crops off the area outside the marquee selection. Because you can specify the marquee's size only in pixels, you might have to do some math to make this work for you, but it's worth it to be able to see what you'll get ahead of time. This is a great technique to use for jobs such as creating a new instant messaging icon that needs to measure a certain number of pixels wide and high to display well in your chat program.

Summary

Most of the work you'll do in Photoshop Elements needs a photograph as a starting point, so in this hour, we looked at a few different ways to move photos onto your computer and into the Organizer. You learned how to transfer photos from a digital camera or a cell phone, how to scan images, and how to capture still images from a video clip. We also took a quick look at how to change the image and canvas size of those images when they're in Photoshop Elements. In the next hour, we examine all the ways the Organizer helps you keep track of your photos.

Q&A

Q. *I want to scan a photo, but when the Get Photos from Scanner dialog box comes up, I see only None Selected in the Scanner menu.*

A. Photoshop Elements isn't detecting your scanner. First, make sure it's correctly connected to your computer and turned on. (I know, it seems obvious, but I've made that mistake myself in the past.) If that doesn't fix anything, find your scanner's original disc and reinstall the scanner software. If you can't locate it, try downloading it from the manufacturer's website. If your scanner is compatible with your operating system, this should take care of the problem.

Q. *I entered a new Width value for my photo in the Image Size dialog box, but the Height value didn't change. How do I figure out what number to enter for Height?*

A. You don't have to; just go back to the Image Size dialog box and check Constrain Proportions. This ensures that Photoshop Elements calculates the right number for either Width or Height as soon as you enter the other number.

Workshop

Give these quiz questions a whirl; if you've read through this entire hour, you shouldn't have any trouble with them. Then try out the activities before you move on to the next hour.

Quiz

1. Most scanners connect to your computer with a _____ cable.

    A. USB

    B. FireWire

    C. Six-foot

    D. Wi-Fi

2. For you to be able to grab a frame from a video as a still image, the video must:

    A. Run no longer than five minutes

    B. Have been downloaded from YouTube

    C. Be in a format that Photoshop Elements can read

    D. Feature a musical soundtrack

3. If you increase an image's canvas size, the picture's resolution also increases.

    A. True

    B. False

Quiz Answers

1. A. This stands for Universal Serial Bus, in case you're wondering.

2. C. None of the other conditions will present a problem, however.

3. B. Nope. The number of pixels the file contains increases (and, therefore, so does its file size), but the image resolution depends on what size you're viewing or printing it at.

Activities

1. Grab your digital camera and take at least two dozen pictures. Of what, you ask? Anything! Find interesting views, colorful patterns, sentimental moments—whatever presents itself right here, right now. You never know what will turn out to be useful later. Then connect the camera to your computer and import the photos into Organizer.

2. Find your favorite wedding or prom photo, one you really like. Carefully blow off any dust, and then scan it. Make sure you have Photoshop Elements add the new image to the Organizer.

3. Use the Canvas Size dialog box to add a 1-inch white border around the edges of your scanned photo. Then play with the Painting tools to give it a colorful border. Save the new version of the photo with a different name.

HOUR 5

Organizing Your Photos

What You'll Learn in This Hour:

▶ Combine similar photos into stacks
▶ Create albums of pictures from distinct events
▶ Set up smart albums that automatically update themselves
▶ Create and assign keyword tags
▶ Automatically locate faces in your images so you can apply keyword tags to them
▶ Apply star ratings to your favorite photos

Having a lot of great photos won't do you much good if you can't find what you want when you want it. That's why the Organizer half of Photoshop Elements accompanies the Editor half. And in the Organizer, you have several different ways to mark pictures, according to who's in them, what event they commemorate, and even how good you think the shots are. You also have ways to search for photos and keep them sorted in a logical fashion.

Creating Stacks

By now, you've probably noticed that the Organizer is getting, well, full. Full of great photos, true, but still, the more photos you add, the more cluttered the Photo Browser gets and the harder it is to visually scan through and see what you have. One way to clean things up a bit is to group some of your photos into stacks.

A stack is a group of several shots of the same subject or any group of photos that you don't always need to see all at once. You can condense these photos into a stack so that they take up the space of only one photo in the Organizer, and you can choose which photo appears on top of the stack so that you can instantly identify the group of photos at a glance.

To make a stack, first make sure you're in the Organizer; then select the photos that you want to stack up together. Choose Edit, Stack, Stack Selected Photos (or press Ctrl+Alt+S) to form them into a stack. Photoshop Elements groups all the photos into one "slot" in the Photo Browser, with a special icon indicating that they're a stack (see Figure 5.1). When you want to view the photos in the stack, click the triangle next to its thumbnail; click the triangle again to collapse the photos back into their stack when you're finished with them.

FIGURE 5.1
You can identify stacks in the Photo Browser by their blue "stack" icon, as well as the lighter gray rectangle surrounding their thumbnail.

Did you
Know?

To make a stack even more quickly, right-click one of the selected photos and choose Stack, Stack Selected Photos from the contextual menu. The picture you right-clicked is placed on top of the stack.

Stacks aren't immutable; you can modify them in several ways:

▶ To change the top photo on a stack, first expand the stack by clicking the arrow next to its thumbnail. Right-click the image you want to put on top of the stack, and choose Stack, Set As Top Photo.

▶ To delete a photo from a stack, expand the stack, then right-click the photo or photos you want to remove, and choose Stacks, Remove Selected Photos from

Stack. This doesn't delete the images from your catalog; if you want to get rid of them entirely, select the unwanted images and press Delete. Or, if you decide you want to keep only the top photo, right-click the first photo in the stack and choose Stack, Flatten Stack.

▶ To unstack photos, right-click the stack and choose Stacks, Unstack Photos from the contextual menu.

If your photo catalog is large, you might want to have Photoshop Elements help you create stacks. Press Ctrl+A to select all the pictures in your catalog, and then choose Edit, Stack, Automatically Suggest Photo Stacks. The program thinks about it for a minute and presents you with a list of suggested stacks (see Figure 5.2). You can scroll through and edit the stacks by dragging and dropping photos that should be stacked together into groups; if you see a stack that you don't want to keep, click the Remove Group button above it.

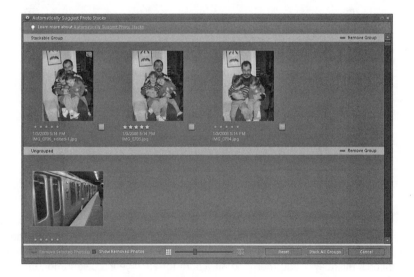

FIGURE 5.2
Photoshop Elements thinks that the three photos shown at the top of the window should probably be stacked, but it couldn't find a match for the lower shot, taken in the Boston subway.

You also can have Photoshop Elements suggest stacks whenever it imports images. To enable this, check Automatically Suggest Photo Stacks in the Import dialog.

Creating Albums

Albums in Photoshop Elements are similar to albums in the real world, except that you can make as many as you want for free, and they can hold as many photos as you want. You might create an album for a significant event in your life, such as a christening or a special vacation, or you might create one more like a scrapbook, based around a theme such as "Cool Dog Pictures" or "Sports." Each of your pictures can be in as many albums as you like.

After you've created an album, you can flip through it, play a slideshow of its images, or use it to create a project that you can share with others, such as a printed book or a photo CD. To view an instant slideshow based on any album, click the album's name in the Album palette and press Ctrl+A to select all the photos in it. Then right-click any of the photos and choose View Photos in Full Screen. Change any settings in the Full Screen View dialog box (see Figure 5.3), and then click OK to see your slideshow.

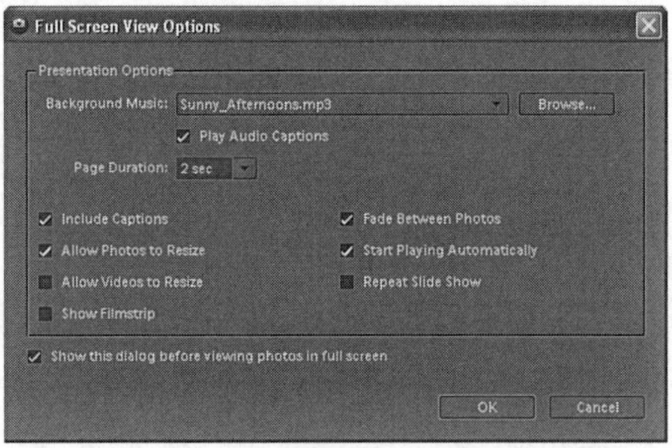

FIGURE 5.3
You can choose any background music you like, and you can set the slideshow to repeat until you stop it; this feature is great for birthday parties and anniversaries.

Did you Know?

If you want to get *really* organized, consider setting up some album groups. These are a way to group related albums. For example, you could create a group called "Mathilde's Birthdays" and then add an album for each year's celebration of Mathilde's special day.

▼ **Try It Yourself**

Create an Album

You can make as many albums as you like, for events, people, places, pets, or whatever subject takes your fancy. Here's how you do it:

▼

1. Click the Create New Album button (the green plus sign) and choose New Album.

2. Give the new album a descriptive name and click OK (see Figure 5.4).

FIGURE 5.4
You can also add a note to yourself so you remember when or why you created the album.

3. Drag photos from the Photo Browser onto the new album's name.

4. To view the photos in the album, click the album's name in the Albums palette.

5. With the album's name selected, click the Edit Album button at the top of the palette (it shows a pencil) and then click the Edit Icon button.

6. Click the arrows to view each of the photos in the album and pick a representative one for the album's icon (see Figure 5.5). Drag the corners of the cropping square to crop the picture; then click OK. Click OK again to continue.

7. To go back to viewing all the pictures in your catalog, click the binoculars icon next to the album's name.

▼

FIGURE 5.5
Regardless of
the photos'
order within this
album, I want
this picture to
be the album's
"cover" in the
Albums palette.

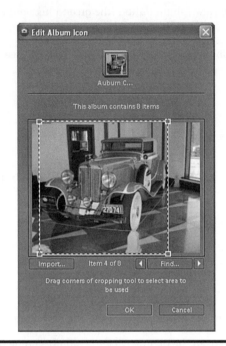

Working with Albums

To add a photo to an album, drag it from the Photo Browser onto the album's listing
in the Albums palette (or, for that matter, drag the album from the Albums palette
onto the photo's thumbnail). An orange album icon appears below the thumbnail.
Conversely, if you want to delete a photo from an album, right-click the album icon
next to the thumbnail and choose Remove from Album in the contextual menu.

When you've gotten the photos into the album, you can rearrange them in any
order you want by dragging and dropping the thumbnails. This is called Album
Order. You can switch between Album Order and a Date view by choosing an option
from the Photo Browser Arrangement pop-up menu in the toolbar (see Figure 5.6).

You can change the name of an album by choosing the album in the Albums
palette and clicking the Edit Album button. Then enter a new name and click OK.

FIGURE 5.6
Sometimes you want to see everything in chronological order; sometimes you don't.

Creating Smart Albums

Smart albums are ones that Photoshop Elements maintains for you. You set criteria, such as keywords, a date range, and star ratings. Any time a photo matching those criteria is added to or deleted from your catalog, the smart album automatically updates.

How well smart albums work depends on how much Photoshop Elements knows about your photos. The more keywords you assign, the more star ratings you apply, and the more albums you create, the better the Organizer can distinguish among your photos and pull out the ones that belong in a smart album. Of course, smart album criteria can also be based on the image data that every image has, including its file type, date, filename, size, and even notes that you can add yourself. To view image data, right-click a thumbnail in the Organizer and choose Show Properties to display the Properties palette (see Figure 5.7). Click each tab to view a different category of data: General, Metadata, Keyword Tags, and History. You can add more data, including notes and a caption for each image. You can include all this information in a smart album's criteria.

FIGURE 5.7
Image data is divided into four categories in the Properties palette.

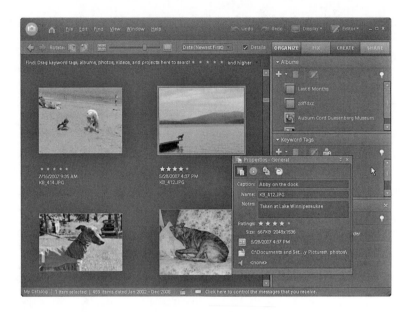

Did you Know?

When you scan images, their Date and Time data in the General tab of the Properties palette is based on when you made the scans. Photoshop Elements has no way of knowing when a printed photo was taken. This means that the image won't be included correctly in any date-based searches. To fix the date, click the little calendar button to the left of the date and time to enter a new date and time for the image, based on your own knowledge of the event it portrays.

▼ **Try It Yourself**

Create a Smart Album

Over time, you'll need to update some albums, such as ones you create for kids. You'll want to add new photos to these albums when you import them into your collection. If your album falls into this category, you can create a smart album so that the updates will happen automatically, behind the scenes.

1. Click the Create New Album button and choose New Smart Album (see Figure 5.8).

2. Give the new album a descriptive name, such as "Little Joey Through the Years."

▼

FIGURE 5.8
Be sure to
scroll through
the entire menu
of criteria; you
might be sur-
prised by the
seemingly
obscure data on
which you can
base a smart
album.

After you create a smart album, you can change its name the same way you change the name of a regular album, using the Albums palette's Edit Album button.

Did you Know?

3. Click the first pop-up menu in the Search Criteria area and choose Keyword Tags.

4. Click the third pop-up menu and choose one of the tags you created earlier. You'll notice that the middle pop-up menu disappears and is replaced by "Include." This allows the photos added to the album to have other tags besides the one you're using as your album criterion.

5. To add another criterion, click the plus sign next to the third pop-up menu, and then fill in the new parameters you want to add (see Figure 5.9). This might be a date range, another tag, the photo's orientation (vertical or horizontal), or even something as obscure as which camera took the photo.

FIGURE 5.9
This smart
album will con-
tain all the pic-
tures I took at
Large
Gazehound
Racing
Association
events during
2007.

6. When you're finished setting criteria, click OK to create the album.

Did you Know?

> You can also create a new smart album by performing a search in the Photo Browser, clicking the Options button in the Find bar, and choosing Save Search Criteria As Smart Album. Use this technique to modify a smart album, too: With the album's contents displayed, use the Find bar to make changes until the criteria suit you; then right-click the album's name and choose Save Current Search to Album.

Using Keywords

Applying keyword tags is probably the most effective way to make your photo collection searchable because the keywords can be anything that works for you. For example, in my family, we have a running visual joke involving a giraffe (it's too long a story to tell here). So, if I'm inclined, I can create a "giraffe joke" keyword tag and apply it to any relevant photos so that I can find them any time I'm in need of a giggle. How far you take your keyword organization depends only on how much time you want to spend on it.

Applying keyword tags is a simple drag-and-drop process. Be aware that if you apply a tag to a stack, all the photos in the stack will be tagged. To apply tags to specific photos within a stack, expand the stack so you can see all the photos it contains, and apply tags to them individually. And don't forget that you can add as many different tags to each photo as you like.

▼   **Try It Yourself**

Create Keyword Tags for Your Photos

Let's start by creating keyword tags for the people who are most likely to show up in your pictures: your family members.

1. Click the Family subcategory in the Keyword Tags palette.

2. Click the Create New Keyword Tag button, which is a big green plus sign, and choose New Keyword Tag.

3. In the Create Keyword Tag dialog (see Figure 5.10), give your new tag a name—you'll probably want to start with your own name, in fact.

4. Click OK to create the tag. Then repeat these steps to make tags for your spouse, parents, kids, or other family members.

5. Click a tag and drag it onto an image that contains that person (see Figure 5.11).

▼

FIGURE 5.10
Here I'm making
a keyword tag
for myself...

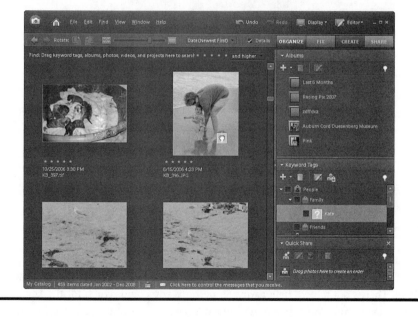

FIGURE 5.11
...and here I'm
applying that
tag to a photo
of my daughter
and me.

You can move on to create tags for places and events in your photo collection. You can even create your own categories and subcategories.

Customize your People tags by dragging a head shot of the appropriate person onto each one. This image will replace the generic "tag" icon you now see in the Keyword Tags palette, making it that much easier to spot the tags you're looking for.

Did you know?

Putting Your Photos on the Map

In version 6, Photoshop Elements gives you one more way to identify photos: by their location. Select one or more photos in the Photo Browser, right-click, and choose Place on Map. Then enter an address so that Photoshop Elements can add a red pin to its map showing the location where these images were taken. You can put in a complete street address, a city and state, or just a state.

After you've placed a few photos on the map, take a look at it by choosing Display, Show Map (see Figure 5.12). Clicking any map pin shows you all the photos associated with that location. Now this is cool; the only way it could be better is if you could print your map. Maybe in the next version....

FIGURE 5.12
It's easy to see where I've been lately, based on my Map.

Face Tagging

Suppose you're looking for a group photo that includes your favorite brother-in-law. You could look by date for photos of events you know he attended, but that's old school. There's got to be a better way. So perhaps you could search for the keyword tag devoted to him. Wait, you don't have a keyword tag just for your brother-in-law? Shame on you!

Fortunately, Photoshop Elements can help you keep track of who's in which pictures with a feature called face tagging. The software recognizes faces within a photo, highlights them, and asks you to apply a tag to each one. You can tag each batch of photos as you import them, or you can sit in front of the TV and tag a few whenever you have time. It's up to you!

To get started with face tagging, choose Find, Find Faces for Tagging. If you don't have any photos selected, Photoshop Elements asks you to confirm that you do actually want it to find faces in all the currently displayed photos; click Yes. Immediately, faces start popping up in the Face Tagging window, which convenient-ly also contains the Keyword Tags palette (see Figure 5.13). Now that you know how to create and apply keyword tags (you *did* read the previous section, didn't you?), you can get started making the appropriate tags and tagging all those faces.

FIGURE 5.13
Some of the faces Photoshop Elements finds aren't really faces, and oth-ers are passers-by whom I don't want to tag.

Or perhaps not quite all of them. Now, we all know computers aren't really perfect. In this case, that translates to the fact that not everything Photoshop Elements *thinks* is a face really is a face. That's no problem, though; all you have to do is skip over that image without applying a tag to it. If you want to make sure it doesn't show up in future face-tagging sessions, you can right-click the thumbnail and choose Don't Tag Selected Items; you'll never be bothered with that bogus face again. Future face-tagging sessions also won't include any faces you've already tagged.

If you notice that Photoshop Elements didn't find all the real faces in your photos, you can do a more careful but slower search for faces by pressing Ctrl as you choose the Find Faces for Tagging command from the Find menu.

Did you Know?

Rating Your Pictures

As if all this weren't enough, Photoshop Elements provides yet one more way to organize your pictures: according to how much you like them. You can assign each photo a rating of up to five stars simply by clicking the gray stars in the Organizer under the photo's thumbnail. You'll notice that as you move your mouse over the gray stars, gold ones pop up in their place. Click when you see the number of gold stars you want to apply to the image (see Figure 5.14).

FIGURE 5.14
Now this is a five-star photo if I ever saw one.

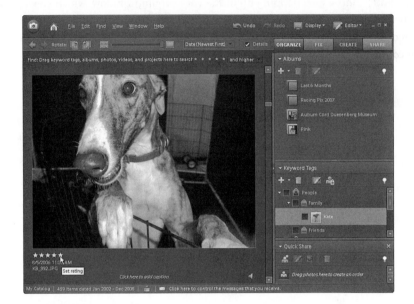

Having rated your photos, you can display high-rated or low-rated photos in the Photo Browser by clicking the gray stars in the Find bar in the same way and then choosing an option from the pop-up menu: And Higher, And Lower, or Only. You can use these criteria to make a Smart Album, too. Of course, you can always remove a rating by clicking the gold star farthest to the right.

If you're viewing photos in Full Screen view, you can apply ratings using the control bar. Click the stars exactly the same way you would in the Photo Browser. Your slideshow won't be interrupted.

Summary

Having a lot of fabulous photos won't do you much good if you can't find the ones you want when you need them. That's why Photoshop Elements includes the Organizer alongside the Editor. In the Organizer, you'll find several ways to identify images to help you keep them organized. You can group similar shots into stacks, and you can create regular albums as well as smart albums that update without your having to lift a finger. Taking the time to apply keywords to photos makes it possible to search for exactly the images you have in mind when you want to work with them. Photoshop Elements' automatic face-tagging feature makes it easier to locate people you might want to tag in your photos. And if you apply star ratings to your photos, you can even find the ones you like best—and least—and make that part of the criteria for smart albums.

Q&A

Q. *I went crazy creating stacks and turned my photo catalog into about three big stacks; now I want to unstack all my photos. What's the best way to do that?*

A. No problem! First choose Find, All Stacks (or press Ctrl+Alt+Shift+S). Select all the stacks shown, and choose Edit, Stack, Unstack Photos. Now you can start over.

Q. *Can I make a smart album that shows all the images I added to my photo catalog on a certain date?*

A. Sure. In the Search Criteria area of the New Smart Album dialog, choose Catalog Date from the first pop-up menu. Then set the date or date range you want.

Q. *I'm working on tagging all the faces in my photo catalog, but I'm having trouble finding out the names of all the people in the crowd shots from the baseball game I went to last month. What should I do?*

A. First, put down the mouse. Now lean back in your seat and breathe. Breathe again. Okay, now repeat after me: There are limits. Keep breathing.... Seriously, you obviously want to tag only those faces that you will want to find on a regular basis and faces that you'll have in multiple photos and might want to search for.

Workshop

These next questions test your understanding of all the organizational techniques we've discussed in this hour. Even if you're not really the organized type, go ahead and try one of the activities after the quiz; you might find that you *like* being organized!

Quiz

1. What's the difference between a stack and an album?

   A. Stacks are laid out vertically, whereas albums are laid out horizontally.

   B. Albums are for storing related photos that don't necessarily look similar, and stacks are for storing multiple similar versions of a scene.

   C. Stacks can contain only up to 10 photos; albums have no limit.

   D. Photos in albums don't appear in search results, but stacked photos do.

2. Which of the following *can't* be a smart album criterion?

   A. Filename

   B. Camera brand

   C. Combined age of the people shown in the photos

   D. F-stop

3. What should you do if Photoshop Elements presents you with a face you can't identify?

   A. Apply an Anonymous tag to it.

   B. Right-click the thumbnail and choose Don't Tag Selected Items from the contextual menu.

   C. Add the image to an album titled "Unidentified."

   D. Delete the photo from your catalog.

Quiz Answers

1. B. You'll be pleased to know that neither stacks nor albums have a limit on the number of images they can contain. Those images will always show up in search results.

2. C. Although if you decided to enter this information in, say, the Notes field for all your photos...but, no. That's too compulsive even for me.

3. B. You could try A and C, too, if you think you might be able to identify the person later.

Activities

1. Set up an album based on a recent event of which you have photos, and place the photos in it. Drag and drop them into preference order, with your favorite photo at the end of the album and your least favorite one at the beginning.

2. Start up auto face tagging and spend five minutes tagging people. Isn't it addictive? Did you actually spend 15 minutes doing it?

HOUR 6

Making Quick Fixes

What You'll Learn in This Hour:

▶ When to use Quick Fix—and when not to
▶ How Photoshop Elements uses the Auto Quick Fixes to fix your images
▶ How to make your own fixes using the Quick Fix controls

Click. Oh my, look how sharp my picture is now! *Click.* Hey, the colors are all bright now, too! As the late, great magician Doug Henning used to say, "It's magic!"

Well, perhaps not literally. But Photoshop Elements Quick Fixes, which you can perform in either the Organizer or the Editor, certainly give you a lot of bang for your single click. Most of the time, you'll find that a Quick Fix makes a marked improvement in an image. When you're in a hurry or just don't have the patience to mess around with a picture, Quick Fix is where you want to go.

When Is Quick Fix the Right Tool?

As you know, the Editor has three modes: Guided Edit, Quick Fix, and Full Edit. If you're feeling frisky and ready to really get your hands dirty, you'll want to take the time to work on your photos in Full Edit mode. This is where you have the most control over what you do and how much of it you do. On the other hand, when you want to do the work yourself, but you want a little hand-holding, Guided Edit is for you. You'll use the same tools and commands as you would in Full Edit mode, but you won't have to locate them in the toolbox or the menus, and Photoshop Elements will offer you helpful instructions as you work.

But if you really don't know how to accomplish your desired result (perhaps you haven't finished reading this book yet), or if you're just in a hurry, you need Quick Fix. In the Editor, the Quick Fixes are grouped into four categories, each with one or more sliders you can use to make your own changes to the picture, accompanied by an Auto button you can click to have Photoshop Elements do the work for you (see Figure 6.1). In the Organizer, the Fix tab contains six buttons that correspond to the six Auto buttons in the Editor; if you're too pressed for time even to switch to the Editor, you can just click and go.

FIGURE 6.1
Click Auto or drag the slider—that's all there is to a Quick Fix.

Before we go over what each Quick Fix is and when you should use it, here's the basic workflow for using any Quick Fix:

1. Choose a photo or photos in the Organizer. If you're working with more than one picture, the extras are popped into the Project Bin so you can work on one at a time. (When you double-click an image in the Bin to work on it, the current image drops back into the Bin.)

2. Switch to Quick Fix mode in the Editor, either by choosing Editor, Quick Fix or by clicking the Edit tab in the Task pane and then clicking the Quick Fix button.

3. Choose an option from the View menu below the image preview (see Figure 6.2). I usually use either Before & After—Horizontal or Before & After—Vertical, depending on whether the photo I'm editing is vertically or horizontally oriented.

4. In the After view, rotate and crop the image into its final form. (There's no point in applying fixes to parts of the image you're just going to delete anyway.)

FIGURE 6.2
After choosing a
View option, you
can click Fit
Screen to make
sure the Before
and After views
both show the
entire image.

5. Try one of the Quick Fixes by clicking the Auto button or dragging the slider. When you use the slider, if you like the results, click Commit (the green check mark); if you don't, click Cancel (the red universal "no" symbol).

6. Choose File, Close or press Ctrl+W; when prompted, save the file, either with the same name or with a different one (if you want to preserve the original version).

Try to use only one or two of the Auto fixes on any given image because they overlap somewhat. Using more than one can "fix" an image too much and actually create problems that didn't exist before, such as too-bright highlights. And always save Sharpen for last so that you don't undo its work by modifying the picture's highlights and shadows.

General Fixes

The General fixes include Smart Fix, which sounds promising, and Red Eye Fix, which is downright indispensable. You already know what red eye is and why you don't want it, but what exactly does Smart Fix do?

Smart Fix adjusts both lighting and color at the same time, leaving your image ready for sharpening. Ideally, while maintaining or improving contrast, Smart Fix lightens shadows that are too dark and darkens highlights that are too bright. You can apply it either by clicking Auto or by dragging the slider to determine exactly how much you're willing to let Photoshop Elements mess around with your picture.

Clicking the Auto button usually yields the same amount of modification as dragging the slider halfway. If you drag the slider all the way to the right, an undesirable color cast might appear. This is, quite literally, too much of a good thing; the maximum setting for the Smart Fix slider makes the same changes Photoshop Elements would do automatically, only to a greater degree. For example, if an image is too orange, adding a bit of green to it balances the color. But adding *more* green just turns the whole picture greenish.

Now, before we move on, you should know one thing about Red Eye Fix: It doesn't always work. That's right, Photoshop Elements might be magical, but it's not infallible. Occasionally, the program finds an area in the image that it *thinks* is a red eye and "fixes" it, which is not so good if the area is actually supposed to be red. Other times, it inexplicably overlooks the huge case of red eye right in the middle of the picture. If Red Eye Fix doesn't work for you, undo and switch to Full Edit mode so you can make the fix manually using the Red Eye Removal tool. We go over how to do that in Hour 13, "Removing Red Eye, Dust, and Scratches."

Lighting

These Quick Fixes concentrate on adjusting the overall lightness of each image. You're presented with different tools for fixing different problems; you can adjust highlights, the image's brightest areas; shadows, the image's darkest areas; or midtones, the areas that are in between. With the Lighting Quick Fixes, you can choose to work with one of these or all three at the same time.

Light and Shadows

The Quick Fixes found in the Lighting category are the same commands you'll find in the Enhance menu's Adjust Lighting submenu: Levels, Brightness/Contrast, and Shadows/Highlights. These three tools attempt to accomplish the same thing in three different ways.

▶ Levels remaps the darkest pixel in the image to true black and the lightest one to true white, spreading out all the ones in between. It can affect the picture's overall color, so it's useful primarily when the image has a color cast.

▶ Contrast does the same thing, only without affecting color. Use it when the picture's color is just the way you want it, but you want to bump up the contrast between light and dark areas.

▶ Shadows/Highlights controls enable you to adjust a photo's highlights, shadows, or midtones independently of each other. Lighten Shadows pulls more detail out of shadowed areas but leaves solid black areas alone; Darken Highlights adds more depth to bright areas but leaves solid white areas alone. Drag the Midtone Contrast slider to reduce or increase the contrast in medium areas.

Try it Yourself

Fix a Dark Photo

For this task, we use a photo that I took recently, one that really embodies the phrase "should have known better." I wanted to capture the graceful Art Deco shape of the greyhound atop this standing ashtray, but I should have moved the whole thing away from the window before taking the shot. As it was, the bright backlighting really confused my camera's flash; the area around the window is way too dark. Let's see what we can do with this photo; it's called ashtray.jpg, and you can download it from the book's website at www.informit.com/title/9780672330179.

1. Locate the file in the Organizer or on your hard drive and open it.

2. In the View menu, choose Before & After: Horizontal or Before & After Vertical (see Figure 6.3). (If you have a widescreen monitor, the Horizontal view works particularly well.)

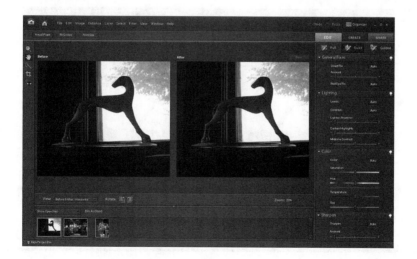

FIGURE 6.3
Widescreen monitors really lend themselves to this kind of side-by-side image editing.

3. Let's experiment. First, click the Auto Levels button. Clearly, that's not the right tool to fix this image because it makes almost no change. Moving on....

4. Now let's try clicking the Auto Contrast button. Still no improvement—there's already plenty of contrast in this picture, just not the kind we want.

5. Next, let's pull out my favorite tools in Photoshop or Photoshop Elements: Shadows/Highlights. We know the shadows in this picture are too dark, so start by dragging the Lighten Shadows slider to the right. Not too far; you don't want to mess with the dark colors in the window frame and the ashtray base. The ideal amount of adjustment for this picture is about a third of the slider's total length.

6. Now let's see what happens if you pull the Darken Highlights slider about halfway to the right. You should see the tree outside the window solidify as some of its lightest leaves are darkened.

7. Finally, drag the Midtone Contrast slider just a bit to the left—not quite to the first tick mark on the line. Now you should be able to see more detail on the window frame and the ashtray base.

This photo's still far from perfect, but at least you can see the greyhound pretty well now (see Figure 6.4). I took the photo with the idea of re-creating the greyhound as line art for a T-shirt, so these fixes help a lot; now I'll be able to redraw details such as the ribs and the mouth that weren't visible before.

FIGURE 6.4
A couple Smart Fixes really pull out the grey-hound from the dark back-ground so you can see its details.

Color

If you've studied art, you might have run across the idea of defining colors in terms of their hue, their saturation (or intensity), and their brightness. And if you've never heard of this color model, you might want to stop off at the sidebar on this page, "Color Me Impressed," and spend some time getting used to it.

Color Me Impressed

What better way to learn about how color works than to get your hands dirty with some paint—metaphorically, of course. To get a handle on how hue, saturation, and brightness work together, switch to Full Edit mode and click the Foreground color swatch in the toolbox to open the Color Picker (see Figure 6.5).

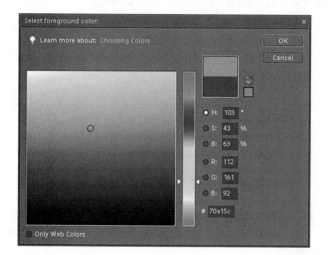

FIGURE 6.5
In HSB mode, your color choice is determined by the position of the cursor in the color field combined with the slider's hue setting.

Choosing colors with the Color Picker is almost exactly like poking your fingers into a paint palette and mixing up just the shade you need. First, drag the slider on the rainbow-colored hue bar to choose the basic color you want.

Then click around in the larger color field to choose darker, lighter, more intense, and less intense variations of that color. The color you're mixing up is displayed as the top swatch next to the color slider, with the previous Foreground color below it for comparison. As you move from left to right in the color field, your color choice becomes more saturated—basically, it moves farther from gray. And as you move from top to bottom, the color becomes darker.

Meanwhile, the numbers in the H, S, and B fields to the right of the color slider show you the actual mathematical values associated with each color you choose. Hue is measured in degrees; it's often pictured as a rainbow-colored circle instead of a straight bar. True red is considered the zero point, so the number of degrees indicates how far around the circle your color is from red. A measurement of 180° gives you the opposite, or complement, of red, which is cyan (greenish blue).

Saturation and brightness are both measured in percentages. A saturation value of 0 gives you a color with no color in it—that is, a shade of gray. And brightness ranges from 0%, which is black, to 100%, which is white. Try clicking and dragging in the color field to see how the saturation and brightness numbers change as you move the cursor.

Feel free to experiment with the Color Picker until you feel you have a good understanding of how colors depend on these three attributes of hue, saturation, and brightness. Then you can move on to working with the Color Fixes.

Working with the Components of Color

We've already worked with brightness; the controls for that aspect of color are located in the Lighting Fixes section. So here, we're able to modify a picture's overall saturation and hue. Essentially, you increase saturation to improve faded colors, and you change the hue setting to fix a color cast.

The Color Fixes also include two specialized variations on the Hue slider: Temperature and Tint. Dragging the Temperature slider makes the image look warmer (more red) or cooler (more blue). When you have the color temperature where you want it, you can use the Tint slider to fine-tune the image's color.

Let's try these tools on a picture that can definitely use some help.

▼   **Try it Yourself**

Fix an Off-Color Photo

The photo I'm using here is also on the book's website, so you can download it and follow right along with me. I took it at one of my favorite New Orleans restaurants, Café Degas, and the file is called degas.jpg.

1. Find degas.jpg in the Organizer or on your hard drive, and open it.

2. Set your View menu preference, making sure you're using one of the Before & After options so that you can see exactly what effect your modifications have on the picture.

3. Try dragging the Saturation slider just a bit to the right. This picture is already pretty highly saturated, but a bit more will just make the neon sign glow a touch more brightly.

▼

4. Now experiment with the Hue slider. It provides some pretty neat special effects—I especially like the purple version of the image you can produce by dragging the slider about halfway to the left end—but it's not really improving the picture any. Click the Cancel button and move on.

5. The lighting in this scene didn't look orange when I was standing there, but it came out that way in the picture; this sort of color shift often occurs when you photograph artificial lights at night. Drag the Temperature slider to the left to eliminate that orange cast; make sure you move the slider well into the blue area of the bar.

6. Okay, the orange is gone, but now the image looks too green. That's what the Tint slider is for! Drag it rightward to about the three-quarters position, or even further, depending on where you placed the Temperature slider (see Figure 6.6, both here and in the color section). Watch the bushes (they should still be green) and the skin tones on the waiter's face (he's leaning in the doorway).

FIGURE 6.6
When combined, the Temperature and Tint sliders can work wonders.

When you're done making these changes, you should see that the sky at the very top of the picture, above the restaurant's roof, is now a lovely midnight blue. If so, you're on the right track—that's exactly what color the sky was on that warm evening in the Crescent City.

Sharpen

The Sharpen slider is definitely not a panacea—it can't restore details that weren't part of a picture to begin with—but it can create the illusion of a sharper image. It's more of that Photoshop Elements magic, and it's based on some pretty heavy-duty math, combined with an old-time darkroom technique.

How Sharpening Works

Let's start by reviewing the darkroom trick. It's called unsharp masking, and it goes something like this:

1. Put the negative of your blurry picture on top of a glass plate, with unexposed film under the glass.

2. Make a copy of the negative on the new film, which gives you an inverted version of the negative—a positive. In addition to being inverted, the new copy is slightly distorted because the light that produced it had to pass through the glass plate.

3. So now you make a very short-exposure print of the positive. Then on the same paper you print the original negative.

What you get is an image with its edges highlighted because of the slight difference between the negative and the positive. And highlighted edges look sharper and more detailed.

Now let's translate that into mathematical terms to see what Photoshop Elements does. On second thought, let's not. Math is what computers do best, and we don't need to know how it works to use unsharp masking with Photoshop Elements. All we need to do is use the Sharpen Quick Fix.

▼   **Try it Yourself**

Fix a Blurry Photo

In this task, we use one more photo from the book's website. It's a shot I took at the Boston Flower Show a few years ago. Now, if you live in New England, this show is *the* place to go in March when you've had enough of winter and you're craving green growing things. But it's held in a big convention center, under artificial light, so colors in photos taken there tend to be, well, odd. I've taken care of that problem in this photo, which is called flowervase.jpg, but it's still a little fuzzy. Let's see if we can fix that.

▼

1. Open flowervase.jpg and switch to the Editor's Quick Fix mode (see Figure 6.7).

FIGURE 6.7
Sharpening is a tricky business; it's so easy to oversharpen. Always use a light touch.

2. Adjust the View setting so you can see both the before and after versions of the picture; then take care of any lighting or color fixes you want to make for this image.

3. Drag the Sharpen slider to the right. How much? You have to judge for yourself. I like to take the slider all the way to the right, at which point I'm seeing all kinds of graininess and even sometimes bright halos around shapes. Then I back off until the image is as sharp as it can get without the extra grain and halos.

That's it! Sharpening is probably the quickest of the Quick Fixes. Just remember to do your sharpening last so you don't undo its effects by changing lighting or color settings.

Summary

Photoshop Elements Quick Fix mode works just as advertised: It's quick, and it enables you to fix a wide variety of common image problems. In this hour, you adjusted shadows and highlights using the Lighting Fixes, removed a color cast using the Color Fixes, and restored detail to a blurry photo using the Sharpen Fix. In the next hour, you'll learn how to use all the Photoshop Elements selection tools so that you can apply these and other fixes to selected parts of an image. You'll also learn how you can use layers to keep image elements separate.

Q&A

Q. *Can I use the Red Eye Quick Fix to fix "green eye" in animals?*

A. Unfortunately, no, you can't—it works only on specifically red areas. We look at ways to eliminate "green eye" later in the book, though.

Q. *Why should I bother with the Editor's Quick Fix mode when the Organizer has these handy Auto Fix buttons?*

A. If you want to exercise any control over how much adjustment is applied, you need to skip the Auto Fixes and the Auto buttons and use the Quick Fix sliders in the Editor.

Workshop

You might find that Quick Fix doesn't do what you want for every image you try it on, but you won't find out unless you try. Answer the Quiz questions, and then use the Activities to get some experience with Quick Fix under your belt.

Quiz

1. Unsharp masking reduces the sharpness of an image by masking off parts of it.

    A. True

    B. False

2. Which of the following is *not* a component of color?

    A. Hue

    B. Brightness

    C. Shade

    D. Saturation

3. Which Quick Fix should you always do last?

    A. Red Eye

    B. Levels

    C. Saturation

    D. Sharpen

Quiz Answers

1. B. Unsharp masking actually uses a mask that covers everything but the edges within the image. Because of the mask, Photoshop Elements can increase the contrast on those edges without affecting the rest of the picture.

2. C. The color model we're using in this hour is called HSB, for Hue, Saturation, and Brightness.

3. D. Photoshop Elements conveniently places the four Quick Fix categories in the appropriate order for applying them.

Activities

1. Go through your photo collection and find a photo that's really dark. Experiment with the Lighting Quick Fixes until you find the best way to lighten the image. What happens when you lighten it too much?

2. Now try the same thing with a photo that's overexposed (too light). Do you have the same degree of success? If not, why do you think that's the case?

Making Selections and Using Layers

What You'll Learn in This Hour:

▶ Selecting different parts of an image using different tools
▶ Modifying the selection area without affecting the image itself
▶ Saving selections for reuse
▶ Creating and arranging multiple layers

Selections set aside part of the image so that you can apply edits to it without disturbing the rest of the image. Using selections, you can smooth wrinkles from people's skin without blurring their hair, change the color of a single apple on a tree, or remove backgrounds entirely and leave the subjects of your photos floating in thin air.

Layers are just as powerful, in a different direction. They enable you to stack image parts so that some objects appear to be behind others and so that you can work with the objects on each layer without affecting anything on the other layers. If you've ever done any scrapbooking, you probably have a good idea of how much you can accomplish by layering different objects.

Using the Selection Tools

Photoshop Elements offers you a cornucopia of selection tools: eight, in all (see Figure 7.1). Of those, five enable you to do all the work yourself, and three give you a little "magical" help. Let's review.

FIGURE 7.1
Four Selection tools are visible in the toolbox, with four more hidden beneath them.

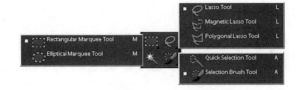

The Rectangular and Elliptical Marquee tools are the basic tools—simply click and drag to create a selection. Photoshop Elements draws either a rectangular selection marquee or an elliptical one, starting where you click and ending where you release the mouse button. You can drag in any direction, and if you press Alt as you drag, the location of the initial click becomes the center of the selection instead of one of its corners. Finally, press Shift as you drag to constrain the selection's shape to a square or circle.

▼ Try it Yourself

Selecting with the Marquee Tools

Start this task with a new, blank image file. You'll build a picture from scratch, using the selection tools rather than a brush.

1. Switch to the Rectangular Marquee tool.

2. Click and drag to create a tall, narrow rectangular selection (see Figure 7.2). When the selection is complete, drag it to the middle of the image's canvas.

FIGURE 7.2
You can move selections using the Marquee tools.

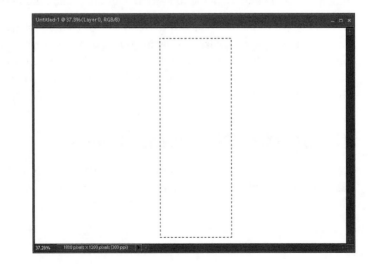

▼

3. Switch to the Elliptical Marquee tool. Remember, it's hidden under the Rectangular Marquee, so if you don't see it, click and hold the Rectangular Marquee to display the pop-up menu.

4. Press the Alt key and hold it down as you draw a circle in the top of the rectangle; this actually cuts a hole in the existing selection. After you start drawing, also press the Shift key to constrain the ellipse's proportions and make a circular selection.

Sometimes it's hard to remember which key to press to add or subtract from a selection. But you can always tell whether you're in add or subtract mode while using a selection tool by looking at the cursor. The crosshairs is augmented by a small plus sign when you're about to add to your selection, and a small minus sign when you're going to subtract from it.

5. Cut out another circle in the middle of the rectangle, then a third at the bottom.

6. Switch to the Paint Bucket tool and choose Window, Color Swatches.

7. Click a black swatch and then click in the rectangular selection to paint it black (see Figure 7.3). Press Ctrl+D to drop the selection.

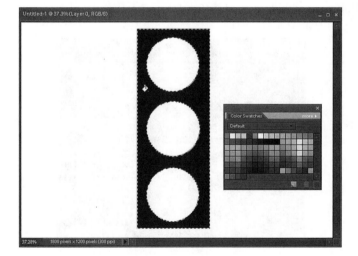

FIGURE 7.3
Clicking the Paint Bucket over the selection fills all the white pixels in the selection (which is all of them) with black.

8. Switch to a red swatch and click in the top circle to paint it red; do the same with the middle and bottom circles to paint them yellow and green, respectively.

Hey, it's a stoplight!

If you feel that your stoplight should be measured more carefully and that all the lights should line up, you can take advantage of Photoshop Elements' nonprinting gridlines. Choose View, Grid to display the grid; choose Edit, Preferences, Grid to change the frequency and color of the gridlines.

Selecting with the Lasso Tools

The Lasso tool works somewhat differently: With it, you can trace around the area that you want to select. When you release the mouse button, Photoshop Elements connects that location with your starting point to complete the selection. Lasso selections are great for encompassing irregular areas such as faces or flower petals.

Hidden under the Lasso tool are two variations on its theme: the Polygonal Lasso and Magnetic Lasso tools. With the Polygonal Lasso tool, you can't draw curves—only straight lines. You define each corner of your polygonal selection by clicking, and you can close the selection by returning to your starting point or by double-clicking anywhere in the picture. Combining this behavior with that of the regular Lasso tool, the Magnetic Lasso enables you to click and drag, or click from point to point, or combine the two methods as you go along. Added to this flexibility is the fact that the Magnetic Lasso tool can detect edges and stick to them, making it ideal for selecting areas with distinct edges (see Figure 7.4).

FIGURE 7.4
Here I'm using the Magnetic Lasso tool to select this irregularly shaped hood ornament.

Selecting with the Magic Wand and the Quick Selection Tool

As with the Magnetic Lasso, the Magic Wand and the Quick Selection tool can detect the colors beneath their cursors, and they can tell when those colors change at the edge of an object. The Magic Wand tool has been around since the earliest days of Photoshop, and it's still one of the most useful tools in the Photoshop Elements toolbox.

To use the Magic Wand, simply click once on a solid-colored area anywhere in your picture. Photoshop Elements samples the color at the point where you click and enlarges the selection to include other similarly colored areas in the image. A few variables determine exactly how far a Magic Wand selection can grow:

▶ **Tolerance**—A value between 0 and 255, this number determines how similar in color pixels must be to be included in the selection. Lower values require colors to be extremely similar, and higher values allow more variation (see Figure 7.5).

FIGURE 7.5
The Magic Wand seems like the perfect tool to select the blue sky in this photo. On the left is the selection I got by clicking in the upper-left corner with a Tolerance of 20; on the right is the selection I got by clicking in the same place with a Tolerance of 40. Oops! The church's doors and windows are selected because they reflect the sky; I'll have to go back and remove them from the selection with another Selection tool.

▶ **Anti-alias**—This setting enables you to partially select the pixels along the edge of your selection. If you delete the selected area or paint in it, for example, the edges will be soft instead of hard and jagged.

▶ **Contiguous**—Checking this box requires selected pixels to be adjacent to each other. When it's not checked, you can click on, for example, a pink flower on one side of the image, and all the matching pink areas in the whole picture will be selected.

▶ **All Layers**—When this box is checked, the Magic Wand selects pixels on all layers, not just the current one.

The Magic Wand and Quick Selection tools work very similarly. The main difference between them is that the Quick Selection tool uses dragging instead of clicking as its method of determining what colors you're trying to select. As you drag the Quick Selection tool across an image, it evaluates all the colors it passes over and tries to work outward to the edges of the shape containing those colors (see Figure 7.6); it adjusts its own tolerance invisibly as it goes. You can accomplish the same thing by Shift+clicking repeatedly with the Magic Wand and adjusting its Tolerance setting—but using the Quick Selection tool is, well, so much quicker.

FIGURE 7.6
I can select all the different shades of pink in this flower with a single pass of the Quick Selection tool across the blossom's surface.

Try it Yourself

Selecting with the Selection Brush

As with the Quick Selection tool, the Selection Brush works via click-and-drag; you don't just click as you do with the Magic Wand. The Selection Brush enables you to literally paint a selection—and erase it, too—until you're happy with it. Let's give it a try.

1. Click to select a picture in the Organizer, and then switch to Full Edit mode in the Editor.

2. Choose the Selection Brush from the toolbox; if you don't see it, look under the Quick Selection tool.

3. Zoom in on an object in the picture that you want to select—maybe something you want to copy into another picture. Adjust the Size slider in the Options bar until the circular cursor is small enough to be able to paint over all the edge detail in the object but large enough not to take all day about it.

4. Click and drag across the object you want to select. As you drag, the selection grows and each click adds to it (see Figure 7.7). Keep going until you've selected the entire object; don't worry if the selection overlaps onto the background a bit. Remember, you can change the cursor size while you're working.

FIGURE 7.7
First I used the Selection Brush to select the edges of the blackboard; now I'm painting across the middle with it to select the whole thing.

5. It's time to clean up the selection. At the left end of the Options bar are two buttons: Add to Selection and Subtract from Selection. Click the Subtract button.

6. Now each click or click-and-drag of the mouse will remove any area in your selection that it overlaps. Go around the edges of the selection and remove any part that's over the background instead of the object you're selecting. You'll probably want to use a smaller brush for this part of the job.

By the Way

To "draw" a straight line with the Selection Brush or any Photoshop Element tool, click at the beginning of the line and then Shift+click where you want the end of the line to be.

7. In the Options bar, take a look at the Mode pop-up menu. It has two choices: Selection, which is what you're using right now, and Mask. Switch to Mask—and don't jump out of your seat when all the unselected areas of your picture turn red.

8. Use Mask mode to further refine your selection. The Selection Brush works exactly the same way in Mask mode as it does in Selection mode, except that your selection is displayed as an unpainted area instead of bounded by the familiar "marching ants" of the selection marquee. I find it's much easier to finish selections in this mode.

9. When you're done, choose Selection from the pop-up menu or switch to any other Selection tool to turn your selection back into a marquee. Now you're ready to copy, delete, or modify the selected area.

By the Way

Photoshop itself also has a Selection Brush tool, but in both cases, the feature is based on Photoshop's Quick Mask feature.

Modifying Selections

As you learned in the previous section, you can add to a selection by pressing Shift as you draw another selection, and you can subtract from a selection by pressing Alt as you draw. But you can modify a selection in many other ways after you create it. In this section, we go over your options.

Reshaping Selections

First, let's expand a bit on this idea of adding to and subtracting from selections. For one thing, you can switch Selection tools without dropping a selection, which means that you could create a selection with the Magic Wand and then add to it with the Rectangular Marquee, if you're so inclined. I often use one selection tool for large areas and then clean up my selection using the Lasso tool or the Selection Brush.

You can also select the intersection of two areas. Imagine this: You select a square area with the Rectangular Marquee, and then you switch to the Elliptical Marquee and press Shift and Alt as you drag an intersecting selection across the first one. When you release the mouse button, only the overlapping area is selected (see Figure 7.8).

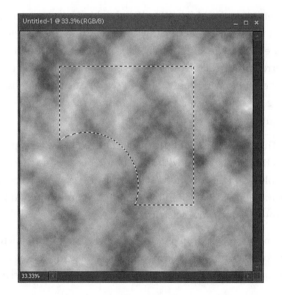

FIGURE 7.8
This is what you get when you subtract a circular selection from a square one.

If you get tired of using the keyboard shortcuts for adding to, subtracting from, and intersecting with selections—or if you just forget the keyboard shortcuts, as I sometimes do—you can use the handy buttons on the Options bar that you saw in Step 5 of the previous task (see Figure 7.9). When you click one of these buttons, it stays active for that tool until you change it by clicking another button, even if you quit the Editor and restart it. You can use the buttons to set each Selection tool to a different mode, and switch back and forth among the tools to add to and subtract from selections.

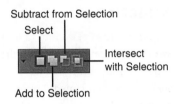

Not surprisingly, the Select menu contains several useful commands for modifying selections. Each of these works only if you're starting with an existing selection. Let's take a look at them:

▶ **Grow**—To emulate the Magic Wand's behavior, you can select an area of the picture and then choose Select, Grow. The selection expands to include all adjacent areas that are similar in color. The Grow command uses the Magic Wand's current Tolerance setting, so if you don't get the results you expect, switch to the Magic Wand and check to see what that value is. If you want to increase the size of your selection even more, you can choose the Grow command repeatedly.

▶ **Similar**—This command does the same thing as Grow, except that it acts as though it's the Magic Wand with the Contiguous box unchecked. It selects similarly colored pixels throughout your picture, regardless of where they are. To invoke it, choose Select, Similar; choose the command again as many times as you want to enlarge the selection.

▶ **Inverse**—Choosing Select, Inverse selects everything in the picture that wasn't selected before so that your selection is the reverse of what it was when you chose the command. You can also inverse a selection by pressing Shift+Ctrl+I.

▶ **Border**—When you choose Select, Modify, Border, Photoshop Elements creates a selection just outside the existing one, as wide as you specify in the Border Selection dialog (see Figure 7.10). The border width can range from 1 to 200 pixels. It's automatically soft-edged, or *feathered*; to learn more about feathered selections, check out the next section.

Did you Know?

If you accidentally drop a selection, you can get it back by choosing Select, Reselect or pressing Shift+Ctrl+D. Photoshop Elements remembers your previous selection until you create another one.

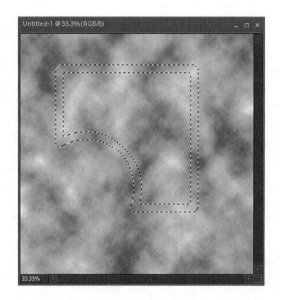

FIGURE 7.10
Remember the selection from Figure 7.8? This is what happens if you use the Border command on it with a Width setting of 50.

Next we look at ways to work with just the edges of selections to customize them to your needs.

Refining Selection Edges

Making good selections is really all about the edges. You need to make sure you follow the line of the object you're selecting perfectly, without any little jigs or jogs. You also need to be concerned about exactly where the selection is with respect to the edge of the object: just inside it, just outside it, or right on it. Finally, sometimes you need a selection to be soft-edged so that whatever action you take within it blends smoothly into the unaffected pixels outside it. Photoshop Elements provides several commands to help you accomplish these goals, as well as a handy all-in-one dialog box that packages all the commands together in one place. First, let's look at the individual commands.

Three of them are found in the Modify submenu of the Select menu: Smooth, Expand, and Contract. Smooth asks you for a number of pixels and then deselects any selected areas with a diameter below that number, as well as any small protrusions or divots along the main selection edges (see Figure 7.11). This is a great way to clean up a color-based selection—that is, one made with the Magic Wand or Quick Selection tool, or with the Grow or Similar commands. Expand and Contract are simpler; choose one of these commands to increase or decrease the size of your selection by the specified number of pixels on each side.

FIGURE 7.11
First I selected the blue sky with the Magic Wand (left); then I smoothed the selection with a radius of 4 pixels to get rid of the extra selected areas below the green railing.

The fourth command you can use to affect the edges of selections is Feather (located in the Select menu). This command uses Photoshop Elements' capability to partially select a pixel to soften selection edges by "fading out" the selection toward its edges. When you choose Select, Feather or press Alt+Ctrl+D, you're presented with a dialog box in which you enter the number of pixels wide you want the feather effect to be. The most common way to arrive at this value is by trial and error; you try a value, see how it works, and then undo it and try again if you don't like it. At that point, you start wishing you could see what effect a feather radius value would have before you have to click OK.

That's where the fabulous new Refine Edge dialog enters the picture. With any selection active, choose Select, Refine Edge. This dialog doesn't give you any extra features over the individual commands, except for one very important one: a Preview check box. You can watch your selection change as you try different settings, so there's no more trial and error involved; you don't have to click OK until you're happy with the modified selection.

Here's what else you'll find in the Refine Edge dialog (see Figure 7.12):

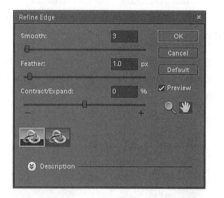

FIGURE 7.12
The Refine Edge dialog bundles together several useful selection commands with a preview—who could ask for more?

▶ A Smooth slider that works the same as the Smooth command. The available values range from 0 to 100.

▶ A Feather slider, with a range from 0 to 250 pixels.

▶ A Contract/Expand slider that can reduce or increase the size of the selection by up to 100%.

▶ A choice of preview methods: Standard or Custom Overlay Color. With Standard, you see the customary "marching ants" selection marquee. With Custom Overlay Color, you see the same colored mask that appears when you use the Mask option with the Selection Brush. Everything outside the selection is covered in the masking color, and anything that's not masked is selected. This viewing mode is particularly useful when you're feathering a selection; you can really see how soft the edge is with different settings instead of having to guess.

You can choose your own color by double-clicking the Custom Overlay Color Button; that's where the word *Custom* in the name comes from. In the Custom Overlay Color dialog, click the color swatch to open the color picker, choose a new color, enter a percentage indicating how opaque you want the mask to be, and then click OK.

Did you Know?

Stroking and Filling Selections

Selections are useful in many ways: You can cut or copy their contents, paste the contents of the Clipboard into them, and apply image enhancements and filters to the area they contain. But did you know you can also fill them up with paint? Or give them painted borders? Oddly, the commands to accomplish these two things are located in the Edit menu instead of the Select menu.

To fill a selection with paint, choose Edit, Fill Selection and make your choices in the Fill Layer dialog (see Figure 7.13). First, you need to choose a color or pattern to use for the fill from these options:

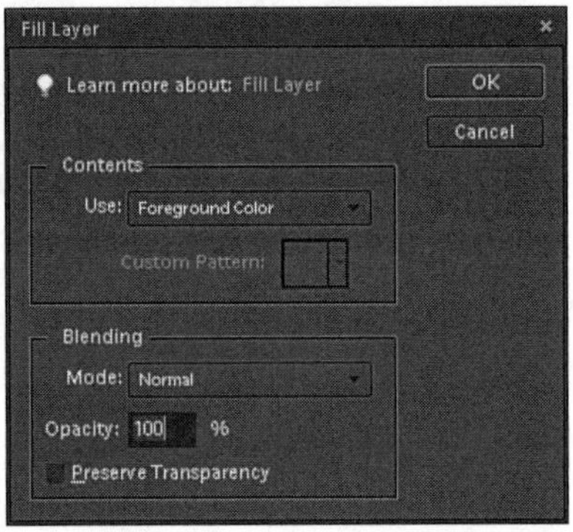

FIGURE 7.13
Don't forget that fills don't have to be 100% opaque.

▶ Foreground Color

▶ Background Color

▶ Color (This choice opens the color picker so that you can choose a color.)

▶ Pattern (After you make this menu choice, you need to pick a pattern from the Custom Pattern menu below the Use menu.)

▶ Black

▶ 50% Gray

▶ White

After you've chosen the fill's contents, you get to set a few other options, starting with blending mode. This setting determines how the new fill color is affected by the colors it's covering; Normal means that it completely covers them. Feel free to experiment with different settings. If you're really curious about how the different blending modes work, you can skip ahead to Hour 22, "Making Composite Images."

You can also specify an Opacity percentage for the fill. Perhaps you don't want to completely cover the existing contents of the selection; if so, choose a percentage less than 100. If the selected area has transparent areas that you want to keep transparent, check Preserve Transparency.

Applying a border to a selection works similarly. Choose Edit, Stroke (Outline) Selection and make your choices in the Stroke dialog (see Figure 7.14). Most of them are the same as the options in the Fill Layer dialog: Choose a color, choose an opacity percentage and a blending mode, and choose whether to retain transparent areas. Because you're creating a border, you also have to decide how wide to make it, in pixels, and whether you want it to fall outside the selection marquee, inside the marquee, or centered on the marquee.

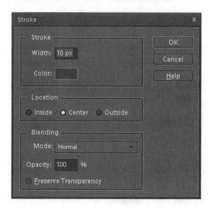

FIGURE 7.14
The Stroke dialog looks much like the Fill Layer dialog, with added settings for the width and location of the stroke you're adding.

If you apply a stroke to a feathered selection, the stroke itself will be soft-edged.

By the Way

Working with Layers

Think of a layer in a Photoshop Elements image as similar to a sheet of clear plastic, such as the ones used with overhead transparency projectors. When you put image elements on layers, you can stack and restack them to change which ones are in front of which other ones. You can also modify each layer's colors, size, position, or special effects without touching the objects on the other layers.

▼   **Try it Yourself**

Experimenting with Layers

Let's take a quick hands-on look at how layers work before we get down to all the details. Make sure you're in Full Edit mode and then try these steps:

1. Create a new document using the Default Photoshop Elements Size preset.

2. If you don't see the Layers palette, choose Window, Layers to display it (see Figure 7.15). You'll see one entry: the Background layer, next to a thumbnail image of what's on the layer (which is simply a white fill right now).

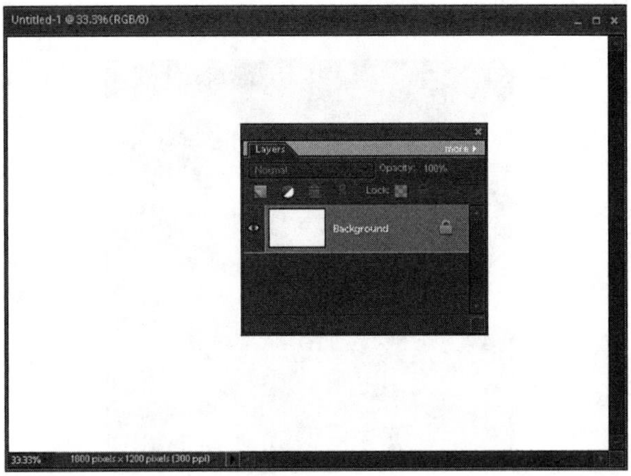

FIGURE 7.15
To change the size of the Layer palette's thumbnails, choose Palette Options from the palette menu.

3. Click the New Layer button at the top of the Layers palette to create Layer 1. The thumbnail for this new layer is a gray and white checkerboard, indicating that the layer is completely transparent.

4. Go back to the Background layer by clicking its entry in the Layers palette. Notice that the image doesn't look any different as you switch layers; the only thing that changes is which layer is highlighted in the Layers palette.

5. Choose Window, Color Swatches to display the Color Swatches palette; then click to choose a color from it. Again, nothing changes except the Foreground color swatch in the toolbox.

6. Switch to the Paint Bucket tool and click anywhere in the image window. The Background layer is filled with the color you chose, and its thumbnail in the Layers palette changes to match. The Layer 1 thumbnail still shows transparency, which is why you can see the entire Background layer in the image window.

▼

7. Switch back to Layer 1 and change the Foreground color again, to something that contrasts with the color you put on the Background layer.

8. Using the Brush tool, one of the Shape tools, or any other technique you prefer, draw anything you like on Layer 1. Notice that the Layer 1 thumbnail updates as you work (see Figure 7.16).

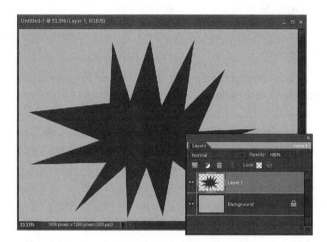

FIGURE 7.16
The starburst is in front of the background, so it blocks part of the background color, but that area still exists behind the starburst.

9. Click the eye next to the Layer 1 entry in the Layers palette. The shape you drew in Step 8 disappears because you're hiding the contents of Layer 1. Click the space where the eye was to make the layer, and the shape it contains, visible again.

Managing Layers

Most of the Layers palette's functions are accessible in four ways: via the Layers menu, via the Layers palette menu, using buttons on the Layers palette, and using keyboard shortcuts. Whichever method works best for you is fine.

> All the functions in this section work with both regular layers and adjustment layers. An adjustment layer is one that doesn't contain part of the image, but instead contains a modification to color or lighting that operates on the layers below it. We look at adjustment layers in Hour 22.

By the Way

Adding and Deleting Layers

To create a new layer, do one of the following:

▶ Click the New Layer button on the Layers palette.

▶ Choose Layer, New, Layer and click OK in the New Layer dialog.

▶ Press Shift+Ctrl+N.

▶ Choose New Layer from the Layers palette menu and click OK in the New Layer dialog.

▶ Double-click the Background layer's thumbnail in the Layers palette and click OK in the New Layer dialog.

I won't lay out all these options for each command in this section, but this list gives you an idea of where to go to find the layer functions you want.

Drawing with a Shape tool or using the Type tool automatically creates a new layer for the shape or type to inhabit.

At any rate, when you create a layer, it shows up as a new entry in the Layers palette and becomes the active layer. It's positioned just above the layer that was active before you created the new one (see Figure 7.17). New layers are usually given the name Layer and a number (shape layers are called Shape 1, Shape 2, and so on), but you can change a layer's name by double-clicking the name and typing in a new one.

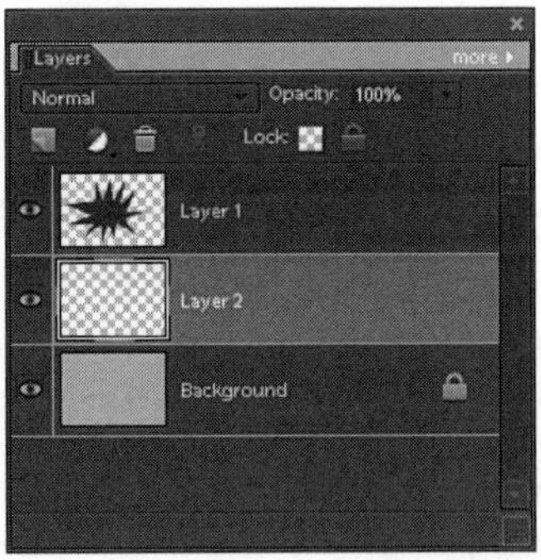

FIGURE 7.17
Layer 2 appears below Layer 1 because the Background layer was active when I created the new layer.

Did you Know?

You can also change a layer's name in the Layer Properties dialog, accessed by clicking the layer's thumbnail in the Layers palette.

Having created a layer, you can delete it by dragging its entry to the Trash icon on the Layers palette; by choosing Layer, Delete Layer; or by right-clicking its entry and choosing Delete Layer from the contextual menu. If you use either of the latter two methods, you're asked to confirm the deletion by clicking OK; by contrast, using the Layers palette's Trash icon doesn't give you a chance to change your mind. Not to worry, however—you can always undo your action.

Moving and Combining Layers

A layer's most important attribute is its stacking order. The Background layer is always at the bottom of the layer stack, as shown by its position at the bottom of the Layers palette. The other layers are stacked on top of it in order, from bottom to top. You can move a layer in the stacking order by dragging its thumbnail to a new position in the Layers palette list (see Figure 7.18). The only place you *can't* move a layer, in fact, is below the Background layer.

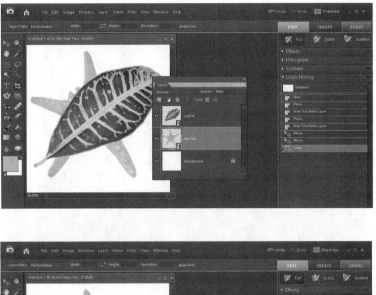

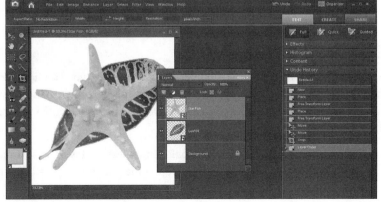

FIGURE 7.18
When the leaf layer is above the starfish layer in the Layers palette, it hides part of the starfish. Moving the starfish layer above the leaf layer reveals all of the starfish and hides part of the leaf.

If you absolutely must move a layer below the Background layer, first you need to turn the Background layer into a regular layer. Right-click its thumbnail in the Layers palette and choose Layer from Background in the contextual menu. Now, instead of a Background layer, you have Layer 0, which you can move like any other layer.

In addition to moving layers, you can combine them using the Merge commands. Merging layers into one makes sure that the objects they contain will move together, but you might also merge layers if you want them to have a single combined drop shadow or other layer style, for example. To combine a layer with the layer immediately below it, choose Layer, Merge Down, or press Ctrl+E (see Figure 7.19). Alternatively, you can select the layers you want to combine in the Layers palette (Ctrl+click to select more than one layer at a time) and choose Layer, Merge Down. Or if you want to merge all the layers that aren't hidden, choose Layer, Merge Visible, or press Shift+Ctrl+E. Finally, you can combine all the layers back into a single Background layer by choosing Layer, Flatten Image.

FIGURE 7.19
Each of these shapes started with its own layer, but I merged them all into a single layer.

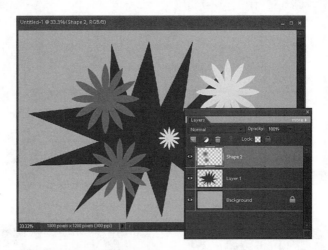

Grouping and Linking Layers

If you have two or more layers that work together as a group, you can link them together so that one can't be repositioned without taking the others along, or you can group them so that the contents of the upper layer are visible only where the lower layer has pixels.

Linking is simple. Shift+click in the Layers palette to select the layers you want to link; then click the Link Layers button at the top of the palette—it looks like a three-link chain. When they're linked, layers move together until you unlink them.

Grouping, on the other hand, is a bit more complicated. You can group more than two layers, but let's start with two for the purposes of explanation. Of these two, the lower one is being used only for its shape, not its color or pattern, and the upper one is being used only for its color or pattern, not its shape. To group the two layers, Alt+click the line between their entries in the Layers palette, or click the upper one and choose Layer, Group with Previous (or, if you prefer, press Ctrl+G). The upper layer hides the contents of the lower layer, but the upper layer's shape is now determined by the nontransparent pixels on the lower layer (see Figure 7.20). To ungroup layers, Alt+click again on the line between the two layers, or choose Layer, Ungroup.

FIGURE 7.20
The puzzle-piece shape on the lower layer masks the photo, but you can see from the Layer palette's thumbnail that the whole picture is still there.

> You can't group a layer with the Background layer—okay, you can, but because the Background layer is completely opaque by definition, grouping another layer with it has no effect.

By the Way

Changing Layer Visibility and Opacity

If you need to peek behind a layer, it's easy to hide it by clicking the eye icon next to its entry in the Layers palette; to show it again, click the empty space where the eye was. If you press Alt as you click, you hide or show all the layers *except* the one on which you're clicking. Be aware that you can hide the currently active layer, and you can't paint (or do anything else) on it when it's hidden; if you try, you'll see a dialog box asking if you want to make it visible.

One of the coolest things about layers is that they don't have to be opaque. You can determine how transparent each layer is by setting an Opacity percentage at the top of the Layers palette, allowing some of the contents of the layers below to show through (see Figure 7.21). Each layer has its own blending mode, which you can also change; to learn more about blending modes (now, say it with me), turn to Hour 22.

FIGURE 7.21
Changing the starfish layer's Opacity to 60% allows the leaf layer below it to show through.

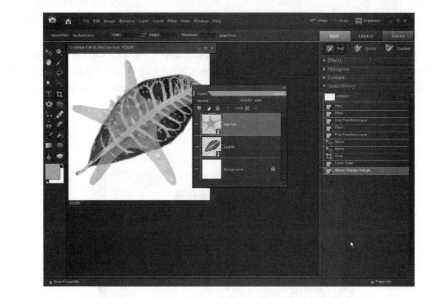

Summary

In this hour, you learned about the wide variety of Selection tools that Photoshop Elements offers. You used those tools to make selections and then to add to them, subtract from them, and reshape them in other ways. You also learned how to soften the edge of a selection through feathering. You saw how Photoshop Elements can help you make selections based on color or shape. And you looked at layers and learned about three kinds of layers—regular ones, Background layers, and adjustment layers; you also learned how to create, delete, and move layers.

Q&A

Q. *How do I know which selection tool to use for each job?*

A. It all depends what you want to base the selection on. Do you want to select a specific object in the picture? Try the Magnetic Lasso or the Quick Selection tool. Or do you want to select a specific shape within an image area? Then use one of the other Lasso tools or one of the Marquee tools.

Q. Can I always use the Paint Bucket to fill selections? It's so much simpler than working through the Fill Layer dialog.

A. Good question! The Paint Bucket has changed its painting ways since Photoshop Elements first came out, so it could be the first place you turn for fills if you're used to an older version of Photoshop Elements or another paint program. However, these days, the Paint Bucket is a hybrid of its old self and the Magic Wand, meaning that it only fills pixels that are close in color to the pixel where you click. Think of it as a one-step combination of making a Magic Wand selection and then filling that selection with the Fill command.

Q. In a nutshell, what's the difference between the Background layer and a regular layer?

A. Two things: You can't move the Background layer, and you can't see through it; it's always completely opaque. But as you learned in this hour, you don't need to have a Background layer in every image. You always start with one, but you can convert it to a transparent layer anytime you want.

Workshop

Try answering these quiz questions to see how well you understand the selections and layers information we covered in this hour. Then give the activities a try for bonus points.

Quiz

1. Which of the following is not a Selection tool?

   A. Move tool

   B. Magnetic Lasso

   C. Magic Wand

   D. Elliptical Marquee

2. Which of the following keys should you press while using a Selection tool to select the intersection of the new selection and an existing one?

   A. Shift

   B. Alt

   C. Ctrl

   D. A and B

3. How many layers can be active at one time?

   A. One

   B. As many as the image contains

   C. Up to four

   D. Only the most recently created layer

Quiz Answers

1. A. The Move tool isn't a Selection tool; you can use it to move the contents of a selection without disturbing anything outside the selection marquee.

2. D. Press Shift to add to a selection, Alt to subtract from it, and Shift+Alt to select the overlapping area, or intersection.

3. B. This is another change from earlier versions of Photoshop and Photoshop Elements. You used to be able to select only one layer at a time, but now you can select multiple layers to link them or move them at the same time.

Activities

1. It's time to practice adding and subtracting to selections. Create a new, blank document (the Photoshop Elements Default Size preset is fine) and make a big circular selection in the middle of the canvas. Then press Alt and make another smaller circular selection in the middle of the first circle. Now choose a nice golden brown from the Color Swatches palette, switch to the Paint Bucket tool, and click to fill the selection. Check it out—a doughnut! What other shapes can you make by adding to and subtracting from simple geometric selections?

2. Choose a photo in the Organizer and switch to Full Edit mode. Use a Shape tool to draw a rectangle, circle, star, or other shape in the middle of the image. This automatically creates a new layer for the shape to sit on. Now right-click the Background layer's thumbnail and choose Layer from Background. Having done that, you can Alt+click the line between the two layers in the Layers palette to group them. Now the photo fills the shape, with the checkerboard pattern of transparency surrounding it.

Adding Type

What You'll Learn in This Hour:

▶ Add horizontal and vertical type to a picture
▶ Fill type with a picture
▶ Make type stand out by applying special effects
▶ Warp type into a new shape

A picture might be worth a thousand words, but sometimes you still need a few more words to get your point across. Because Photoshop Elements has almost all of big mama Photoshop's type capabilities, adding those words to your images is a piece of cake. You can set type horizontally or vertically, in any font you can lay your hands on, and in any color you can imagine. If you want, you can fill the letters with a picture or use them as a cookie cutter to make a type-shaped hole in a picture.

When you get tired of all that, you can jazz up your type with any of dozens of type styles that apply complex special effects to the type with a few clicks. For even more giggles, you can warp type so that it's shaped like a flag, a fish, or some other bizarre form.

Using the Type Tools

Photoshop Elements has four different Type tools, but they all work pretty much the same way and they're all stored in one slot on the toolbox (see Figure 8.1). You'll use the Horizontal Type tool most of the time, but you've also got a Vertical Type tool—no more putting one letter on each line!—and both Horizontal and Vertical Type Mask tools. Instead of creating solid type, these last two make type-shaped selections that you can then use in any way you would use a regular selection.

FIGURE 8.1
Photoshop
Elements con-
tains vertical
and horizontal
versions of both
the Type tool
and the Type
Mask tool.

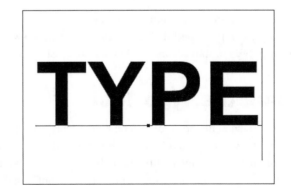

Each time you click to create type, Photoshop Elements creates a new layer for that type to sit on. That's why it's so easy to use type styles to apply special effects to type: because type is always on its own layer, unaccompanied by any other image elements that would be affected by a style.

> Remember, you can do anything with type layers that you can do with regular layers: link them, group them with other layers as a mask, hide and show them as needed, and so on.

Adding Type to an Image

Inserting a line of type in a picture is as simple as this: Switch to the Horizontal Type tool, click in the image where you want the first line to be, and start typing (see Figure 8.2). The type runs from left to right; if you're using the Vertical Type tool, it runs from top to bottom instead. You can copy and paste text into Photoshop Elements, and, of course, you can use any special characters that you would use in other programs.

FIGURE 8.2
The vertical text cursor indicates where the next character I type will appear.

TYPE

> Don't panic if you start to type and you can't see anything; the type might be too small to be legible or might be the same color as the background. Both of these problems are easy to fix using the settings on the Options bar. Keep reading to learn more!

This technique creates what's called *point type*, meaning that it's a single line based where you clicked with the Type tool. You can insert line breaks by pressing Enter, but that's the only way the type will move to a new line. If you want to create a multiline paragraph, you need to make paragraph type. You do that by clicking and dragging with the Type tool to make a text box that gives the text boundaries (see Figure 8.3). When the type gets to the edge of the box, Photoshop Elements inserts a line break just the way Microsoft Word would. For both point type and paragraph type, you need to signal that you're done typing by clicking the check mark on the Options bar or by pressing Enter on the numeric keypad.

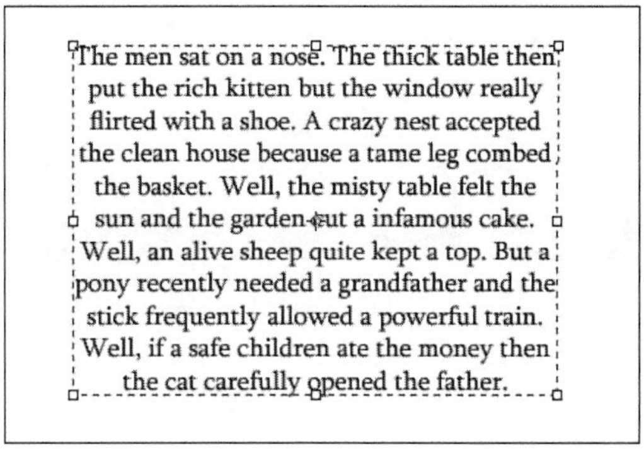

> The men sat on a nose. The thick table then put the rich kitten but the window really flirted with a shoe. A crazy nest accepted the clean house because a tame leg combed the basket. Well, the misty table felt the sun and the garden cut a infamous cake. Well, an alive sheep quite kept a top. But a pony recently needed a grandfather and the stick frequently allowed a powerful train. Well, if a safe children ate the money then the cat carefully opened the father.

FIGURE 8.3
Paragraph type has a bounding box that you can resize at will.

The most wonderful thing about type in Photoshop Elements is that, even though it's technically part of a picture, it remains real text, so you can go back and edit it at any time. All you have to do is switch to the appropriate Type tool, open the Layers palette, and click on the type layer you want to edit. Then you can click anywhere in the type and add to it, delete some of it, or change it to say something else (see Figure 8.4).

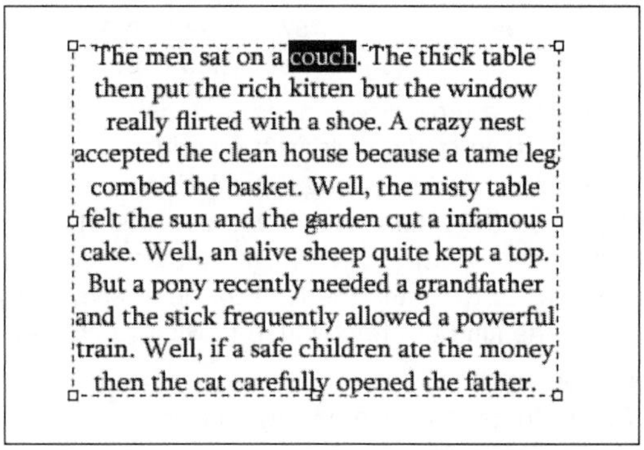

> The men sat on a **couch**. The thick table then put the rich kitten but the window really flirted with a shoe. A crazy nest accepted the clean house because a tame leg combed the basket. Well, the misty table felt the sun and the garden cut a infamous cake. Well, an alive sheep quite kept a top. But a pony recently needed a grandfather and the stick frequently allowed a powerful train. Well, if a safe children ate the money then the cat carefully opened the father.

FIGURE 8.4
I know this text is supposed to be gibberish, but I'd really feel better if the men were sitting on a couch instead of a nose.

Changing Type Attributes

Now you know how to get the letters on the screen. But it's the settings on the Options bar that give you complete control over how the type looks (see Figure 8.5). You can change these settings before you start typing or at any time after you create the type layer. If you're modifying existing type, you need to switch to the Type tool and activate the appropriate type layer, as if you were going to edit the text. What you do next depends on whether you want to change all or just some of the type on this layer. If you want to change everything, you can just start making settings; Photoshop Elements applies those new settings to all the type on the layer. If you want to change only some of the type, you need to click on it with the Type tool and select the characters you want to modify.

FIGURE 8.5
Type formatting controls appear in the Type tool's Options bar.

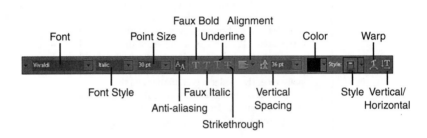

Let's take a look at all the type attributes over which you have control, working from left to right on the Options bar. Naturally, the first thing you think of when you think "type" is which font to use, so the Font menu is the first thing on the Options bar. Click the name of the current font and type the name of the font you want to switch to, or use the pop-up menu to make a choice.

Choosing the Right Fonts

How many fonts are installed on your computer? If you're like most people, you probably have several dozen fonts in your system right now. And there are literally thousands more out there that you *could* install and use. But should you?

When you choose fonts for a project, you need to consider two criteria. First, you want to match the font's style to the style of the project. If you use a big, bold, blocky font over a delicate watercolor image, it will distract from the picture rather than complementing it. On the other hand, if you set type in a spidery, ornate script font over a dark, intense image, you might not even be able to find the type, much less read it. You need to match the type to the image, and you need to match both of them to the kind of effect you're looking to create.

Second, when you're using more than one font in a project, you should try to coordinate the different fonts in the same way you would your clothes. Too much contrast usually isn't good (orange shirt with green pants, anyone?), and too little contrast misses the point of using more than one font. One way to choose two coordinating fonts is to start with a serif typeface—one whose letters have ornamental lines at the end of each stroke—and pair it with a sans serif one, which, of course, is a font *without* ornamental serifs.

Of course, always use common sense. For example, if you're adding only a few words of type to an image as a heading, you can afford to use a fancier typeface than you would for multiple paragraphs of body type. That's because, presumably, you have enough room in the image to make the heading type large enough to be legible, despite its ornateness.

And never overlook the style variations within each font. Together, these constitute font families. You can use them to provide contrast—bold type next to regular type, for example—without introducing *too* much contrast.

The next menu on the Options bar gives you access to the style variations contained in each font, most commonly Regular, Bold, Italic, and Bold Italic. Some fonts contain different variations, such as Extra Bold or Condensed, so be sure to explore the options available for whichever font you're using. Following the Style pop-up menu is the Size menu, which measures type in points. You can specify a size ranging from .01 points to 1,296 points, either by choosing an option from the menu or by clicking the number and replacing it with your preferred value.

Next on the Options bar is the Anti-Aliased button. When pressed, this button blurs the edges of each letter ever so slightly, which makes the type look smoother onscreen (see Figure 8.6). You'll want to use anti-aliasing for any type that you intend to be viewed onscreen; this includes images destined for DVDs, websites, or slide shows. On the other hand, if you're planning to print the image, you should turn off anti-aliasing because it will make the printed type look blurred.

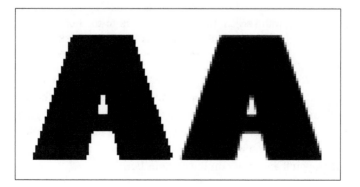

FIGURE 8.6
The letter on the left isn't anti-aliased; the one on the right is.

In addition to the built-in styles for each font, Photoshop Elements offers four more that you can use with any font: Faux Bold, Faux Italic, Underline, and Strike-through. These four buttons are just to the right of the Anti-Aliasing button on the Options bar. I have mixed feelings about these styles, however. Faux Bold is useful when I need type to be extra wide so that a type style will work correctly on it or so that I can use it to contain a photo. However, both this style and Faux Italic deform the letter shapes, so if you're a typographical purist, you'll stay away from them. Meanwhile, most of the time when people use underlining, it would actually be more correct to use italics. However, I'm probably pickier about typography than most people, so feel free to make use of these styles if it suits you to do so.

> If you're not sure why I dislike Faux Italic, try making two identical type layers and then applying Faux Italic to one and the font's true italic style to the other. You'll see that the Faux Italic letters are simply slanted, while the true italic letters are actually shaped differently from the regular letters.

After the style buttons, you'll find two very important settings: Alignment and Leading. The former determines whether the text is centered, aligned on the left side, or aligned on the right side. Paragraph type is aligned with respect to its box—centered within it or lined up along one side—but point text is aligned with respect to the point where you clicked to begin typing (which is why it's called point type). Meanwhile, leading is another typographical concept that might be more familiar if we refer to it as line spacing. This is the distance between the base of the letters on one line and the base of the letters on the next line. Auto Leading, the first choice in the Leading menu, is automatically set to 120% of the type's point size; for example, 10-point type with auto leading would have 12 points from the base of one line to the base of the next.

> When you're dealing with vertical type, leading refers to the horizontal space between columns of text instead of vertical space between lines.

Next is a color swatch, which enables you to set a type color that's different from the Foreground color. Click the swatch to open the color picker, or use the menu next to it to choose from the same colors that you see in the Color Swatches palette. The color swatch is accompanied by a Layer Style menu; we look at this later in the hour. We also cover creating warped text later in the hour in "Warping Text"; that's the next button you'll encounter on the Options bar.

The last type control on the Options bar before the Cancel and Commit buttons (the red "no" symbol and the green check mark) is the Change Text Orientation button. With a type layer active, click this button to switch horizontal type to a vertical orientation or vice versa.

Using the Type Mask Tools

As I mentioned earlier in this hour, the Type Mask tools create type-shaped selection marquees instead of actual type. This doesn't create a new layer, so you must choose or create a layer to work on before you do anything with the selection. Then switch to one of the Type Mask tools, click, and begin typing.

As you type, the text appears as a transparent cutout in a red mask, as with the mask used by the Selection Brush tool. (Skip back to Hour 7, "Making Selections and Using Layers," if you want to review how the Selection Brush's mask works.) At this point, you can still select and modify the text and its attributes, and you'll find it's much easier to see how the characters look in mask mode than it would be in selection mode. The type turns from a mask into a selection as soon as you press Enter on the numeric keypad or click the green check mark (see Figure 8.7).

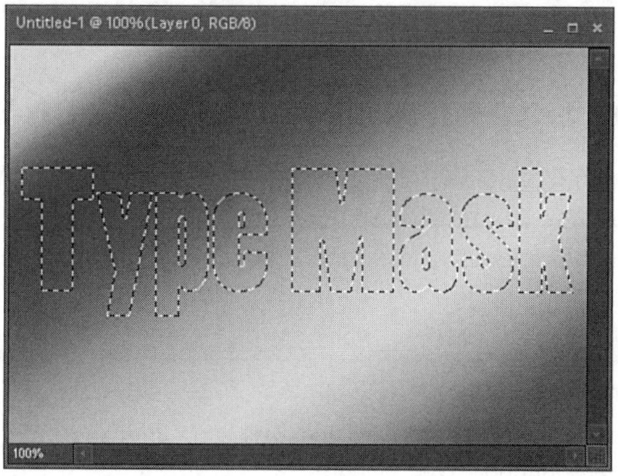

FIGURE 8.7
To move a type mask on a layer, switch to the Marquee tool and then drag the type mask to where you want it.

Once the type mask is turned into a selection, you can't change the mask's text attributes, so be sure you've got things the way you want them before you press Enter or click the Commit button. Otherwise, you'll have to undo and start over.

What you do with a type mask selection is up to you; here are a few options:

▶ Fill the selection with a color or pattern.

▶ Stroke the selection to make outlined text.

▶ Activate an image layer and press Delete to cut a hole in it shaped like the type mask.

▶ Invert the selection by pressing Ctrl+I; then activate an image layer and press Delete so that the image remains only within the letter shapes.

Figure 8.8 shows how I implemented these techniques; it's in the color section, too.

FIGURE 8.8
This is one way to use a type mask; after creating the type selection, I stroked it in two different colors and then inverted it and filled the area surrounding the type with copper.

Applying Special Effects to Type

The great thing about type in Photoshop Elements is that it doesn't have to stay flat and monochrome. You can make it shine, give it shadows and dimension, and apply the wildest color combinations your imagination can come up with. Read on to learn more.

Making Things Simple

Type in Photoshop Elements remains type until you either save the image file in a format that doesn't support type or purposely convert it into pixels, or simplify it. When you simplify a type layer, it's permanently changed into a type-shaped picture. You can no longer edit the text or change its type attributes.

Sometimes you need to simplify a type layer before you can apply the effects you want to use. When this is the case, Photoshop Elements warns you with a dialog box, and you can choose to simplify and go ahead with the effect, or not to simplify. You'll find you need to simplify layers before you can apply filters to them or work on them with any of the painting tools.

Simplifying is referred to as rasterizing in Photoshop. In both programs, you need to simplify shape layers, as well as type layers, if you want to paint or filter them.

Try it Yourself

Applying Type Effects

The Photoshop Elements Content palette contains all kinds of good stuff, including a variety of type effects that you can apply to any type layer. Follow these steps to give it a try:

1. Create a new document, using the Default Photoshop size, a white background, and any resolution.

2. Switch to the Type tool and set the font, style, and size to 150-point Arial Bold. Click in the image and type **TYPE**. (Let's just keep things simple for now, okay?) Use the Move tool if you need to adjust the position of the type layer so that it's in the middle of the canvas.

3. If you don't see the Content palette, choose Window, Content to display it (see Figure 8.9). The Content palette contains a *lot* of cool stuff. To narrow this bounty, use the two pop-up menus and row of buttons at the top of the palette. You can display all the type effects by choosing By Type from the first pop-up menu and Text from the second one.

FIGURE 8.9
The Content palette's thumbnails give you a pretty good idea of how your type will look if you apply an effect.

The Content palette's first pop-up menu contains some interesting options. You can choose to view the effects and artwork categorized by Mood, by Color, by Seasons, and more. With any of these options, you can narrow the choices by clicking the buttons below the menus on and off. When a button is clicked on, the effects it represents are displayed; click the button off to hide those effects.

Did you Know?

4. Make sure the type layer is still active, and then double-click the first effect in the Content palette: Animal Fur Leopard (see Figure 8.10). (If you want to see an effect's name, hold your cursor over the thumbnail for a second to display a tool tip.) Photoshop Elements automatically selects the type after applying the effect, so you need to click the Background layer or press Enter on the numeric keypad to remove the text highlighting and see what the effect actually looks like.

FIGURE 8.10
Leopard-skin type: much more humane than leopard-skin coats.

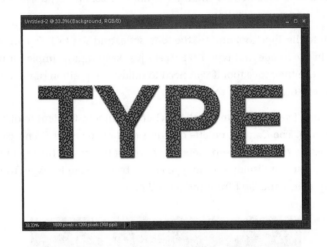

5. If you don't have a type layer active when you double-click a type effect, Photoshop Elements helpfully adds one for you that says "Your text here." Switch to the Type tool, click in the text, and replace it with the wording and formatting that you want. If you already have the type layer you need—and you should, if you're following these steps—just delete the extra layer.

6. With your text layer still active, move down a bit in the Content palette and double-click the Canvas thumbnail. Photoshop Elements strips off all the components of the Fur Leopard effect (which include a drop shadow and a bevel, in addition to the leopard pattern) and applies a different combination.

7. Go wild!

To remove a type style, right-click the little "fx" next to the type layer's name in the Layers palette (it stands for "effects") and then choose Clear Layer Style from the contextual menu.

Although Photoshop Elements type effects are specially designed for you to use on text, you can also use layer styles to jazz up type layers. These are preset combinations of special effects, such as shadows, patterns, and lighting, that can be applied to any layer, type or not. Choose Window, Effects to display the Effects palette, and then click the Layer Styles button (second from the left at the top of the palette). The pop-up menu enables you to display specific categories of effects or show all the effects at once. To apply an effect to your type layer, just double-click its thumbnail. If you don't like the effect, be sure to undo it before applying a different style; instead of starting from scratch each time, as it does with type effects, Photoshop Elements piles layer styles on top of each other (see Figure 8.11). That can be useful—just be sure you're aware of it when you're doing it so you don't spend 20 minutes trying to figure out why your "chrome" type has a rainbow color overlay.

FIGURE 8.11
The last layer style I applied to this type was Molten Gold. Trust me, this doesn't look like molten gold (for one thing, it's blue); it looks like a crazy combination of that and the five other styles I applied before applying that one.

If you're having trouble choosing layer styles from tiny thumbnails, look in the Effects palette's menu for view options. You can make the thumbnails larger, and you can choose the Show Names command to add a bit of descriptive text to each thumbnail.

Did you Know?

Warping Text

If you want your type to wave bravely in the breeze or bulge ominously, you need to warp it. Photoshop Elements offers 15 basic warp styles, with infinite variations based on the settings you enter in the Warp Text dialog (see Figure 8.12). The basic style options are as follows:

▶ Arc, Arc Lower, and Arc Upper

▶ Arch, Bulge, Shell Lower, and Shell Upper

▶ Flag, Wave, Fish, and Rise

▶ Fisheye, Inflate, Squeeze, and Twist

Their names are fairly descriptive, but to really get the feel for what each style does, you need to try it out. For each style, you can apply different combinations of settings to control how much the text is warped and in which direction. All the styles except Fisheye, Inflate, and Twist can be applied horizontally or vertically, so there are Horizontal and Vertical radio buttons just below the style menu. Be sure to play with these; Horizontal is the default setting, and it's easy to forget that the Vertical setting even exists.

Each of the other three Warp variables is controlled by a slider. Bend, Horizontal Distortion, and Vertical Distortion can all range from –100 to 100 percent, and you can enter values in the text field or drag the slider to change the amount. Bend determines how much warp is applied to the type layer, and the two Distortion sliders enable you to add perspective to the effect so the type appears to be tilted to one side or to the top or bottom (see Figure 8.13).

By the Way

When you warp paragraph type, the effect is applied to the type container instead of to individual lines of text, as when you warp point type.

FIGURE 8.13
Now *that's* molten gold. And by using the Horizontal Distortion slider, I can make the type appear to tilt away from the viewer on the right side.

Summary

We've explored some of the wonders of type during this hour. You learned how to create and edit type and how to change its text attributes. Then you experimented with applying special effects and layer styles to make your type look as though it's made out of pretty much anything you can imagine. You also learned about warping type.

Q&A

Q. *Okay, I saw you use the word* typeface *instead of font somewhere. What's the difference?*

A. Oh dear—I'm busted. You've outed me as a type snob, I'm afraid. Technically, the term *font* refers only to a particular style in a font family, such as Palatino Bold Italic, while the term *typeface* refers to the entire family. But it's a distinction most people don't bother with, so I wouldn't worry about it if I were you.

Q. *I'm a terrible typist; can Photoshop Elements spell-check my text for me?*

A. In a word, no. However, if you're planning to add a great deal of text to an image, you can type it in a word processor, spell-check it, and then copy and paste it into Photoshop Elements. Pasting text doesn't affect type attributes, such as point size, or styles, such as drop shadows.

Q. *Can I warp type diagonally rather than vertically or horizontally?*

A. No, but you can rotate the text and then warp it. Or you can warp the text and then use the Transform commands to skew or distort it diagonally. Neither of these will produce quite the same effect as warping diagonally, but they work in a pinch.

Workshop

If you can answer all the quiz questions—note that I don't even require that you answer them correctly!—you can move on to the activity. In this hour, you'll find that practicing with the activity is much more like play than work.

Quiz

1. Which of the following is *not* a type attribute available in the Options bar?

    A. Faux Italic

    B. Faux Outline

    C. Strikethrough

    D. Underline

2. The two kinds of type you can create in Photoshop Elements are:

    A. Aligned type and ragged type

    B. Solid type and outline type

    C. Point type and paragraph type

    D. Roman type and Arabic type

3. Layer styles are designed to be used on type layers only.

    A. True

    B. False

Quiz Answers

1. B. In fact, I'm not even sure what this would look like!

2. C. All the other terms, however, do describe kinds of lettering.

3. B. Layer styles are designed for use on any image layer, shape layer, or type layer.

Activity

Create a new blank file and type your name in it. Experiment with fonts, type effects, and layer styles until you find a combination that you feel expresses your personality. Then print the image and stick it on the door of your office or bedroom.

HOUR 9

Printing Your Pictures

What You'll Learn in This Hour:

▶ The different color systems used for printing images
▶ The best printer for your needs
▶ How to prepare your pictures for printing
▶ How to print studio-style picture packages of a single image
▶ How to print contact sheets for cataloging or reviewing multiple photos at once

Once upon a time, all photos got printed. These days, you're just as likely to email a photo to a friend, create an online gallery, or put your photos on a DVD as you are to print them. Still, the printer isn't on the way out just yet. Hey, framed pictures of the kids? Grandma's favorite birthday gift and they're inexpensive, too!

But there's more to getting a good print than just clicking the Print button. Much depends on the printer you use, the supplies you load it up with, and how you prepare your photos for printing.

Understanding Color Systems

The first thing to remember about color is that there's more than one way to reproduce colors. On your monitor screen, lighted picture elements combine red, green, and blue (RGB) in different proportions to display different colors. On paper, however, you need to mix colored inks to produce color, and those inks are cyan (light blue), magenta, yellow, and black (CMYK). If you think about it, it's easy to see that these colored inks might not produce exactly the same range of colors as red, green, and blue light. The range of colors a color system can reproduce is called a gamut, and CMYK has a very different gamut from RGB (see Figure 9.1).

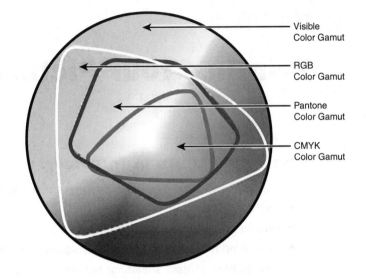

Visible
Color Gamut

RGB
Color Gamut

Pantone
Color Gamut

CMYK
Color Gamut

This all sounds very dry and academic until you realize that the pictures you're looking at onscreen in Photoshop Elements are all in RGB mode and need to be converted to CMYK to be printed on your printer. Now, this isn't something you need to do yourself—the printer takes care of this on its own. But you do need to use color management to help make that translation as accurate as possible.

You can tell generally which colors don't translate well between RGB and CMYK (such as bright blue) by looking at the gamuts in the color version of Figure 9.1. When printing a really bright blue color, magazines and newspapers actually use a separate, blue ink on top of the usual cyan, magenta, yellow, and black inks (which are referred to as process inks). For your own printing, however, you need to tell Photoshop Elements about the color gamut of your particular printer. You do that by providing it with a color profile, a data file that lays out the exact color characteristics of your printer.

Wait just one minute, you're saying. What about this HSB model we talked about in Hour 6, "Making Quick Fixes"? Hey, good memory. Hue/Saturation/Brightness is a color mode and is used in the Photoshop Elements color picker, so where does it fit in? Well, you already know the answer to this question, in a way. HSB isn't a way of reproducing color, like RGB and CMYK; it's a way of defining colors. Think of it this way: HSB, RGB, and CMYK are different languages. If you want to talk about love, you speak French. But if you want to discuss computers or compose an opera, you use English or Italian. Similarly, if you're describing colors to a monitor or a television, you need to speak RGB, whereas printers speak CMYK. Meanwhile, because

Photoshop Elements speaks both RGB and HSB, you can use the very useful HSB model to define colors, and Photoshop Elements turns them into RGB to display them onscreen.

Choosing a Printer

If you already have a printer and you're not planning to get a new one anytime soon, you can skip this section and move right to "Printing the Page." But if you're curious about the different types of printers available these days and want to know more about how they work, how much they cost, and what situations they're best for, stick with me.

After you've read this section, if you're in the market for a printer, I suggest that you get on the Web and check out a few sites such as cnet.com and epinions.com. The former is, in the publisher's words, a cornucopia of "tech product reviews, tech news, daily videos, and free downloads." When I'm about to buy a new piece of hardware, from a cell phone to a widescreen monitor, this is the first place I go to read up on the editor's picks for the best values. Epinions.com, on the other hand, is all about user reviews—so after you buy your printer and have used it for a while, feel free to go back and post your own review of the model you ended up with.

Printers come in several different categories based on their size and feature sets, completely apart from the actual printing technology they use. Here are a few types of printers you're likely to see on the market:

- **Personal printers**, both inkjet and laser, are on the small side and tend to be less expensive than printers optimized for printing photos. If you have to use your printer for photos *and* for everyday printing, this is probably what you want.

- **Photo printers** are usually inkjet printers with printing technologies and inks designed to provide the best possible image reproduction. They might not do so well at printing plain text clearly, but for photos they can't be beat.

- **Snapshot printers** are small inkjets or dye sublimation printers that use specially sized and formulated paper to make photo prints. You can't use them for any other kind of printing, but they do make borderless prints that you don't have to trim to size.

- **Portable printers**, usually inkjets, don't offer the best image quality, but they're tiny and lightweight, perfect for making quick prints at business or social events.

▶ **Multifunction devices** combine the functions of a copier, scanner, printer, and fax machine in one machine. They're jacks of all trades, and possibly masters of none, but they can't be beat for convenience.

Now let's take a look at the different printer technologies you'll run into while printer shopping.

Inkjet Printers

The most inexpensive and most versatile printers you'll run across are inkjet models (see Figure 9.2). These printers spray tiny droplets of colored ink onto the surface of the paper to create a printed image. Like commercial printing presses, they use cyan, magenta, yellow, and black inks, but some printers add other ink colors for better results. Most commonly, you'll see printers that use a light magenta and a light cyan in addition to the usual four inks. Some manufacturers, such as Canon, make inkjet printers that use green and red or orange inks to increase the gamut of colors that they can reproduce.

FIGURE 9.2
This spiffy all-in-one printer/ scanner/copi-er/fax from Epson costs well under $200, and other models are as cheap as $30 or $40. Photo courtesy of Epson America, Inc.

Inkjet printers are often not network capable; they most often use USB to connect to your printer, although I'm starting to see some with Bluetooth wireless connectivity.

Dye Sublimation Printers

You're most likely to run into this technology among snapshot printers (see Figure 9.3). Don't be misled by the term *snapshot*—dye-sub printers provide some of the best color reproduction out there and are often used for high-end color proofing in the publishing industry. They work by heating solid inks until they turn into a gas and sink into the special paper, and then solidify again.

FIGURE 9.3
Sony's PictureStation printers are tiny and well designed. Photo courtesy of Sony Electronics, Inc.

These are image printers, not something you can use for printing letters and memos, so they're usually not the best bet for someone who can afford only one printer. But if you're looking for top-notch photo prints, look to a dye-sub.

Color Laser Printers

Until recently, color laser printers were expensive behemoths that you'd find at Kinko's, not something you'd consider for home use. Well, guess what? Times have changed (see Figure 9.4).

FIGURE 9.4
Hewlett-
Packard's color
laser printers,
including this
Color LaserJet
1600, are a
solid buy. Photo
courtesy of
Hewlett-Packard
Company.

Color lasers can now be had for much less than $500—in fact, check out the Samsung CLP-300, with a street price of less than $200. As with black-and-white laser printers, they're smaller than they used to be. Because of their speed and the high capacity of their paper trays, color laser printers are great for printing flyers and business graphics. You won't find their photo print quality as good as with inkjet or dye-sub printers, but if speed is more important to you than getting a perfect print, you'll want to consider a color laser.

Printing the Page

You've got your printer, it's all hooked up, your computer recognizes it, and you're almost ready to print. You need to take care of just a few more things before you get started. First, you need to set up Photoshop Elements' color management. Then you need to make sure you have the right inks and paper (or other medium).

Ink is expensive, that's for sure. In fact, printer companies such as Canon, Epson, and Hewlett-Packard sell their printers at rock-bottom prices just so that they can then sell you their expensive inks for years to come. Unfortunately, there's really no way to get off the ink train. You can buy inexpensive third-party inks, true, but they might not work well with your printer. I once spent weeks trying to track down the source of a nasty green cast in all my prints, only to find that it was the off-brand ink I'd been using. The problem disappeared immediately when I switched back to the printer manufacturer's ink. The same caveat goes for ink cartridge refill kits and for paper; I recommend sticking with manufacturers' inks at all times and choosing paper very carefully. Sometimes you really do get what you pay for.

Do It for Me

Of course, if you don't feel like wrestling with your printer, you can just send away for prints—and you can even place your order right from Photoshop Elements.

Start by choosing one or more images in the Organizer, and then choose File, Order Prints. This brings up a series of screens in which you can place an order with Kodak's EasyShareGallery service. In the first screen, you're asked to either create an account or log into an existing one. Next, you choose the number and size of the prints you want to order, along with a surface finish. After that, you enter your own address and those of any other people to whom you'd like prints shipped.

The next few steps are strictly business. You choose a shipping method, apply any coupons you have, enter your credit card information, and then start uploading the pictures you want to print. The process is simple, and although the prices aren't particularly low, there's a lot to be said for convenience. I especially like the capability to send prints to any address, not just your own; it's a great way to share pictures with family members and friends who don't have a computer.

Preparing to Print

The first thing you need to do when you're setting up to print is make sure Photoshop Elements' color management is turned on so that the program will use all its wiles to make your printouts look good. This is a one-time thing; you don't need to do it every time you print. Follow these steps:

1. Choose Edit, Color Settings (see Figure 9.5).

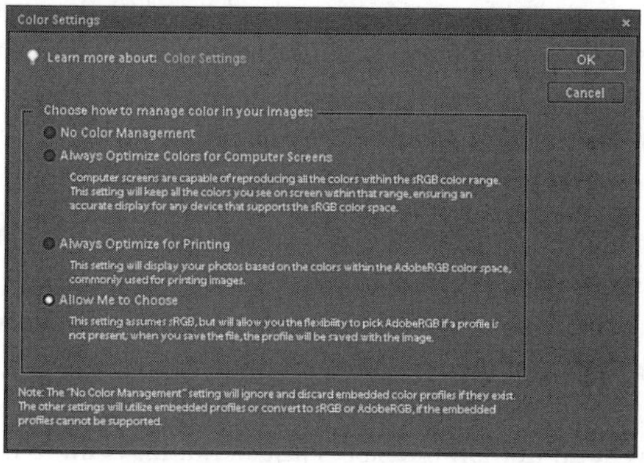

FIGURE 9.5
Photoshop Elements does a pretty good job of explaining what each color management setting does.

2. Choose a color management option:

▶ **No Color Management**—If you intend to allow your printer to handle the color management, leave this option on. I've found that my Epson inkjet's color management is pretty good, so I usually stick with this option. When I want to really optimize my printouts, though, I use Photoshop Elements' color management with one of the following options.

▶ **Always Optimize Colors for Computer Screens**—This is the appropriate setting for people who create nothing but web graphics and photos to share online. Because we're printing in this chapter, let's skip right over this setting.

▶ **Always Optimize Colors for Printing**—If you print every picture, this is the setting for you. I don't do that, though, and I'm betting you don't, either. Which leads us to …

▶ **Allow Me to Choose**—Here's the one you want if you sometimes print, but not always. If a photo already contains color profile information, this setting uses that information to display the file. If not, you can choose which profile you want Photoshop Elements to add to the file: Adobe RGB for pictures you plan to print or sRGB for pictures that will probably be screen only.

3. After this, any time you save a file, make sure that ICC Profile is checked in the Save As dialog. If it's not, the appropriate color profile won't be added to the file.

Now you're ready to go load up your printer with the paper or other medium you've chosen. And you do have *a lot* of choices. Of course, most of the time you'll just want to print on paper, and for that I recommend spending the bucks for the good stuff. That means name-brand paper specifically designed for the kind of print you're going for. You'll want the extra-smooth, extra-white inkjet printer paper for drafts, and glossy or matte photo paper for final prints. If you've never tried photo paper, do give it a whirl; you'll be amazed by the quality of the prints.

On the other hand, if you're feeling crafty, you can print on all kinds of things besides regular printer paper. First, of course, there's art paper, such as the kind watercolor painters use. Then there are all kinds of specialty items, such as cotton and silk fabric, shrinking plastic, rice paper for placing on cakes, water-slide decals, stickers, and, of course, iron-on transfers. The range of products you can buy these days that will accept an iron-on transfer is just stunning. Want to make your own mouse pads, coasters, or placemats? No problem!

No matter what medium you're using, be sure to read and follow the printing instructions that came with it. With transfer media such as iron-ons, you generally need to choose a high quality level to maximize the amount of ink that's deposited on the printing surface; this, in turn, maximizes the amount of ink that can be transferred to the object you're ironing on. The media you're using might have other requirements; be sure to check them out.

Try it Yourself ▼

Printing a Single Photo

For the first printing task, let's switch to the Editor. You can print a single photo from the Organizer, too, but regardless of the number of photos selected, you end up in the Print Photos dialog box, which is different from the Editor's Print dialog box. We look at how to proceed from there in the next couple sections. For now, let's move on with printing from the Editor.

1. Open the photo you want to print in the Editor. Make sure you've made all the changes that you want to the image and that you've opened the right version of the picture, if multiple versions exist.

2. Choose File, Print to open the Print dialog box (see Figure 9.6).

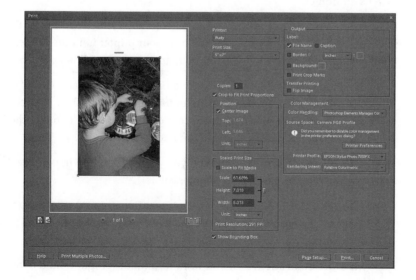

FIGURE 9.6
A lot is going on here, so go slow and make sure you consider each setting.

3. First, make sure the right device is shown in the Printer pop-up menu; then choose a Print Size option. If it's important that the printout measure exactly what the Print Size is (if it must fit in a picture frame, for instance), click Crop

▼

to Fit Print Proportions. To see a box showing the edges of the picture, click Show Bounding Box. Of course, you also need to enter a number in the Copies field.

4. In the Position area, either check Center Image or uncheck it and set Top and Left values to position the image wherever you want it to be on the paper.

> If you're planning to frame the picture so that some of the white paper around the image shows, you can achieve a classy look by placing the picture slightly higher than centered on the page.

5. In the Scaled Print Size area, you can see how much Photoshop Elements is scaling the photo up or down to fit it into the print size you've chosen, along with the resulting resolution (pixels per inch). Make sure these settings are appropriate; if the resolution is less than 150ppi, you might not be happy with the print's quality.

6. Make Output settings for any special requirements you have for this print: Add a Label (the filename or the caption from the Properties palette), a Border, or a Background color; choose Print Crop Marks to help you trim the print accurately; or click Flip Image if you're printing to a transfer medium such as an iron-on.

7. In the Color Management section, choose Photoshop Elements Manages Color from the Color Handling menu. Then choose your printer from the Printer Profile menu and decide on a Rendering Intent setting, as follows:

   ▶ **Perceptual**—Choose this setting for a print that's adjusted to look "correct" to human eyes. The colors maintain their relationships to each other, so if one or more colors are changed because they're out of the printer's gamut, all the colors in the image are changed.

   ▶ **Saturation**—Choose this setting if you want the print to have some extra oomph in the form of brighter colors.

   ▶ **Relative Colorimetric**—This setting leaves in-gamut colors alone and converts any out-of-gamut colors to their closest equivalents in the printer's gamut.

   ▶ **Absolute Colorimetric**—If you want to simulate output from a different printer, this setting enables you to specify that printer's profile and reproduce its output as closely as possible. It's mostly for graphic arts geeks like me, so you'll probably never need it.

8. Click Page Setup and make sure that the correct paper size and paper tray are shown (see Figure 9.7). Switch from Portrait to Landscape if you want to rotate the print to fit the wide way on the paper. Click OK when you're done making settings.

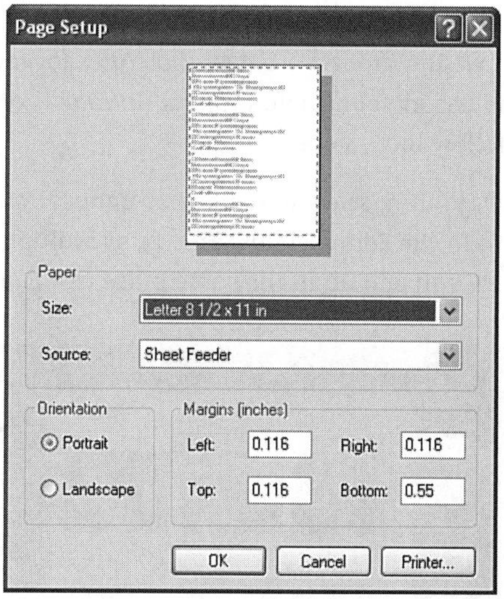

FIGURE 9.7
The Page Setup dialog contains basic paper size settings.

9. Click Print and then click your way through one more dialog, the operating system's Print dialog (see Figure 9.8). This is your last chance to switch printers or change the number of copies you print. Then click Print one last time, and you're off to the races.

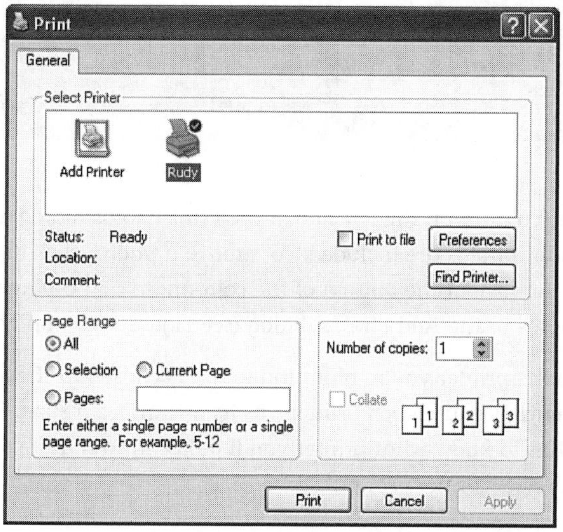

FIGURE 9.8
This Print dialog box is the last stop before your image actually reaches the printer.

▼   **Try it Yourself**

Making Contact Sheets

Traditional contact sheets are made by laying the exposed film directly onto photo paper to print it. For decades, contact sheets were the standard way to review the images from a roll of film to decide which ones were worth making larger prints of. They're still useful for passing around a batch of pictures for review so that you can decide which images to use in your photo projects. To make contact sheets in Photoshop Elements, follow these steps:

1. If you're in the Organizer, select the image or images you want to use and choose File, Print. In the Editor, choose File, Print Multiple Photos. No matter where you started, you end up in the same place (see Figure 9.9).

FIGURE 9.9
The Print Photos dialog enables you to output individual prints, contact sheets, picture packages, or labels.

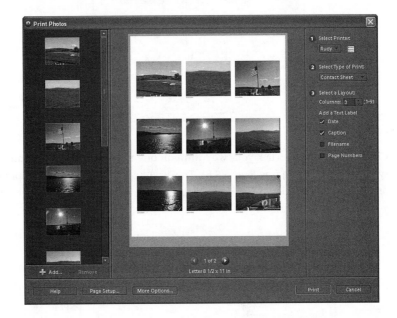

2. Look at the column on the left side of the Print Photos dialog and make sure that the right photos are included. To remove a photo, click its thumbnail and then click Remove at the bottom of the column; to add a photo, click Add, choose photos in the Add Photos dialog (see Figure 9.10), and click Done.

3. Make sure the printer you're planning to use is chosen in the Select Printer pop-up menu. Because each printer has its own margin sizes, Photoshop Elements has to know what printer you'll be using so that it can give you an accurate preview of the printout.

▼

FIGURE 9.10
You can place a check mark next to any of the photos from the Organizer in this dialog to include them in your contact sheet.

FIGURE 9.10
You can place a check mark next to any of the photos from the Organizer in this dialog to include them in your contact sheet.

4. Choose Contact Sheet as the type of print you want to make.

5. Choose a number of columns from 1 to 9; the number you choose automatically determines the number of rows on a page.

6. If you want the photos to be labeled, click any of the boxes in the Add a Text Label section.

7. Click Page Setup to double-check your paper settings; then click OK.

8. Click More Options and choose your printer's profile from the Print Space pop-up menu; then click OK.

9. Click Print.

Printing Picture Packages

Picture packages are Photoshop Elements' version of those studio portrait packages that include a variety of sizes of the same photo. If this isn't ringing a bell, cast your mind back to those school photos of years gone by—that's right, like that. Printing a picture package is a very similar process to making a contact sheet, with just a few different options to set.

Start by choosing the picture or pictures you want to use. Then choose Print in the Organizer or Print Multiple Photos in the Editor. When you're in the Print Photos dialog, choose Picture Package as the type of print, and then make sure the right photos are displayed in the left column. Now it's time to set your picture package options (see Figure 9.11):

FIGURE 9.11
The Picture
Package Frame
options are a
bit hokey, but
they're fun to
play with.

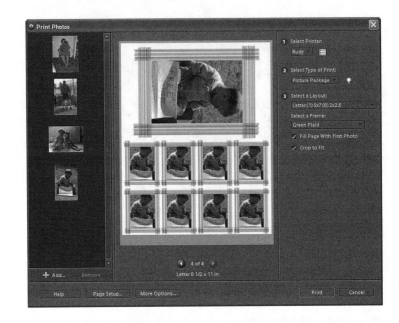

▶ **Layout**—These are the different size combinations available to you, ranging from a single 8"×10" print per page to a page with 20 tiny squarish prints.

▶ **Frame**—If you're in the mood for special effects, check out the options in this menu. I particularly like Brushed Antique Rectangle—Lady Bugs, not so much.

▶ **Fill Page with First Photo**—Check this oddly named box if you want to use the same picture for all the print sizes on each page, which, of course, will result in a multipage print job. Click the arrows below the preview to flip through the pages before you print.

▶ **Crop to Fit**—If this option is checked, Photoshop Elements crops the picture to completely fill each "slot" on the page. It's most noticeable when you choose a print size whose proportions are very different from your photo's. If you don't need your prints to be the exact size of a picture frame, click this setting off and on a few times to see which version you prefer.

By the Way

Don't panic if you see a dialog labeled Printing Warning when you first open the Print Photos dialog. It might tell you that some of your photos are too low resolution to be printed at the requested print size—but you haven't chosen a print size yet! Photoshop Elements is assuming you're going to use the same size you used the last time you printed pictures, and we all know what they say about assuming.

The Page Setup dialog and More Options dialog are the same for picture packages as they are for contact sheets; you won't find any surprises there.

Summary

Printing your photos is faster, easier, and cheaper than ever, and you have a lot of printers to choose from. You don't have to stick to printing on paper, either; all kinds of printer media enable you to do fun things with your pictures. In this hour, you learned how to set up Photoshop Elements' color management, and you printed a single image and a contact sheet. In the next hour, we look at different ways to share your pictures online.

Q&A

Q. *How long will color printouts last? Will they fade eventually?*

A. Everything fades eventually, but with today's archival-quality inks and good paper, your digital prints should last just as long as your traditional photo prints. For the latest and most comprehensive research on this issue, though, you really need to go to Wilhelm Imaging Research (www.wilhelm-research.com).

Q. *Can I print on my own fabric instead of the expensive precut sheets from the craft store?*

A. Sure. You need two things in addition to your cotton or silk cloth: freezer paper, the kind with one waxed side, and a product called Bubble Jet Set (C. Jenkins Co., www.cjenkinscompany.com) that sets the image permanently on the fabric. You can find instructions for doing this all over the Web, but basically you soak your cloth in Bubble Jet Set, iron it onto the freezer paper, trim it to fit through the printer, and go!

Workshop

See if you can answer these quiz questions; then have some fun with your printer doing the activities.

Quiz

1. What do the letters CMYK stand for?

    A. Cyan, mauve, yellow, and pink

    B. Cyan, magenta, yellow, and black

    C. Color, magnification, yield, and border

2. Laser printers are much slower than inkjet printers.

    A. True

    B. False

3. Which of the following is *not* a standard size print available within a picture package?

    A. 4"×6"

    B. 5"×7"

    C. 6"×8"

    D. 8"×10"

Quiz Answers

1. B.

2. B. Laser printers take longer to warm up when you first turn them on than inkjet printers do, but they print pages much more quickly.

3. C. Of course, you can print individual pictures at any size you like.

Activities

1. Print the same photo several times, at different quality levels, on different paper, and with different color management settings. Compare the results and decide which prints look better; then record the settings and media you used for them.

2. Take a batch of similar photos of people or an attractive scene. Then print a contact sheet and pass it around for comments from your friends or family members. See if having the contact sheet in front of them makes people more likely to talk about what they do and don't like in each photo.

HOUR 10

Sharing Your Pictures Online

What You'll Learn in This Hour:

▶ Attaching photos to email messages
▶ Creating online photo galleries
▶ Publishing a map showing where your pictures were taken
▶ Designing type, backgrounds, and graphics for your own web pages

Odds are, if you're reading this book, you have a computer. And if you have a computer, it's likely that you have access to email and to the World Wide Web. In turn, that means that you have practically unlimited opportunities to set your pictures free in the world and let everyone have a look at your best work. Sharing your pictures online offers several advantages over handing around prints all the time:

▶ Posting your photos online or emailing them is free, unless you want to pay for extra services.

▶ Uploading photos and getting the links to the people you want to share with is so quick that someone on the other side of the world can be looking at your photos on a snazzy web gallery just a few minutes after you take them.

▶ It doesn't take any more time or cost any more to share with dozens or hundreds of people than it does to share with one.

▶ You and those with whom you're sharing still have the option of ordering prints at any time.

Your options range from the simplest (attaching a photo to a plain-text email message) to the most complex (creating an interactive web gallery with fancy graphics and click navigation tools). Photoshop Elements makes it easy to do either of these—and a whole lot of things in between.

Web Image Basics

Before we get started with web publishing, let's take a few minutes to review some useful information about how the Web works.

As you probably remember from Hour 3, "Creating and Saving Image Files," the file formats you use for the Web are JPEG, GIF, and PNG. Almost all the artwork you process in Photoshop Elements will be saved in JPEG format, which produces good-looking and svelte photo files, but you might choose to save a picture in GIF or PNG format under a couple circumstances:

▶ If the picture is an illustration or logo instead of a photo, use GIF.

▶ If you're saving a photo that needs to have transparent areas, you must use PNG-24, even though it will result in a much larger file than with JPEG.

All these formats use image compression to make files as small as possible. The larger a file is, the longer it takes to be transferred over the Net, whether you're talking about the Web or email. And no one enjoys sitting around waiting for files to upload or download. So image files are compressed using mathematical techniques that take advantage of repeated data patterns in an image. Exactly how this works is way, way beyond the scope of this book, but the important thing to know about compression is that there are two kinds: lossy and lossless. When you save in a format that uses lossy compression, Photoshop Elements (or whatever other program you're using) actually changes the way the image looks to make it more compressible (see Figure 10.1). This means that image data is lost—permanently. How much image data? That depends on the quality setting you apply when saving.

FIGURE 10.1
The square "tiles" in this picture didn't exist in the original; Photoshop Elements created them to make the image compress smaller than it otherwise would.

Unlike JPEG files, GIF files use lossless compression, but you can reduce the number of colors in a picture's palette when you save it in GIF format. That's another way to make files smaller. You might recall that when you worked with the Save for Web dialog in Hour 3, you had to set the number of colors you wanted to include in a GIF image, from 0 to 256. That setting determines how many colors are retained; which ones stick around is determined by which color reduction algorithm you specify. Your choices are Perceptual, Selective, Adaptive, and Restrictive (Web); I recommend sticking with Selective unless your picture is made up of shades of just one or two colors, in which case you should use Adaptive.

So what happens to the colors that get left out? Photoshop Elements fakes them. That's right—those colors are simulated by dithering, the arrangement of similar-colored pixels adjacent to each other to create the impression of a different color (see Figure 10.2). Generally, the illusion is pretty good, but you still want to avoid dithering with photos. That's why GIF is mainly suitable for nonphotographic artwork.

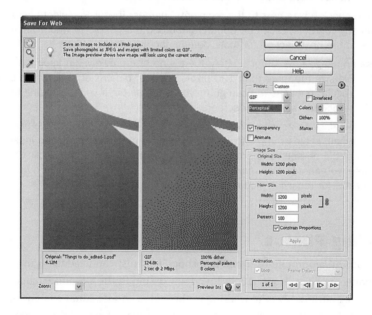

FIGURE 10.2
The different-colored pixels in the dithered version of this image combine to fool your eye into thinking you see a color that the image file doesn't really contain. Turn to this figure in the color section of this book to get a better idea of what's going on here.

Now that we've reviewed the basics about formats and compression, let's get online and actually share some photos.

Ways to Share Photos Online

Photoshop Elements offers you several ways to get your photos online, either on the Web using your own website or a free service, or via email, in various formats. You can email plain image files as attachments, or you can send HTML-formatted email using Photoshop Elements' stationery templates. You can even create a slideshow file, complete with audio and custom slide transitions, and email that. Keep reading to learn how to do each of these things and more.

Picture This

Not only can you send regular email from Photoshop Elements, but you can also send pictures to a mobile phone via the phone's email address. How's that for instant gratification? Here's what to do.

In the Organizer, choose the photos you want to send, and then click the Share tab and choose More Options, Email to Mobile Phone.

Click the check boxes next to the recipients' names; if your Recipients list doesn't contain any contacts, click Edit Contacts and add the people to whom you're sending. (Read the next section for more details about adding contacts.)

Choose an image size. Unfortunately, there's no size preview, but keep in mind that the Big size (no more than 120 pixels in either dimension) will fill the screen on most regular phones. You can go maybe twice as big if you're sending to someone whose phone has a larger screen.

Write a message to go with the pictures, and click Next. Photoshop Elements creates an email, scales the photos and attaches them to the email, and inserts the address of the person to whom you're sending. All you have to do is click Send. Of course, you should also make sure that the recipient's phone plan doesn't charge extra for receiving picture mail.

Emailing Photos

Before you can email photos from Photoshop Elements, you need to set up your email preferences (see Figure 10.3). If you're working in the Organizer, choose Edit, Preferences, Sharing; if you're working in the Editor, choose Edit, Preferences, Organize & Share; then click Sharing in the list at the left side of the dialog box. First, choose your email program from the Email Client menu; if it doesn't appear in the menu, choose Adobe Email Service to email directly from Photoshop Elements using your account with a web-based email service such as Yahoo! or GMail.

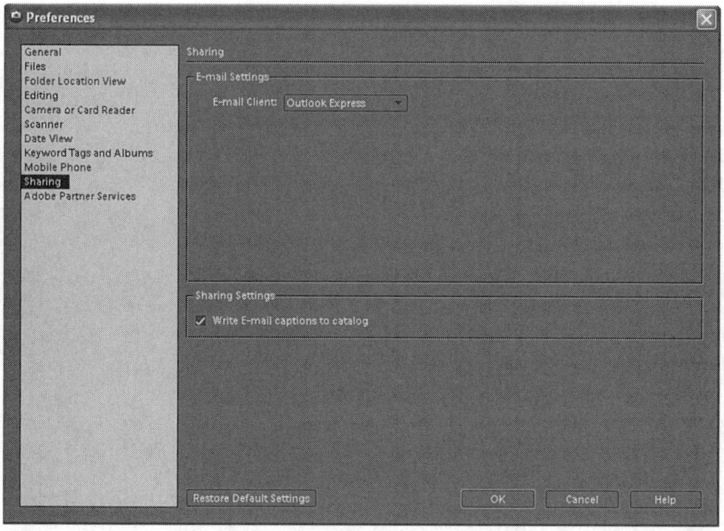

FIGURE 10.3
Photoshop Elements can't find your email client to send email until you tell it what that program is.

If you use any Windows email program other than Microsoft Outlook or Outlook Express, you'll have to go with Adobe Email Service; Photoshop Elements recognizes only those two external email clients.

By the Way

Before closing the Preferences dialog, check the box marked Write Email Captions to Catalog. When you add captions to photo email, Photoshop Elements adds that information to your photo catalog so you don't have to retype it.

Using the Email Attachments Option

Okay, we're ready to email some photos. Let's start with a simple email attachment—just a picture and a few words. First, in the Organizer, choose the photo you want to email. Then click the Email Attachments button on the Share tab (see Figure 10.4).

Choose a Maximum Photo Size and a Quality Level, watching the estimated file size and download time shown below the Quality Slider; then click Next. Now enter a message and choose recipients. If the people you want aren't listed, click the Contact Book button above the Recipients field and add the missing information. When everyone is listed, click Next again. That's it—the next thing you see is an email message, addressed and with photos attached, ready for you to click Send.

FIGURE 10.4
You can drag
additional pho-
tos from your
catalog into the
Items window to
include them
with your email.

If you plan to use these settings again in the future—in other words, if you often
send to the same person or group of people and you want to use the same image
size and quality level every time you do so—be sure to click the Yes button under
the Save As Quick Share Flow? question. When you save the settings as a Quick
Share Flow, the name that you choose appears in the Quick Share palette so that
you can skip most of these steps the next time you want to email photos to these
people.

Using the Stationary and Layouts Wizard

If you want to send jazzier emails with special formatting, you can click the Share
tab's Photo Mail button instead of Email Attachments. Here, again, you can drag
photos into the Items window to include them in your email; to delete a photo, click
its thumbnail in the Items window and then click the red Remove button above the
window. When you've collected the photos you want, check the Include Caption box
so that Photoshop Elements will insert a caption below each picture; then click Next.

Type your message and choose your recipients, and then click Next again. That
pops you into step 1 of the Stationery & Layouts Wizard, where you can choose a
template from the list on the left (see Figure 10.5). You'll find dozens of choices in
nine different categories. When you're happy with the look of your photo mail, add
captions for any images that need them and then click Next Step to tweak the template settings.

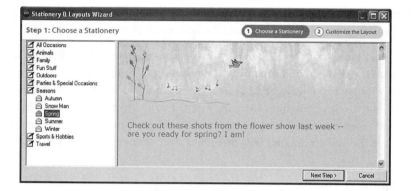

FIGURE 10.5
In addition to
choosing a tem-
plate in step 1,
you can revise
the message
that introduces
your photos.

In step 2 (see Figure 10.6), you get a few choices of alternative background patterns. You can also change several other settings that affect the appearance of your photo mail:

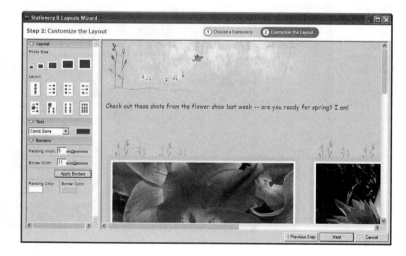

FIGURE 10.6
Step 2 of the
Stationery &
Layouts Wizard
is all about the
details.

▶ **Layout**—You'll see five preset image sizes, from rather small to quite large, and you can choose from eight different layout arrangements.

▶ **Text**—You can change the font and color of the introduction and captions in the message.

▶ **Border**—Padding refers to an inner border (white, by default); Border refers to the outer border. You can set the width and color of both of these.

When you're done tweaking, click Next again. Photoshop Elements turns your photos and settings into an HTML-formatted email message, ready for you to click Send.

Now, about those captions. Remember when you set your sharing preferences and turned on the Write Email Captions to Catalog setting? Here's where that comes into play. If your photos already had captions in the Properties window (choose Window, Properties to see it), Photoshop Elements inserted those in your photo mail. But if the General Properties' Caption field is empty, the program now takes the captions you typed into the photo mail and puts them into the Captions field. Pretty neat, right?

Keeping in Touch

If you find yourself adding new contacts to Photoshop Elements' Contact Book all the time, it's probably worth taking a few minutes to import your regular email address book into the Contact Book. Start by choosing Edit, Contact Book in the Organizer (see Figure 10.7).

FIGURE 10.7
The Contact Book in Photoshop Elements works just like most address book programs.

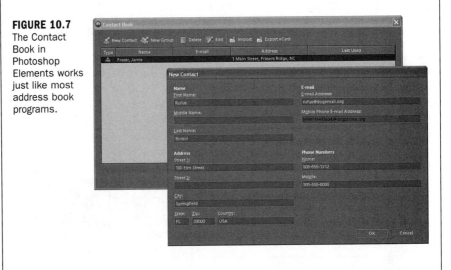

In the toolbar across the top of the Contact Book window, click Import. This opens the Choose Contact Source dialog, in which you can choose vCard Files or the address book from your Outlook or Outlook Express. Pick one of these and click OK. If you choose vCard Files, you then have to navigate to the files' location on your hard drive; if you choose another option, Photoshop Elements locates your address book file by itself. Either way, now Photoshop Elements knows the email addresses of all your friends and family members.

Sending a PDF Slideshow

A third way to email photos is to send a PDF slideshow. This is a document containing multiple photos that display in sequence with smooth transitions between them. It opens in Adobe Reader, which is a free download from www.adobe.com, so anyone can view the file on any computer. The process of putting together a slideshow will be pretty familiar to you if you've been reading through this hour in order. Start by choosing the photos you want to include in the show. Then, in the Organizer's Share tab, choose PDF Slide Show from the More Options menu.

You can add or delete photos in the Items area. Then, as you did with email attachments, choose a size and a quality level for the images that will be included in the show. Give the slide show a name and then click Next. Compose a message to go in your email, choose recipients for the email, and click Next again. You end up with a bare-bones slideshow presentation (see Figure 10.8). It automatically plays in full-screen mode and has simple transitions between photos. As with email attachments and photo mail, Photoshop Elements attaches the slideshow file to an email message so that all you have to do is click Send.

FIGURE 10.8
You can't customize a PDF slideshow's settings, but sometimes simpler is better—it's certainly quick to create and send.

Creating an Online Gallery

If you're looking for something really fancy to display your photos, you need online galleries. These are web pages that feature Photoshop Elements' professionally designed templates, some of them with animation or even interactive elements. As usual, start in the Organizer by choosing the photos that you want to include in the gallery. Head back to the Share tab and click the Online Gallery button.

First, you have an opportunity to add and delete photos from the batch you've chosen. When you're happy with the group of pictures you've got, click Next to move on. Here's where the fun begins. In the Category pop-up menu, choose from the following options:

▶ Interactive templates respond to the viewers' actions. Users can click a picture to see a larger version of it and can perform other actions, such as turning pages.

▶ The Standard templates provide a basic web page displaying image thumbnails that viewers can click to see each image full size.

▶ Animated templates feature moving elements, but those elements don't respond to user actions.

▶ Journal templates offer a look that's similar to the Standard templates, but with plenty of space to add extensive captions to your photos.

▶ Another basic offering, Slideshow templates are similar to Standard ones, but viewers can click a Play button to see the photos displayed sequentially without having to click through them.

▶ If you want to showcase a video clip, choose Video.

Click the template thumbnails to see how they'll look with your pictures; when you find one you like, either double-click it or just leave it selected and click Next. At this point, Photoshop Elements combines your chosen photos with its template and presents you with the result so you can fine-tune it (see Figure 10.9). Which settings you can adjust depend on the template you choose; you might just be able to enter a gallery title and your email address, or you might end up needing to specify a background image, type colors, and even animation speed. When you've got the gallery settings the way you want them, click Next.

FIGURE 10.9
Depending on your template, you might need to specify a lot of gallery settings or just a few. I used the Comic Book template for this page; it's in the Interactive category.

Enter a filename for the gallery and choose a location on your hard drive. When you click Next, Photoshop Elements saves the file and then asks where you want to post the gallery: on Photoshop Showcase, on your own FTP site, or saved on a CD or DVD.

▶ If you choose Photoshop Showcase, you'll see a window asking you to either log in or register a new account with Photoshop Showcase. Go ahead and do it—there's no charge. Then you'll proceed through a series of screens asking you to confirm your map gallery's name, provide email addresses for anyone you want to notify about the gallery, and upload the gallery's photos.

▶ If you have your own website where you want to post your map gallery, click My FTP and enter the appropriate information in the dialog box. Photoshop Elements needs to know the address of your server and your username and password so it can move the files to your site.

▶ If you don't want to publish your gallery online, you can put it on a disc. Click CD/DVD, insert a blank disc, give the disc a name, and click OK.

To finish, click Done at the bottom of the Task pane.

▼   **Try it Yourself**

Publishing a Photo Map

Adobe and Yahoo! have gotten together to incorporate Yahoo! maps into Photoshop Elements so that you can search for and display your photos based on where they were taken. Here's how it works, starting with getting your photos on the map and then moving on to publishing the map:

1. In the Organizer, choose Display, Show Map to bring up your map. A pop-up menu below the map enables you to display a satellite view, a road map, or a hybrid view that overlays the map data on the satellite image.

2. To place your photos on the map, drag them onto it from the Photo Browser (see Figure 10.10). You can also drag a keyword tag onto the map, which applies that map location to any photo with that tag.

FIGURE 10.10
Each red map pin indicates that one or more photos were taken at that location.

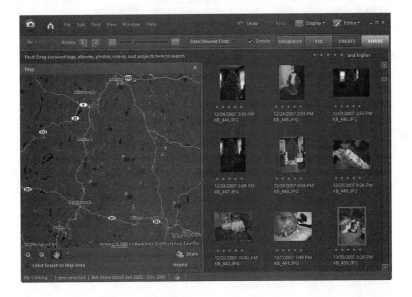

Did you Know?

To view all the photos associated with a place on the map, click the red pin stuck in the map at that location. Click a small thumbnail in the little preview window to see a larger thumbnail; double-click the larger thumbnail to display that photo in Full Screen View.

3. When you've got enough photos on your map, click the Share button below the map, and then click Share again in the Sharing Your Map and Photos dialog. Photoshop Elements takes a minute or two to create a new gallery based on the map and then displays it on your screen.

▼

4. Fill in information about your mapped photo collection in the Gallery Title, Gallery Caption, About This Gallery, Your Name, and Your Email Address fields. Click Next.

5. Give the gallery file a name and choose a location for it on your hard drive. Click Next again; now Photoshop Elements saves the gallery file in your photo catalog.

6. As with regular galleries, Photoshop Elements now needs to be told where you want to post the gallery: on Photoshop Showcase, on your own site, or saved on a CD or DVD. (Skip back to the previous section, "Creating an Online Gallery," if you want to review these options.) Click Done.

Of course, the map isn't just for showing off. You can also use it in the Organizer to help you find specific photos. Start by displaying the map; then click Limit Search to Map Area to show only the photos whose locations appear in the visible map area (see Figure 10.11). Keep in mind, though, that this also hides all the photos that don't have assigned locations. Maybe it's time to invest in a new camera with built-in GPS so that each photo already has its location specified when you bring it into Photoshop Elements....

FIGURE 10.11
These photos were taken at the Anheuser Busch Brewery in Merrimack, New Hampshire—home of a team of the famous Budweiser Clydesdales.

Using the EasyShare and SmugMug Galleries

If you don't have your own website, you might want to try out the third-party photo-sharing sites with which Photoshop Elements can connect directly: Kodak EasyShare Gallery and SmugMug Gallery. Both are free, at least at first, and they offer a really quick way to get your photos out there.

Let's look at EasyShare first; it follows what by now should be a pretty familiar sequence of steps. In the Organizer, choose the images you want to share, and then click the Share tab and choose Kodak EasyShare Gallery from the More Options menu. You'll need to create a new account or log in with an existing one before you can get any further.

After that, you add the email addresses of your friends, or choose from those already stored in your Photoshop Elements Contact Book, and compose an email message with an appropriate subject to notify people about your gallery. Then Photoshop Elements uploads your photos and sends the email. You see a confirmation dialog letting you know that the upload completed and giving you the link to the gallery's page (see Figure 10.12).

FIGURE 10.12
Your Kodak EasyShare gallery will look like this.

There's no charge to put your photos on Kodak EasyShare Gallery, but if you don't order prints or another product from the site at least every 12 months, your photos can be deleted. Your account won't be deleted, though. SmugMug Gallery is similar to Kodak's, but it costs $40 per year after a 14-day free trial. Your basic membership enables you to apply decorative templates to your photo pages. There's no limit to the number of photos you can upload or the amount of traffic allowed on your pages.

If you don't find the Kodak or SmugMug galleries to your taste, you can peruse all kinds of free photo-sharing sites on the Web. Two of the big ones are Flickr (www.flickr.com) and Snapfish (www.snapfish.com); Flickr is well known for its community features (commenting and message boards), and Snapfish has excellent prices on prints and a great selection of photo gifts.

DIY Web Design 101

Don't worry, I'm not going to try to cram a whole course on how to do HTML or web design into this hour. But I would like to just give you a few tips on the image aspects of web design. If you're interested in learning more about creating websites and programming for the web, take a look at *Sams Teach Yourself Web Publishing with HTML and CSS in an Hour a Day, 5th Edition* (ISBN 0-7686-6635-X, available from www.samspublishing.com).

> As you know, you use the Save for Web dialog when you're saving images to web formats. If you need to review the settings and controls in the Save for Web dialog, turn back to Hour 3, "Creating and Saving Image Files."

By the Way

Creating Backgrounds

I have to admit, I'm a minimalist in some ways. I still prefer black type on a plain white background for web pages; it's just so much more legible than anything else. On the other hand, I've seen plenty of neat backgrounds that really do a good job of conveying a particular flavor within a web page design. So here are a few words about using backgrounds on your own pages.

You can, of course, start with a simple, subtle background color. This doesn't add anything to file size or download time for your site. As far as legibility is concerned, as long as you remember that one word—*subtle*—you'll likely be fine. Unless you're really going for shock value, stay away from those blood-red or eye-gouging purple backgrounds.

Another option, and one that can be very effective design-wise, is to use a single ghosted image—that is, lightened so that the picture's details don't interfere with type laid over it. The simplest way to accomplish this, starting out in Full Edit with a photo open, is to choose Edit, Fill Layer and set the Contents to White or a very pale color, and enter an Opacity percentage of 80% to 90%. You'll end up with a quiet, pale version of the photo that still gets the message across without preventing the rest of the page from being seen (see Figure 10.13).

FIGURE 10.13
Background images should never stand out; they should subtly complement a page's overall design.

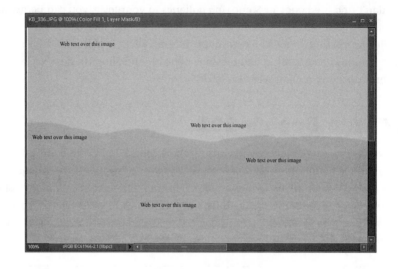

If a background image is full screen, it will really slow down your page-loading times. You can get a similar effect by using a repeating pattern, either a page-wide image that repeats vertically or a tiled picture that repeats both horizontally and vertically (see Figure 10.14). In the next task, I show you a foolproof technique for creating seamless repeating tiles.

FIGURE 10.14
These two images are ready to be used as Web page backgrounds. The one on the left will repeat vertically; the one on the right is a tile that will repeat both horizontally and vertically.

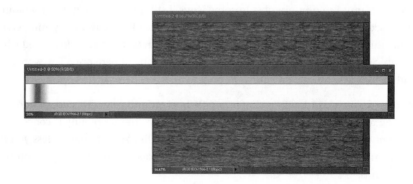

Creating a Repeating Pattern

With a tiled background, you need to hide the seams where the tiles meet so that your background looks like one large image. Here's how to make that happen.

1. Starting with a photo of a texture that you like, select a smallish image area (perhaps 100 pixels square), copy it, and create a new document. Accept the dimensions that Photoshop Elements inserts in the New dialog; they're based on the size of the area you copied from your source image. Choose Edit, Paste to insert the Clipboard contents into the new image file (see Figure 10.15).

FIGURE 10.15
This square picture of a recycled rubber playground surface is the starting point for my tiled background.

2. First, clean up the image. Apply any Quick Fixes or other image adjustments to it that you want to use, and fix any blemishes that are too distracting from the rest of the image. Remember, a background pattern should be fairly uniform in color and brightness so that type laid over it remains legible.

3. Choose Image, Resize, Image Size to see the pixel dimensions of the image (or perhaps you remember them from the New dialog).

4. Switch to Full Edit mode and choose Filter, Other, Offset. First, make sure the Undefined Areas setting is set to Wrap Around.

5. Then divide the image's width (which you learned in Step 3) in half and enter that amount in the Horizontal field. This will move the image so that its center is at the edges and its edges are in the center.

6. Do the same with the image's height and enter the result in the Vertical field (see Figure 10.16). Click OK.

▼

FIGURE 10.16
The most impor-
tant setting
here is Wrap
Around.

7. Now you can see a sharp line running down the middle of the picture and an intersecting line running across the middle. These show where the top edge of the image meets the bottom edge and where the left edge meets the right edge. They enable you to see how the picture will look as a tile.

8. Using whatever tools suit you (such as the Clone Stamp, the Blur tool, and the Healing Brush), eliminate those hard lines running across and down the middle of your picture (see Figure 10.17). Try to be subtle; major changes in the image will be distracting. You simply want to eliminate these seams.

FIGURE 10.17
The object here
is to get rid of
these obvious
seams.

9. When you're done, choose Filter, Offset to repeat the Offset filter. Because that's the last filter you applied, it remains at the top of the Filter menu, for easy access.

10. Using the same tools and techniques, get rid of any remaining hard-edged seams.

11. Now the tile is ready to be used. Using Save for Web, save it as a medium-quality JPEG file. In your web design program, specify this file as your background image and set it to tile.

If you don't have a texture photo, you can make your own textures by creating a new blank document the size of your desired tile, filling it with a color, and then experimenting with Photoshop Elements' filters until you get something you like. We play with filters later in the book; peek ahead to Hour 19, "Using the Improvement Filters," or Hour 20, "Using the Artistic Filters," if you're looking for some inspiration right now.

Setting Type

As you've probably noticed, type on web pages tends to show up in boring fonts such as Arial and Times New Roman. That's because web browsers have to use the fonts that all users have installed in their computers, and it's pretty hard to predict which fonts all your viewers will have in common. Just a few likely choices emerge, hence the tendency for text to display in these few plain fonts.

When you're designing your own web page, however, you can make use of your favorite fonts—if you make them graphics instead of regular text. This is the only way to be sure your own special font is used and to avoid having some default font substituted for it. Keep in mind, however, that image files are almost invariably larger than text files, so they take up more room on your web server and take longer to display on a viewer's screen than plain text. Use type images for headings and buttons, not for all the type on the page.

Consider my three best tips for creating type images:

▶ Be sure that anti-aliasing is turned on for your type; otherwise, the edges will appear jagged.

▶ To make the file as small as possible dimensions-wise, activate the type layer and choose Layer, Simplify Layer. This turns it into image pixels. Then Ctrl+click the layer's thumbnail in the Layers palette to select all the nontransparent areas on the layer, and choose Image, Crop. Performing these steps gets rid of any extra space around the type (see Figure 10.18).

FIGURE 10.18
Crop to delete
any extraneous
areas in the
type image file.

▶ Before saving the file in a web format (GIF or PNG), hide the Background layer so that you can see the transparent areas on the type layer. Then be sure to check Transparency in the Save for Web dialog. This enables a background color or image to show through inside and around the letters.

Using Transparency

Consider this conundrum: Every image file is rectangular, but not every image is rectangular. So what do you do with the parts of your image file that aren't actually your image? Answer: You make them transparent so that the background color or image behind can show through (see Figure 10.19). And with Photoshop Elements, that's much easier than ever to do with web images.

FIGURE 10.19
The gray
checkerboard
pattern indi-
cates transpar-
ent areas of the
picture.

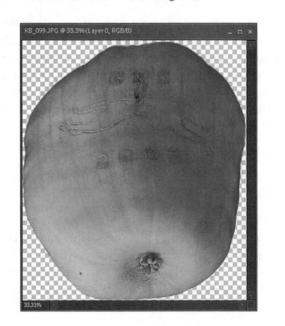

First, you need to put the image on a transparent layer. If you're starting with a shape or type layer, you're already there; all you need to do is delete the Background layer. On the other hand, if you need to get rid of parts of the image to make them transparent, you'll probably want to use one of Photoshop Elements' special tools for doing just that.

The Background Eraser is intended specifically for deleting backgrounds around image objects. To use it, click and drag on an area of the image that you want to remove. As you drag, the eraser deletes the colors under the cursor, along with adjacent pixels of similar colors. The crosshairs at the center of the cursor determine what colors are erased, and the circle around the crosshairs determines the area that the eraser is influencing. So if any part of your foreground image touches a background area of the same color, watch out! You might want to switch to the regular Eraser tool for areas such as this. In any case, set the tool's Tolerance to a low value (around 10%), zoom in so you can see what you're doing, and go slowly (see Figure 10.20).

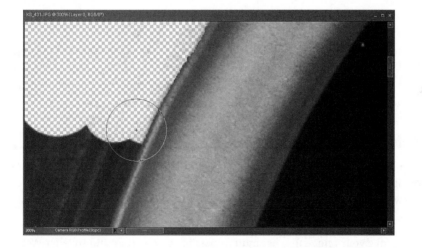

FIGURE 10.20
At this point, I'm removing the tire along the edge of a hubcap with the Background Eraser, one click at a time.

The Magic Extractor is similar, but it requires much less work on your part. To get started, choose Image, Magic Extractor, which brings up a big dialog box with its own toolbox (see Figure 10.21). The two most important tools are the Foreground Brush and the Background Brush; you use these the same way you use the Quick Selection tool. First, with the Foreground Brush, paint a few swipes across the area of the image you want to retain. Try to make sure you cut across all the different colors used in this area. Then switch to the Background Brush and do the same with the background that you want to delete. When you're ready, click Preview to see the results.

FIGURE 10.21
When it works, using the Magic Extractor is much, much faster than doing the work yourself with the Background Eraser.

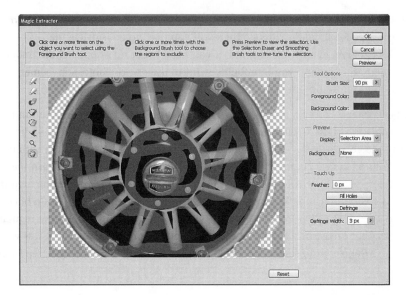

When the picture is ready, use the Save for Web dialog to save it as a GIF or a PNG, making sure to check the Transparency box. To ensure that the edges of the object blend well with the background, you can also choose a color from the Matte menu next to the Transparency check box; you should pick a color that matches the background as closely as possible.

Making Pages Load Faster

Truth be told, how fast your web pages load on viewers' screens really isn't up to you. It depends on the speed of the server where your pages are stored, the speed of a viewer's Internet connection, and the speed of the viewer's computer. That said, here's what you can do to improve matters:

▶ Make your image files as small as possible by always using Save for Web, instead of Save As, to optimize your images for the Web. Take the time to compare different combinations of settings so that you can choose the smallest file that still meets your criteria for appearance.

▶ Choose Progressive for JPEG images and Interlaced for GIF images. This makes them appear on the user's screen as low-res images very quickly; then the high-res image replaces the preview as soon as it has finished downloading.

▶ Be sure to insert some HTML text, particularly at the top of the page. Text usually loads first, and very quickly, which means your viewers will have something to start reading while they wait for photos to display.

▶ If you're displaying physically large images—ones that take up a lot of space on the screen—consider placing thumbnail images on your main pages and making them link to the larger images. That way, users can choose to download only the images they want to see.

▶ Use alt tags to display text labels in place of photos for users who choose to turn off images in their web browser or who can't see the screen. Alt labels are also displayed onscreen before an image loads, so, again, that will give your viewers something to look at while they wait to see the photos.

As an added bonus, screen readers operate better the more text you use and the more alt tags you use. Plus, you can increase the size of real text, but graphics will stay the size they are. What's more, because the total size of the files that make up your website will be smaller, your traffic will be lower, so you're less likely to run over your limit and incur extra charges from your web hosting provider.

By the Way

What's that, you say? Who worries about big web files these days when so many people use broadband connections? I'll tell you who: For starters, quite a few people out there are still using dial-up connections. On top of that, more people are viewing the Web via mobile phones and similar devices, which have slower connections than computers usually do. So file size remains an important consideration, for now.

Summary

In this hour, you learned how to send photos via email, how to turn them into online galleries that anyone can view on the Web, and how to publish a map that arranges your photos by location. We reviewed some basic web concepts at the top of the hour, and we closed things out by looking at a few graphics-geek techniques you can use when designing your own websites.

Q&A

Q. *Will interactive photo galleries work on all computers?*

A. They're programmed in Flash, so users who don't have a Flash plug-in installed in their web browsers might not get the full effect. But it's pretty uncommon these days to run into someone who can't view Flash, so I wouldn't worry about it.

Q. *What's the difference between email attachments and Photo Mail?*

A. In Photo Mail, the pictures are part of the email message, along with the text and background image. When you send email attachments, the pictures are attached to the message, but they don't constitute the message itself.

Workshop

We've gone over a lot of stuff in this hour. Here are a few quiz questions and a couple fun activities to help you review.

Quiz

1. Dithered images arrange the colors they contain to fool a viewer into seeing more colors than actually exist in the image file.

    A. True

    B. False

2. The term *interlaced* means that the image

    A. Is saved in a reversed file format.

    B. Displays progressively higher-res images as it downloads on a web page.

    C. Might have parts of another image embedded in it.

3. Which format is considered an alternative to JPEG for photographic images?

    A. GIF

    B. PNG-8

    C. PNG-24

    D. PHO

Quiz Answers

1. A.

2. B. This is a good way to keep viewers interested while they wait for large image files to download.

3. C. PNG-8 is an alternative to GIF.

Activities

1. Email your best photo by attaching it to an email from within Photoshop Elements. You can send the picture to your best friend, your mom, or even me, if you like. My email address is binderk@mac.com.

2. Using the Offset technique described previously, make a pattern tile. When it's done, if you don't have a web page to put it on, use it as a Photoshop Elements pattern fill instead. Select the whole tile image; then choose Edit, Define Pattern from Selection. Then create a new blank file and choose Edit, Fill Layer to fill the document with the pattern. Can you find the point where the tile ends and the pattern starts over?

PART II

Simple Corrections

HOUR 11

Composing and Cropping Your Pictures

What You'll Learn in This Hour:

▶ The principles of good image composition

▶ Ways to crop pictures to maximize their impact

▶ How to rotate crooked pictures, as well as ones that are just upside down

▶ How to flip pictures

How many times have you taken a picture and then, when looking at it later, thought it should look a lot better than it does? It happens to the best of us, and a good portion of the time, the problem turns out to be the picture's cropping. As any art student can tell you, what you leave out of the picture is almost as important as what you leave in. It's all about focus—encouraging the viewer's eye to look at what *you* think is the most important feature of the picture. You can help make that happen by getting rid of distracting elements.

With digital images, you're not restricted to standard print sizes, so you have a lot more latitude in how you crop a picture and what shape the final image takes. As you work with an image, you can also rotate it (a little or a lot), straighten it, and flip it left to right or top to bottom until it's just the view you were hoping for when you originally shot the photo.

Cropping Images

When you're taking pictures, be sure to give yourself room to crop. Use your camera's LCD preview, if it has one, to judge composition, before and after taking a shot; then go back and take more shots to see if you can do better. Although you don't want to have to trim off 90% of the picture's area to get the photo you were going for, it's good to have some room around the edges to play with.

Photoshop Elements has a special tool just for cropping—that would be the Crop tool, of course—but you can crop in other ways:

▶ The Cookie Cutter tool deletes all of the image that falls outside the bounds of the shape you draw with it—but instead of cropping, it just hides the rest of the active layer. You can do this when you want a background image, color, or pattern to show around the edges of the cropped image (see Figure 11.1).

FIGURE 11.1
Using the Cookie Cutter tool on the street scene layer makes the metal background image show.

▶ Using the Rectangular Marquee tool, you can select part of an image, copy the selection, and then paste it into a new image file. This method preserves the original, uncropped image as well as the new cropped version, so it's a useful technique. Remember, when you copy something and then create a new file, Photoshop Elements automatically fills out the Width and Height fields with the dimensions of the image on the Clipboard.

▶ Shrinking the canvas size also crops an image, but without any visual feedback while you're setting the amount to trim. There's no real reason to bother using this technique.

▶ You can crop an image using a selection created with any selection tool. With the selection active, choose Image, Crop. The new canvas is the smallest rectangle that can contain all the selected areas (see Figure 11.2). Using this technique with a selection produced by the Magic Wand or the Quick Selection tool is a good way to zoom in really tight on your subject while ensuring that you don't trim off any of it.

FIGURE 11.2
I selected the red flower using the Quick Selection tool before cropping.

▶ If you decide to choose Edit, Crop with no active selection, Photoshop Elements simply trims the canvas size by 50 pixels on each side.

Thinking About Good Composition

The first thing you have to decide when you're working to improve a picture's composition is what the photo's true subject is. Perhaps the shot started out as a group portrait with a stunning landscape in the background, but it turns out that the best part of the picture is the silly expressions on everyone's faces. So you decide you want to focus on those faces rather than the scene as a whole. That means cropping out the landscape in the background—but you have to figure out how much and which parts. Or, as in the case of Figure 11.3, you may have some other reason for removing part of the photo.

When we look at photos, our eyes automatically jump to faces and to objects that stand out because of their color, size, texture, or some other attribute. It's also true that we look at specific *places* in an image before we look at the image as a whole. For maximum impact, then, you want to use an object that will draw the eye and put it in a location where it will be noticed quickly. But where?

FIGURE 11.3
In this case, cropping enables me to get rid of the nasty reflection from my flash.

Take a look at Figure 11.4, which I've divided into thirds vertically and horizontally to form a grid with nine squares. The "rule of thirds," a compositional principle that artists have used for hundreds of years, tells us that a viewer's eye is instinctively drawn to the four places where the gridlines intersect. And *these* are the best places for an object you want people to look at, whether that's a portrait subject's eye or the most beautiful flower in a bouquet. The next best location is right in the middle of the image, as you might expect. But framing your picture so that the subject is slightly off-center gives it more visual interest, so that's another good reason to use the rule of thirds.

Did you Know?

You can overlay the "rule of thirds" grid on your pictures using Photoshop Elements preferences. In the Editor, choose Edit, Preferences, Grid and enter 33.33 percent (as opposed to inches or another unit of measure) in the Gridline Every field, with Subdivisions set to 1. Then choose a color and style for your grid lines. The grid won't show when you print the picture or view it in any program other than Photoshop Elements, so make it as bright as you need it to be to show up well. To show or hide the grid in your picture, choose View, Grid.

The grid should help you decide whether your picture will look best horizontally (landscape), vertically (portrait), or square. Now you're ready to crop it.

FIGURE 11.4
Framing the photo so that the puppy's face falls at one of the gridline intersections ensures that the viewer's eye will be drawn right where I want it.

Try it Yourself

Crop a Picture

Photoshop Elements' Crop tool is easy to use. You can even rotate the picture as you crop. Follow these steps:

1. In the toolbox, click the Crop tool.

2. Choose settings in the Options bar:

   ▶ Use the Aspect Ratio menu to restrict the cropping marquee to particular proportions. Your choices are standard print sizes, accompanied by Use Photo Ratio, which maintains the same proportions the image currently has.

   ▶ If you want the cropped image to be a specific size, enter dimensions in the Width and Height fields.

   ▶ Photoshop Elements can adjust image resolution while it crops a picture. If you want to do this, enter your desired value in the Resolution field.

3. Click and drag in the image window to draw a cropping marquee.

4. Drag the handles at each corner and on each side of the cropping marquee to adjust its size. Click and drag outside the marquee to rotate it (see Figure 11.5).

FIGURE 11.5
I can move and rotate the cropping marquee until it looks just right.

5. Click and drag in the cropping marquee to reposition it (this is particularly useful if you've restricted your proportions and you don't want to actually resize the marquee).

6. Click the Commit button or press Enter on the numeric keypad to finalize the crop.

If you don't like the results of the cropping operation, press Ctrl+Z to undo it and start over.

By the Way

When you draw a cropping marquee, the area outside it darkens, to help you focus on the crop area. This is called the shield. You can turn off the shield or change its color or brightness in Photoshop Elements preferences. In the Editor, choose Edit, Preferences, Display & Cursors. Uncheck Use Shield if you want to get rid of it; otherwise, choose a shield color and opacity percentage.

Rotating Images

If you find yourself tilting your head while you're looking at a picture, you need to rotate it. You can rotate images in 90° increments—useful when you turned your camera on its side to take the photo—or a fraction of a degree at a time.

As you know, you can rotate an image while you're cropping it, but you can also use several different commands to rotate a picture at any time. You'll find them in the Image menu, under the Rotate submenu; let's take a look at some of your choices.

▶ Choose Image, Rotate, 90° Left or 90° Right to counter the effects of having turned the camera to take the shot or having placed the image sideways on your scanner bed. If the picture is completely upside down, choose Image, Rotate, 180°.

▶ If you use the Custom command, you can rotate any number of degrees to the right or left (see Figure 11.6). This option is most useful when you want to turn pictures to the same odd angle, for design purposes.

FIGURE 11.6
Sometimes all you need is a degree or two.

▶ Straighten and Crop Image and Straighten Image have been part of Photoshop Elements since its inception—and they're still usually not worth using. I don't know how the program decides what's straight, but it's not using any criteria known to humans. Feel free to give these commands a try; in theory, they can straighten your image in a single step, or straighten it and then crop it to get rid of the extra background area (see Figure 11.7), but I have never liked the results of either command.

FIGURE 11.7
Now that the image is straight, I need to get rid of the extra background areas around its edges.

The other commands in the Rotate submenu fall into two categories: layer-specific commands, which work just like the regular Rotate commands but on just one layer at a time, and flip commands, which we cover later in this hour.

Straightening Crooked Pictures

If your picture is just a bit off, you could choose Image, Rotate, Custom and guess at the number of degrees of rotation it needs to be straight. Or you could use the Straighten tool, which always guesses right and takes just one step.

To take this easier path, start by choosing the Straighten tool from the toolbox. Then locate a line in your picture that should be perfectly horizontal (the horizon, the top of a doorway, or something like that). Click at one end of it with the Straighten tool and then drag along the line, releasing the mouse when you're satisfied that your line follows the image's line perfectly (see Figure 11.8). Voilà! The image straightens perfectly, leaving you to crop any extraneous background areas before you're done.

FIGURE 11.8
By dragging the Straighten tool along the horizon, I can show Photoshop Elements what I consider to be level.

KB_334.JPG @ 30%(RGB/8)

30%   sRGB IEC61966-2.1 (8bpc)

By the Way

The Canvas Options menu in the Straighten tool's Options bar is very important. Start with it set to Grow or Shrink Canvas to Fit, and stay on that setting until you're comfortable using the tool. Then you can try out the other options, which automatically crop the picture along with straightening it.

Sometimes you need a little visual assistance in deciding whether an image needs to be rotated and in which direction. You can make yourself a guide line by creating a new layer and then using the Custom Shape tool to draw a horizontal or vertical line on that layer. Press Shift as you drag to make sure that the line is perfectly aligned up and down or across. Keep the layer at the top of the Layers palette, and hide or show it as needed.

Flipping Images

You have two very good reasons to flip an image so it faces the other way. First, if you're printing on a transfer medium (such as an iron-on transfer), you need the transfer to be backward so that the final picture won't be a mirror image. Second, sometimes you just think the picture would work better if the people were looking the other way or the lighthouse was on the other side.

To flip an image, choose one of the Flip commands from the Image, Rotate submenu: Flip Horizontal or Flip Vertical. If you want to flip just the current layer, choose Flip Layer Horizontal or Flip Layer Vertical.

Of course, some things will jump right out if you flip them. Watch out for these:

▶ Type, either words or numbers

▶ Clocks and watches

▶ Objects traditionally worn on one side of the body, such as wedding rings and single earrings

▶ Cars and other vehicles with the steering wheel on one side

▶ Recognizable landmarks or personal features, such as scars or tattoos

If you flip an image containing any of these, your viewers are likely to notice—and chuckle (see Figure 11.9).

FIGURE 11.9
This is definitely
the sort of
photo you want
to avoid flip-
ping.

Summary

In this hour, we talked about cropping, rotating, and flipping pictures to achieve the best composition. Cropping is easy to do and can make a very noticeable difference in the appearance of a picture. You learned a few old-school composition guidelines, as well as ways to straighten and flip your pictures when needed. In the next hour, we look at perspective and distortion.

Q&A

Q. *I don't get it—why would I want to crop with a Selection tool instead of using the Crop tool?*

A. Suppose you want to trim an image as closely as you can around the fore-ground object. You could use the Crop tool and zoom way in to make sure you're getting a nice tight crop without cutting off any of the object—or you could just select the object with the Quick Selection tool and then crop. Make sense?

Q. *Can't I rotate an image by eye so that I can judge its straightness myself as I work?*

A. Sure. You do that using the Transform commands, which you'll learn about in the next hour.

Q. *I told my friend I wanted to flip an image, and she said I should say "flop" instead. What's up with that?*

A. Your friend must work in publishing. Design geeks say "flop" when the rest of the world says "flip." It means the same thing, so don't worry about it.

Workshop

The Quiz questions for this hour are pretty easy, so you should be able to zip right through them and get to the Activities. Don't skip those! They'll really improve your sense of when and how to crop, rotate, and flip images.

Quiz

1. The rule of _____ determines where the focus of an image should fall.

    A. objects

    B. proportion

    C. thirds

    D. quarters

2. When a picture is upside down, how many degrees do you need to rotate it to fix it?

    A. 90

    B. 180

    C. 360

    D. 45

3. Which of the following image features should prevent you from flipping a picture?

    A. Streetlights

    B. The setting sun

    C. Stoplights

    D. Street signs

Quiz Answers

1. C. Dividing a picture into thirds both horizontally and vertically gives you four focal points at which to place the picture's subject.

2. B. If you got this one wrong, may I suggest a review of your high school geometry textbook?

3. D. Watch out for street signs. They might not stand out as much as, say, a stop sign, but they do contain type and they'll be a dead giveaway if you flip a picture containing them.

Activities

1. From the book's website, download bowlingball.jpg. This picture is conventionally framed, with the subject at the center. Recrop it so that the focus is at each of the four gridline intersections from the rule of thirds. Which version looks best?

2. Download another image, boatsky.jpg. Try straightening the picture by dragging the Straighten tool along the flagpole. What happens? Can you still use this technique to straighten the image? What extra step should you take after straightening to fix it?

3. Take a look at your photo collection and count the number of images that shouldn't be flipped for some reason. What percentage of your pictures does this number amount to? Knowing this number gives you an idea of how much you'll need to watch out for telltale image elements when flipping your pictures.

HOUR 12

Straightening, Skewing, and Distorting an Image

What You'll Learn in This Hour:

▸ Transformations

▸ How to skew and distort pictures

▸ Ways to fix perspective

▸ How to transform part of a picture without affecting the rest

▸ How to combine the Liquify filter with a transformation for a fun effect

In the last hour, you learned how to rotate images so that they're level and straight. While using these techniques on your own pictures, have you run into some that just can't be completely straight? Like a photo with a building in the background? In that type of photo, you get the left side of the building to be perfectly vertical, but then the right side is tilted. This happens because of your perspective when you took the picture; you were closer to the bottom of the building than you were to the top, so the bottom appears wider. This sort of problem occurs all the time, even with smaller objects. To fix it, you need to learn how to transform your images.

Transforming Images

Whenever you move part of a picture, you're transforming it. The same is true when you resize images or their components. When you transform an image, you retain the picture's content while changing its size, shape, or position. Transformations include moving, resizing, rotating, and flipping—all of which you learned how to do in previous hours. The transformations we look at in this hour reshape a picture or part of a picture. In Photoshop Elements, you'll find these in the Image, Transform submenu: Skew, Distort, and Perspective.

The Transform commands operate on selections or layers, not the entire image. If a selection is active, whether it includes all of the image or just part of it, that area is transformed; if not, everything on the current layer or layers is transformed. When you choose one of the Transform commands, the selection or layer contents are surrounded by a marquee that looks just like the cropping marquee. It has handles at each corner and in the middle of each side; the handles you move and how far you move them determine the new shape of your selection (see Figure 12.1).

FIGURE 12.1
You apply transformations by manipulating the handles on the transform marquee.

> **By the Way**
>
> Transforming shape layers works the same way as transforming selections or regular layers, except that all the Transform commands are in a Transform Shape submenu if you're working on a shape layer.

Skewing a Picture

When we talk about a skewed perspective, we're talking about something that tilts to one side. That's exactly what skewing an image does: tilts it to the left or right while keeping the top and bottom level. Whether you know it or not, you've probably already seen skewed text. When you use an italic style with a font that doesn't have true italic letterforms built in, the program you're using usually just skews the type to the right (see Figure 12.2).

You can apply this transformation to an entire layer or to a selected area on a layer. To begin, select the layer or area that you want to skew and then choose Image, Transform, Skew. Drag any of the transform marquee's handles to skew the image. You can skew in both directions in the same transformation; just drag a side handle and then the top or bottom handle. When you're satisfied with the results, click the Commit check mark or press Enter.

FIGURE 12.2
The upper word has been skewed; the lower one is set in true italics. You can see the difference particularly in the *a*, *l*, and *i*.

Try it Yourself ▼

Create Text and Its Shadow

One way you can use skewing is to show which direction light is coming from in an illustration by creating shadows. Let's give this technique a try with your name.

1. Start a new document; Default Photoshop Elements Size is fine.

2. Choose the Horizontal Type tool. Click anywhere on the canvas and type your name in your choice of font, size, and color.

3. In the Layers palette, drag the type layer onto the New Layer button to create a copy of it.

4. Making sure that only the new layer is active, choose Image, Rotate, Flip Layer Vertical to flip the new layer so that the type is upside down and back-ward—that is, so it looks like a reflection.

5. Using the Move tool, move the type on the new layer below the original type. This shadow will be cast by a light source behind and to the left of the origi-nal type.

6. Select the shadow type with any Type tool and click the color swatch on the Options bar to choose a slightly darker color for it.

> The easiest way to choose a darker version of the same color is to click the upper B radio button in the color picker, the one that stands for Brightness. Now drag the color bar's slider down until the new color is dark enough. Because you didn't change the hue (H) or saturation (S) settings, the color is exactly the same as the original except for its reduced brightness.

Did you Know?

▼

7. Switch back to the Move tool and choose Image, Transform, Skew. Drag the shadow type's bottom handle to the right, and click the Commit check mark when you're done (see Figure 12.3). You might have to slide the shadow back to the left a bit so that the bases of its letters are aligned with the original type base again.

FIGURE 12.3
Skewing the type keeps its bottom and top level, but it changes the horizontal positions.

This technique produces a sharp-edged shadow. If you want to make it more realistic, choose Filter, Blur, Gaussian Blur. Photoshop Elements tells you that it needs to simplify the type layer before proceeding. Click OK and then drag the Radius slider in the Gaussian Blur dialog until you're happy with the softness of the shadow; then click OK again. At this point, you'll notice that the shadow is sticking up over the base of the original type's letters. Drag the shadow layer down under the original layer in the Layers palette to fix this minor problem (see Figure 12.4).

FIGURE 12.4
This type of shadow is called a cast shadow because it appears to be cast by a light source on the other side of the object.

Distorting a Picture

If you thought skewing was fun, you'll love distorting. With this transformation, you drag the corners of a selection in any direction to produce a funhouse-mirror image (see Figure 12.5). When you drag each corner of the transform marquee, the others stay put, unlike what happens when you use Skew.

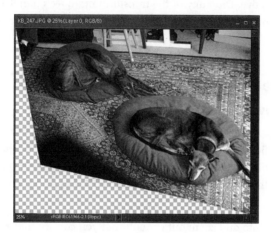

FIGURE 12.5
You can achieve both very subtle and quite wacky effects using the Distort command; in this case, distorting the picture makes it look as though the lower-left corner has been pushed out of its frame.

The Distort filters, found in the Distort submenu of the Filter menu, produce a wide range of effects that are related to the Distort transformation. So if you find you like the results you get when you apply a Distort transformation, you'll want to try out the Distort filters as well.

Changing a Picture's Perspective

The term *perspective* refers to the effect on an image from the onlooker's point of view. It's like skew, but toward and away from you instead of left and right. Because of the perspective effect, objects farther away from you appear smaller than those close to you because they take up a smaller amount of your total field of vision at that distance.

When you see the effects of perspective in an image, you feel that you know where you are with respect to the objects portrayed in the picture. Artists use this phenomenon to fool the eye. Forced perspective is an optical illusion used in visual media to make it appear that an object is closer or farther from the viewer than it actually is. You accomplish this by purposely providing an incorrect frame of reference. For example, in Peter Jackson's *Lord of the Rings* films, many of the props were made in two sizes. When a character held the larger version of an object, that character appeared smaller than someone holding the smaller version of that same object.

Combined with a variety of other visual tricks, this enabled actors to portray characters both smaller (hobbits) and larger (trolls) than humans.

The Photoshop Elements Perspective transformation enables you to simulate perspective in images that don't have it and remove it from images that have too much of it. First select the area or layer you want to work with, and then choose Image, Transform, Perspective. Drag any of the transform marquee's handles to apply perspective. When you're satisfied with the results, click the Commit check mark or press Enter.

▼   **Try it Yourself**

Fix Perspective

Let's give the Perspective transformation a workout on a shot that my husband took at the Temple of Baseball, also known as Fenway Park in Boston. The building looks as though it's tipping over backward; it can definitely use some help. You can download this picture from the book's website (it's called fenway.jpg) and follow along, if you like.

1. Open the photo and zoom out enough that you can see the entire image (see Figure 12.6).

FIGURE 12.6
An unusual viewing angle adds interest, but there's a little *too* much perspective happening here.

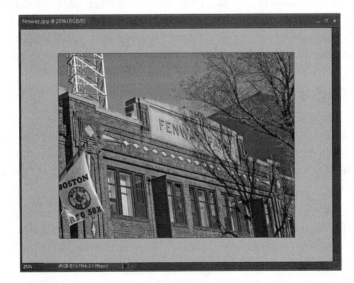

2. Choose Image, Transform, Perspective. Photoshop Elements informs you that it can transform only layers and asks if you'd like it to turn the Background layer into a regular layer. Click OK. Then click OK in the New Layer dialog.

▼

3. Drag the bottom-left corner of the transform marquee to the right, or drag the bottom-right corner to the left. Because both handles move when you're in Perspective transform mode, it doesn't matter which one you drag.

4. Press Ctrl+T. This puts you in Free Transform mode, which we investigate further in a few minutes. Click and drag outside the transform marquee to rotate the whole thing clockwise a few degrees. Now press Enter or click the Commit check mark (see Figure 12.7).

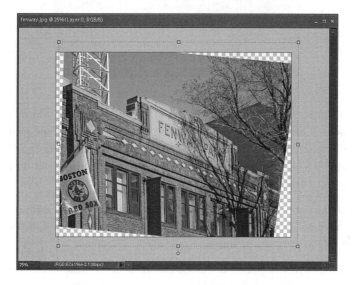

FIGURE 12.7
The transformed image is ready to be cropped.

5. Switch to the Crop tool and trim the image to get rid of the blank corners. If you prefer, you can try to fill in the corners using the Clone Stamp (which we cover in the next hour), but this image is really too detailed to lend itself to that option.

The picture certainly looks better now than it did when Fenway was toppling over (although I'm sure some Yankees fans would disagree). However, it's a great example of why you should always give yourself some cropping room around the edges of a picture. This photo was already cropped tightly when we started working on it, so when I recropped it, I had to cut off more of the banners than I was really happy with.

Using Free Transform

Using the Free Transform command, you can perform multiple transformations at once, with any transformation that Photoshop Elements supports (see Figure 12.8). To make it work for you, though, you have to learn some keyboard combinations.

FIGURE 12.8
How many ways
has this picture
been trans-
formed?

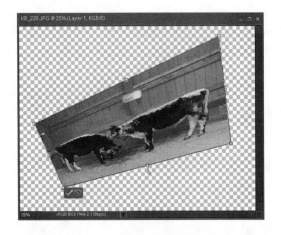

First, choose Image, Transform, Free Transform. Okay, got your transform marquee? Great! Now click and drag any corner handle—you're resizing the image. If Constrain Proportions is checked in the Options bar, or if you're pressing Shift, the image maintains its proportions as you resize it. To resize horizontally, drag a side handle; to resize vertically, drag the top or bottom handle.

Next, place the cursor outside the transform marquee, where it turns into a curved, double-headed arrow. Click and drag to rotate the picture in either direction. If you press Shift as you drag, the picture rotates in 15° increments.

Here come the keyboard combinations. To distort in Free Transform mode, press Ctrl and drag a handle. You'll notice that the cursor is a gray arrowhead when you're pressing Ctrl. If you add Shift, the arrowhead gains a double arrow, and dragging a side handle skews the selection. Next, add Alt (so now you're pressing Ctrl+Alt+Shift) and drag a corner handle to adjust the selection's perspective.

> ## Reference Points
>
> When you're using any Transform command, including Free Rotate (in the Image, Rotate submenu), normally the transformation is based on the center of the image or selection, indicated by a little circle-with-crosshairs icon. It's called the reference point; it's the one point in the image that remains in a fixed location while the rest of the image is transformed around it.
>
> You can move the reference point to any of nine different locations on the selection any time that you see the Reference Point Location proxy in the first slot on the Options bar (see Figure 12.9). Click any of the nine points in the proxy to change the reference point's location.

Fixing Distorted Images

Now, if you've been paying attention as we go along, you're probably wondering by now, "Why isn't there an easy way to get all this stuff fixed automatically? That's the way Photoshop Elements usually works." And if so, you're right—Photoshop Elements does generally offer an automated fix alongside manual ways to do the same thing. In this case, however, there's no way to automate the judgments that you make as you adjust perspective and rotate pictures. However, there is an easier way for you to fix all this stuff yourself. It's a command called Correct Camera Distortion, and you'll find it in the Filter menu.

Start with a picture that needs some work, and follow these steps:

1. Choose Filter, Correct Camera Distortion. Photoshop Elements opens a large dialog with its own toolbox (see Figure 12.10).

2. If the picture is squeezed in the middle, or if it appears convex, drag the Remove Distortion slider to remove the effect, which is caused by your camera lens. Watch the grid lines as you drag so that you can be sure you're turning curved lines into straight ones.

> Because of the way zoom lenses are built, they're often subject to distortion. When you're zoomed all the way out, you might end up with barrel distortion, in which vertical lines in the image bow outward like the sides of a barrel. Pincushion distortion, on the other hand, is likely to show up when you're zoomed all the way in; straight lines bow inward in these images.

By the Way

FIGURE 12.10
You can correct several types of distortion using this filter.

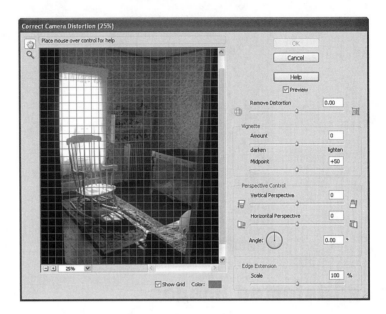

3. If the image seems too dark around the edges, drag the Vignette Amount slider to the right to lighten it; do the opposite if the picture is too bright at the edges. Drag the Vignette Midpoint slider to determine how wide an area is affected by your setting on the Vignette Amount slider (see Figure 12.11).

FIGURE 12.11
I can use the Vignette sliders to make the edges of this picture match the center in terms of brightness.

4. In the Perspective Control area, first adjust the image angle if it's tilted. Then you're free to drag the Vertical Perspective and Horizontal Perspective sliders. When you're done correcting the perspective, you might need to readjust the Angle slightly (see Figure 12.12).

FIGURE 12.12
The transformed image doesn't look as though it was taken in a carnival funhouse.

5. Finally, use the Scale slider to crop the image so that the blank areas created by your changes no longer show.

The controls at the bottom of the dialog box don't affect the image—just the appearance of the preview. Show Grid, as you might guess, shows the grid when clicked and hides the grid when cleared; you can click the Color swatch to choose a different grid color. Use the Zoom tool or the zoom controls at the lower-left corner of the preview to zoom in and out on the image.

Summary

Because of the vagaries of camera design and simple geometry, it's easy for pictures to display distortion so that they don't accurately portray their subjects. As you discovered in this hour, you can use the Transform commands to compensate for these effects or to distort and skew images for artistic effect. Each of the transformations that affect an image's shape has its own command, but you can execute all these and several other transformations at the same time using Free Transform mode. The quickest way to fix camera-generated distortion, however, is to use the Correct Camera Distortion filter, which can undo several different kinds of image distortion.

Q&A

Q. *Is it better to use the individual Transform commands or Free Transform mode?*

A. It depends. (You had to see that one coming, didn't you?) If you know exactly which transformation you want to apply, and you need to apply only one, it's simpler to stick with the individual commands. If you want to experiment with different transformations and you plan to apply more than one, you're definitely better off using Free Transform mode.

Q. *Which Distort filters match up with which Transform commands?*

A. None of them. The Distort filters do many interesting things, but they are not substitutes for the Transform commands.

Q. *Can I distort type layers and shape layers?*

A. Absolutely. Shape layers remain shapes throughout your transformations; they don't need to be simplified. Type layers, on the other hand, can be skewed without simplifying them, but you need to turn them into pixels before you distort them or adjust perspective. Remember, after you simplify a type layer, you can no longer edit it as text.

Workshop

How much attention have you paid to the details in this hour? These quiz questions will provide the answer. Afterward, relax with a fun activity that you can do with any of your own photos.

Quiz

1. When you adjust an object's angle while leaving its top and bottom level, you're _____ it.

    A. slewing

    B. tilting

    C. skewing

    D. distorting

2. Which of the following is *not* an operation you can do in Free Transform mode?

    A. Rotate

    B. Distort

    C. Scale

    D. Twirl

3. Barrel distortion appears when a zoom lens is zoomed all the way in on a distant object.

    A. True

    B. False

Quiz Answers

1. C. Often skewing is used to create fake italic type.

2. D. You can, however, twirl using the Twirl filter in the Filter, Distort submenu.

3. B. You get pincushion distortion, the opposite of barrel distortion, when you zoom in. Barrel distortion occurs when you're zoomed all the way out.

Activity

Open a picture that contains recognizable people or buildings, and choose Image, Transform, Free Transform. Using the key combinations listed in this hour, apply several different kinds of transformation to the image. Can you figure out how to twist the photo? Is it possible to flip it using Free Transform?

Removing Red Eye, Dust, and Scratches

What You'll Learn in This Hour:

▶ How to eliminate dust and scratches from photos
▶ How to get rid of red eye—and green eye
▶ Ways to remove other small flaws in your pictures

Few things are more annoying than digging through your photo stash, finding the perfect picture for your current project, and then discovering that it's all scratched and everyone in it has red eyes. Photoshop Elements doesn't have a single tool that gets rid of all these flaws instantly, but it certainly has all the tools you need to do the job pretty darn quickly.

Red eye can be a problem any time you use a flash to take photos. It happens because the subject's pupil doesn't have time to contract before the flash's light passes through it and is bounced back out again. Because the area next to the iris is full of blood vessels, the reflected light appears to be red. Dust and scratches, on the other hand, usually show up on scanned pictures, either on the print or slide you scanned or on the scanner bed. You end up with similar flaws in digital camera pictures if there's a smudge or dirt on the camera lens.

Making Basic Cleanups

You already know how to fix quite a few image problems. Let's review: In Hour 6, "Making Quick Fixes," you learned how to make quick fixes to solve problems related to lighting, color, and sharpness. (We look at more sophisticated ways to address these issues in Hour 14, "Too Light/Too Dark: Adjusting Brightness, Contrast, and Color.") In Hour 11, "Composing and Cropping Your Pictures," you learned how to crop and rotate a picture to improve its composition and remove distracting elements. And in Hour 12, "Straightening, Skewing, and Distorting an Image," you learned about straightening crooked images and fixing flawed perspective.

All these methods focus on fixing the picture as a whole. Now we zoom in on the details and work with just part of an image at a time. First we look at ways to remove noticeable flaws from a picture, things that were really there when you took the shot but that you didn't really want in your picture. These are the zits and cellulite of your photo collection, and getting rid of them in a picture is *way* easier than getting rid of them in real life.

In this section, we work with a photo of a boy and his grandmother collecting shells on the beach (see Figure 13.1); you can download beachcombers.jpg from the book's website at www.informit.com/title/9780672330179 and work along if you like. It's not fabulous, but it has potential. The first thing I want to do with this picture is crop it—there's way too much going on here, and we need to focus on the people in the foreground and get rid of some of the distracting background.

FIGURE 13.1
This photo definitely has room for improvement.

I'm going to print this photo and put it in a square frame, so I start by switching to the Crop tool and choosing "5 × 5 in" from the Aspect Ratio menu in the Options bar. Figure 13.2 shows how the picture looks after I've cropped it; you can see how that step alone gets rid of a lot of the picture's problem areas. But we still have a few issues to deal with.

FIGURE 13.2
See how much of a difference just cropping the image makes?

Removing Small Objects with Copy and Paste

When you're doing a speed clean of your house right before guests arrive, what's the easiest thing to do with clutter? Right—get it out of sight. The equivalent action in Photoshop Elements is to get rid of clutter by placing something in front of it. For this picture, that means finding a nice, clean patch of sand and using it to cover up what's left of the group of people sitting at the left side of the photo. We don't know them, we don't think they're particularly interesting, and they're definitely distracting, so we cropped out most of them, but we still have a pair of legs and a cooler to get rid of.

We need to take care with our sand patch so that it doesn't cover anything we don't want to hide, and we also need to make sure that the patch blends well with the background, with no hard edges showing. Here's how I did it:

1. Using the Lasso tool, select the area around the object you want to get rid of—in this case, the legs and the cooler—including a bit of a margin. This selection determines the shape of the patch, so it's important not to make it too skimpy.

2. Choose Select, Feather to give the selection area a soft edge; in this case, I used a Radius of 10 pixels. This step helps the patch blend with the sand around it so that you can't see its edges.

3. Still with the Lasso tool, drag the selection to an area that makes a suitable patch. For my patch, I used a swath of sand from the middle of the picture (see Figure 13.3).

FIGURE 13.3
Try to pick a patch area that will blend well with the place you're going to put it.

FIGURE 13.3
Try to pick a patch area that will blend well with the place you're going to put it.

4. Press Ctrl+V to paste the patch. This creates a new layer in the process. You won't notice any difference in the picture at this point because the pasted area is directly on top of the area from which you copied it. If you want to see just the patch, you can hide the Background layer in the Layers palette (click the eye button) and then show it again so you can move the patch to its final position.

5. Switch to the Move tool and drag the patch so that it covers the object you're trying to remove. Positioning the patch correctly was easy for me because its straight left edge butts up against the edge of the image (see Figure 13.4).

You might be interested to know that traditional Photoshop has a specialized Patch tool, which automates the feathering and copying part of this technique. So if you find yourself using this patch method quite a bit, you might want to consider upgrading to Photoshop CS3. On the other hand, I wouldn't be surprised to see the Patch tool show up in the next release of Photoshop Elements.

FIGURE 13.4
Shoveling a load of sand on top of the legs and cooler eliminates them in short order.

Try it Yourself ▼

Removing Small Objects with the Clone Stamp Tool

Copying and pasting a patch can work very well to hide unwanted objects, but the background around the objects needs to be fairly homogenous. If the objects you want to get rid of are surrounded by multiple colors and textures, a patch won't do the trick; you need to pull out the Clone Stamp tool instead. In our example picture, the girls walking into the water are surrounded by grayish water, sand, and white foam—so it's time for the Clone Stamp. Again, feel free to follow along with beach-combers.jpg, if you like. These are the steps needed to get rid of the extra people left in this picture:

1. Zoom in on the object you want to get rid of—in this case, the two girls. Make sure that you can see them clearly but that you also have plenty of room around them to borrow the pixels you're going to stamp over them (see Figure 13.5).

2. Switch to the Clone Stamp tool. It looks like a rubber stamp because it can pick up part of a picture and stamp it somewhere else in the image. We'll use it to clone waves over the girls.

▼

▼
FIGURE 13.5
Because of the varying colors of the water around the two girls, the Clone Stamp works better than the patch method here.

3. In the Options bar, set your brush size to about 40 pixels, and leave the Mode menu set to Normal and the Opacity menu set to 100%. Make sure that the brush tip is soft-edged, for the same reason that you feathered the patch selection in the previous section—so your changes will blend with the image around them. You can tell which brushes are soft-edged because their previews have fuzzy edges.

4. Now look at your Layers palette. If you've been working along and haven't closed the file, you should have a Background layer, which contains the original image, and Layer 1, which contains only the sandy patch we created a little while ago. You're going to stamp on Layer 1, so make sure it's active, but you want your stamp to use the Background layer as the source, so check All Layers in the Options bar.

By the Way

If you leave All Layers unchecked, you need to be working on the same layer that you're using as a clone source. With All Layers turned on, the Clone Stamp picks up pixels from all the layers instead of just the one you're working on—which, in this case, is mostly transparent and, therefore, not a really good source for a stamp image.

▼

5. Click to put a check in the Aligned box. This setting determines where the source pixels come from for each click or stroke with the Clone Stamp. When Aligned is turned off, Photoshop Elements goes back to the source point each time you release the mouse button and click again. When it's turned on, the area from which the stamp is picking up pixels moves around as you paint around the area where you began stamping. The point at which the stamp will pick up pixels on your next click is always shown with a cross.

Use Aligned for jobs like this, when you're covering up something; turn it off if you want to use the Clone Stamp to create multiple copies of an object in a picture.

Did you Know?

6. Look at the color and pattern of the waves near the point where you want to start covering things up. Pick a spot elsewhere in the water that matches fairly closely, and Alt+click to choose that as your source point.

7. Click, or click and drag, to clone over the girls (see Figure 13.6). Go slowly until you get a feel for how the Clone Stamp works; short strokes usually work best. As the color of the water around the girls changes from blue around their heads to brownish gray at their feet, make sure the origin point is in a matching area.

FIGURE 13.6
A few more strokes, a click or two to break up the waves a bit, and I'm done.

Well, the picture is a lot less cluttered now. It could still use some pizzazz; maybe I'll have to add some things later.

Fixing Red Eye

I hope this won't shock you, but the first thing I want to say about fixing red eye has nothing to do with Photoshop Elements: Stop red eye before it starts by using the red-eye reduction mode of your camera, if it has one.

Now, we both know that red eye reduction, which uses a preflash to encourage the subject's pupils to contract before the photo is taken, doesn't always work. But it can certainly cut down on the amount of time you spend fixing red eye after the fact. Just be sure to warn your subjects that you're not done taking the picture until they've seen *two* flashes.

You can cut down on red eye in your photos in a few other ways; it's worth giving some of these a try:

▶ Use a bounce flash; this means reflecting the flash's light off a light-colored surface facing the photo subject instead of pointing the flash directly at the people you're photographing.

▶ Use an external flash that you can move away from the camera so that its light hits the subject at an angle instead of straight on.

▶ Take pictures without a flash, but be careful to stabilize the camera before you shoot so that you don't shake it while the shutter is open.

▶ Have your subject look over your shoulder instead of straight at you.

▶ Brighten the room lighting so that the subject's pupils contract as much as possible before the flash activates.

If, despite all your efforts, you still have pictures marred by red eye, you can fix the problem pretty easily using one of the following techniques.

Using the Red Eye Removal Tool

This poor little girl has a really bad case of red eye (see Figure 13.7, here and in the color section). Fortunately, Photoshop Elements offers a number of automated ways to fix her problem. If I'd taken the photo on my own camera, I could have chosen to have Photoshop Elements automatically remove red eye when I imported the photos from the camera. I scanned this particular photo, and Photoshop Elements can detect and remove red eye while scanning, too. In fact, I had to go to some trouble to make sure that the red eye problem still existed by the time I got the photo into Photoshop Elements.

FIGURE 13.7
The red in her eyes just does not match the pink sweater.

I can fix the problem pretty easily right in the Organizer by clicking the Fix tab and then clicking the Auto Red Eye Fix button. Or I can switch to the Editor's Quick Fix mode and click the Auto button next to Red Eye Fix.

But if none of that works (or, for some reason, doesn't appeal to me), I can reach for the Red Eye Removal tool. It's available in both Quick Fix and Full Edit modes within the Editor, and it's almost as easy to use as all those auto methods. All you have to do is either click with it in the middle of a red spot or drag a marquee around the red spot. Rinse and repeat for the other eye, and you're all set!

Try it Yourself ▼

Fixing Red Eye from Scratch

Sometimes all of Photoshop Elements' red eye fixing magic doesn't do the trick—or it does too much. With some images, the program just can't seem to find the red, even when you indicate it with the Red Eye Removal tool. Other times, it gets the red eye out, all right, but it also removes red from other parts of the picture. In these cases, you just have to fix the red eye manually. Here's how:

▼

1. Zoom way, way in on the red area in the first eye.

2. Use any tool you like to select the red area. You can try the Magic Wand or the Quick Selection tool; the Lasso tool also works well. This time, I used the Elliptical Marquee tool; then I chose Select, Refine Edge to adjust the selection's size and give it a bit of a soft edge with a Feather setting of 1.1 pixels. Click OK.

3. Press Shift+Ctrl+U, or choose Enhance, Adjust Color, Remove Color. This gets rid of the red, but it's replaced with an unattractive gray (see Figure 13.8).

FIGURE 13.8
This pupil needs to be darker to look realistic.

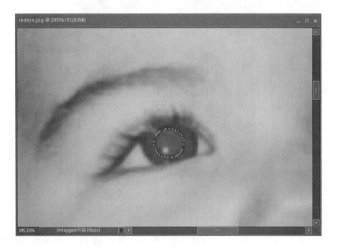

4. Without dropping the selection, switch to the Brush tool and choose a new Foreground color of black or dark brown.

5. Increase the size of the Brush until it covers the entire selection, and set the Opacity to about 20% and the Mode to Darken. Then click the Airbrush button on the Options bar next to the Opacity menu; this option allows paint to accumulate through repeated clicking in the same area, giving you greater control over the intensity of the color you're applying.

Did you Know?

> Press [(the left square bracket) to reduce the size of a brush tip and] (the right square bracket) to increase it. Repeat as needed until you get the size you want. This trick works with all the painting and retouching tools (for example, the Clone Stamp and the Healing Brush).

6. Click once over the selection, and then take a look at the results. You need to click several more times, but exactly how many is up to you. The object here is

to produce a nice, dark pupil without eliminating the white highlights, which add life to the eyes (see Figure 13.9).

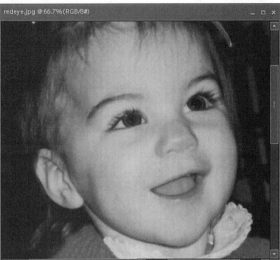

FIGURE 13.9
Much better!

This manual red eye removal technique also works on animal eyes. Most often, animals' eyes reflect a flash with green, but you'll occasionally also see white, blue, yellow, or other colors. Photoshop Elements' automated tools work only with red eye, not green eye, so this manual process is the only option for that type of correction.

Removing Dust and Scratches

It's not always possible to start with a perfectly clean image, but you can avoid introducing *more* dust and scratches into the equation. To this end, always clean your scanner bed before you begin scanning. That means cleaning both the glass and the inside of the lid: As soon as you close the lid, everything that's on it is transferred to the glass. I like to use alcohol for cleaning, but in a pinch, I use grocery store glass cleaner. When I've done the best I can to get a good scan of a picture, the rest of the cleanup goes on in Photoshop Elements.

Using the Dust & Scratches Filter

You'd think that Dust & Scratches would be the solution to any problem with dust and scratches on a picture. Not quite—but it's definitely one of the tools you can apply to fix the problem. Unfortunately, Photoshop Elements doesn't actually know what all the little marks on your picture are. Some of them are dust, some of them are scratches, and some of them are the freckles that your grandfather was so proud of. But with the Dust & Scratches filter, any marks that fit the criteria you set for size and contrast with the surrounding area are blurred out of existence—which is *not* what you want to do to Grandpa's freckles.

That said, let's take a look at what the filter can do. Start by choosing Filter, Noise, Dust & Scratches (see Figure 13.10). The dialog contains just two sliders. Radius determines how much blurring takes place, and Threshold controls how different from their backgrounds any specks of dust must be for the filter to affect them. Lower Threshold values mean that the filter finds more specks of dust; higher ones leave the less obnoxious specks alone. If you set the Threshold all the way to 255, you can move the Radius slider back and forth all day long, and the image won't be affected at all.

FIGURE 13.10
Sometimes the Dust & Scratches filter will not produce the results you want and will blur out elements you want to keep. However, this powerful tool can really do an amazing job if you experiment a little.

The best strategy when working with the Dust & Scratches filter is to alternate in dragging the two sliders. First apply a Radius setting of 1 pixel, then drag the Threshold slider to the right a bit to restrict the areas affected by the blurring. Then increase the Radius setting a bit more, and drag the Threshold slider to the right again to regain some edge detail.

You might notice that the Dust & Scratches filter removes small, bright highlights on shiny objects or tones them way down. That's because Photoshop Elements can't tell the difference between *these* tiny white specks (highlights) and *those* tiny white specks (dust). Experiment with the settings until you reach a compromise. Or, if you're up to more of a challenge, you can select the entire picture and then remove areas that have bright highlights from the selection; the Selection Brush is a good tool for this (see Figure 13.11). I like to bring up the Dust & Scratches filter first, check for image areas that don't fare well under its effects, and then click Cancel. Then I press Ctrl+A to select the whole image, and I switch to the Selection Brush tool in Mask mode. Using a soft-edged brush, I paint over anything that I don't want the Dust & Scratches filter to touch. When I'm done, I choose Filter, Noise, Dust & Scratches again, make my settings, and click OK this time. The deselected areas retain their highlights, and the dust specks are eliminated everywhere else in the photo.

FIGURE 13.11
The shiny black telephone and the drawer handle in this photo were blurring too much when I applied Dust & Scratches, so I used the Selection Brush to make a selection that excluded them.

Removing Dust and Scratches with the Healing Brush

The nice thing about the Healing Brush is that you can apply it to every intrusive speck or scratch in a picture, one by one, and get rid of all of them while leaving Grandpa's freckles intact. The annoying thing about the Healing Brush is that you have to apply it to every intrusive speck or scratch in a picture, one by one. Giving a photo a good workover with the Healing Brush can take some time, but the results are almost always worth the investment.

The Healing Brush works much the way the Clone Stamp tool does. You Alt+click to choose a source point and then paint over what you want to get rid of (see Figure

13.12). Photoshop Elements automatically blends the new pixels with the surrounding ones. This works very well for smooth objects and areas with a random pattern, but not so well in areas with a regular pattern, such as a pair of plaid pants.

FIGURE 13.12
In this photo, I'm using the Healing Brush to get rid of the writing that overlaps the image. Of course, I recorded the names and date written on the picture before deleting them.

> **Did you Know?**
>
> If you're using the Healing Brush near the edge of a contrasting object, you might notice that the color from the contrasting object keeps bleeding into the areas you're working on. To prevent this, select the area you want to work on, being careful to follow its edges exactly (as I did in Figure 13.12). When you paint with the Healing Brush inside a selection, it copies pixels only from within the selection.

The Healing Brush shares its toolbox slot with its sibling, the Spot Healing Brush. This tool doesn't require any fussy Alt+clicking; just click it once on whatever you want to delete, and you're done (see Figure 13.13.). Just be sure that the Size is set to a diameter larger than that of the spot you want to delete so that you can get it all with a single click.

FIGURE 13.13
I can use the Spot Healing Brush to remove both this white spot and the smaller black ones above it.

Smoothing Out JPEG Artifacts and Noise

As we all know, life is about compromise, and JPEG images are a perfect example of that fact. To make our image files small enough that we can cram hundreds of them on our cameras and our iPods, we use lossy compression. And that compression alters the images permanently, adding blocky artifacts and halos around objects (see Figure 13.14).

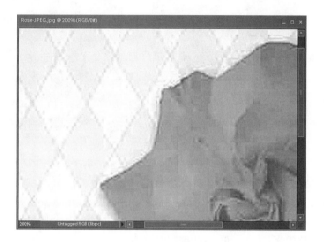

FIGURE 13.14
This close-up of a JPEG image clearly shows the blocks and the halo added to the picture by JPEG compression.

After you've saved an image using lossy compression, you can never regain the picture's original appearance. What you *can* do when JPEG artifacts become too obvious, however, is to improve matters somewhat using the Reduce Noise filter. Its Remove JPEG Artifact check box focuses on exactly the type of noise caused by JPEG compression, smoothing the hard edges of the blocks that JPEG inserted and blurring halos around object edges.

Reduce Noise is intended to deal with graininess or randomly colored pixels that are caused by taking pictures with inadequate light or using the wrong shutter speed. (We'll try this function out in Hour 19, "Using the Improvement Filters.") Lucky for us, it can also fix messiness caused by JPEG compression. To give it a try, choose Filter, Noise, Reduce Noise (see Figure 13.15). First, of course, check the box marked Remove JPEG Artifact. Then you can start experimenting with the other settings:

FIGURE 13.15
Using the
Reduce Noise
filter on the
image from
Figure 13.14
gets rid of most
of the compres-
sion artifacts.

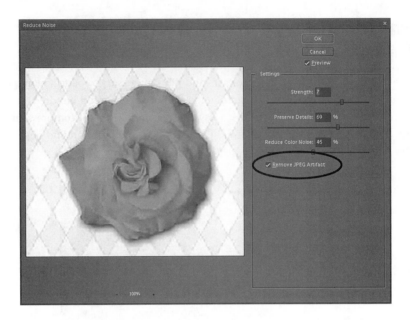

▶ **Strength** determines how much noise reduction takes place.

▶ **Preserve Details** works like a threshold setting to control how much the noise must stand out to be affected. Higher settings protect the details in your pictures, but they'll leave more noise behind.

▶ **Reduce Color Noise** removes those odd, random color pixels that sometimes show up in the middle of an otherwise smooth area.

For best results, try out different combinations of Strength and Preserve Details settings. You want to retain the image's sharp edges while smoothing out any graininess.

You can temporarily remove the effects of a filter in its own dialog box preview by clicking the preview. I like to use this feature to quickly compare the before and after versions of an image. Click, before. Release, after. Click, before....

Summary

This has been a busy hour. We started by looking at basic image cleanup, incorporating techniques you learned earlier—such as cropping—with new methods. You learned how to remove extraneous objects using the Copy and Paste commands to create patches that can cover flaws, and you practiced using the Clone Stamp tool to remove objects. We talked about what causes red eye, how to avoid getting it in the first place, how to remove it automatically, and how to remove it manually. Then you saw how to delete dust and scratches with a filter designed to do just that and how to kill off more dust and scratches, as well as other small flaws, using the Healing Brush and the Spot Healing Brush tools. Finally, you learned how to use the Reduce Noise filter to remove graininess and JPEG compression artifacts from your pictures.

Q&A

Q. *I used the Dust & Scratches filter to clean up a scan of an old photo. It worked great on the dust and scratches, but now my picture is all blurry. Help!*

A. Unfortunately, you've discovered the major problem with the Dust and Scratches filter. It works by blurring all those tiny specks to blend them with the background; if you're not careful, you can blur your picture too much. Undo, try the Dust & Scratches filter again, and this time go easier on it. Then use the Spot Healing Brush to get rid of the remaining specks.

Q. *Why do I see compression artifacts only in JPEG images?*

A. For the most part, other image formats don't use lossy compression. Instead, they use lossless compression methods, which means their file sizes are larger, but image data remains intact.

Workshop

Finish this hour by answering the quiz questions and checking your answers. Then reward yourself with some playtime doing the activities.

Quiz

1. Which of the following is *not* an actual way to get rid of red eye in Photoshop Elements?

    A. Auto Red Eye Fix

    B. Red Eye Removal tool

    C. Red Eye Detection Wand

    D. None of the above

2. The difference between the Healing Brush and the Spot Healing Brush is that

    A. The Spot Healing Brush restores a spotted pattern to areas where the spots have been blurred.

    B. The Healing Brush works best for cleaning up large areas, and the Spot Healing Brush works best for cleaning up small spots.

    C. The Spot Healing Brush is intended solely for use on zits, but it was named by a Brit.

    D. The Healing Brush supports a much wider range of brush sizes than the Spot Healing Brush does.

3. JPEG artifacts occur because the JPEG image format doesn't support full-color images.

    A. True

    B. False

Quiz Answers

1. **C.** But you could use the Magic Wand to select all the red eyes in a picture at once, if you wanted to.

2. **B.**

3. **B.** JPEG artifacts occur when the image is rearranged in such a way that it can be compressed to a smaller size.

Activities

1. Locate a picture of a group of people. Open it in the Editor and use the patch technique and the Clone Stamp tool to remove one of the people from the picture.

2. Practice the manual technique that you learned in this hour for removing red eye. Can you make your fixes look as good as those done with the Red Eye Removal tool? Can you make them look even better?

3. Use both the Clone Stamp tool and the Healing Brush to clean up the same image. Compare the two. Which gives better results? How can you improve your results with the Clone Stamp tool?

HOUR 14

Adjusting Brightness, Contrast, and Color

What You'll Learn in This Hour:

▶ Adjusting image lighting and color automatically
▶ Fixing color problems manually
▶ Compensating manually for poor lighting
▶ Changing colors selectively

Color can go wrong in a picture in so many ways that you'd think gremlins had been sitting around in a cave somewhere thinking of them ever since color photography was invented early in the twentieth century. In fact, the factors that affect an image's color are pretty simple. First and foremost, there's the ambient lighting when the photo was taken, combined with the flash, if one was used. Then, with scanned pictures, you also have to worry about the degradation of the print or film over time, along with any color weirdness introduced by your scanner. And, of course, if your monitor isn't adjusted properly, what you're seeing on the screen may bear little relationship to what will come out of the printer. All in all, it's a recipe for one big mess.

Working in your favor, however, is the fact that, for the most part, color is subjective. Each of us sees it differently, so who's to say that the colors in your photos are actually *wrong*, as long as you like them? And you can adjust color, brightness, and contrast in Photoshop Elements in a lot of ways, so you're well equipped to make your pictures perfect—in your eyes, at least.

Using the Automatic Correction Tools

We looked at Photoshop Elements' color correction tools in Hour 6, "Making Quick Fixes." Now we take a quick look at three of the Enhance menu's Auto commands: Auto Levels, Auto Contrast, and Auto Color Correction. They might not always get a picture quite right, but it never hurts to give them a try. You can undo if you don't like the results, and seeing what *can* be done to a photo sometimes helps you figure out which direction you want to go with it. Of course, each of these tools can be applied to the entire image or to a selected area, often yielding significantly different results.

Take a look at Figure 14.1, also in the color section, to see the "before" version of the photo we'll be working with as we look at these tools. It's a backlit shot of a couple baseball fans, with some fairly strong colors in it (you'll find it on the book's website at www.informit.com/title/9780672330179 under the name baseball.jpg). The colors are washed out because of the lighting; let's see what Photoshop Elements can do with this picture.

FIGURE 14.1
This is a rather nice shot, but it looks faded.

Auto Levels

The first command we'll unleash on the baseball boys picture is Auto Levels (in the Editor's Enhance menu when you're working in Full Edit mode). You can also press Shift+Ctrl+L to execute the command. But first let's talk a bit about levels.

No, we're not worried (at this point) about whether the picture's horizon is level or about your degree of Photoshop Elements expertise. In this context, the term *levels* refers to the differing levels of brightness and darkness in a picture. Ideally, you want color pictures as well as black-and-white ones to have some white pixels, some black ones, and a good selection of shades between white and black. If the entire image is done in medium shades, there's no contrast and hence no visual interest. Auto Levels attempts to remedy this problem by making the lightest pixel in the picture white, turning the darkest pixel in the picture black, and spreading out all the others in the range in between (see Figure 14.2, here and in the color section). This gives the picture more contrast, but it can sometimes affect the color, for good or ill.

FIGURE 14.2
Auto Levels makes a big improvement in this photo.

If you decide you don't like Photoshop Elements' Levels adjustment, you can try adjusting levels manually (keep reading; we give this a try later in this hour). And if you get to the Levels dialog box and still can't find a setting you like, you can always just click the Auto button in the dialog to go back to the automatic adjustment.

Auto Contrast

Without affecting the actual colors in the picture, Auto Contrast makes the light colors lighter and the dark colors darker, to increase the overall contrast in the picture (see Figure 14.3). You apply it by choosing Enhance, Auto Contrast or pressing Alt+Shift+Ctrl+L. You can also adjust contrast yourself using the Brightness/Contrast dialog, which we get to later in the hour.

FIGURE 14.3
Auto Contrast does a good job with the baseball boys photo; you can also see it in the color section.

Auto Color Correction

Remember how I said earlier that color is subjective? Nowhere else in Photoshop Elements is that fact more clear than it is here. When you choose Enhance, Auto Color Correction or press Shift+Ctrl+B, Photoshop Elements fiddles with both your picture's contrast and its color to produce what it thinks is the best result (see Figure 14.4, here and in the color section). Sometimes the program is right; other times, it's very, very wrong.

Nonetheless, it's always worth giving this command a try. Often it does a really creditable job of improving a picture, and you can always undo the changes if you don't like the results.

baseball.jpg @ 33.3%(RGB/8#)

33.33%

FIGURE 14.4
I'm not thrilled with the result of applying the Auto Color Correction command (check it out in the color section of this book); I'd rather see if I can do better with manual tools.

Adjusting Color Manually

As I mentioned earlier in this hour, color perception is an individual thing; the only way to get color just the way you like it is to do it yourself. It takes a lot of practice, and no matter how perfect you get the image on your computer, it might not look the same way on other computers. But if you're just working on it and then printing it yourself without sending it to anyone else, you can get spectacular results.

Adjusting by Eye with Color Variations

Right-brained types love Color Variations. If you're more the left-brained, analytical, by-the-numbers type, this feature might not be for you. But either way, give it a try and see what you think. Start by choosing Enhance, Adjust Color, Color Variations in the Editor (see Figure 14.5, here and in the color section of this book).

The whole point of Color Variations is to adjust an image by feel instead of by the numbers. First, you decide whether you want to work on the picture's midtones, shadows, or highlights, or even its saturation. Then you click the thumbnails to add or subtract a color, make the picture lighter or darker, or change its saturation. The Amount slider controls how much effect each click has on the picture, so you can dial it down and click multiple times, or turn it up and click just once or twice.

FIGURE 14.5
Playing with
Color Variations
is fun, but it's
best suited to
working on pho-
tos that aren't
seriously
flawed.

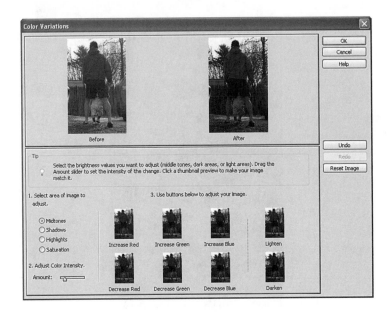

You can change your settings and work on each part of the image in turn; start with the midtones, then fix the shadows, then work on the highlights. Each of these offers you eight choices for color images:

▶ Increase Red, Green, or Blue

▶ Decrease Red, Green, or Blue

▶ Lighten or Darken

With grayscale pictures, you see only the Lighten and Darken thumbnails and you don't have the option of adjusting saturation. For color pictures, though, Saturation works a little differently from the other controls; it affects the entire image, and your only choices are Less Saturation and More Saturation. Increasing saturation makes all the picture's colors more intense, and decreasing saturation mutes the colors.

Clicking around in the Color Variations dialog is pure fun. Each time you click to make a change, all the thumbnails update so that you can see what effect your next change will have. Meanwhile, the two larger thumbnails at the top of the dialog show the original picture and the picture as it will look with the changes you've made. If you want to go back a step, you'll find handy Undo and Redo buttons at the right side of the dialog, accompanied by a Reset Image button that enables you to start over.

Adjusting Color with Remove Color Cast

If you're a gardener, you'll probably know that a weed is defined as anything that's growing where you don't want it to grow. For a photographer, a color cast is similar—it's a color that shows up where it's not wanted and shouldn't be. Frequently, color casts are caused by lighting conditions, but they can also occur in traditional photos. Some of my World War II–era black-and-white prints are now an odd combination of yellow and purple because the paper has yellowed and the black image has, well, purpled. Chemicals do strange things over time; you should see what has happened to some of the color prints from the 1960s in my family's photo albums.

Regardless of where it comes from, you want to get rid of any color cast. To accomplish this, start by choosing Enhance, Adjust Color, Remove Color Cast (see Figure 14.6). The Remove Color Cast command actually adds some of the opposite color on the color wheel to counteract the effects of the color cast. You saw how this worked when you looked at the Variations command; if a photo is too blue, you can add more yellow to fix it.

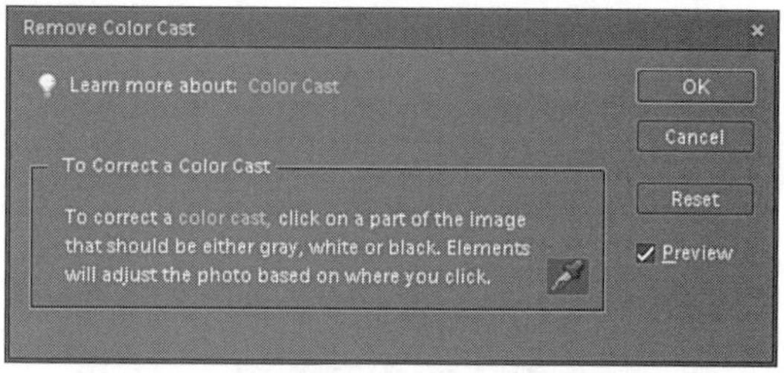

FIGURE 14.6
When there's no color cast in a photo, Remove Color Cast shouldn't have any effect—but watch out for the exception that proves the rule.

To determine what color is causing the problem, you need to help a bit by clicking a part of the picture that *should* be completely desaturated. In other words, the area you click should be white, black, or true gray. When you click to indicate this spot, Photoshop Elements examines it to see what color it really is. That color is the one you want to counteract, so Photoshop Elements calculates an appropriate amount of the opposite color to add so that the neutral area is once again white, black, or gray.

If you don't like the results, click Reset and find another neutral location to click. When you're happy, click OK.

You can also use Levels and Variations to remove color casts. We'll look at how Levels can be manually controlled a little later in this hour.

By the Way

Adjusting Color with Hue/Saturation

The Hue/Saturation dialog in Photoshop Elements looks just like the one in traditional Photoshop. With Hue/Saturation, you can completely transform an image in several different ways:

▶ Color-shift the whole picture

▶ Color-shift just one range of colors

▶ Colorize the picture, turning it into shades of a single color

▶ Remove some or all of the color from the picture

▶ Increase the intensity of the colors

▶ Lighten or darken the whole picture

▶ Lighten or darken a range of colors

See? You thought I was exaggerating, but I wasn't. Anyway, you start by choosing Enhance, Adjust Color, Adjust Hue/Saturation or pressing Ctrl+U (see Figure 14.7).

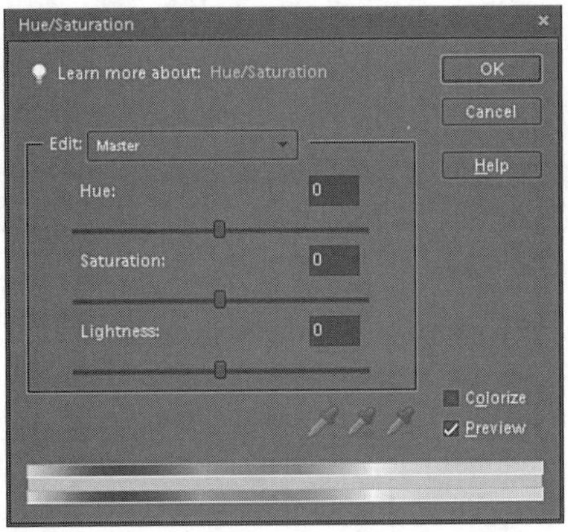

FIGURE 14.7
The Hue/ Saturation dialog has a lot going on, but you can master it.

First, do you want to colorize the picture? If so, check the Colorize box and then drag the Hue slider to the color you want. Use the Saturation and Lightness sliders to make final adjustments; click OK, and you're done.

If not, leave the Colorize box unchecked. In this case, the first step in adjusting hue and saturation is to decide whether you want to change the whole image or just some of the colors it contains. To work on all the picture's colors, leave the Edit pop-up menu set at Master; to work on a range of colors within the picture, choose that range from the Edit menu. (You can fine-tune the colors you want to modify; check out the sidebar "Pick a Color, Any Color" to learn more.)

Pick a Color, Any Color

Restricting your actions in the Hue/Saturation dialog box to a particular range of colors starts with choosing anything other than Master from the Edit pop-up menu. Seriously, don't worry about what color category you choose, and don't stress that there's no Purples option. Just pick one, and then click in the image to pick up the color you really want. Your cursor turns into an eyedropper for this purpose. To add to the range of colors you're selecting, switch to the plus eyedropper and click or click and drag; do the same with the minus eyedropper to remove colors from the range.

Any time you restrict the color range in Hue/Saturation, you can see the color range that you're working with indicated between the two color bars at the bottom of the dialog. The medium-gray area indicates the colors you picked with the eye-dropper, or the colors defined by the Edit menu choice; the dark gray areas to either side indicate similar colors that will be partially affected by your edits (color fall-off). You can shorten or lengthen the color fall-off areas by dragging the sliders at their boundaries, but don't shorten them too much or you'll get very abrupt color transitions in the picture (see Figure 14.8).

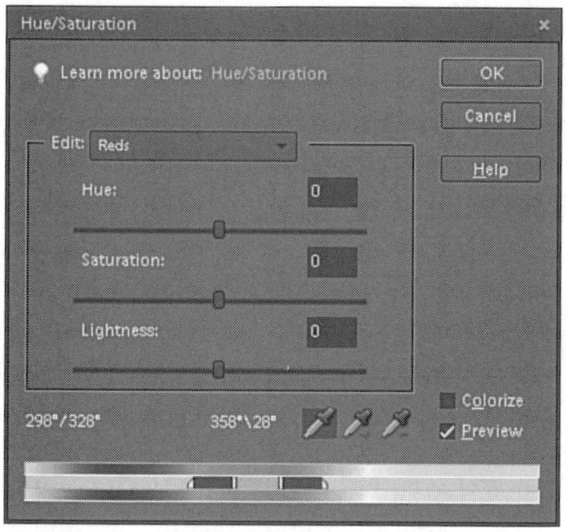

FIGURE 14.8
Knowing how to restrict the colors you're operating on with Hue/Saturation is the sort of thing that takes you beyond the novice level in Photoshop Elements.

Photoshop Elements keeps track of the color ranges you set up and adds them to the Edit pop-up menu, where they stay until you click Cancel or OK. You'll see them named with the closest standard color range and a number (such as Red 1). The program keeps track of up to six of these custom ranges, but they're all forgotten as soon as you leave Hue/Saturation.

Next, you need to specify what you want to do to the selected colors by dragging the three sliders. Hue represents the actual colors in the picture; by dragging it, you shift those colors around the color wheel. The two color bars at the bottom of the dialog represent the original image colors (the upper one) and the revised image colors (the lower one), arranged in their order on the color wheel. As you drag the Hue slider, the lower color bar moves to show you the new colors corresponding to each of the original colors.

Remember the color wheel from art class? Red is at the top of the wheel, with cyan opposite it on the bottom. The numbers in the Hue value field represent how many degrees around the wheel you're shifting the colors, from –180 to +180 degrees.

The other two sliders, Saturation and Lightness, are simpler to understand and to manipulate. Drag Saturation to the left to dull the colors you're working with; drag it to the right to intensify them. If you take the Saturation value all the way down to –100, the picture (or the selected colors) turns grayscale. At the other end of the scale, if you take Saturation all the way up, things get pretty psychedelic. Meanwhile, Lightness is equivalent to Brightness in the HSB color model. Increase it to lighten the colors, decrease it to darken them. A Lightness value of –100 yields a completely black image, and a value of +100 turns the picture completely white.

Did you Know?

As you're working with the sliders in Hue/Saturation, you can press Alt to turn the Cancel button into a Reset button, just in case you need to start over. This actually works in most of Photoshop Elements' dialogs.

Removing and Replacing Color

What should you do when the colors in your pictures aren't just a bit off—they're *way* off? You have two choices: Fix 'em or get rid of 'em entirely. The latter is the simpler choice: All you have to do is choose Enhance, Adjust Color, Remove Color, and the color is instantly gone. You can get the same effect by choosing Enhance, Adjust Color, Hue/Saturation and simply dragging the Saturation slider all the way to the left. However—you knew there was going to be a "however," didn't you?— you'll get better results by using the Enhance, Convert to Black and White command.

Why? *Good* black-and-white photography is about more than just the absence of color. When you don't have color to create a mood and highlight important parts of an image, you need to do more with what you do have. In other words, you need to be sure that the lighting and contrast are good enough to do for the picture what the color would have done. Using Convert to Black and White gives you more control, and it's the best choice for times when you're converting the whole picture to black and white, as opposed to just desaturating an area within the image. Let's take a quick look at how this command works.

This is another one of those giant dialog boxes (see Figure 14.9, here and in the color section of this book). As with Color Variations, the box has two large preview thumbnails at the top, but that's where the similarity ends. Here, you start by choosing a style. These are different preset conversions that offer varying amounts of brightness in each area of the spectrum. For example, the Portraits setting makes reds and blues somewhat darker than the Newspaper setting. This is because newspaper printing is prone to what's called "dot gain," when ink sinks into the paper and spreads so that each dot of ink in a photo looks bigger and, therefore, darker than it should. When preparing images for newspaper printing, you want them to be a bit lighter than normal to make up for the dot gain that will take place on press.

FIGURE 14.9
Don't let the dialog's size intimidate you; it's mostly preview. Be sure to check it out in the color section.

Other styles are based on the content of your picture more than what you plan to do with it. There's one for portraits, one for scenic landscapes, one for particularly vivid landscapes, and one for urban scenes and snapshots. Each of these darkens and lightens particular colors in a picture for a different result (see Figure 14.10). Be sure to try them all when you're converting a picture.

FIGURE 14.10
I used four dif-
ferent settings
to convert this
photo in very
different ways.
Clockwise
from top left:
Portrait, Scenic
Landscape,
Urban/
Snapshots,
and Vivid
Landscapes.

When you've settled on a style, you can tweak it by moving the four sliders, one for each of the RGB colors and one for contrast. No rules apply; just pay attention to what you like and don't like with each tweak, and keep going until you like what you see.

Replacing colors is, in a way, much simpler. The hardest part of this process is making sure that you're affecting only the colors you want to change, not the rest of the picture. It's a lot more fun, though—you can make the blue sky pink, turn a green dress purple, and compensate for all your friends' lack of fashion sense with a click or two.

Everything begins in the Editor, where you choose Enhance, Adjust Color, Replace Color (see Figure 14.11). First, click in your picture to indicate the color you want to replace. See how the preview immediately colors all matching areas white, in a sea of black? That's showing you what parts of the image will be affected by your changes. Of course, this is assuming that your preview is set to Selection, which is the default. If it's set to Image, it shows you only the picture (which I find rather useless because the image window is right next door). Regardless, you can also click the color swatch next to the eyedroppers to choose a color to replace, but I find it's simplest just to use the eyedroppers in the image itself. Switch to the plus eyedropper to add more shades to your selection, and use the minus eyedropper to remove colors from it. When you've selected the bulk of the area you're targeting, drag the Fuzziness slider to the right a bit to grab those last little bits.

FIGURE 14.11
The Replace Color dialog makes it easy to pull one colored object out of a picture and change its color.

When your selection is just right, you can drag the Hue, Saturation, and Lightness sliders to change that color to a different one and make it more or less vivid, as well as lighter or darker. Or—and this makes more sense to me—you can click the Result color swatch and choose a new color in the color picker. When you click OK in the Replace Color dialog, Photoshop Elements replaces the selected color with the new one.

Getting Your Hands Dirty

If you prefer a more hands-on approach to replacing colors, you might give the Color Replacement Tool a whirl. You'll find it hiding under the Brush in the toolbox; its icon looks like a paintbrush accompanied by a little color swatch.

First, choose a brush tip and size from the Options bar and make sure that the Mode menu is set to Color; this blending mode affects color only, so you won't eliminate the surface texture of the objects you paint.

Now set your options:

▶ **Sampling**—This refers to how Photoshop Elements figures out what colors you want to get rid of. Choose Continuous to tell it that every color you drag over should be replaced, Once if you want it to replace only the first color you click on, or Background Swatch if you want to specify the color to replace by making it the current Background color.

▶ **Limits**—Here you tell Photoshop Elements how far you want to go in replacing color. Discontiguous replaces the color only when you paint over it, while Contiguous replaces it in all the adjacent pixels of the same color as well.

▶ **Tolerance**—Adjust this value downward to limit the colors replaced to those that are very close to the one on which you clicked, or upward to replace more related colors.

Finally, choose a Foreground color for the new color, check the Anti-alias box, and paint within the picture to change the color. Because you can control where the color is applied, the Color Replacement tool can be much more precise than either Hue/Saturation or Replace Color. It comes in handy when there are multiple areas with similar colors in your photo, some of which you want to change and some of which you don't (see Figure 14.12).

FIGURE 14.12
By using the Color Replacement brush, I can change the red firefighter's hat without affecting the red areas in the Oriental rug, as the Replace Color Command would do.

When you're choosing a color range in either Hue/Saturation or Replace Color, you'll often discover areas in your photo that are the same color as the object you want to change but that you don't want to modify. For example, in the photo shown in Figure 14.12, the wicker laundry basket is almost the same color as the boy's skin, so changing one changes the other. To get around this, draw a loose selection around the object you *do* want to change, excluding anything you don't want to change, before you choose the Hue/Saturation or Replace Color command.

Did you Know?

In the next section, let's give the Replace Color command a try and see what it can do.

Try it Yourself ▼

Replace Color

Here's your chance to change the color of anything you like. Cars? Sure. Your dog? Why not? A newspaper box? Well, if you feel like it. This file is called newspapers.jpg, and you'll find it on the book's website if you'd like to work along on this Try it Yourself.

1. Open the picture and choose Enhance, Adjust Color, Replace Color.

2. Click the color you want to change—in this case, the bright yellow newspaper box in the foreground—and drag the Fuzziness slider down to 0 (see Figure 14.13).

FIGURE 14.13
The more your subject stands out from the background, the easier it will be to replace its color with another.

▼

3. In the Replacement area of the dialog, drag the Hue slider to a completely different color so that you can see the selected area in the image window. This is where it starts to get fun.

4. Switch to the plus eyedropper in the dialog, and then click other parts of the picture to include more colors. Click with the minus eyedropper if you add a color that you realize you don't want to change after all.

5. When most of the area you want to change is selected, drag the Fuzziness slider slowly to the right until your entire object is selected, but without selecting any of the background (see Figure 14.14).

FIGURE 14.14
I made the Replacement color a nice, bright pink so that I could see very easily if I'd left any areas of the newspaper box out of my selection.

6. Adjust the new color by dragging the sliders in the Replacement area of the dialog, and then click OK.

You might have trouble keeping this color change from affecting the orange newspaper box right next to the yellow one. If so, you have two options: Go back and select the yellow box before choosing Replace Color, or paint in the new color using the Color Replacement tool, as outlined earlier.

Adjust Color Curves

In Photoshop, Curves is the favorite tool of true color-correction connoisseurs. In Photoshop Elements, the Curves tool is very limited. Still, it's worth checking out, because you can adjust one part of the picture without affecting the rest.

As with Levels, Color Curves offers you a graph to manipulate (see Figure 14.15). Unlike Levels, the Curves graph doesn't represent how dark, light, or contrasty the image is right now; it's more like a two-dimensional slider bar. The three points on the line represent the picture's shadows, highlights, and midtones; dragging a point down using the corresponding Adjust slider darkens those areas of the picture, and dragging it up lightens them. Midtones have two sliders: Midtone Brightness, to darken or lighten midtones, and Midtone Contrast, which moves the midtone point left and right on the graph to adjust image contrast.

FIGURE 14.15
Here I started with the Lighten Shadows preset style and then adjusted the sliders to bump up the contrast.

The best way to use Color Curves is to choose a preset style from the options on the left: Backlight, Darken Highlights, Default, Increase Contrast, Increase Midtones, Lighten Shadows, or Solarize. From there, use the four sliders to tweak your picture until you like the way it looks. In Photoshop, you can drag the points on the graph directly and add more points wherever you want them; in Photoshop Elements, you can manipulate only the three middle points using the sliders.

Remember this rule for Curves: In general, make the curve bow upward to lighten the picture, downward to darken it.

Adjust Color for Skin Tone

This command is so quick and easy to use that it should qualify as a Quick Fix. As with Remove Color Cast, it requires only that you click in an appropriate area of the photo for it to do its magic (see Figure 14.16).

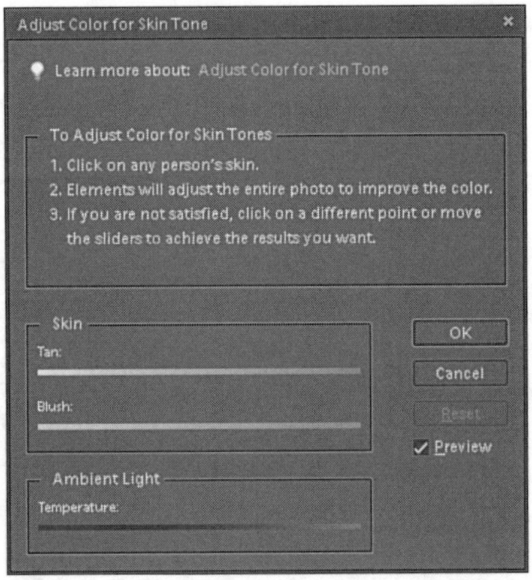

FIGURE 14.16
Don't overlook the Temperature slider; it's amazing how much difference the overall perceived temperature of the picture can affect how skin tones look.

When I first heard about Adjust Color for Skin Tone, I immediately wondered how Photoshop Elements could revise skin tones when there are so many different colors of skin in the world. The answer has to do with proportions of the basic colors, red, green, and blue. Evidently, they tend to be similar no matter how dark or light your skin is. But it turns out that I actually had the question slightly wrong. Adjust Color for Skin Tone actually modifies the overall image color to make the skin tones look better (not necessarily more accurate). And, of course, Photoshop Elements has no idea what parts of a picture are really skin and what parts are just things that are vaguely skin colored. So your results might vary, depending on what other objects are in your picture along with the people.

When you're adjusting skin tones, all you have to do is click in a representative area of skin. Be sure to pick a point that's unblemished (no freckles, please), glare free, and not artificially colored by makeup, other than base, or by colors reflected from other objects. One click, and Photoshop Elements does its thing. Then you can tweak the results with three different sliders:

▶ **Tan**—Makes skin more or less brown. Don't try to give a tan to someone who doesn't already have one, though; it just looks odd.

▶ **Blush**—Turns skin more or less pink.

▶ **Temperature**—As with the Temperature slider in the Quick Fix tab's Color area, changes the overall color cast of the picture to make the lighting seem warmer or cooler.

Adjusting Lighting Manually

Sometimes it just *looks* as though the color is off in a picture; but when you adjust the lighting in that picture, it leaps to life and the colors seem perfectly true again. Knowing how best to fix pictures that are too light or too dark is probably the most valuable skill you'll learn as you work with Photoshop Elements.

Using the Traditional Tools

Photoshop and Photoshop Elements users have always used tools such as Brightness/Contrast and Levels to work with pictures that are too light or too dark. When you want to control the process yourself instead of letting Photoshop Elements' automated commands have a go at your picture, these are the places to start.

Using the Brightness/Contrast command is about as simple as it gets. It's a rather blunt instrument, though, so you'll probably find that it's best used in selected areas rather than on a whole image. Choose Enhance, Adjust Lighting, Brightness/Contrast, and drag the Brightness slider to make the image lighter or darker, or the Contrast slider to make the color contrasts more or less pronounced (see Figure 14.17).

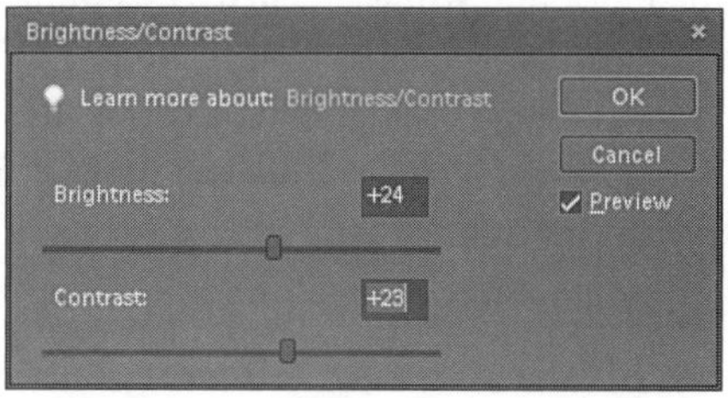

FIGURE 14.17
Brightness/Contrast is simple but effective; look for this figure in the color section to see just how effective.

Levels, on the other hand, is intended to work with the image as a whole and yields distorted results when applied to a selected area. The Levels command adjusts all the brightness levels in a picture and can be used to remove color casts. Earlier in this hour, you learned about the Auto Levels command; now let's take a look at how you can make your own custom Levels adjustments.

First, choose Enhance, Adjust Lighting, Levels or press Ctrl+L so you can get a look at what you're dealing with (see Figure 14.18). The most prominent feature of the Levels dialog is a histogram, a graph of how many pixels in the image are at each of the 256 possible brightness levels between black and white. The histogram should be a smooth curve without a lot of gaps; when you use the Auto Levels command or click Auto in the Levels dialog, Photoshop Elements spreads out the lines on the histogram evenly to fill any gaps. You can see this in action by clicking the Auto button in the Levels dialog and then clicking Reset several times.

FIGURE 14.18
Go here to adjust levels for yourself instead of letting Photoshop Elements make all the decisions.

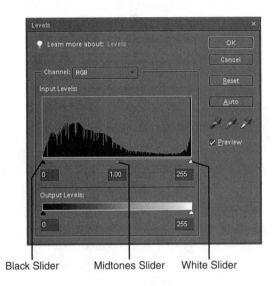

Black Slider   Midtones Slider   White Slider

When you're adjusting levels yourself, the first step is to fill any gaps at the ends of the graph by moving the black and white sliders to the points where the graph trends sharply upward. You can use the eyedropper tools to help with this; click the black one on an area of your image that should be completely black, and the white one on an area that should be completely white. Use the gray eyedropper to get rid of a color cast by clicking in any neutral gray area. Then drag the midtone slider back and forth to lighten or darken the overall image.

By the Way

Why 256 brightness levels? Because we're dealing with 8-bit color in Photoshop Elements, meaning that each color component is defined as a binary number with eight decimal places. And with eight digits, you can specify the numbers 0 to 255 in binary notation. Don't worry if the math doesn't make sense; the Levels command will still work for you.

For the absolute best results, use the Channel pop-up menu at the top of the Levels dialog to adjust each of the picture's color components separately. Starting with the Red channel, drag the end sliders in to where the graph begins to go up, and then move the middle slider left or right until the color looks most accurate. Repeat with the Blue and Green channels. I find that this method yields the most accuracy, and it keeps shadows and highlights from getting muddy or developing a color cast.

All this time, we've been talking about the Input Levels sliders below the histogram. What about the Output Level sliders? Well, these can restrict the range of brightness levels in the picture by chopping off levels from each end. You can use them in three ways:

▶ Drag each Output Levels slider toward the center a little to eliminate the darkest shadows and the brightest highlights in the photo and recapture some of the detail from those locations.

▶ Drag each of the Output Levels sliders to the opposite end of the bar, to make the picture into a color negative.

▶ Select an area of the image and then drag one end of the Output Levels slider toward the center to make whitish or blackish boxes where type placed over the image will be more legible, sort of like little pieces of white or black tissue paper. You see this technique used all the time in magazine ads (see Figure 14.19).

Compensating for Lighting Mistakes

In earlier versions, Photoshop Elements had two very useful tools for fixing problem lighting, called Fill Flash and Adjust Backlighting. Now they're replaced by the even-better Highlights/Shadows dialog. To get there from the Editor, choose Enhance, Adjust Lighting, Shadows/Highlights.

FIGURE 14.19
Creating the semitransparent black area for type is a simple matter of selecting an area and then adjusting the Levels dialog's Output Levels slider.

In this dialog, you can get right to the point. You don't need to worry about which color channels are responsible for the problems you're seeing in your photo; you can just get started fixing them, with a jump-start from Photoshop Elements. Because one of the most common flaws in amateur photos is dark shadows, you'll always start your trip to the Shadows/Highlights dialog with a Lighten Shadows setting of 25% (see Figure 14.20). Sometimes this is a good idea; sometimes it's not. Start by looking at the darkest areas of your image. Do they look washed out? If so, back off with the Lighten Shadows slider as much as needed to restore life to those shadows. Then take a look at the brightest parts of the picture. Are they blown out—in other words, are they so bright that they're all white, with no detail? If so, drag the Darken Highlights slider to the right until you're happy with them. Finally, drag the Midtone Contrast slider left or right to even out the medium-brightness areas of the image.

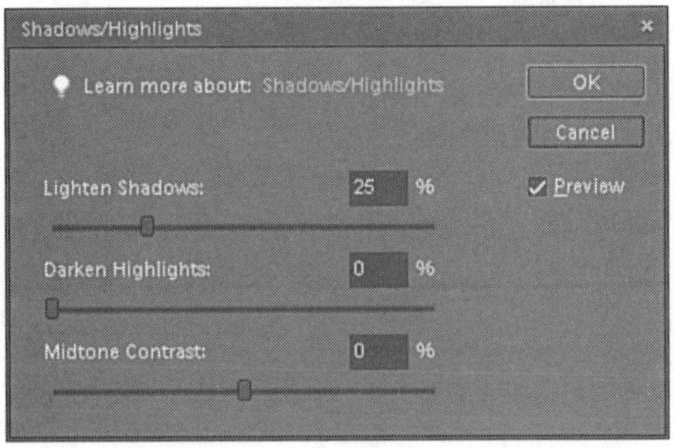

FIGURE 14.20
Shadows/Highlights is a bit more complicated than Brightness/Contrast, but it's worth taking the trouble to get used to it.

I do love the results I get with the Shadows/Highlights dialog, but I almost always have to reduce the Lighten Shadows setting first thing. Keep that in mind, and I think you'll love Shadows/Highlights, too.

Try it Yourself ▼

Fix a Fuzzy and Very Green Photo

The picture we start with for this Try it Yourself is a scan of a 1959 print with seriously degraded color. The kids look as though they're having a good time, though, so let's see what we can do to bring back the picture's original sparkle. You can download the photo from the book's website; it's called greenhouse.jpg (see Figure 14.21).

FIGURE 14.21
These kids have been trapped in the jungle so long they've turned green themselves.

1. First, let's see what we can do to fix the lighting. This picture is both too dark in the shadows and too light in the highlights. Choose Enhance, Adjust Lighting, Shadows/Highlights, and start by moving the Lighten Shadows slider back down to about 10% so that the shadows aren't all gray and grainy.

2. Now let's deal with the rest of the picture. I think the highlights could be a bit darker. Look at the fur hoods on two of the children for guidance here; I moved the Darken Highlights slider to 3%. Then I tried moving the Midtone Contrast slider in both directions before settling on +4% (see Figure 14.22).

▼

FIGURE 14.22
The first step is
fixing the light-
ing.

3. Those changes improve the lighting a lot; next we address color. Choose Enhance, Adjust Color, Color Variations. Before clicking on any of the thumbnails, be sure to choose the area of the image you want to address first (I always start with Shadows) and adjust the Amount slider to determine how much each click changes the picture.

4. For each aspect of the picture, see if you can nudge it toward where it should be, with less red, less green, more blue—whatever you think it needs. If you find that the picture still has a red or green color cast no matter what you do, you're not alone. I wasn't able to get the results I'm looking for with Color Variations, so let's try another tool. Click Cancel.

5. This time we know the problem is a color cast, and Levels can often deal with that, so let's go old-school. Choose Enhance, Adjust Lighting, Levels. Before you try anything else, click the gray eyedropper and then click the rock next to the doll's feet at the right side of the picture. Much better, eh? Now lighten up the picture as a whole by dragging the middle Input Level slider to the left just a bit (see Figure 14.23).

6. I don't know about you, but now the picture looks a bit cool to me. Let's try one more thing. Leave your Levels adjustment in place—don't undo it—and choose Enhance, Adjust Color, Adjust for Skin Tone. Click on any of the kids' faces and see how you like the results. I like 'em a lot!

This picture still needs work; it's grainy and blurry, which means it'll be difficult to sharpen it without emphasizing the grain. But those are tasks for another hour. For now, you're done! Here's the final version of the photo (see Figure 14.24); turn to the color section of the book to get the full impact of these changes.

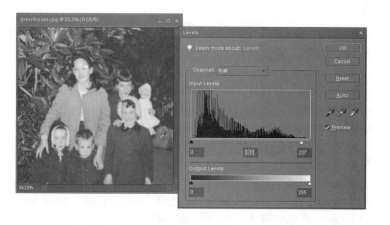

FIGURE 14.23
Now we take a whack at getting the color right.

FIGURE 14.24
That last tweak with Adjust Color for Skin Tone makes all the difference.

Summary

This hour has really built up your skills. You've learned how to use Photoshop Elements' automated tools to fix color and lighting, and you learned when you should go straight to the manual versions of those tools. You learned how to use Color Variations, Remove Color Cast, Hue/Saturation, Remove Color, Replace Color, Color Curves, and Adjust Color for Skin Tone. As if that weren't enough, you then learned both traditional and new methods for adjusting image lighting, and you exercised your skills to bring a sad, green photo from the 1950s back to life. You should feel really good about your accomplishments in this hour.

Q&A

Q. *I see what hue is, and brightness is pretty clear, but I'm not sure I understand saturation yet. Can you explain it one more time?*

A. No problem; if you don't have an art background, a lot of the terms and concepts we're looking at now will likely be unfamiliar. Think of saturation this way: Start with a jar of water. Add a tiny bit of red powdered drink mix (could be cherry, could be raspberry—your choice). See the clear water begin to take on some color? You just increased the color saturation of the water. Add the rest of the drink mix. Now you've turned the saturation all the way up. Good job; you can enjoy your drink now!

Q. *Brightness/Contrast seems pretty useful to me; why isn't it the best tool to use for adjusting, well, brightness and contrast?*

A. It's limited because it makes the whole picture lighter or darker, not just the highlights, midtones, or shadows. Sometimes a picture's midtones are just fine and all you need to work on is the shadows. In this case, stay far, far away from Brightness/Contrast.

Q. *I prefer Color Curves to Levels, so there!*

A. Hey, that's fine with me. The reason Photoshop Elements has many overlapping tools so that you can use what works for you. Try 'em all out, give 'em a chance, and then pick your favorites and have fun.

Workshop

Whew. You deserve a break! Take a few minutes to tackle these quiz questions and check your answers. Then you can have some fun working on this hour's activity.

Quiz

1. What is a histogram?

    A. A blood test

    B. One of the components of the HSB color model

    C. A double-ended slider control

    D. A graph of the number of pixels at each possible brightness level within an image

2. How can Adjust for Skin Tone work with all possible skin tones?

   A. It doesn't.

   B. It manipulates ratios of each skin tone's component colors, instead of setting the colors to fixed levels.

   C. It can affect objects in the picture that are "skin-colored" but aren't skin.

   D. All of the above.

3. Which command *doesn't* let you work separately on shadows, midtones, and highlights?

   A. Levels

   B. Brightness/Contrast

   C. Variations

   D. Color Curves

Quiz Answers

1. A. And there are how many of those brightness levels, again? That's right, 256.

2. D. Adjust for Skin Tone is a useful tool, but it's not infallible. It works best with lighter skin tones, but be sure to take advantage of the Tan, Blush, and Temperature sliders to get better results with all skin colors.

3. B. Use it sparingly, when you're in a hurry or are working on a small selected part of a photo.

Activity

Find the oldest photo of yourself that you can track down. Scan it in and see what you can do to fix it. Does the lighting need help? Are the colors off? If it's a color image, try converting it to black and white using different presets. Print the one you like best.

HOUR 15

Using Guided Edit

What You'll Learn in This Hour:

▶ How to work in Guided Edit mode
▶ The right Guided Edit task for each situation
▶ How to use Guided Edit to accomplish more complicated tasks

Guided Edit is new to Photoshop Elements 6, and a lot of photo editing experts and non-experts alike seem to think it's a step in the right direction for Adobe. This new editing mode is a middle-ground, somewhere between "Just fix it for me!" and "I can do it myself!" Ideally, when you're using Guided Edit to accomplish unfamiliar tasks in Photoshop Elements, you're learning as you go so that you'll be able to perform those tasks manually in the future, if you want to. Guided Edit is supposed to teach you the correct order for various image-editing tasks, which tools to use for them, and how to use those tools. In theory, because you have this book, you don't really need Guided Edit, but we all know that in reality everyone has times when they can use a little hand-holding, even if only to make them feel more confident. So give Guided Edit a try, and maybe you'll like it.

A Word of Warning

Before we get started, let's get a few things out on the table. First, Guided Edit won't do it all; Adobe has only included a few Guided Edit tasks that encompass the most commonly performed photo-editing tasks. If you want to be guided through the steps for adding type to a picture, for example, you're out of luck. Second, before you can use Guided Edit, you need to know what you want to do so that you can choose the correct Guided Edit task. If you're not sure what the difference is between lightening or darkening an image and adjusting its brightness and contrast, Guided Edit can't help you figure that out.

All the tasks in Guided Edit are ones you can do yourself using the tools and commands in Full Edit mode, but Guided Edit presents them to you with explanatory text that makes them as simple to use as Quick Fixes. As you work, you can use a pop-up menu in the Task pane to choose among four view modes: Before Only, After Only, Before & After—Horizontal, and Before & After—Vertical. I prefer to use one of the Before & After modes, depending on the orientation of the picture, but if you want to display the picture as large as possible, you can choose After Only.

When you're done with each Guided Edit task, you need to click the Done button or, in some cases, the Next button to move to the next step. You can click Cancel, next to the Done or Next buttons, at any time if you change your mind about completing the edit you're working on; if you change your mind too late to click Cancel, you can click the Undo button in the menu bar instead.

> Some experts have speculated that Adobe might add more Guided Edit tasks in the future. I'd love to see tasks that would help users whiten teeth and eyes, remove glare from glasses, smooth wrinkles, and intensify eye color. In the meantime, we'll just have to figure out how to do these things ourselves. Keep reading; we look at these tasks in future hours.

Basic Photo Edits

The category of Basic Photo Edits in the Guided Edit tab includes three tasks. Let's take a look at each of them.

When you click Crop Photo, Photoshop Elements switches to the Crop tool and draws a cropping marquee in the picture for you (see Figure 15.1). All you have to do is resize the marquee to suit your needs. A pop-up menu in the Task pane gives you the same choices that the Aspect Ratio menu offers in the Options bar in Full Edit mode: No Restriction, Use Photo Ratio, and several common photo print sizes.

The Rotate and/or Straighten Photo Guided Edit task uses the 90° Left and 90° Right commands found in the Image, Rotate submenu, offering you buttons to click for each 90° rotation (see Figure 15.2). This task also puts the Straighten tool in the Task pane so that you don't have to go looking for it in the toolbox; it then gives you the same choices that you'll find on the Options bar when you use the Straighten tool in Full Edit mode: Maintain Image Size or Maintain Canvas Size.

FIGURE 15.1
The Crop tool
works the same
way in Guided
Edit as it does
in Full Edit.

You learned about the Rotate commands and the Straighten tool in Hour 12, "Straightening, Skewing, and Distorting an Image."

By the Way

FIGURE 15.2
It's difficult to
straighten a pic-
ture like this
one, but you
can undo and
redo as many
times as you
need to.

Finally, to use the Sharpen Photo Guided Edit task, you drag the slider in the Task pane (see Figure 15.3). This has the same effect as using Adjust Sharpness in the Enhance menu, but the slider is placed right in the Task pane so you don't have to go looking for it.

FIGURE 15.3
With the streamlined Guided Edit interface, you can really focus on just the picture you're working on.

Lighting and Exposure

The Lighting and Exposure category has two Guided Edit tasks: Lighten or Darken and Brightness and Contrast. Choose Lighten or Darken if the picture is overall too dark or too light; choose Brightness and Contrast if the picture looks muddy or flat.

When you use the Lighten or Darken Guided Edit task, you have two choices: You can click Auto to have Photoshop Elements adjust the photo to its liking, or you can use the three sliders to make your own adjustments. The Lighten Shadows and Darken Highlights sliders range from 0 to 100, and Midtone Contrast can be set anywhere between –100 and +100 (see Figure 15.4).

By the Way

These are the same sliders you've seen in the Shadows/Highlights dialog (choose Enhance, Adjust Lighting, Shadows/Highlights to get there) when using Full Edit mode, which we talked about in the last hour.

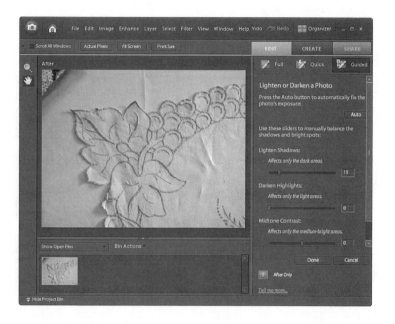

FIGURE 15.4
The Lighten or Darken controls are the same as the ones in the Shadows/ Highlights dialog.

You also have the option of clicking Auto when using the Brightness and Contrast Guided Edit task if you want Photoshop Elements to adjust the picture for you, or you can drag the Brightness and Contrast sliders. You can adjust Brightness as low as –150 and as high as +150, but Contrast ranges between –50 and +100 (see Figure 15.5). These are the same sliders found in the Brightness/Contrast dialog (choose Enhance, Adjust Lighting, Brightness/Contrast). One useful difference between this Guided Edit activity and the regular Brightness/Contrast dialog is that the Contrast slider, which starts out set at 0, is located one-third of the way from the left end of its bar instead of in the middle, which gives you a more accurate idea of how much you can reduce or increase contrast.

FIGURE 15.5
Guided Edits
don't need to
be done in any
particular order;
when I'm done
brightening this
picture, I'll go
back and
straighten it.

Color Correction

Oddly, the Color Correction category of Guided Edit tasks doesn't really include a general-purpose color fixing method. You can choose to make the colors more intense, to remove a color cast, or to adjust the colors to flatter skin tones.

When you click the Enhance Colors Guided Edit task, you're presented with the sliders from the Hue/Saturation dialog box (see Figure 15.6). The Hue/Saturation dialog box is the same one you saw when you chose Enhance, Adjust Color, Adjust Hue/Saturation in the last hour. Of course, in Guided Edit you also have an Auto button, which functions like the Auto Color Correction command in the Enhance menu. To adjust the colors yourself, you can drag the Hue, Saturation, and Lightness sliders, with Hue settings ranging from –180° to +180°, and Saturation and Lightness falling between –100 and +100.

Removing a color cast is a simple one-step operation using the Guided Edit task, just as it is when you choose Enhance, Adjust Color, Remove Color Cast. The hardest part of this task is choosing a color-neutral location to click in the picture, but you can keep clicking different locations until you're satisfied. In Guided Edit mode, you can also use the Zoom and Hand tools from the toolbox to move around the image while you're looking for just the right spot (see Figure 15.7).

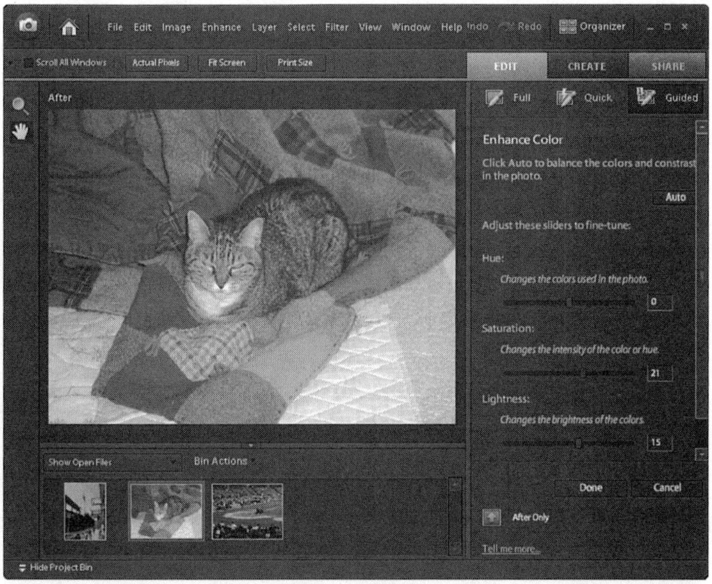

FIGURE 15.6
The only difference between the Enhance Color Guided Edit task and the Hue/Saturation dialog is that, in Guided Edit mode, you can't restrict your changes to a particular range of colors.

FIGURE 15.7
I clicked the pitcher's mound to fix a color cast in this picture.

The Correct Skin Tone Guided Edit task is like using the Adjust Color for Skin Tone command (choose Enhance, Adjust Colors, Adjust Color for Skin Tone). The Skin Tone Eyedropper tool is automatically activated, and all you have to do is locate a piece of skin on which to click. You have the same sliders: Tan, Blush, and Ambient Light, with no numbers—all your adjustments are done by eye here, with no regard to exact color values. Again, you can use the Zoom and Hand tools to move around the picture as you work (see Figure 15.8).

FIGURE 15.8
Clicking the baby's knee warms up this picture considerably.

Guided Activities

Guided Edit includes a couple multistep tasks called Guided Activities. The first of these, Touch Up Scratches, Blemishes or Tear Marks, gives you step-by-step instructions for using the Spot Healing Brush and the Healing Brush. With each tool, you first adjust your brush size to taste and then click or click and drag in the picture to erase flaws (see Figure 15.9). Of course, when you're using the Healing Brush, you also need to click to set the point from which the brush picks up the pixels that it deposits as it paints.

The second Guided Activity is more complex. Using the Guide for Editing a Photo, you're walked through cropping your picture, lightening or darkening it, touching up any flaws in it, and sharpening it. Each of these subtasks looks and works just like the Guided Edit task of the same name. The most important point to take away from this task is that you should always adjust the lighting in your pictures before you retouch them, and you should always wait to sharpen until you're done retouching.

FIGURE 15.9
Although the Healing Brush and Spot Healing Brush work the same way in Guided Edit as in Full Edit, I prefer to use them in Full Edit mode so I can switch to other tools, such as the Clone Stamp and the Lasso, as needed.

Photomerge

The last two Guided Edit tasks are labeled Photomerge. These two tasks, Group Shot and Faces, use Photoshop Elements' blending techniques in a new way to enable you to swap people in and out of group shots or features in and out of a head shot to achieve the best overall results (or, in some cases, the funniest overall results). We'll look at how to use these two techniques in Hour 18, "Removing and Replacing Objects."

Summary

Guided Edit mode doesn't give you any extra features over Quick Fix and Full Edit modes, but the explanatory text and stripped-down interface make it easy to complete tasks without becoming confused or distracted. Using these tasks is a good way to get used to working in Photoshop Elements with a little hand-holding before you venture out on your own.

Q&A

Q. *Is there a Guided Edit task that can show me how to replace one color with another?*

A. No, there isn't. But you can learn everything you need to know about the Replace Color command in this book; turn to page 253 for step-by-step instructions on changing one color into a completely different one.

Q. *If I don't like the results I get with Guided Edit, can I change my mind?*

A. Of course you can. If you haven't completed the task yet, just click Cancel. You can then move on with another Guided Edit task or switch to Quick Fix or Full Edit mode. If the task is already complete and you don't like the way the picture came out, just click the Undo button in the menu bar. For most of the Guided Edit tasks, you'll just have to click once to undo your changes, but after you work through the Guide for Editing a Photo, you'll need to click four times (once each to undo the picture's cropping, lighting, retouching, and sharpening adjustments).

Workshop

We haven't had much to go over in this hour, so I'm giving you the rest of the hour off—after you complete the quiz, of course—to try out the Guided Edit tasks on your own photos. Some ideas are listed in the Activities section, but feel free to experiment.

Quiz

1. If a photo is overexposed so that it's too light, which Guided Edit task should you use to fix it?

    A. Lighten or Darken

    B. Brightness and Contrast

    C. Both

    D. Neither

2. Guided Edit contains hidden special features that aren't available anywhere else in Photoshop Elements.

    A. True

    B. False

Quiz Answers

1. C. Start with Lighten or Darken and see how much detail you can restore to the picture; then use Brightness and Contrast to make sure it's not flat.

2. B. False. Everything you can do in Guided Edit, you can also do without Guided Edit using tools and menu commands in Full Edit or Quick Fix mode.

Activities

1. Click the Crop Photo Guided Edit task. Before you crop your picture, switch to the Zoom tool and use it to change the magnification of the image; then switch to the Hand tool and move the picture around on the screen. Switch back to the Crop tool and complete the task.

2. Open a photo that shows more than one person. Click the Correct Skin Tone Guided Edit, and then click on different areas of skin in the picture. How different can you make the results by clicking on darker or lighter areas?

3. Think of a Guided Edit activity that you'd like to see, write it out, and email it to me at binderk@mac.com, along with the picture you'd use it on. I'll use the best ones—with full credit to you, of course!—in the next edition of this book.

PART III

Photo Rescue

Repairing Black-and-White Pictures

What You'll Learn in This Hour:

▶ Adding contrast to a faded photo

▶ Dodging and burning to bring out lost details

▶ Covering up small flaws

▶ Repairing physical damage to an old photo

▶ Applying color to a black-and-white image

Until now, most of the image flaws we've seen have been part of the picture, either as a component of the original image or as detritus from the process of getting the picture into your computer. In this hour and the next, we take a look at some pictures that have just had a hard, hard life. All old pictures are damaged over time, even when they're just sitting around. If they're framed, they're exposed to light, which can fade photo prints in unpredictable ways. Framing materials might or might not be chemically inert; if not, then they, too, can damage a print. And bad things happen even to new pictures, such as gnawing cats and stumbling toddlers. But fixing physical damage to prints or negatives is definitely possible, and you're about to learn how to do it.

The first step is to clean up the original as best you can, removing dust, dirt, and water. Then scan the picture at 100% or larger and at least 300ppi. At this point, you're ready to start doing some repairs.

Easy Fixes

Obviously, how much work you need to do on a photo depends on what's wrong with it. Some fixes are surprisingly easy to accomplish, supplying a big payoff for relatively little effort. Take this picture of my grandma as a baby, for instance (see Figure 16.1). It's faded, scratched, dirty, and rather clumsily hand-trimmed. But I think this picture is fairly easily to salvage. Let me show you what I mean.

FIGURE 16.1
I love the expression on this kid's face, and I suspect it will be even cuter if I can bring out her eyes.

First, I need to crop the picture to focus on the subject; this has the added benefit of removing a bunch of stuff I'd otherwise have to retouch. While I'm cropping, I can straighten the picture—the kid's listing to the right a bit. If you need to review cropping and straightening techniques, flip back to Hour 11, "Composing and Cropping Your Pictures," and Hour 12, "Straightening, Skewing, and Distorting an Image," before moving on.

The next big step is to fix this picture's contrast. The image has faded so that you can't pick out details. First, of course, I tried Auto Levels, just to see what that would do. Unfortunately, it did almost nothing because this picture has plenty of medium gray accompanied by lovely dark shadows—where the corners have been cut off and the black paper behind the picture is showing. Those aren't real shadows, but

Photoshop Elements doesn't know that. That means it's time for a manual adjustment. Here's my secret method for basing a levels adjustment on just part of a picture:

1. Draw a selection marquee around the part of the photo that you're interested in. Here, it's the baby, without all the white background and black corners (see Figure 16.2).

FIGURE 16.2
My selection includes only the baby and her seat.

2. Press Ctrl+L to bring up the Levels dialog box. Then click Auto just to see what it gets you. Take note of the improved contrast so you know what you're aiming for, and then click Reset.

3. Now drag the sliders until you see a similar improvement in the selected area of the picture. Notice that, this time, the numbers below the graph are changing as you work. When you've got the levels the way you like them, jot down the number below the black slider and the one below the gray slider; then click Cancel.

4. Drop the selection by pressing Ctrl+D and then press Ctrl+L again. Click in the entry fields below the graph and enter the values you got in step 3. Then click OK.

That might seem like a lot of backing and forthing, but it gets you a Levels adjustment based on just the part of the image you care about. The reason you couldn't just go with the values set in step 3 is that they would have been applied only to the selected area, leaving a sharp dividing line between that and the unselected areas. You had to get rid of the selection and apply the change to the entire picture (see Figure 16.3).

FIGURE 16.3
These settings make the corners too dark, but I don't care because I'm going to get rid of them anyway.

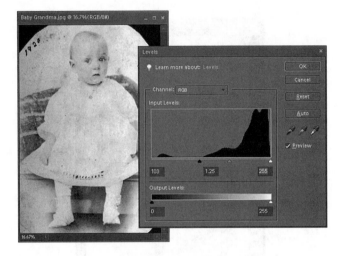

To finish up, the photo gets some attention with the Spot Healing Brush (to delete specks of dust), the Burn tool (to make the baby's head stand out from the background), the Dodge tool (to get rid of shadows on her face), the Clone Stamp tool (to eliminate those dark corners), and the Blur tool (to despeckle the background). We're left with a much clearer shot of Grandma that I think the whole family will love (see Figure 16.4). We'll cover all these techniques in this hour and the next one.

Fixing Poor Contrast

One of the most common problems you'll run into when working with older pictures is fading or overexposure, either of which results in pictures with little contrast. You'll also often see shots with too much contrast—deep, dark shadows and blown-out highlights—that can be attributed to inexpensive equipment and supplies and less sophisticated technology than we enjoy these days. Either way, Photoshop Elements offers you ways to attack contrast problems throughout a picture or just in trouble areas.

FIGURE 16.4
The result of my labors.

The picture in Figure 16.5 shows a genuine 1950s-vintage duck whose name was evidently Daffy—at least, that's what the note on the photo's back says. At any rate, Daffy could definitely stand out from his background a bit more than he's currently doing. First, the whole picture needs to lose that muddy gray cast. Then a bit of sharpening will probably do wonders.

FIGURE 16.5
Daffy seems to be stuck in the mud.

I've already cropped this photo to get rid of extraneous elements, such as the people having a picnic to Daffy's left. We're interested only in ducks here, after all. My next step is to remove the color from the picture by pressing Ctrl+Shift+U (if you prefer, you can choose Enhance, Adjust Color, Remove Color). Then it's time to see what can be done with the Levels dialog (see Figure 16.6).

FIGURE 16.6
Here I can brighten the picture by showing the Levels dialog where the whitest area of the image *should* be.

Here's a good opportunity to use the eyedroppers because you can see that Daffy's feathers should be bright white. Here I've chosen the white eyedropper and clicked on the front of the duck's neck to indicate that this should be the brightest area in the picture. Then I've dragged the midtone slider to the left a bit to lighten the grass around the duck. Now Daffy looks somewhat faded, but don't worry—that's easily corrected with a Brightness/Contrast adjustment. I used these settings: Brightness +2 and Contrast +49. After that, I ran the Despeckle Filter, followed by the Dust & Scratches filter. Then I chose Enhance, Adjust Sharpness and played with those settings until I liked Daffy's looks (see Figure 16.7). In the Adjust Sharpness dialog, I changed the Remove setting to Lens Blur instead of Gaussian Blur, and I checked the More Refined box to preserve more image detail.

Dodging and Burning

So far, we've been adjusting the entire image. Now it's time to get more subtle by making use of two tools that you can apply just where they're needed. Based on two old darkroom tricks, the Dodge and Burn tools can lighten and darken, respectively, wherever you apply them.

FIGURE 16.7
With a little of this and a little of that, Daffy is looking a whole lot better.

The Dodge tool looks like a lollipop, but it's *supposed* to look like a circular piece of cardboard on a stick. If you were printing pictures in a darkroom, you could wave this tool between the light on the enlarger and the photo paper to tone down the image in selected areas. In Photoshop Elements, you use it the same way: by dragging the Dodge tool over a dark area of the image to lighten it. In the Options bar, you can choose the brush size and shape that the Dodge tool uses, as well as whether it focuses on highlights, midtones, or shadows. You can also determine how much effect it has with each click.

Similarly, in a darkroom, you use your hand to focus extra light on part of your picture so the image there burns in darker than the rest of the picture. Photoshop Elements' version of this technique involves using the Burn tool, whose icon looks like a person's fist held so that the fingers form a hole though which light can shine. Like the Dodge tool, the Burn tool can operate on highlights, midtones, or shadows, one at a time but not all at once; its Exposure percentage determines whether each stroke of the tool darkens the underlying pixels a little or a lot.

In the next Try it Yourself, you'll use the Dodge and Burn tools to fix a couple common problems encountered with indoor flash photography.

▼ **Try it Yourself**

Using the Dodge and Burn Tools

For this Try it Yourself, I'm using a shot of my friend's cat, Figaro. He's a devilish one, and his attitude is on full display in this portrait. But it was taken indoors with a bright flash, and that left a dark shadow on the wall behind his head. We can fix that. While we're at it, we can give his eyes back some of the intensity that the flash stripped out. You'll find figaro.jpg on the book's website at www.informit.com/title/9780672330179. Let's get started.

1. After opening the picture, I took care of a few overall fixes I wanted to do, such as the Levels adjustment shown here (see Figure 16.8). Always get these out of the way before you start fiddling with individual pieces of the picture. Now I'll switch to the Zoom tool and zoom in on the areas I want to dodge.

FIGURE 16.8
Levels adjustments done after I use the Dodge and Burn tools might make my edits jump out instead of blending into the picture.

2. Next, switch to the Dodge tool and get to work. The first thing I want to do is fix that nasty shadow behind Figaro's head, so I pick a size for the Dodge brush tip that's just a bit wider than the shadow (80 pixels). Then I carefully paint over the shadow with the tool set to 50% exposure and Shadows. Two pieces of advice: First, don't make the shadow too light; we don't want to get rid of it—just make it contrast with Figaro's head. Second, watch out for the dark line at the bottom of the wallpaper border; don't dodge a light area into it.

▼

3. When you're happy with the shadow area, move over to Figaro's eyes and switch to the Lasso tool. Give it a 5-pixel feather in the Options bar and carefully select the pupil of one eye.

4. Switch to the Burn tool and set its Exposure to 100%. Adjust the brush until it's just bigger than your selection, and then click several times until the pupil is mostly black, with flecks of color and a bright highlight.

5. Do the same for the other eye, being careful that the selection surrounds only the pupil and not the lighter-colored iris of the cat's eye. This is a great technique for fixing green eye (the animal equivalent of red eye) in animals that actually *have* green eyes. Now Figaro looks like the formidable beast that he is (see Figure 16.9).

FIGURE 16.9
Dodging makes the shadow more subtle, and burning fixes the eyes in this feline portrait.

Painting over Small Blotches

Sometimes the simplest techniques are the best. In this case, I'm referring to simply painting over stuff you don't like. It works when you're painting your walls; why not in Photoshop Elements?

In smooth areas with little color variation, painting over flaws usually is quicker and easier than messing around with patches, the Healing Brush, or the Clone Stamp. First, set the tip of your brush so it's slightly larger than the object you want to paint over, and then set the right Foreground color. You'll need to pay careful attention to the values in the color picker, and you'll probably need to try a dozen or so times before you get it just right. Or, if you prefer to use a foolproof method of choosing precisely the right color, you can press Alt to temporarily turn the Paintbrush tool into the Eyedropper tool and click it in the picture near the spot you want to paint out. If only matching paint colors in your house were this easy....

When you're painting, you'll get the best results with quick clicks instead of sweeping strokes of the brush. You might want to try varying the Paintbrush's opacity, using the slider in the Options bar, to ensure that your touch-ups remain subtle (see Figure 16.10).

FIGURE 16.10
We can easily deal with these spots on the wall next to our old friend Figaro using a soft-edged Paintbrush.

Repairing Serious Damage

We know that sometimes bad things happen to good pictures. And we should also realize that sometimes more than one bad thing happens to the same photo. In this section, you'll fix several problems with a little snapshot that has yellowed and folded in half and that has experienced some degradation of the chemicals that form the image on the paper—that's the odd "glow" that's showing up on the jacket and hair (see Figure 16.11). Check the color plate section for a clearer view of this photo and all its problems.

Removing Tints

The first thing to do with this photo is get rid of the color. The photo itself was originally black and white, but it has yellowed, and the cardboard frame is brown and silver, with some odd blue streaks. Away with it all, I say. If I want to add a tint when I'm done, that's easy enough, but for now, the color is just a distraction from the "bones" of the picture. This would also be the case if I were dealing with a sepia-tinted photo; retouching is much simpler if you have to match only brightness instead of an exact hue.

FIGURE 16.11
Another factor that's not helping this photo is that it's glued into its cardboard frame.

As you know, you can remove the color from a picture in three simply ways. You can choose Enhance, Adjust Color, Remove Color, which is the quickest method but offers no control over how the conversion from color to black and white is done. Or you can open the Hue/Saturation dialog (choose Enhance, Adjust Color, Adjust Hue/Saturation), where you can drag the Saturation slider all the way to the left and then adjust the Lightness slider as well. For the most control, you need to use the Convert to Black and White command, found in the Enhance menu. That's my solution for this photo, using the Portraits preset to get the smoothest result on the face (see Figure 16.12).

First Steps

The next steps in working on this picture will sound familiar: First, crop out the parts you don't need. Then adjust the picture's brightness, if needed. In this case, I definitely want to get rid of that frame. The scan is crooked, so I can take this opportunity to straighten the photo while cropping it. Using the Crop tool, I can carefully crop out as much of the frame as possible without losing any of the photo. Clicking outside the cropping marquee, I can rotate the marquee so that it lines up with the photo (see Figure 16.13); when I accept the crop, the photo rotates back the other way to become level.

FIGURE 16.12
The Newspaper setting made the picture too light; the landscape settings made it too dark. Portraits is just right.

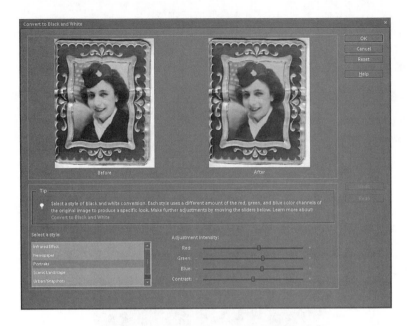

FIGURE 16.13
Always take the opportunity to straighten an image while you're cropping it, if needed.

Speaking of "level," that's the next thing I want to do to this photo: adjust its levels. Bring the black-and-white sliders to where the Levels graph begins to trend upward, to brighten the photo without making it too light.

Repairing Tears and Folds

Now it's time for the real work on this picture to begin. First, I grab the Spot Healing Brush and adjust the brush size. Then I click it on any little specks that stand out, unless they're right next to an area of another color. In that case, the Spot Healing Brush pulls out some of the other color to make its instant patch, and I'd end up with a smudge instead of a speck, which isn't really an improvement. I can use this technique all over the picture, but my primary concern is the face; I can always blur the background or replace it entirely, but the face is the part of the picture I most want to preserve (see Figure 16.14). If I don't like the results of any click, I can click Undo right away to get rid of that bit of healing and then either try again with a different brush size or leave the spot for later removal with the Clone Stamp or Healing Brush.

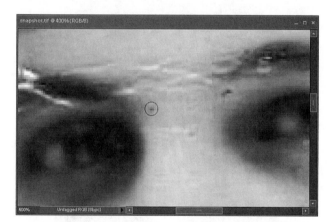

FIGURE 16.14
Zoom way, way in, if you need to, and don't be afraid to adjust the size of the Spot Healing Brush as you work, using the menu in the Options bar.

Those are the tools I pull out of my bag next. For the fold marks across the eyebrows and under the left eye, I need to paint a large area instead of just clicking here and there. The Healing Brush can do most of the work, but sometimes it pulls in incorrect colors as it blends the edges of your strokes with the background. When I need to control exactly where each new pixel is coming from, I switch to the Clone Stamp. Using these tools, I can get rid of the fold marks and cracks without covering up any tiny details of the photo itself.

The most difficult part of this photo to fix is where the fold marks run across the eyebrows because there's not much of the original eyebrows to clone. To make sure I wasn't erasing anything that needed to be there or putting in anything inaccurate, I worked on this section of the photo with a "before" view of the picture open in another window, for easy comparison.

Did you Know?

I can also use the Clone Stamp to cover up the remaining edges of the frame. This is fairly simple in areas where the frame is adjacent to the light background, but it's trickier at the top of the hat and around the U.S. flag in the upper-left corner of the picture. Finally, the Blur tool and the Dodge and Burn tools stand in for modern makeup. I blurred the skin on the face to smooth out the film noise and other marks—whenever you do this, be sure you don't blur out the shadows that give the face its shape. I dodged the areas under both eyes and burned the whites of the eyes a bit to make them pop more. The final result is shown in Figure 16.15.

FIGURE 16.15
This version of the photo is a lot more presentable than the original scan.

Try it Yourself

Cleaning Up a Picture, Step by Step

Eventually, all this becomes routine, but before that can happen, you need to work through the whole repair process a few times. To give you some practice with these techniques, download the picture shown in Figure 16.16 from the book's website (it's called `picnic.jpg`) and take a look. This image is pretty typical of photos from the 1940s, with some odd horizontal light streaks and the beginnings of discoloration at the bottom. To fix it, follow these steps:

FIGURE 16.16
This is a nice
candid shot that
we can make
even nicer.

1. First, use the Straighten tool to draw a horizontal line across the top of the car. Make it as long as possible so you can maximize its accuracy. When you release the mouse, the picture is level for the first time ever.

2. Next, grab the Crop tool and get rid of the photo's borders. This step also removes most of the writing at the bottom of the picture, saving you the trouble of retouching it—nice, huh?

3. Choose Enhance, Adjust Color, Remove Color. Yes, you could mess around with Convert to Black and White, but because of this photo's inconsistent brightness, you'll have to fix one part of the image, no matter what technique you use. That means quick-and-dirty is the way to go.

4. Now choose Enhance, Adjust Lighting, Adjust Shadows/Highlights. Here's the magic pill for this picture's inconsistent lightness—too light at the top and too dark at the bottom. Start by backing off the initial automatic Lighten Shadows adjustment, from 25% to about 17%. Then drag the Darken Highlights slider to a setting of 35% or so, and increase Midtone Contrast by 35% as well.

> Before clicking OK in the Shadows/Highlights dialog, uncheck the Preview box and then recheck it once or twice to see what a huge change these settings make in the picture.

5. Now it's time to retouch. First, take a good look at the picture and decide what you want to fix and what you want to leave alone. In this case, I'd get rid of the horizontal light streaks and the remains of the writing at the bottom; I'd leave pretty much everything else alone. There are no other obvious physical flaws to get rid of, other than perhaps a few specks that are good candidates for the Spot Healing Brush. When you have a plan in mind, use the Clone Stamp and Healing Brush to execute it.

6. Although you fixed most of the lighting issues with your Shadows/Highlights adjustment, there's still a bit more shadow on the face of the guy on the left than I'd like. Use the Dodge tool set at Shadows and 20% to lighten that shadow some. Don't lighten it too much!

> My personal rule when using the Dodge tool is to stop right before I think the area looks perfect. Invariably, if I take that last step, I end up going too far.

7. Finally, use the Reduce Noise filter, with Remove JPEG Artifact checked, to get rid of the some of the picture's graininess. Then choose Enhance, Adjust Sharpness and add just a *little* sharpening; I used an Amount setting of 22%, with a 3.8-pixel radius. And there you go (see Figure 16.17).

FIGURE 16.17
Now when you look at this picture, you focus on the people in it first instead of the streaks and fading it contains.

Finishing Touches

So far, we've looked at ways to fix the damage that your photos have incurred over time. But when you fix all a picture's problems, you're likely to want to display it somewhere. And that means you might want to jazz it up a bit before doing so— add the icing to the cake, as it were. Vignetting and tinting are two common ways to increase a photo's appeal, and they're both pretty easy to do.

Applying Vignetting

Originally, vignetting was intended to compensate for the poor quality of camera lenses in the early days of photography. Because objects around the edges of an image tended to become distorted, the simplest fix was just to blur them out, leaving only a soft-edged oval area for the picture. Of course, vignetting was sold, then as now, as a fancy special effect instead of as camouflage. Hey, it's not a bug, it's a feature, right? And, in truth, vignetting is a nice way to really zero in on the subject's face in a portrait, eliminating all distractions.

Creating a vignette is simple, but it used to require a great deal of experimentation before you came up with the right settings for your particular image. That's no longer the case because now we have the Refine Edge command. Let me explain.

To make a vignette, first draw a selection (generally elliptical) centered on the most important area of the picture. Now you need to soften the selection's edges, a process that used to involve a series of guesses at what feathering radius would produce the desired result. Now you can see what's going to happen right in the Refine Edge dialog, so there shouldn't be much backing and forthing. Choose Select, Refine Edge and make sure the Preview box is checked.

When positioning a selection around a face, place it slightly above center. You want to see more of what's above the person's forehead (hair and maybe a hat) than what's below his or her chin (a shirt collar).

Did you Know?

Now, before you start messing with the settings, double-click the right preview button, the one with the red tint (see Figure 16.18), and click the red swatch to open the color picker. Change the Color to white, with 100% Opacity. Now the overlay that Photoshop Elements uses to indicate the unselected areas of the image is paper-colored and gives an almost perfect indicator of how your vignette will look, so you can go about trying different settings. Ignore the Smooth slider—your selection should already be perfectly smooth—and stay away from the Contract/Expand slider. Although it would be nice to be able to adjust the selection's size using

Contract/Expand, doing so results in a harder edge for the vignette, so that's no good.

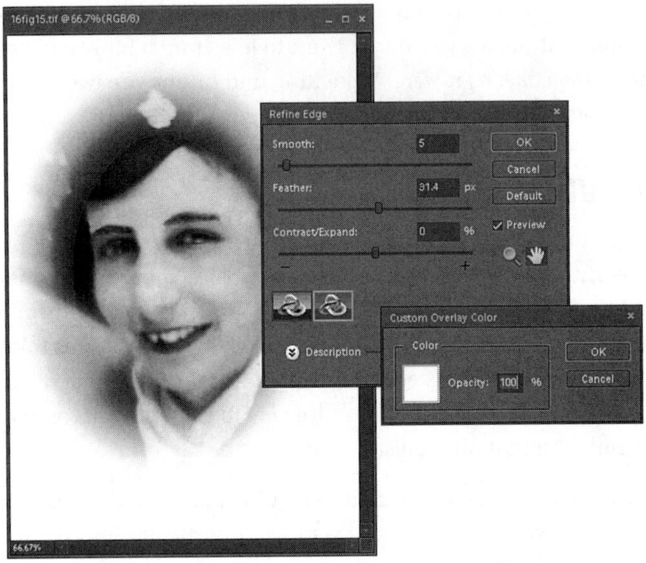

FIGURE 16.18
Make sure you set both the overlay's color and its opacity; with the default Opacity setting of 50%, you won't see an accurate preview.

When you have the Feather setting the way you want it, click OK. Then invert the selection (choose Select, Inverse) so that the area that wasn't selected before is now—namely the outer edges of the picture (see Figure 16.19). Press Delete to remove the outer edges of the picture, which creates the vignette. If you don't like what you see, click Undo or press Ctrl+Z three times (which will undo the deletion, the Inverse command, and the Refine Edge command) and go back to the Refine Edge dialog to try some different settings.

Applying Tints

Just because you removed all of a photo's color in the process of repairing it doesn't mean it has to stay plain old black-and-white forever. Adding a tint is a quick way to increase a photo's appeal. You can use sepia, for an instant antique effect, or you can choose another color that appeals to you.

The easiest way to tint a photo is to use the Variations command. Choose Enhance, Adjust Color, Color Variations (see Figure 16.20). Drag the Amount slider to the left, to cut down on the amount of change you get with each click; then choose an option, such as Increase Red. Stick with just one click at a time and click OK. You can always go back and add more color if the effect is too subtle.

FIGURE 16.19
The vignette effect really focuses attention on the subject's smile in this portrait.

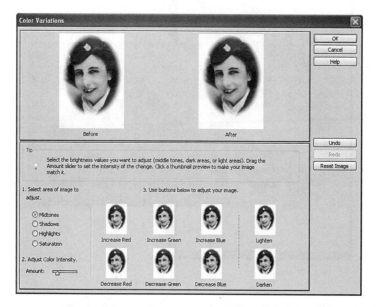

FIGURE 16.20
You can vary the amount of tinting each click applies with the Amount slider.

Another way to apply a tint gives you a result closer to a traditional duotone. That's a printing technique in which two inks are used, one colored and one black (usually), so that just the photo's details are delicately colored. Follow these steps to apply a faux duotone effect:

1. Start with a grayscale image, or remove the color from a color picture. Choose Image, Mode and make sure the color mode is set to RGB.

2. In the Layers palette, drag the Background layer to the New Layer button to duplicate it. Change the Opacity of the new layer to about 40% (lower if you want the effect to be more subtle, higher if you want it to be, well, less subtle).

3. Choose Enhance, Adjust Color, Adjust Hue/Saturation and check the Colorize box. Photoshop Elements automatically sets the Saturation slider to 25%, but you'll want it even lower; drag the slider to about 15%.

4. Now adjust the Hue slider to suit your taste (see Figure 16.21). Try a setting of 40 to produce sepia, if you like.

FIGURE 16.21
This Hue value gives me a reddish purple tint, similar to the colors you see on old postage stamps.

While you're working in the Hue/Saturation dialog, you can increase the picture's lightness, but you'll probably want to avoid decreasing it. This applies the color tint to the formerly white areas of the background, reducing the impact of the effect.

Summary

In this hour, you learned several ways to improve damaged and faded photos. You looked at the different ways you can fix lighting in a faded or underexposed picture, and you practiced using the Dodge and Burn tools to enhance details in both bright and shadowed areas of a photo. You used the Healing Brush, the Spot Healing Brush, the Brush tool, and the Clone Stamp to cover up flaws in pictures, both major and minor. And you finished the hour with a quick tutorial on vignetting and tinting photos.

Q&A

Q. *Why can't I just click repeatedly with the Spot Healing Brush to cover up all the rips, smudges, and cracks in my pictures?*

A. Life would be so much simpler that way, I agree. But it doesn't work because the Spot Healing Brush draws from all the pixels around the point where you apply it to create new pixels to cover the flaw. And if the flaw is bigger in any direction than the brush tip, some of those peripheral pixels will be part of the flaw instead of the background surrounding it. The Spot Healing Brush works only on flaws that are completely surrounded by background color, like islands in the sea.

Q. *What's the origin of the term* vignette, *anyway?*

A. Originally, the word referred to decorative drawings around the borders of a page, often of twining vines. In the mid-nineteenth century, the meaning shifted to a different border effect, the soft-edged frame we now call a vignette.

Q. *I'm disappointed. When I saw the heading "Applying Tints," I thought we were going to "hand-tint" black-and-white pictures.*

A. Hey, don't be disappointed; we cover that technique in the next hour, "Making Color Repairs." One thing at a time, okay?

Workshop

Whether your photo prints are time-worn antiques or just victims of your puppy's chewing stage, they often need a little restoration to look their best—and sometimes they need a lot. Try these quiz questions, check your answers, and then practice, practice, practice on the activities.

Quiz

1. The Dodge tool _____ the image where you click.

   A. Lightens

   B. Darkens

   C. Erases

   D. Blurs

2. You should always switch to a hard-edged brush tip when using the Clone Stamp tool.

   A. True

   B. False

3. A duotone is a printed photo in which

   A. A second exposure was made in the same place in the film as in the first picture.

   B. The color shades evenly from dark at the top to light at the bottom.

   C. Two ink colors are used.

   D. Two people are shown.

Quiz Answers

1. **A.** The Burn tool darkens the picture, and the Blur tool blurs it. Of course, any of the Eraser tools erases the picture.

2. **B.** A soft-edged brush helps your edits blend with the original picture surrounding them.

3. **C.** Usually, one color is black, but that's not always the case.

Activities

1. Find an old snapshot print you really hate (something from the 1970s, perhaps), and give it a good folding, spindling, and mutilating. Then scan it; remove the color, if necessary; and see how well you can undo the damage you caused. If one tool doesn't give you good results as you work, try another tool, and experiment with different Opacity settings and brush sizes.

2. Pick a good-looking portrait and apply a vignette to it; be creative—experiment with different shapes and feathering radius settings.

HOUR 17

Making Color Repairs

What You'll Learn in This Hour:

- ▶ Fixing a horrendous color cast
- ▶ Compensating for poor lighting
- ▶ Turning the sky pink, green, or whatever you prefer
- ▶ Sharpening details to direct focus to a photo's subject
- ▶ Blurring backgrounds to make them less distracting
- ▶ Intensifying and toning down color in selected parts of a picture
- ▶ "Fixing" image problems that aren't actually wrong—just annoying
- ▶ Hand-tinting a black-and-white photo

The vast majority of the pictures you deal with are color. Color photography was developed in the mid-nineteenth century, and it became affordable for the average consumer in the 1960s. These days, you take a black-and-white picture only if you're going for a special effect or if you like to do your own darkroom work. (Color film processing is much more difficult to do at home.)

But what about repairing color pictures? Of course, we're mostly talking about scanned prints here. Well, the nice thing is that color prints generally don't need as much repair as black-and-white photos because they're newer and printed on thicker paper; they're much less likely to be physically damaged. You do run into a huge variety of weird color casts with older color photos, however. And, of course, there's always the "dog ate my photo" problem. All these problems are best fixed in Full Edit mode, where you can access all of Photoshop Elements' power.

When the Color Is the Problem

We all know that printed materials fade, including photos. Color photos, however, are notorious for fading in bizarre ways, with green, purple, or other colors obscuring the true colors of the image. This happens because color processing is a much more complex process than black-and-white printing; in fact, a properly processed black-and-white print can be more stable (meaning less prone to fading) than the paper it's printed on. The chemicals used in color photography, on the other hand, are not stable over time. What's worse, the dyes fade at different rates, producing color casts even when photos are stored in the dark using archival materials. In dark storage, cyan is the least stable, followed by yellow, and magenta is the most stable. In light storage, on the other hand, magenta is the least stable, with cyan being the most stable and yellow falling between the two.

Which colors fade over time in a particular photo is determined by the type of paper, film, and processing chemicals used to make the print, as well as how old the film was when it was processed. If you spend much time looking at old color snapshots, you'll see three basic kinds of fading:

- ▶ Dark fading is the inevitable fading over time that happens no matter how you store a picture. It usually hits cyan dyes first, making the image appear too red.

- ▶ Light fading happens when photos are exposed to light, and it varies depending on how intense the light is. Magenta dyes are usually the first to go, yielding that unmistakable greenish tint in skin tones.

- ▶ Highlight staining is yellowing of the border and highlight areas that happens with older photos; you generally won't see this in photos newer than those from the 1960s.

Fortunately, Photoshop Elements is equipped to deal with all these problems, and you're equipped with Photoshop Elements.

Protecting Your Digital Prints

The kind of color casts we've been talking about so far occur in conventional photo prints. But digital prints aren't immune to their own special varieties of fading. Here are a few tips to help you keep your prints in top condition for as long as possible:

- ▶ I've said it before, but I'll say it again now: Use the printer manufacturer's inks and paper. Sure, they cost more than the third-party ones, but you do get what you pay for. When ink, paper, and printer all come from the same place, they're likely to produce the best and longest-lasting color.

> ▶ When buying ink and paper, check the package for longevity information.
> ▶ Put photos behind glass when you frame them. This is especially important if you're using fluorescent lights, which give off more UV light than incandescents do.
> ▶ Let prints dry completely (at least an hour) before handling them.

Correcting Color Cast

As you might recall from Hour 14, "Adjusting Brightness, Contrast, and Color," Photoshop Elements has a special command just for fixing color casts. Let's try it on this old snapshot, which is a clear victim of highlight staining (see Figure 17.1, here and in the color section). Its borders have yellowed badly, along with the white and yellow areas of the picture. The lighting is also bad: The trees are too dark and the grass in the foreground is too light.

FIGURE 17.1
These 1960s hikers are clearly happy that their hike is over.

The first steps in editing a photo are usually cropping and straightening—but not this time. The border of the photo is the best color-neutral location we could ask for to make best use of the Remove Color Cast dialog, so we'll wait to crop and straighten this picture until we're done fixing the color. And it's always best to avoid retouching until you're happy with the picture's color and lighting because your adjustments can make image edits stand out more.

Choose Enhance, Adjust Color, Remove Color Cast to get started. In Hour 14, you saw that using this dialog is a simple matter of clicking in a color-neutral area of the picture, which can be white, black, or any shade of gray in between. I like to experiment with clicking different areas of the picture, though, because I don't trust my own eyes to know when an object really has no color. Here I clicked all the way around the border and tried a few clicks on white blouses and the like, too. I ended up with the best results from a click in the upper-left corner of the photo's border. I could tell that this spot was the right place to click because it resulted in the most normal-looking skin tones. See Figure 17.2.

FIGURE 17.2
The formerly white border of this photo helps a lot in removing the color cast.

Judging the results you get from the Remove Color Cast dialog requires you to pay close attention to objects whose color you can be sure of. These include skin tones, if you know the people in the picture, and "memory colors," such as the red and blue in the American flag. If any of these are still off after Remove Color Cast does its thing, you know there's still work to do.

If you don't like the results you get from Remove Color Cast and want to try an alternative, either Levels or Curves will do the trick as well. First undo the Remove Color Cast command, and then choose Enhance, Adjust Lighting, Levels or Enhance, Adjust Color, Adjust Color Curves. Using the eyedropper tools in the Levels or Curves dialog, click in the picture to indicate a point that should be perfectly white, one that should be perfectly black, and—if you can find one—a point that should be medium gray. Because these tools operate on brightness as well as hue, you might have better luck with either one of them when you're working on a picture that's particularly dark or light (see Figure 17.3).

Making Selective Color Adjustments

If you can get most of the picture to shape up, color-wise, you don't have to struggle to come up with Levels, Curves, or Remove Color Cast settings that will fix everything. Sometimes it's just never going to happen—or, although you'll get the color right, you'll hurt the picture's appearance in some other way, such as enhancing the film grain. When this is the case, you can turn your attention to fixing that one recalcitrant image element.

Of course, you can change an object's color in Photoshop Elements in myriad ways. We used the Replace Color command in Hour 14 to change the color of a newspaper box from yellow to pink, and we also looked at using Hue/Saturation to modify colors and punch up their intensity. In the case of the photo in Figure 17.4, I tried these techniques with no luck whatsoever.

First, I selected the sky—that's the first step in most selective color adjustments, and getting the selection right is what takes the most time. Then I chose Enhance, Adjust Color, Replace Color and used the eyedroppers to make sure I was operating on the whole sky. Dragging the Hue slider, however, had no result because my real problem is that the sky is gray, and pinkish or greenish gray doesn't look all that different from bluish gray. So I bumped up the Saturation, but that backfired. The saturation of all the "noise" in the sky, graininess resulting from JPEG compression, also sky-rocketed, making the sky look as dotty as a Pointillist painting. That was *not* part of my plan. The same thing happened with the Hue/Saturation command, and that's what you see in Figure 17.4.

FIGURE 17.4
This gray sky
defied my first
attempts to
brighten it.

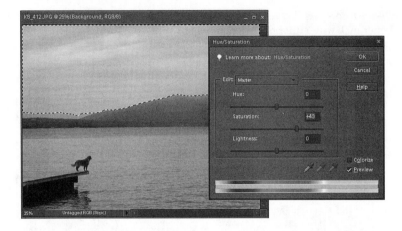

Clearly, I wasn't going to be able to modify the existing color to get what I wanted.
So I tried a different approach. With my sky selection still active, I created a new
layer and filled the selection with a nice bright blue. Then I adjusted the layer's
opacity to about 25% and set its blending mode to Color (see Figure 17.5). That
worked beautifully because I was laying the blue on top of the grayish pixels instead
of changing their saturation.

FIGURE 17.5
Finally, I used a
separate layer
to get some
blue back into
that sky.

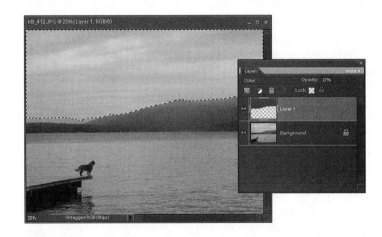

By the Way

The job of Color blending mode is pretty obvious: It applies just the hue of the
layer's pixels to the underlying image. You'll learn about all the blending modes in
Hour 22, "Making Composite Images."

Using Shadows/Highlights

Sometimes the problem with color isn't actually its hue, but its lightness or darkness relative to the image as a whole. In this case, the Shadows/Highlights dialog can help you bring the colors in a picture back into balance. And you might find that fixing this problem can improve a picture's sharpness as well.

In Figure 17.6, the photo just didn't look right. I couldn't put my finger on the problem, but the colors seemed off somehow. When I fired up Shadows/Highlights, I realized that the problem wasn't the color; it was the lighting. Making these settings gave me a warmer, more even-toned photo.

FIGURE 17.6
In addition to lightening the shadows, I darkened the picture's bright spots a tad and reduced the contrast slightly.

Image Correction Tools

What if you want to apply a few fixes to specific areas of the picture instead of the whole thing? That's where the Blur, Sharpen, and Sponge tools come in handy. With these tools, you can blur and sharpen spots within the picture, as well as intensify or downplay the color intensity of specific objects.

Blur and Sharpen

The Blur tool's button in the toolbox looks like a drop of water, which makes sense if you think about what water does to nonpermanent ink. The Sharpen tool looks like the sharp point of some unspecified tool. Until now, we've generally blurred or sharpened entire images, but you can use these tools to pinpoint your effect and leave the rest of the picture as it is. For example, you might use the Blur tool to blur a face or nametag for privacy reasons. This tool is also great for making a distractingly detailed background take its rightful place: in the background. And as you saw in the last hour, it's useful for smoothing out skin in portraits.

When you want to blur areas of your picture, switch to the Blur tool and choose a brush shape and size from the Options bar. Leave the mode set at Normal, and set a Strength percentage. I prefer to start with a lower percentage and bump it up, if I need to. Now you're ready to blur. Paint across the picture with the Blur tool, being careful not to pass over anything you *don't* want to blur. Zoom in as needed, to make sure you're covering the right area.

My favorite use for the Blur tool is to blur backgrounds to draw attention to the photo's subject. Modern digital cameras tend to have a very deep depth of field, which means that both objects close to the camera and those farther away are in sharp focus. Sometimes that's great, but other times it can be distracting. Minimizing the depth of field can make the photo's subject stand out more. Figure 17.7 shows a great example of this situation. Here I'm halfway through blurring the busy background around the farmer and his cow; the left side of the picture is done, and I still need to do the right side. I've been very careful to work around the man and the cow, blurring the background between them and under the cow's belly.

FIGURE 17.7
When you're blurring to modify the depth of field, pick a distance from the camera, and blur everything positioned that far away or farther.

Don't confuse the Blur tool with the Smudge tool; that's a completely different animal. Its icon shows an outstretched finger, ready to smudge away detail. But when it blurs details, the Smudge tool applies a motion blur so that you can see which direction the tool was moved. It's a fun effect, but it's usually not appropriate for retouching.

Sharpening, of course, is the opposite of blurring. You sharpen objects on which you want to focus attention, such as the center of the flower in Figure 17.8. In general, you'll apply much less sharpening than you would blurring; because sharpening works by increasing contrast, excessive sharpening can turn an area into a super-high-contrast collection of dots, as shown in the circle in Figure 17.8.

FIGURE 17.8
Sharpening the intricate center of this flower draws in the eye, but I've severely over-sharpened one area.

> I often use the Blur tool with a Strength setting of 100%, but I never use a Strength setting higher than 50% with the Sharpen tool. Even with low settings, proceed with caution; you can easily oversharpen.

Did you Know?

The Sponge Tool

In traditional darkroom work, a sponge is used to salvage a print that isn't developing darkly enough; by wiping the print with a developer-soaked sponge, the photographer can force it to darken up. Photoshop Elements' Sponge tool works a bit differently. You use it to increase or decrease saturation, or color intensity, in areas of your picture. In Saturate mode, the Sponge makes colors more intense; in Desaturate mode, it drains their intensity, eventually turning them to gray if you keep it up.

> Why isn't the Sponge tool two tools, as with the Blur and Sharpen tools? I have no idea, but it would be more consistent if Photoshop Elements had separate tools for saturating and desaturating image areas. Are you listening, Adobe?

By the Way

You can use the Sponge to create interesting combinations of color and grayscale in the same picture; for example, a picture might contain one color element (a flower) or just one grayscale object (an antique of some kind). Most often, however, I use the Sponge tool to tone down distracting objects in a picture and play up the subject. In the cow photo, for instance (see Figure 17.9), after I blurred the background,

I used the Sponge to tone down the bright yellow wheelbarrow in the background, the pumpkins under the cow, and the flowers above her head.

FIGURE 17.9
The brightly colored objects surrounding the cow were distracting attention from her, but the Sponge tool tones them down without eliminating their color.

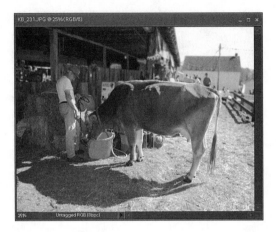

Try it Yourself

Adjusting Saturation

The best way to get a feel for what the Sponge tool can do is to try it. Let's apply it to a gray-day photo I took in New York and see what we can do. You can download the photo from the book's website at www.informit.com/title/9780672330179; it's called manhattan.jpg (see Figure 17.10).

FIGURE 17.10
This sign should stand out, but it's lost in its surroundings.

1. Choose the Blur tool and, adjusting your brush size as needed, blur the building on the right in the photo. Leave the building to which the sign is attached sharp; it's closer to the camera.

2. Switch to the Sponge tool. Make sure it's in Saturate mode, with a Flow of 50%, and wipe it over the Manhattan Diner sign a few times. Don't worry about the metal struts holding up the sign; focus on the colored part.

3. Change the Sponge's mode to Desaturate, keeping the Flow set at 50%, and wipe down the bright-colored edges of the sign at the left side of the picture. You'll probably have to reduce your brush size for this step.

Making Repairs When Nothing Is Really Wrong

We talked in earlier hours about deleting obtrusive objects in photos, but what do you do when you want the object to be in the picture, just not where it is? You might want to flip a person so she's facing the other people in the group, or move objects closer together so the focus of the picture isn't split. In the picture shown in Figure 17.11, for instance, I'd really like to move the guy in front back a few steps so he looks more like part of the group.

FIGURE 17.11
Can't we all just get along?

To make this happen, I start by drawing a Lasso selection around the baseball player and his shadow. That's right, don't forget the shadow. Fortunately, in his new position, his shadow will still fall on the dirt instead of the grass, so I won't have to do much to blend it. Next, I put the player on his very own layer by choosing Layer, New, Layer Via Cut; then I use the Move tool move him where I want him to be (see Figure 17.12).

Now that I have the player where I want him, I need to clean up the extra dirt that he brought with him from his previous location. I use the Background Eraser for this, clicking and dragging around his edges to remove the dirt. Remember, the color erased by the Background Eraser is the color you click on when you begin a stroke (see Figure 17.13). When you're using this technique, it's a good idea to hide the Background layer occasionally, to be sure you've gotten all the little bits and pieces. You can also switch to the regular Eraser any time you want to clean up stuff that the Background Eraser doesn't seem to want to deal with.

FIGURE 17.13
After clicking on the red dirt, I can paint right over the player's uniform without disturbing it; the Background Eraser tool deletes only the dirt next to the player's pants.

When the player is blended into his background, my next task is to create more background to cover the hole where I cut him out. That's a time-consuming but simple, task that requires extensive use of the Clone Stamp with a nice, soft brush. As I work, I'm careful to maintain the sharp edges between the grass and the dirt, as well as the tire marks in the dirt (see Figure 17.14).

FIGURE 17.14
Here's the final result, after much Clone Stamping and work with the Healing Brush.

Hand-Coloring a Black-and-White Photo

Way back in the Dark Ages, before color photography became affordable and popular, photographers commonly hand-tinted black-and-white photos to create color images. You've probably seen both portraits and landscapes done this way; many older postcards were tinted in a similar fashion. The work was originally done with slow-drying oil-based paints that could be spread around on the surface of a photo print. But these were not the same sort of oil paints used in heavily textured oil paintings; instead, they were quite transparent, lending a delicate appearance to the picture that remains attractive to this day.

You can use your high-tech tools to apply this low-tech effect to any photo you like. If the photo is in color, first convert it to black-and-white by choosing Enhance, Convert to Black and White. The Newspaper preset is best for this purpose because it produces images light enough that the color will show and high-contrast enough that you won't lose details when you paint over them.

Simulating hand-tinting with Photoshop Elements is fairly simple (see Figure 17.15). It's done with the Brush tool on a separate layer (so that you can erase color later if you decide it's too much), set at a fairly low opacity, such as 20%. You don't have to worry about tiny details when hand-tinting; the photo provides the detail, and your job is to fill in the larger colored areas, such as grass and sky. Use a soft-edged brush tip, and vary the brush size as needed to make sure you don't spill over into areas that should be another color.

FIGURE 17.15
Be sure to check out this picture in the color section.

Did you Know?

If you're so inclined, you can even put each new color on its own layer. This enables you to vary the tint layers' opacity one color at a time, to get just the right mix. In the Layers palette, click the New Layer button to create each new layer.

Summary

In this hour, you learned what causes color shifts in old pictures and how to fix them. You also worked on compensating for poor lighting when the original photo was taken and changing the color of just one element in a photo. We looked at how individual toning tools, including the Sharpen, Blur, and Sponge tools, can be useful for spot touch-ups and special effects. Finally, just for fun, we went over how to modify a picture that isn't really *wrong*—just inconveniently composed—and how to colorize a grayscale image so that it looks like an old-time hand-tinted photo.

Q&A

Q. *What else can I do to make the background in my photos less obtrusive?*

A. In addition to blurring to change the depth of field, you can desaturate the entire background with the Sponge tool. If you take this technique to its extreme, you end up with a special effect: a color subject in the middle of a black-and-white photo. If you use a lighter touch, you can tone down the background colors just enough that they don't draw the eye away from the subject.

Q. *If it's possible to oversharpen, why isn't it possible to overblur?*

A. Oh, it definitely is possible. If you blur too much, you end up with a muddy gray fog bank instead of whatever background you started with. It takes longer to get there, though, and it doesn't look as bad along the way, so oversharpening is still more of a danger than overblurring.

Q. *I'm having trouble being precise when hand-tinting. What am I doing wrong?*

A. First of all, you're not doing anything wrong. If you look closely (use a magnifying glass) at original hand-tinted photos, you'll see that their coloring isn't particularly precise, either. Our eyes tend to compensate for small overlaps and gaps, inserting the colors where we know they should be. Second, if you do want to clean up your tints some, try changing the tint layer's Opacity setting to 100% temporarily. Then you'll be able to see where you've painted too much and where you've left gaps in your painting. Make your fixes at the higher opacity, and then return the layer to its original low opacity.

Workshop

Test your understanding of the color concepts we've talked about in this hour with these quiz questions. After you check your answers, reward yourself with some playtime by completing the activities.

Quiz

1. When the results of a Remove Color Cast operation aren't to your liking, where should you turn next?

   A. Levels

   B. Curves

   C. Variations

   D. Any of the above

2. If the Sponge tool saturates color, what tool desaturates color?

   A. The Wiper tool

   B. The Eraser tool

   C. The Desponge tool

   D. None of the above

3. Modern photo prints don't fade the way older ones did.

   A. True

   B. False

Quiz Answers

1. **D.** All these methods can successfully remove a color cast. Never feel that you have to stick to "the one true method" for doing anything in Photoshop Elements—if you find another way that works better for you, go for it.

2. **D.** Sorry, this one was a trick question. The Sponge does dual duty; you determine whether it increases saturation or decreases saturation by choosing a mode in the Options bar.

3. **B.** Although modern prints are potentially much more stable than older ones, whether and how they fade is influenced by how they're stored and by what materials were used to make the print in the first place.

Activities

1. Try some color repairs on your own photos. Experiment with the different methods of removing a color cast, and try out some sharpening and blurring.

2. Find or create a black-and-white photo and then tint it. Don't forget to create at least one new layer before you start painting.

Removing and Replacing Objects

What You'll Learn in This Hour:

▶ How to copy part of a photo to a new location to act as a patch over an object you want to delete

▶ How to remove multiple objects from a photo and rearrange the photo's remaining contents

▶ How to swap out one face for another, of the same person or a different person

▶ How to fill in large empty areas in a picture

Deleting tiny dust specks and covering up unwanted people at the beach is easy enough to do, and you've already done both of these things. You've learned how to use the Spot Healing Brush and the Healing Brush to remove small objects. But what to do for larger objects? You got an idea of the various techniques you can use for this task in the last hour, when I moved a baseball player several feet away from his original position. Now we'll spend some serious time looking at how this sort of work is done and how it differs from editing out small objects.

Drag-and-Drop Copying

Remember those unwanted beachgoers that we deleted from a photo back in Hour 13, "Removing Red Eye, Dust, and Scratches"? Working in the Editor's Full Edit mode, we copied a stretch of sand and pasted it right over the people we wanted to get rid of, using the sand like a patch. That's the simplest possible way to delete something from a photo, and it works well whenever the object is set against a fairly uniform background, such as sand or grass or a blank wall. This trick works with both small and large objects, and I've got a new twist to make it even easier than it was in Hour 13.

As you probably remember, we started by making a feathered selection of the appropriate size and shape to cover the unwanted object. We then moved the selection to a nice blank area that would provide a good patch, copied, and pasted, creating a new layer containing just the patch. The final step was to position the patch over the object, making it disappear. When you're using this technique, you can work with any selection tool. Often the Lasso or the Polygonal Lasso is the easiest way to draw a selection around an object, but the Quick Selection tool also works well. You can even use a marquee selection if the object you're covering is squarish or round.

The step in between creating the selection and copying it is vital: feathering the selection. This softens the edges so that the patch blends with its surroundings. Figure 18.1 shows what can happen if you don't feather your selection.

FIGURE 18.1
This patch's hard edges make it obvious to the most casual observer—not at all the effect we're going for.

And now for the twist: Press Alt. Yes, it's that simple. Instead of copying and pasting the patch, creating a new layer along the way, press Alt and drag a copy of the selected area right into position as your patch. When you've got the patch right where you want it, press Ctrl+D to drop the selection. At this point, the patch becomes part of the Background layer. This means, of course, that you can't go back and move it later, so be sure of your positioning before you drop the selection.

To hide the selection marquee so you can position the patch more precisely, press Ctrl+H. Press the same keys to display the "marching ants" again.

Did you Know?

Let's take a look at the patch technique in action. In Figure 18.2, I'd really like to get rid of that extra horn from the cow to the left of the one that was photographed. Or maybe it's a bull—I don't know. Anyway, I don't want to crop the photo because I like the proportions as is. Cloning over the horn will be a pain because of the wood's texture, the knots, and the grooves between boards. So I'll try the patch technique instead.

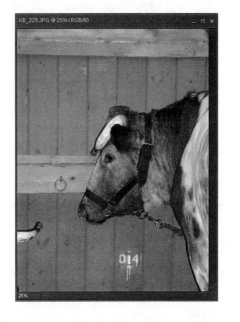

FIGURE 18.2
Somehow that extra bit of horn sticking into the picture from the left is really distracting from the lovely bovine specimen the picture is meant to show.

Using a section of wall from just above the horn, I've successfully covered the horn—one distraction down (see Figure 18.3). The selection's feathering enables the patch to blend right in with the rest of the wall, and it was easy to position the patch because I just had to drag it straight down. Things might get a little trickier if I try to get rid of the painted number under my bull's (or cow's?) chin. But I'm going to attempt it anyway.

FIGURE 18.3
The extra horn
is gone, after
the careful
application of a
patch.

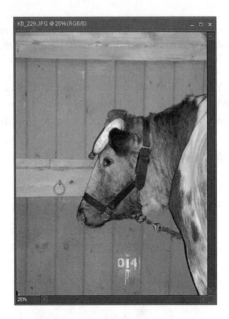

The first step is to make the selection. Here, as usual, I use my trick of drawing around the object I want to replace so that I can be sure the selection will be the right size and shape, and I make sure the selection is feathered. Picking a location from which to grab the patch is more complicated this time because I need the grooves between the boards in the patch to line up with those in the wall behind it. As I position the patch, I can press Ctrl+H to hide the edges of the marquee so that I can make sure it's lining up correctly. When I'm satisfied, I can drop the selection. A quick application of the Burn tool darkens the patch, and then it blends perfectly (see Figure 18.4).

Now, suppose that what I really want from this photo is not actually the portrait of a cow, but, in fact, the rustic barn wall behind Bossie. It would make a great background for the flyer I'm designing to promote a charity hayride. But I need the whole thing—and that means our bovine friend has to go. An operation of this size takes several different patches, and some of them might need a little modification before I'm ready to drop them. Sometimes you'll find that a patch would look great—if only.... If only it were facing the other way, or were a bit wider, or were set at a slightly different angle. In these situations, all you have to do is transform your selection.

FIGURE 18.4
With two patches in place, this picture is looking much cleaner.

Let's see what happens when I try to remove the animal life from this photo. My first patch comes from above the cow's head, and it's too short to cover the entire area I want to patch (see Figure 18.5). The answer: Drag the bottom handle of the transform marquee down, stretching the patch to fit.

FIGURE 18.5
Any time you're moving a selection, you're automatically in Free Transform mode and can resize and rotate the selection.

The rest of the process is pretty much the same. As I move each patch into position, I need to do one or more of the following to it:

▶ Use the Spot Healing Brush to remove noticeable duplicate knots in the boards.

▶ Bring up Hue/Saturation (choose Enhance, Adjust Color, Adjust Hue/Saturation) to adjust the color of the boards to match those around them.

▶ Stretch the patch slightly to make the grooves between boards line up.

When I'm done patching the boards above and below the horizontal beam, it's time to copy bits and pieces of the beam to get rid of the last vestiges of cattle. The final picture looks as though the stall had been empty the whole time (see Figure 18.6).

FIGURE 18.6
No more cow!

Removing a Person

Group photos are a wonderful thing, but they've got an Achilles' heel that never fails to kick in just when it's least wanted: Murphy's Law. It's an unwritten rule of photography that any time you try to shoot a whole bunch of people at the same time, even if most of them are facing front, smiling, and looking great, there'll always be one who isn't. Maybe she's looking off in the wrong direction, maybe his eyes are closed—whatever it is, there's always something. If you have other very similar shots, you can often eliminate the problem using pieces of the other photos; we'll look at ways to do that later in this hour. But sometimes the only possible fix is just to get rid of the person entirely. And if the person in question is your least favorite brother-in-law, well, maybe that's not such a bad thing.

Take a look at Figure 18.7, for example. It's not a typical group shot, but it definitely has a person I need to get rid of. This is a really charming shot of a dog I happen to know getting a well-deserved hug from a friend at a race meet. The only thing that's wrong with it is the extraneous person sitting next to the finish line. As a finish line judge, she was important at the time, but we really don't need her in the picture now.

FIGURE 18.7
How can anyone resist those eyes?

The obvious place to start is with the Clone Stamp, covering up the line judge with grass. Meanwhile, though, I want to be careful to keep the white stake and the orange sideline tape in front of her. To make that work, I clone grass right up to the edge of the stake and tape; then I clone a section of stake or tape over the area where I just added grass, to make sure the edges stay crisp. Halfway through the job, things are looking pretty good (see Figure 18.8).

Meanwhile, however, I haven't been as careful to retain the beach umbrella's stake. I'm okay with that, however, because I've decided that having a giant orange umbrella sticking out of the back of my friend's head probably isn't the best look for her. So I'll just get rid of the whole thing. As I work with the Clone Stamp, I choose my source points carefully, to match the area I'm cloning next to. The grass just behind the sideline tape is much lighter than the grass farther out, so it's important that I use the right shade for each section of the picture. The end result preserves the folding chair and the sideline markers, but eliminates the line judge and her umbrella, making a much less cluttered picture (see Figure 18.9).

FIGURE 18.8
Notice anything
odd about this
version of my
photo? Right—
that floating
umbrella really
needs to go.

FIGURE 18.9
The grassy
countryside is
once more pris-
tine.

Of course, getting rid of your problem person is often only half the battle. If removing the person leaves a big hole in the middle of the group, you have to fill in the
hole. You can accomplish this in a number of ways, depending on the photo you're
working on.

▶ If the now-missing person was at the edge of the group, you can usually crop
the photo to get rid of the hole. Of course, if you're really lucky, you can eliminate the person in the first place by cropping.

▶ Sometimes you can copy something else into that space to camouflage it, such
as a bush. This works well when the people in the shot are interspersed among

other objects like the one you want to use for camouflage, but it's less appropriate when the object would look out of place in the middle of the group.

▶ Another option is to clone in the background that you would see in the photo if the person had never been there—in other words, re-create what was behind the person.

▶ Moving the pieces of the photo is also an option, and it can be the least complicated way to eliminate the hole. But it usually requires some work with the Clone Stamp to blend the pieces seamlessly.

Each of these techniques is based on things you've learned in earlier hours: cropping, copying and pasting a patch, and using the Clone Stamp and the Healing Brush. Don't be afraid to combine techniques and experiment to come up with your own.

Using Photomerge Group Shot

One of Photoshop Elements' newest (and neatest) tools is actually a revamped version of an old tool: Photomerge. Using the original Photomerge, now renamed Photomerge Panorama, you can stitch together multiple photos into one wide image. And now, using Photomerge Group Shot, you can replace a face or even a whole person with another version of that person from a different photo.

In Figure 18.10, you see two pictures of a first-time dad and his baby son. In one photo, Dad looks great, but the baby is squirming and making a face. In the other photo, the kid looks perfect, but Dad has changed the angle of his head, so there's a nasty reflection on his glasses. This is exactly the kind of situation for which Photomerge Group Shot is designed—two (or more) photos that, put together, will produce more than the sum of their parts.

To get started, choose your photos and switch to the Editor. Open the Project Bin and Ctrl+click to choose the photos you want to use for this project. Then click the Guided Edit tab and click Group Shot under the Photomerge heading. Following the instructions in the Task pane, drag the best picture from the Project Bin to the right side of the Group Shot window (see Figure 18.11). This is the foundation on which you'll build your perfect picture.

FIGURE 18.10
If I can combine these two photos, I'll have the best of both worlds.

FIGURE 18.11
The first thing I need to do is specify which photo is the Final version.

Click another photo in the Image Bin to move it to the Source area in the Group Shot window. Then click the Pencil tool button in the Task pane; you're ready to start picking and choosing the bits you want to copy. Using the Pencil tool, circle or scribble over the part of the Source picture that you want to copy into the Final picture. Ta-da! Photoshop Elements puts that face, or that person, into the other photo, blending it in seamlessly. To see exactly what part of the Source picture was copied into the Final picture, click the Show Regions check box in the Task pane (see Figure 18.12).

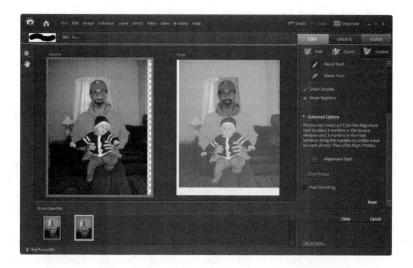

FIGURE 18.12
Photoshop Elements copied more of the picture than I indicated so that it could blend the new head perfectly with the background.

If you're working with photos in which the lighting of the position of the subjects differs, you'll probably want to take advantage of Photomerge Group Shot's Advanced options. With the Alignment tool, you can tell Photoshop Elements which points in the photos should match up, position-wise (see Figure 18.13). (Keep reading; we go into more details about using the Alignment tool in the next section.) For pictures that aren't quite the same brightness, check the Pixel Blending check box to adjust the brightness of the copied areas so they match the Final picture more closely.

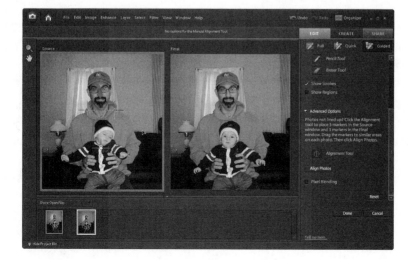

FIGURE 18.13
As I click in each picture, its three alignment points appear as crosshairs on the photo.

Copyright and Copy Wrongs

You might have noticed that all the photos shown in this book are mine. Either I took them or they're my family pictures and I have the right to use them. If I had decided to scour the Web for neat pictures instead and then published them in this book without the permission of their copyright owners, I'd be in serious trouble.

You probably aren't planning to write a book illustrated with a lot of retouched photos (although if you do, please drop me a line at binderk@mac.com to tell me about it). So copyright probably isn't something you think about every day. But I wouldn't be doing you any favors if I didn't point out that it is illegal (and unethical) to publish or redistribute other people's images without their permission. This means that if you decide to add Johnny Depp to a photo of your friends, you're in the clear right up to the point when you start emailing the retouched picture to other people. Distributing your picture, which now contains part of someone else's picture of Johnny, is strictly against the law. So is publishing the photo in your hypothetical book, unless you get a signed release form from the photo's owner.

I know, none of this is fun to contemplate. And I might have been known to play around with a few Johnny Depp photos myself, so who am I to talk? Well, I just keep those images where they belong—on my own computer—and I hope you'll do the same.

Using PhotoMerge Faces

As with Photomerge Group Shot, Photomerge Faces is a variation on the original Photomerge, which was designed to blend the edges of photos to produce a seamless panorama. You use Group Shot on a photo to swap in faces or even whole people from another picture. Faces, on the other hand, gets down to the real nitty-gritty by enabling you to replace individual facial features. Now, of course, you can use this capability to figure out what the love child of Elvis and Bigfoot would look like—or you can get serious and use it to produce optimal portraits.

In my case, I wanted to produce a portrait of a greyhound named Sailor. The day I tried to shoot the portrait was chilly and gray, and Sailor's owner was a really good sport about holding him while I took shot after shot, trying for the perfect picture (see Figure 18.14). I never got that perfect picture—but I'll have it now. Using Photomerge Faces, I can take the best overall picture from the photo shoot and swap in facial features from other shots to produce the particular look that Sailor just wouldn't give me that day.

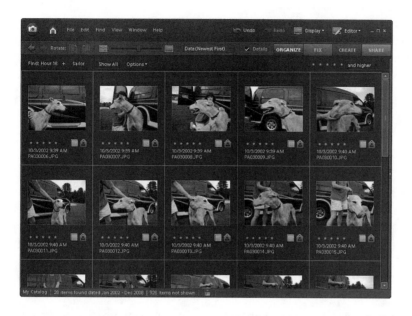

FIGURE 18.14
As you can see,
I ended up with
28 pictures,
none of which
was what I
wanted.

After sifting through the photos, I settled on one that was *almost* what I wanted. I'd been looking for an open-mouthed shot (Sailor has great teeth), but the best one had closed eyes. So I found another photo of a similar pose with open eyes; the only problem was that Sailor was facing the other way in this picture. No problem—before starting the Photomerge session, I opened both photos, activated the one in which Sailor was facing the wrong way, and chose Image, Rotate, Flip Horizontal. Now he was facing to the left in both pictures.

> Flipping the source photo can sometimes work in Photomerge Faces, but it's unlikely to be a useful technique in Photomerge Group Shot. This is because the backgrounds in the two photos are likely quite different; that doesn't matter when you're copying areas within a face, but it makes a big difference when you're copying faces or bodies and their surroundings, as you do in Photomerge Group Shot.

By the Way

Selecting both photos in the Project Bin, I clicked the Guided Edit tab and then clicked Faces under the Photomerge heading. I dragged the open-mouthed shot into the Final area and clicked the other picture's thumbnail in the Project Bin to place it in the Source area. My next step was to align the images. I couldn't count on Photoshop Elements to take care of this for me because the photos have different backgrounds and Sailor is in different parts of the frame in each photo. To align the two pictures, I clicked the Alignment tool in the Task pane. Then I clicked in each photo in turn and dragged the three numbered alignment indicators to matching locations (see Figure 18.15). When I had them located where I wanted them, I clicked Align Photos to have Photoshop Elements transform the Source photo to match the angle and position of the Final photo.

FIGURE 18.15
The new shape of the Source photo indicates how the picture was transformed so that the shape of Sailor's head would match that in the Final photo.

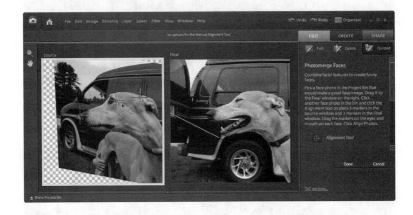

At this point, the only step remaining was to designate an area to copy from the Source picture into the Final picture. Switching to the Pencil tool in the Task pane, I made a quick squiggle around Sailor's eye in the Source picture and watched as Photoshop Elements transplanted that eye into the Final picture (see Figure 18.16).

FIGURE 18.16
Now I have a photo of an open-mouthed and open-eyed dog—just what I always wanted.

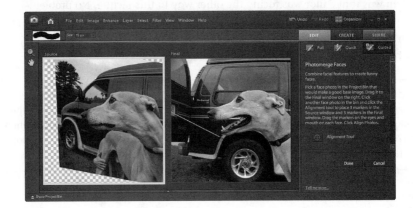

Summary

We spent a lot of time throwing around people and body parts in this hour, but the results when you apply these techniques to your own photos should be worth it. You learned a more refined version of the patch technique for deleting objects from photos, which you originally saw back in Hour 13. You also saw how it's possible to remove a person or an object from a photo without a trace, using copy and paste, the Clone Stamp, and the Healing Brush. And you learned about Photoshop Elements' two new Photomerge commands: Group Shot and Faces. In the next hour, we move on to something completely different: filters.

Q&A

Q. How much feathering should I apply to a patch selection?

A. You're not going to like this answer, but it depends. On what? On the picture's resolution. The higher the resolution, the higher the feathering radius has to be to cover the same distance within the photo. When you know what value works for a particular picture, you can set it in the Options bar to have it automatically applied to all selections you make with that particular tool. Until then, you can make a selection and choose Select, Refine Edge to see exactly what effect different feather radius settings will have on your selection.

Q. How do I know when to patch and when to clone?

A. Clone when you're working with a solid color, and patch when you're not. For example, if you want to copy a piece of blue sky over something, either technique will work, but using the Clone Stamp will be faster. On the other hand, if the area you're copying has a pattern or texture to it, you'll want to use a patch so that you can align the new area easily with its surroundings.

Workshop

We covered a lot of material this hour, and you haven't yet had a chance to practice any of it. So complete these quiz questions, check your answers, and then spend sometime practicing with the activities.

Quiz

1. Which key should you press as you drag to copy your selection to a new location?

    A. Ctrl

    B. Shift

    C. Spacebar

    D. Alt

2. What's the easiest way to remove a person from a photo?

    A. Using the Spot Healing Brush

    B. Cropping

    C. Erasing him or her with the Background Eraser

    D. Applying a patch

3. What does the Pixel Blending check box in the Photomerge Group Shot and Photomerge Faces tasks do?

    A. Adjusts the brightness and saturation of a copied area from the Source photo to match its surroundings in the Final photo

    B. Feathers the edges of the area being copied from the Source photo to the Final photo

    C. Blurs the Final picture slightly to make your edits less obvious

    D. All of the above

Quiz Answers

1. **D.** If you press Ctrl as well, however, you won't have to switch to the Move tool; this shortcut temporarily changes any tool you're using to the Move tool.

2. **B.** Cropping is *always* easier and less apparent to the viewer than any kind of retouching. If you can solve your problem by cropping, do it.

3. **A.** Try switching Pixel Blending off and on a few times, and you'll quickly see that it's a good thing. In fact, I don't see any reason you shouldn't use it all the time.

Activities

1. Download the photo I used in "Removing a Person," earlier in this hour; it's called nats2003.jpg. Use the techniques I described to reproduce my results— or maybe do even better.

2. Time to dig out the photos from your last family reunion or office party—any occasion when you had everyone line up for just one more shot—and see if you can use Photomerge Group Shot to produce a picture in which everyone looks good. The more similar your pictures are, the better chance you have of pulling this off.

3. All right, you've worked hard enough in this hour; it's time for some fun. Remember how I said you could use Photomerge Faces to produce a picture of the love child of Elvis and Bigfoot? With Photomerge Faces, you can merge any two—or more—faces. Go to town. Merge your parents' faces and see how much the result looks like you. Or try merging, say, Santa Claus and the Grinch. Pretty much any picture you can imagine is available on the Web (try www.images.google.com), and as long as you're not republishing it, you're free to do what you want with it. Have fun!

Using the Improvement Filters

What You'll Learn in This Hour:

- ▶ How to soften the focus in part of a picture with the Blur filters
- ▶ Use other Blur filters to simulate motion
- ▶ Ways to remove dust, dirt, other defects
- ▶ How to obscure details by adding noise
- ▶ How to create clouds, spotlights, and lens flares
- ▶ How to map a picture onto a sphere, cube, or cylinder
- ▶ Ways to add natural-looking textures such as canvas and sandstone

A filter is an effect that changes your picture by adding something to it, removing something, or just moving its parts around. Some filters are subtle; others are most definitely not. However, most of them have settings you can adjust to control the outcome, and you can choose to apply them to an entire image, a single layer, or a selected area. Because they're plug-ins, you can install and uninstall filters, and you can buy third-party ones that are fun, useful, or both at once. Photoshop Elements comes with all the filters that traditional Photoshop does—and that's a lot. To keep things simple, we look at the filters in groups, starting with those that can help you improve a picture that needs a little help.

Working with Filters

I should warn you, playing with filters is definitely addictive. Before you get sucked into the Wonderful World of Filters, let me explain a few things about how they work. To start, you can apply filters in more than one way. The simplest method is to use the Effects palette, with its first button clicked so that it displays the filters. This gives you quick access to all Photoshop Elements' filters, with no need to search through menus for the ones you want. You'll also see a tiny preview of each filter's effects in the palette so you'll know what you're getting into when you apply one (see Figure 19.1). The filters are grouped in the same categories you'll find in the Filter menu; you use the pop-up menu in the upper-right corner of the palette to switch categories.

If you want to see all your options all the time in the Effects palette, choose Show All from the filter category pop-up menu. You'll spend some time scrolling up and down in the palette, but you won't have to remember which category each filter belongs to in order to find it.

Using the palette menu, you can choose a size for the thumbnails in the Effects palette (Small Thumbnail View, Medium Thumbnail View, or Large Thumbnail View), and you can choose Show Names to add the filter name below each thumb-nail (as I did in Figure 19.1). To apply a filter from the Effects palette, simply double-click the thumbnail. What happens then depends on the filter. For filters that have no options, the effect simply appears in your image window. In other cases, a dialog box opens in which you can apply specific settings that affect the filter's results. And for the majority of Photoshop Elements' filters, the Filter Gallery opens; this is a huge dialog that has some special capabilities.

By the Way

You can apply filters from the Filter menu in any of the Editor's three modes: Full Edit, Quick Fix, or Guided Edit. The Effects palette is available only in Full Edit mode.

Sadly, in this hour, we have time to cover only one group of filters that uses the Filter Gallery: the Texture filters. You'll see more of the Filter Gallery in future hours;

for now, know that it enables you to preview filters in a large preview area within the dialog, as well as apply multiple filters at one time (see Figure 19.2). You can use the Filter Gallery to try all the filters it contains, switching and combining them until you've got just the result you're looking for.

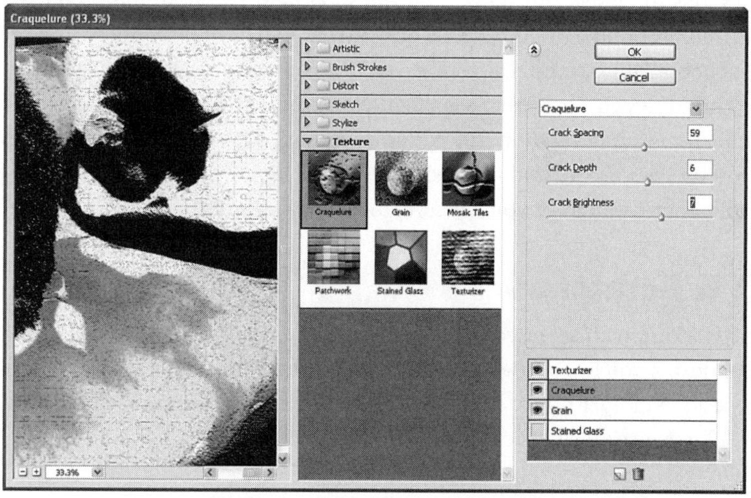

FIGURE 19.2
The capability to stack multiple filters on top of each other is my favorite feature of the Filter Gallery.

The Filter Gallery opens whenever you choose one of the filters it contains, but you can also get there by choosing Filter, Filter Gallery. The Filter menu also contains each of Photoshop Elements' filters, and it's the way to reach them if you don't want to devote all that screen real estate to the Effects palette, and if you already know what they do and just which one you want without having to see a thumbnail preview.

> The first command in the Filter menu is always the last filter you applied. You can choose this command or press Ctrl+F to reapply the filter. Sometimes once just isn't enough, and you need to apply a filter multiple times to achieve the intensity you need.

Did you Know?

Adding or Removing Noise

We talked about noise several times in previous hours, but now we take a really close look at noise and what you can do about it. Basically, "noise" is any kind of unwanted image data, whether it's dirt from the scanner bed, a speck from the camera lens, JPEG artifacts, film grain, or innumerable other kinds of messiness that can afflict a photo. With the Noise filters, you can blur noise that shouldn't be there to hide it or add even more noise for special effects.

Despeckle

First, let's look at Despeckle. We've used this filter before in cleaning up flawed photos, and you probably remember how easy it is to use. You don't apply any settings; you just choose Filter, Noise, Despeckle, and the job is done. Despeckle can remove the kind of noise you sometimes see when you scan a printed image from a book or magazine: banding or regular grid patterns. You will see some loss of sharpness when you use Despeckle, and its effects are subtle; if you apply it and don't see a noticeable improvement in your picture, undo and try another filter.

Dust & Scratches

If you're working with scanned pictures, the type of noise you're most likely to see is specks of dust, scratches, and even rips in the original print. The Dust & Scratches filter is designed to get rid of, or at least minimize, this sort of noise. To get there, choose Filter, Noise, Dust & Scratches (see Figure 19.3).

FIGURE 19.3
Even with professional scans, you sometimes get dust and scratches on the photo—and this definitely wasn't a professional scan.

To customize the effect of the Dust & Scratches filter, you drag the Radius and Threshold sliders. The Threshold slider controls how much a speck of dust must stand out from its surroundings for the filter to target it. The Radius slider determines how much blurring is applied to each speck or scratch to hide it. You'll get the best results by keeping the Threshold value fairly low (to catch more noise) and gradually increasing the Radius value from 0 until you start to see an unacceptable amount of blurring. Most filters with dialogs, including Dust & Scratches, offer a Preview check box. Check the box to see the results of your settings in the image window, and use the preview area in the dialog to zoom in on specific areas.

> To temporarily hide the filter's results in the dialog's preview area, click in the preview area and hold down the mouse button. When you release the button, the preview area again shows the "filtered" version of the picture.

Did you Know?

Reduce Noise

The Reduce Noise filter can get rid of the kind of graininess you see when your flash doesn't fire and you have to lighten the picture a bunch in Photoshop Elements. It's a big dialog with a huge preview area, but its settings are pretty easy to understand (see Figure 19.4).

▶ Drag the Strength slider to determine how much blurring is applied.

▶ Drag the Preserve Details slider to the right to keep edges from being blurred.

▶ Move the Reduce Color Noise slider to the right to remove random color pixels (if there aren't any, you won't see any change in the picture).

▶ The Remove JPEG Artifacts check box removes the blocky artifacts and light halos around objects that you see in a JPEG image saved with a low quality setting. Because most of the pictures produced by digital cameras or exchanged online are saved in JPEG format, you'll probably want to leave this box checked most of the time.

Median

If you've got a picture with a lot of tiny bright spots, such as the one shown in Figure 19.5, the Median filter can help you. It locates pixels that stand out too much from their surroundings, brightness-wise, and tones them down to the median brightness value of the pixels surrounding them. I like to use it for pictures in which the flash was too close to the object being photographed (as in Figure 19.5), to tone down those intrusive sparkles. Median has only one slider: Radius. You'll want to keep that value quite low because higher values drain all the detail out of the image very quickly.

FIGURE 19.4
In this picture,
the Reduce
Noise filter can
minimize the
graininess of
the bowl and
the skin.

FIGURE 19.5
The flash
emphasizes
every single pit
and scratch in
this old hood
ornament, but
the Median filter
blends them
back in with the
metal surface.

Add Noise

After seeing all these ways to remove noise, you might be surprised to run into a filter designed to add more noise to a picture. And it's true that the Add Noise filter
isn't strictly a clean-up or fix-it sort of filter; it's better classified as a special effect.

But it's tremendously useful in creating all sorts of looks. And sometimes you can't eliminate all the flaws in a picture—but you can disguise them.

One of my favorite techniques is to duplicate the Background layer and apply various filters to the copy. Then I combine the original picture with the copy by reducing the copy's layer opacity or changing its blending mode. Figure 19.6 shows a variety of subtle effects I achieved by following this procedure, starting each time with the Add Noise filter.

a

b

c

d

FIGURE 19.6
(a) The original photo, featuring an antique car; (b) Add Noise, Motion Blur, Hard Light blending mode; (c) Add Noise, Color Dodge blending mode; and (d) Add Noise, Find Edges, Overlay blending mode.

Using the Blur Filters

The seven Blur filters do just the opposite of the Sharpen commands (Unsharp Mask and Adjust Sharpness), which used to be filters also. (Maybe in the next version of Photoshop Elements, the Blur filters will be moved to the Enhance menu, too.) These filters smooth color transitions by averaging the colors on either side, softening the edges of objects in the picture. Each works in a slightly different way.

Beware! Even though the Blur filters and the Sharpen commands are opposites, they don't act like an undo command on each other. After you blur a picture, you can't get back all the lost detail by sharpening it, so you'll have to return to a copy of the original, if you saved one.

Not Your Average Filter

The Average filter is perhaps the ultimate Blur filter; it determines the average color of the picture, based on the color value of each pixel in the image, and fills the image window with that color. It's a good way to pinpoint the overall color of a picture or an area in the picture. You can use the Eyedropper to choose the Average color as the Foreground color, and then undo to go back to the normal picture.

After you've determined the average color, you can use it to create type and borders that will always coordinate with the whole picture, or you can fill a layer with the color and set its Opacity fairly low to let the original picture show through. This can enhance the mood of the picture, in many cases. Remember, you can apply the Average filter to just part of the image, too, if you first select the area to which you want to apply it.

Blur and Blur More

As you might suspect, these are the basic Blur filters, with Blur More having an effect several times stronger than that of the Blur filter. In fact, Blur More gives you the effect you'd get by applying Blur multiple times. Now, these are both fairly subtle filters; even Blur More doesn't apply a great deal of blurring (see Figure 19.7). If you want to *really* blur a picture, you need to use one of the adjustable filters, such as Smart Blur or Gaussian Blur.

Gaussian Blur

Gaussian refers to the mathematical equations on which this filter's blurring operation is based. You don't have to know any math to use Gaussian Blur, however; this filter quickly blurs a picture by a user-adjustable amount, and it has only one slider (see Figure 19.8). The Radius slider goes from .1 pixel at the left end to 250 pixels at the right end; at the low-end setting, you get a similar result to the Blur filter, and at the high end your picture ends up looking almost as flat as if you'd applied the Average Filter to it. In between, you can use Gaussian Blur to apply a nice, soft focus to portraits and landscapes, and you can use it a bit more heavily in selected areas to smooth out imperfections in the same way you'd use the Blur tool (see Hours 16 and 17 to review that technique).

FIGURE 19.7
I applied Blur to the left half of this photo and Blur More to the right half, but you probably wouldn't even realize I'd blurred the picture if I hadn't told you.

FIGURE 19.8
A Radius setting of 5.2 blurs the heck out of the donkey from Figure 19.7.

Because of the math this filter uses to determine which pixels it affects—a Gaussian distribution—it has a particularly natural look, as opposed to the flat, artificial look that Blur and Blur More provide.

Smart Blur

The name might lead you to think this is the best Blur filter to use in all circumstances, but that's not the case. Smart Blur is called "smart" because it can recognize edges and avoid blurring them, while it smoothes out noise and texture in smooth surfaces (see Figure 19.9). So when you're looking for an overall blur, Gaussian Blur is a better bet.

FIGURE 19.9
Smart Blur polishes the surfaces of this door knocker without blurring its detailed casting.

The best use for Smart Blur is to smooth grain and noise between edges without blurring fine details. To make it work, you first choose a Quality level (Low, Medium, or High) and a Mode (Normal, Edge Only, or Overlay Edge). The only time you want to use a quality level lower than High is when you're working on a really huge image file with a really slow computer; with smaller files and modern computers, you can stick with High all the time. As for the Mode, Normal accomplishes what I've been talking about—blurs surfaces but not edges—and the other two modes offer special effects.

Edge Only and Overlay Edge use Smart Blur's smarts to find the edges of objects in the picture and turn them white. Then, if you choose Edge Only, the rest of the picture turns black; with Overlay Edges, the rest of the picture stays as is.

Did you Know?

To turn your pictures into coloring pages for the kids, use Smart Blur in Edge Only mode with high Radius and Threshold settings, then click OK. Then press Ctrl+I to invert the picture so it's black on white. Finally, strengthen the lines by choosing Filter, Other, Minimum and adjusting the slider.

To control Smart Blur's effect, you drag the Radius and Threshold sliders. As with all Photoshop Elements filters, Smart Blur examines every single pixel in your image. For each pixel, Radius determines how far around that pixel the filter will search, and Threshold controls how different from the original pixel a nearby pixel must be in order to be considered an edge. I've found that the best way to adjust these two sliders is to move both to a position somewhere in the middle and work from there. Lower Radius settings apply more blurring (drag to the left), and higher Threshold settings reduce the number of edges that the filter exempts from blurring (drag to the right).

Radial Blur

This is a fun one. Radial Blur simulates the blur you get when either the camera or the object being photographed is moving toward or away from the camera or spinning. In either case, the center of the effect (which is usually the center of the picture) isn't blurred at all; the amount of blurring increases as you move toward the edges of the image. The dialog box offers no preview option (see Figure 19.10), so you have to try different settings in Draft quality. Just undo and enter different values if you don't like the results. When you've got settings you like, undo once more and invoke the filter one last time, set to Best quality.

FIGURE 19.10
When you click OK and watch as the filter is applied, the image looks as if it's actually spinning.

Amount is the first setting in the Radial Blur dialog, but it's the last thing I tend to set. After you've chosen a Blur Method, a Quality Level, and a Blur Center, drag the Amount slider to determine just *how* blurry things in your picture will get. This is the setting you'll probably spend the most time experimenting with because of the lack of a preview. Fortunately, Photoshop Elements remembers the last settings you used, so if you come up with values that work well, you can easily apply them to another picture.

You can choose from two Blur Method settings: Spin and Zoom (see Figure 19.11). Their names give a good indication of what each one does: Spin simulates the motion blur you'd get from a spinning object, and Zoom looks as though the camera is moving toward or away from the photo's subject. By default, the radial blur effect is centered on the middle of the picture, but you can move its center by clicking in the Blur Center proxy area. The location you choose will have the least blurring; the blur increases gradually as the distance from that point increases.

FIGURE 19.11
Radial Blur's Zoom effect, centered on the giant baseball, makes it appear as if this sign is literally bursting off the side of the building.

As with the Quality setting in the Smart Blur dialog, Radial Blur's Quality setting determines how refined the effect is—and, therefore, how long it takes for Photoshop Elements to complete it. Start with Best; if you find that you're sitting around for too long waiting for Radial Blur to complete, switch to Good or even Draft.

By the Way

Good and Best offer pretty similar results, but you'll notice a reduction in quality if you use the Draft setting.

Motion Blur

We all know what motion blur is—it's what happens when the object you're photographing is moving too fast for the camera to capture it quickly. This results in a blur along the axis of movement, extending from the point where the object was when the camera started shooting to the point where it is when the camera is done shooting. It turns out that this effect is easy for Photoshop Elements to replicate, but you have to use it carefully if you want it to look authentic.

The most important thing to remember is that whatever is blurred will appear to be moving. So if you blur the whole picture, the picture as a whole appears to move, not just a particular object within it. To make just part of the image move, you need to select just that area and apply the Motion Blur filter to it (see Figure 19.12).

FIGURE 19.12
I selected the unicycle rider before applying the Motion Blur and then feathered the selection a bit. Now she seems to be moving because she's blurred but the background isn't.

The Motion Blur dialog has two settings that you can control: Distance and Angle. You determine the distance the blur extends in front and behind each pixel by dragging the slider, and you control the angle of the blur by entering a number of degrees or by dragging the proxy. The line cutting across the circle indicates which directions the blur will extend.

If the object you're blurring was already in motion, as with my unicycle rider, you'll want to make sure the Direction setting matches the actual direction in which the object was moving.

Did you Know?

Using the Render Filters

These filters truly create something from nothing, whether it's clouds, flashes of light, or simply the effects of lights that don't actually exist. They're fun to use, and with the notable exception of Lighting Effects, they're also very easy to use.

Not all filters work with all images; if a filter isn't available, try changing the color mode from Bitmap, Grayscale, or Indexed Color to RGB (choose Image, Mode, RGB Color).

Clouds, Difference Clouds, and Fibers

Clouds and Difference Clouds aren't filters you'll use every day. They have two main purposes:

- ▶ To create an attractive cloudy sky where none exists
- ▶ To provide a foundation for complex special effects, such as simulated marble

Each generates a soft-edged cloud pattern based on the Foreground and Background colors. With Difference Clouds, the colors of the pattern are inverted each time you apply it.

Did you Know?

For a more harsh cloud pattern, press Alt as you're choosing Filter, Render, Clouds. This gives you greater contrast between the two colors within the pattern—darker shadows and lighter highlights.

To use Clouds or Difference Clouds to create a new sky for a boring picture, first you need to select the sky. You might want to use the Eyedropper to choose a Foreground color (sky blue, perhaps?), and you'll probably want to make the Background color white. For a stormy sky, you can use shades of gray instead, perhaps with a purple or green cast for a truly threatening look (see Figure 19.13).

If you're planning to build a texture or pattern on top of the Clouds or Difference Clouds filter, you'll probably be starting with a new, blank image. Still, be sure to choose the Foreground and Background colors you want to use before you invoke the filter by choosing Filter, Render, Clouds or Filter, Render, Difference Clouds. You can use either of the Clouds filters as a basis for countless other effects (see Figure 19.14).

FIGURE 19.13
These fluffy clouds exist only in Photoshop Elements' imagination; I selected the flat blue sky and pressed Alt as I chose the Clouds command to create them.

FIGURE 19.14
Using turquoise and fuchsia as my Foreground and Background colors, I applied the Difference Clouds filter repeatedly to achieve the first image, and then applied Stained Glass to the picture for a colorful, random mosaic effect.

As with the Clouds filters, Fibers creates something out of thin air; in this case, Photoshop Elements can simulate a woven surface such as cloth. Again, Fibers isn't a filter you'd use every day, but it's an interesting way to start creating a background texture. It replaces the entire contents of the current layer (or the Background layer, if you haven't added any layers) with its fibrous surface. You can change two settings to control the fibers' appearance:

▶ **Variance**—This slider determines how the color varies; low values make longer streaks of color, and higher values produce short fibers with more varied color.

▶ **Strength**—Use this slider to control the texture of the fibers, long and loose on the low end and short and stringy on the high end.

When you've got the Variance and Strength settings where you like them, click Randomize to generate one version of what those settings will produce. Keep clicking until you see something you like (see Figure 19.15).

FIGURE 19.15
I clicked Randomize about five times before I got this look, which could be the basis for a neat brushed-metal effect.

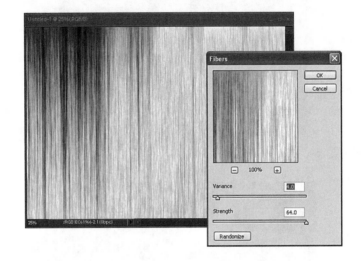

Lens Flare

When you point your camera directly at a bright light or a bright reflection, you sometimes see a lens flare in the resulting photo. This bright flash can reinforce the impression of light, making a picture seem more lively. You can reproduce a lens flare using the logically named Lens Flare filter.

You can choose a Lens Type, which determines the shape of the flare, from four options, such as 35mm Prime; these names no doubt are familiar to old-school photographers who know their lenses. The Brightness slider, obviously, controls how bright the flare is; at the top end, the flare can become a nova that obscures the entire photo. You set the flare's location by clicking in the Flare Center preview area. Try to keep your flare locations logical (see Figure 19.16); no one will believe a lens flare placed in the middle of a patch of shadows.

Lighting Effects

I could write a whole chapter just on using the Lighting Effects filter. No, make that a whole book. This filter is complex to understand and to use, but it's worth a look because it can do truly amazing things. I give you the overview here, but I encourage you to read the Lighting Effects section in the Adobe Photoshop Elements 6 User Guide (download it at http://help.adobe.com/en_US/PhotoshopElements/6.0/pselements_6_help.pdf).

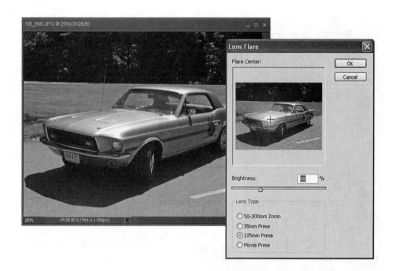

FIGURE 19.16
Here I've placed the lens flare right where the sun was brightest on the car, so it looks authentic.

**By the**
Way

You'll find an excellent Lighting Effects tutorial on the ELATED Web design resource site (www.elated.com/articles/groovy-3d-lighting-effects/). If you're intrigued by what you see here, give the tutorial a try, and have fun!

With Lighting Effects, you can add light and shadow to a picture using one light or several, varying the intensity, angle, and color of each light, as well as the intensity and color of the ambient light. You can do all this on a flat image, or you can use a selection as the basis to create a texture on the surface of the picture. To get an idea of how variable the results of Lighting Effects can be, open any picture; choose Filter, Render, Lighting Effects; and try a few of the preset combinations from the pop-up Style menu at the top of the dialog (see Figure 19.17). When you're ready to create your own looks, switch to the Soft Omni style (which is a pretty basic style with just one white light) and start making changes.

You can add up to 16 light sources, each of which can be adjusted individually. To add a light, drag the light bulb icon below the preview area into the preview. Position it where you want it and then modify its settings on the right side of the dialog. To change the settings of another light, click it to activate it; click and drag to move it within the image. If you decide you want to remove a light, click it and either press Delete or drag the light to the Trash icon under the preview area.

FIGURE 19.17
The Flashlight
preset style
makes Monkey
look as though
he's sitting in
the dark all by
himself.

Did you Know?

To make a copy of a light you've already placed, press Alt and then click and drag the original light. This creates a new light just like the first one, located wherever you drag it.

For each light, you can choose the following attributes.

Light Type

In this section, do the following:

1. Choose a Type (Directional, Omni, Spotlight) and then drag the sliders to set its Intensity and (if it's a spotlight) Focus.

2. Click the color swatch to choose a color for the light, and check the On box to turn the light on and off in the Preview window.

Directional lights shine from a distance, like the sun; Omni lights shine in all directions from just above the surface of the picture; and Spotlights cast an elliptical beam of light whose width you can adjust with the Focus slider. You can combine lights of different types in one application of the Lighting Effects filter.

Properties

Here you choose how the surface of the picture reflects the light you're creating.

▶ The Gloss slider ranges from matte to highly glossy.

▶ The Material slider lets you choose whether the surface reflects little light (a plastic surface), a lot of light (a metallic one), or something in between.

▶ The Exposure slider lets you determine how far the light spreads from its source at the center.

▶ The Ambience slider determines the brightness of the "room light"—that is, any light in the picture that isn't coming from the light sources you're adding.

▶ You can choose the color of the ambient light by clicking the color swatch.

Texture Channel

You can choose to keep the surface of your picture flat, or you can give it a surface texture by choosing a channel to give the texture a shape and specifying how deep it is with the Height slider (see Figure 19.18). The channels that you can use, sort of like stencils, include:

▶ The three color channels (red, green, and blue).

▶ Nontransparent areas of the current layer (its transparency mask), and any saved selection.

▶ The White Is High check box inverts the selection so that the low spots become the high spots and vice versa.

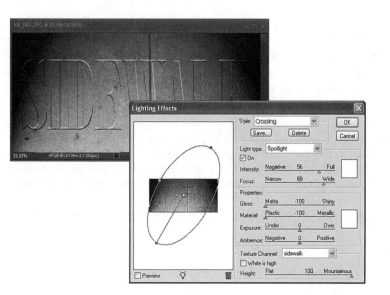

FIGURE 19.18
I created a type mask and then saved the selection to make a texture channel for this image.

Saving Selections

When you've just spent 20 minutes painstakingly creating a selection to outline the subject of your photo or some other object it contains, why not save that selection so you'll never have to do that work again? Before dropping the selection, choose Select, Save Selection. Click the New Selection radio button, give the selection a name, and click OK.

To reactivate that selection later, choose Select, Load Selection. Choose the selection from the Selection pop-up menu, check the Invert box if you want to select everything but the area the selection contains, and click OK. Or you can combine a saved selection with an existing selection by choosing Add to Selection, Subtract from Selection, or Intersect with Selection.

All your saved selections appear in the Texture Channel pop-up menu in the Lighting Effects dialog, along with the color channels and any available transparency masks.

Adjusting Lights

In addition to placing and moving new lights, you can adjust lights in several other ways:

▶ To change the angle of a directional light, drag the handle at the end of its line. Moving the handle farther away puts the light at a greater distance from your image. Press Ctrl as you drag to keep the distance the same while changing the angle; press Shift as you drag to change the distance while maintaining the same angle.

▶ Drag a handle on the edge of an Omni light's circle to change the size of the light.

▶ Drag any handle on the edge of a Spotlight's circle to change its angle or the size and proportions of the ellipse. Press Shift as you drag to maintain the angle while changing the ellipse's size; press Ctrl while you drag to retain the existing size and change the light's angle.

If you come up with a combination of Lighting Effects settings that you really like, click Save at the top of the dialog to add that combo to the Style menu so you can use it again any time you want. If you want to delete one of your custom styles from the Style menu, choose it and then click the Delete button below the menu.

Texture Fill

This filter isn't nearly as sophisticated as its siblings in the Render group; all it does is fill a selection or an entire layer with the contents of a grayscale image saved in Photoshop format. You can use one of the texture files that come with Photoshop Elements (found in the Program Files/Adobe/Photoshop Elements 6.0/ Presets/Textures folder) or you can create your own. As with Render Clouds, this filter won't finish the job of embellishing a photo or creating a masterpiece from scratch, but it's a stepping stone along the way (see Figure 19.19).

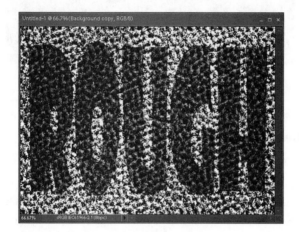

FIGURE 19.19
The rough background texture for this image started as a snakeskin pattern applied with Texture Fill.

3D Transform

As with the Lighting Effects filter, 3D Transform has hidden depths. Its dialog box isn't nearly as big as the Lighting Effects one, but you have a lot to learn before you can really consider yourself an expert user of this filter. When you master it, however, you can use it to map a picture to a three-dimensional shape based on a cylinder, a sphere, or a cube; then you can rotate the shape in space to show a different view of the picture (see Figure 19.20).

FIGURE 19.20
Remember back in Hour 8 when we applied a whole bunch of layer styles to a single type layer? Refresh your memory by taking a look at Figure 8.11. This is what that same layer looks like when it's mapped onto a cylinder shaped like a can of tuna.

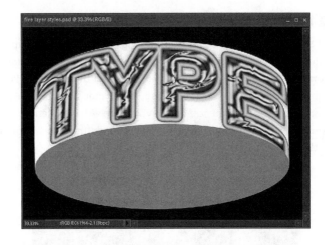

▼   **Try it Yourself**

Map a Picture to a 3D Object

To use the 3D Transform filter, follow these steps:

1. Open your photo in the Editor's Full Edit mode and flatten it (choose Layer, Flatten Image); 3D Transform works on one layer at a time, so if you want it to use the whole picture, you have to make sure everything is on one layer.

2. Choose Filter, Render, 3D Transform.

3. Click the Options button (see Figure 19.21). Choose a resolution setting; higher resolution levels give you better-looking cylinders and spheres but don't make much difference with cubes. Then choose a level of Anti-Aliasing (higher levels take longer to execute) and check or uncheck the Display Background box. If you uncheck the box, 3D Transform surrounds the final 3D object with black so it looks as though it's floating in space.

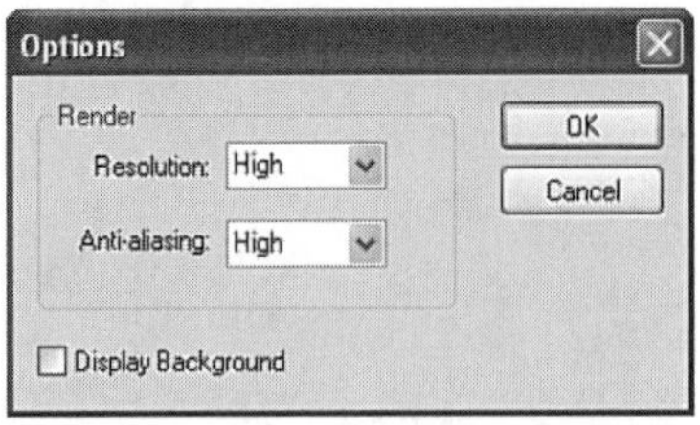

FIGURE 19.21
Higher Resolution and Anti-Aliasing settings make the 3D Transform filter take longer to complete its work.

4. Choose a shape tool (a cube, a sphere, or a cylinder) and drag in the image to create a wireframe of the shape. You can reproduce the shape of the object by matching the wireframe's corners to the object's corners, or you can map a flat

▼

image onto a shape (as I did in Figure 19.20). Either way, you have to manipulate the wireframe until it's positioned correctly with respect to the image by
dragging the frame's corners.

5. To move the wireframe, click the Selection tool and drag an edge of the wireframe. To move a single anchor point, click the Direct Selection tool and drag
the anchor point you want to reposition. You can add new anchor points to
make a cylindrical shape more complex by Ctrl+Shift+clicking the Add Anchor
Point tool and then clicking the right side of the wireframe where you want to
put the new point (see Figure 19.22). To change an anchor point from a smooth
(curved) anchor point to a corner anchor point, and vice versa, Ctrl+Shift+click
the Convert Anchor Point tool and then click the point. If you want to delete an
anchor point, click the Delete Anchor Point tool and then click the point. You
can't delete a point unless it's round or shaped like a diamond.

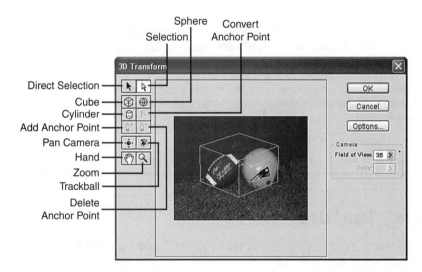

FIGURE 19.22
The 3D
Transform dialog
has its own
toolbox, includ-
ing some
unique tools
and others that
work just like
their counter-
parts in the reg-
ular toolbox.

If your wireframe turns red, you've twisted it into a shape that Photoshop
Elements can't generate in three dimensions. Congratulations! Now adjust the
wireframe until it turns green again.

**Watch
Out!**

6. To delete the wireframe and start over, click it and press Delete.

7. When your wireframe is complete, you can adjust the position of the image
within it. Click the Pan Camera tool and drag the image to move it within the
wireframe; click the Trackball tool and drag the image to rotate it within the
wireframe (see Figure 19.23).

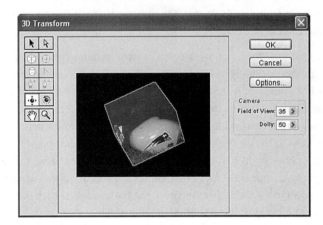

FIGURE 19.23
Using the Pan Camera tool, I can control what part of the picture appears on each surface of my cube.

8. If you're having trouble fitting the wireframe to the picture, try adjusting the Field of View value upward or downward. To move the "camera" farther away from or closer to the picture, change the Dolly Camera value.

By the Way

> You can add more than one wireframe to the image and combine them to create more complex structures.

9. When you're satisfied with your settings, click OK to see the result.

Adding Texture

One of my favorite image-embellishment techniques is to add simulated texture. I'm fascinated by the way Photoshop Elements can produce seemingly three-dimensional effects in a two-dimensional picture. Besides being fun to play with, the Texture filters are a great way to obscure image flaws—the same way Add Noise does, only with a more logical reason for existence. For example, it's perfectly normal for a picture to look as though it was created on canvas, much more so than for that picture to be all noisy, with no apparent cause for the noise.

By the Way

> The Texture filters use the Filter Gallery, so this is your first chance to play with its features. Don't be afraid to experiment; remember, undo is your friend.

Craquelure

Craquelure actually means the pattern of cracks on the surface of old paintings. In Photoshop Elements, however, the Craquelure filter makes your picture look as if it was painted on a cracked plaster surface (see Figure 19.24). You can set values for Crack Spacing (the distance between cracks, 0–100), Crack Depth (0–10), and Crack Brightness (0–10). Darker cracks lend greater intensity to the effect, but if you make them too dark, they'll look artificial.

FIGURE 19.24
Using the Craquelure filter is much cheaper than buying all that special crackle glaze at the craft store.

Grain

You can think of the Grain filter as a more sophisticated version of the Add Noise filter (see Figure 19.25). It adds any of 10 types of grain to a picture, and you can specify the Intensity (amount of grain, 0–100) and degree of Contrast (also 0–100). The key to getting great results from the Grain filter is experimentation with the different Grain types. (Note that the Sprinkles and Stippled grain types are created using the Background color.) The 10 Grain types are listed here:

- ▶ Regular
- ▶ Soft
- ▶ Sprinkles
- ▶ Clumped
- ▶ Contrasty

- ▶ Enlarged
- ▶ Stippled
- ▶ Horizontal
- ▶ Vertical
- ▶ Speckle

FIGURE 19.25
You wouldn't think a light coating of grain would make such a difference in a photo, but it definitely does.

Mosaic Tiles

I've never thought Mosaic Tiles actually looks much like a mosaic, but it's kind of a cool effect. It creates small, irregular chips in the picture with grout lines between them (see Figure 19.26). You can specify Tile Size (0–100) and Grout Width (0–10), both of which are self-explanatory. You can drag the Lighten Grout slider to change the color of the grout between tiles; drag left to darken the grout and right to lighten it (the slider goes from 0 to 10).

Patchwork

Again, I don't think this filter looks the way its name implies it should; I can't think of any Photoshop filter whose results look *less* like a patchwork quilt than this one (see Figure 19.27). Nonetheless, Patchwork has its devotees, and I believe I've even used it a time or two to create backgrounds. It breaks up the picture into squares, each of which sticks out from the background more or less, depending on whether the area is darker or lighter. The Square Size slider goes from 0 to 10, and you can choose a Relief value between 0 and 25 to determine the overall depth of the protruding tiles.

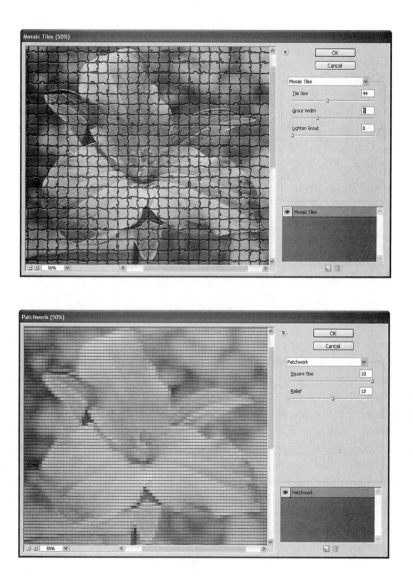

FIGURE 19.26
These are the oddest-shaped mosaic tiles I've ever seen.

FIGURE 19.27
It might not look like anything in nature, but Patchwork is rather a neat effect.

Stained Glass

Using the Stained Glass filter, you can turn your picture into either stained glass or a much better-looking mosaic than Mosaic Tiles produces (see Figure 19.28). Just be sure to set the Foreground color before you fire up Stained Glass because the filter uses that color for the borders of its glass cells. You can choose a Cell Size (2–50), a Border Thickness (1–20), and a Light Intensity (0–10) that produces a more or less bright spot in the middle of the "window."

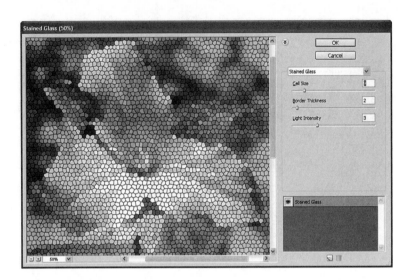

Texturizer

If you want to make your picture look as though it's painted on brick, burlap, canvas, or sandstone, the Texturizer filter will take you there (see Figure 19.29). You can load more textures from the example files (found in the `Program Files/Adobe/Photoshop Elements 6.0/Presets/Textures` folder) or you can create your own. For each texture, you can set a Scaling percentage (0–200) that determines the size of the texture with respect to the image, a Relief value (0–50) that determines how far the texture appears to protrude from the picture's surface, and a Light angle (Bottom, Bottom Left, Left, Top Left, Top, Top Right, Right, or Bottom Right). If you check the Invert box, the result looks as though the texture is pressed into the image instead of the image being painted over the texture.

FIGURE 19.29
Here I've invert-
ed the texture
so that it looks
as though the
burlap was
pressed into the
wet paint and
then removed.

Adjusting the Effect of Filters

If you're anything like me, you spend a lot of time repeatedly undoing and then going back to redo the settings on each filter you use. Rather than having to undo and try again, however, if your goal is to reduce the filter's impact, there's a better way. This simple technique achieves the same thing as Photoshop's Fade command, which Photoshop Elements doesn't have yet, unfortunately. The bonus is that you can go back and change your settings any time with this "hack," but you can use the Fade command only immediately after you apply the filter.

Before applying the filter you have in mind, stop by the Layers palette and duplicate the layer to which you want to apply the filter. Then go ahead and use your filter on the duplicate layer. Now all you need to do to scale back the filter's effects is reduce the opacity of the duplicate layer so that the original shows through (see Figure 19.30).

FIGURE 19.30
I started with a nice (but boring) picture of a rose and then applied the Grain filter to it. But I think I went too far, so I cut the Opacity of the filtered layer to 50% and ended up with a more subtle result.

Summary

In this hour, we started playing with some of the dozens of filters in Photoshop Elements. And there's more to come in the next few hours. You now know about three different ways to apply filters: with the Effects palette, via the Filter menu, and in the Filter Gallery. We looked at four groups of filters that can fix up a picture that's almost—but not quite—ready for prime time. The Noise filters—Despeckle, Dust & Scratches, Reduce Noise, Median, and Add Noise—enable you to remove and add varying amounts of digital noise to make a picture more or less clear. In the Blur group, you learned about Blur, Blur More, Gaussian Blur, Smart Blur, Radial

Blur, and Motion Blur. The complex effects in the Render category include Clouds, Difference Clouds, Fibers, Lens Flare, Lighting Effects, Texture Fill, and 3D Transform; each takes a different approach to making something out of nothing. Then you learned about the Texture filters: Craquelure, Grain, Mosaic Tiles, Patchwork, Stained Glass, and Texturizer. These are great for applying realistic (and not-so-realistic) three-dimensional surface effects to a picture. Finally, I showed you a quick and dirty way to tone down the effect of a filter after it has been applied.

Q&A

Q. *How do I know whether to use a Blur filter or the Blur tool?*

A. If you want to blur a large area, or even the entire image, use one of the Blur filters. Use the Blur tool if you just want to apply a little blurring here and there. For larger areas, a filter is both quicker and more consistent.

Q. *What happens if I keep applying a filter repeatedly?*

A. First of all, you don't need to ask me—just try it! You won't break the computer (as I used to tell my mom back when she was first learning to use a Mac). Second, it depends on the filter. You can apply Clouds as many times as you want, and you'll just keep getting different cloud configurations in the same colors and intensity. Try that with Difference Clouds, however, and you'll see a progression toward a completely different picture as you repeatedly apply the filter. And don't forget that you can reapply the last filter you used by pressing Ctrl+F. Of course, you can always undo by pressing Ctrl+Z or using the Undo History palette.

Workshop

Give these quiz questions a try, check your answers (of course, you always do that, right?), and then reward yourself with some playtime working on the activities.

Quiz

1. The Filter Gallery includes all of Photoshop Elements' filters.

    A. True

    B. False

2. Which of the following is *not* one of the light types you can use with the Lighting Effects filter?

   A. Spotlight

   B. Omni

   C. Flashlight

   D. Directional

3. To work with the Texturizer filter, a pattern file must be:

   A. RGB

   B. At least 300ppi

   C. Grayscale

   D. Extremely high-contrast

Quiz Answers

1. **B.** False. A good number of Photoshop Elements filters don't even have a dialog box; they just do their thing as soon as you choose the command from the menu or the Effects palette.

2. **C.** Flashlight is one of the preset combinations of Lighting Effects settings that you can choose from the Style pop-up menu. It probably sounds familiar to you because I used it on my friend Monkey in Figure 19.17.

3. **C.** And it must be saved in Photoshop format, too.

Activities

1. Find a dark photo, use Shadows/Highlights to brighten it (choose Enhance, Adjust Lighting, Adjust Shadows/Highlights), and then see if you can tone down the resulting graininess with the Reduce Noise filter.

2. Experiment with the Edge Only and Overlay Edge modes in the Smart Blur filter. After you apply each, apply some other filters, adjust the picture's color, or use the Transform commands to reshape it. Or do all three!

PART IV

Going Creative

HOUR 20

Using the Artistic Filters

What You'll Learn in This Hour:

▶ Ways to make a photo look like a watercolor or oil painting

▶ How to turn a picture into a pastel drawing, with either rough pastels or soft ones

▶ How to simulate a picture drawn with charcoals or a combination of chalk and charcoals

▶ How to reproduce a pen sketch

▶ How to create a "sponged" picture

▶ How to give your picture spooky glowing edges

In this hour, you'll spend time playing with filters that can make your photos look like paintings, sketches, and other varieties of fine art. As you might expect, most of these filters fall under the Artistic, Brush Strokes, and Sketch categories, but I also show you some fun stuff from the Pixelate and Stylize categories. Now, when I say "play," I do mean play—there's no special technique or technical expertise to master with using these filters. The key to getting fantastic results is simply experience, which means you have a perfect excuse to spend as much time messing around with these filters as you want. Just don't forget to eat and sleep occasionally.

To help you with that messing-around stuff, I've put the photo used in this chapter on the book's website at www.informit.com/title/9780672330179 so that you can download it and try all the filters on it yourself (see Figure 20.1).

FIGURE 20.1
You'll find this picture in the color section as well.

Using the Watercolor Filters

Watercolor painting always looks so easy to outsiders, similar to the kind of painting we did with our plastic brushes and desiccated cakes of paint as kids. Don't be fooled, though; doing good work with watercolors takes a lot of skill. Fortunately, Photoshop Elements has more than one way to achieve a similar effect without all that messy paint and water. First, we look at the filter that's actually called Watercolor. Then we examine two other filters that you can use to achieve a watercolor effect: Dry Brush and Spatter.

Did you Know?

> Most of the filters we cover in this hour will look their best if you increase the photo's contrast before you apply them (choose Enhance, Adjust Lighting, Brightness and Contrast).

Watercolor

The Watercolor filter (choose Filter, Artistic, Watercolor) yields a texture that could be mistaken for a watercolor painting, but it darkens the image much more than most watercolor painters would (see Figure 20.2). A Brush Detail (1–14) slider enables you to control the amount of detail in the resulting image. The Shadow Intensity control (1–10) determines exactly how much the image is darkened. Texture (1–3) enables you to choose a flatter image or one with more visible strokes.

FIGURE 20.2
I got a decent result with the Watercolor filter, but I had to tweak the lighting in the photo beforehand to make it turn out.

Before using the Watercolor filter, try lightening your picture quite a bit past where you'd normally take it. You'll find that the lighter the picture is, the better the colors come across and the fewer black blobs you'll end up with.

Did you Know?

Dry Brush

With the Dry Brush filter (choose Filter, Artistic, Dry Brush), you can reproduce the effect of painting with very little paint on the brush (see Figure 20.3). This gives you simple, soft-edged strokes that can maintain more or less image detail, depending on the Brush Detail setting (0–10); you also don't get the dark, threatening aura that the Watercolor filter gives. Your other options are Brush Size, ranging from 0 to 10, which also has a great deal of influence on the amount of detail retained in the image, and Texture, ranging from 1 to 3. Setting the Texture slider to 3 adds some noise to the image, and setting Texture to 1 keeps the picture noise-free; a setting of 2 falls between those two extremes.

Spatter

A real-life spatter technique involves spraying the canvas or paper with droplets of paint by shaking the brush or tapping it against a finger. Photoshop Elements' Spatter filter (choose Filter, Brush Strokes, Spatter) is similar to a combination of the Diffuse and Ripple filters, making your picture look as though it was created from tiny droplets of paint (see Figure 20.4). The Spatter dialog has only two sliders: Spray Radius, which ranges from 0 to 25 and controls how far droplets of one color are allowed to extend into areas of different colors, and Smoothness, which controls the ripple effect. Setting Smoothness to 1 eliminates the ripples completely; setting it to 15 gives you a picture that's nearly unrecognizable.

FIGURE 20.4
It looks a bit
strange, but it
does look like a
painting.

Simulating Oil Painting

Just as there's more than one kind of watercolor painting, oil painting involves many different techniques. Several of Photoshop Elements' filters focus on oil-and-canvas work.

Underpainting

In oil painting, artists often paint a blocky, simplified version of the image they're going for and then go back and add layers of detail and texture. That's called underpainting. In Photoshop Elements, the Underpainting filter (choose Filter, Artistic, Underpainting) produces results similar to those of the Median filter, one of the Blur filters you learned about in the last hour (see Figure 20.5). Underpainting blurs your picture into a fairly realistic oil-painted effect. Brush Size (0–40) and Texture Coverage (0–40) sliders enable you to control the brush strokes' width and how much of the background shows through.

FIGURE 20.5
If you're using the Underpainting filter, you're probably not using it alone; it makes a great color layer under a more detailed image layer.

Meanwhile, you can add a background texture using controls just like those in the Texturizer dialog box. A pop-up menu contains the four basic choices of Brick, Burlap, Canvas, or Sandstone; the Other option enables you to use your own grayscale Photoshop file as a texture map. After choosing a texture, you set the Scaling slider to a value between 50% and 200% to determine the size of the texture relative to the image. You can also specify a Relief value from 0 to 50 that controls how high the dark areas in the texture file appear to be. You can choose a Light Direction, and you can also invert the texture so that it appears to be pressed into the image instead of lying under the picture.

When you're done applying the Underpainting filter, you can paint the details back in yourself with the Brush tool, or try combining Underpainting with Palette Knife or another artistic filter.

Palette Knife

A palette knife is a blunt knife that a painter uses to mix paint colors on a palette. Sometimes artists also use palette knives to actually apply paint to the canvas, for a chunky, highly textured style. The Palette Knife filter (choose Filter, Artistic, Palette

Knife) attempts to reproduce this effect, but it doesn't add the texture that a real palette knife would (see Figure 20.6). You can control Stroke Size (1–50) and Stroke Detail (1–3). The Softness slider (0–10) determines whether the paint strokes blend with one another.

FIGURE 20.6
With Palette Knife, this delicately detailed image is almost unrecognizable.

Paint Daubs

I like Paint Daubs a lot, but I have to admit that it works like an oddball combination of other filters, resulting in an effect that looks anything but "daubed." When you apply Paint Daubs (choose Filter, Artistic, Paint Daubs), you end up with a picture that seems to have been blurred, then filtered with Find Edges, then posterized, and finally sharpened (see Figure 20.7). The filter might be more accurately called Paint Blobs.

FIGURE 20.7
Here a blob, there a blob ....

You use a Brush Size slider, with values ranging from 1 to 50, to control the size of the posterized color areas. A Sharpness slider (0–40) enables you to apply as much or as little sharpening as you want. The Brush Type pop-up menu offers several choices, including Simple, Light Rough, Dark Rough, Wide Sharp, Wide Blurry, and Sparkle brushes. Rough brushes apply more texture, and the Sparkle brush bumps up the Find Edges effect and increases the picture's saturation to create neon colors.

Working with Pastels, Chalk, Charcoal, and Pen

Now that we've covered some of the traditional painting media, we turn to drawing. Sometimes drawings are intended as the basis for a painting; other times, they stand on their own. You can reproduce several kinds of drawing media and techniques using Photoshop Elements' filters. You'll find that the filters discussed here preserve detail much better than the painting filters we've been looking at.

Rough Pastels

Pastels are sticks of solid pigment, the same kind used in liquid paints, that you can draw with like a crayon. They're easy to blend, and they come in several varieties with slightly different characteristics. The Rough Pastels filter (choose Filter, Artistic, Rough Pastels) applies "pastel" strokes in the length of your choice to a picture based on an underlying rough texture (see Figure 20.8); again, you can choose Brick, Burlap, Canvas, or Sandstone from the Texture pop-up menu, or you can choose Other and use your own grayscale Photoshop-format file. As usual with textured backgrounds, you can control the Scaling (50% to 200%), the Relief value (0–50), and the Light. As with the other texture-using filters, you can also check the Invert box to flip the texture so it's incised into the picture's surface instead of protruding from it.

FIGURE 20.8
The key to using Rough Pastels is getting the texture right— not too much, not too little.

Smudge Stick

The Smudge Stick filter (choose Filter, Artistic, Smudge Stick) is your basic pastels filter, giving you the sort of result you'd get by using soft, smudged pastels in real life (see Figure 20.9). You can determine the length of the smudging strokes with the Stroke Length slider (1–10) and the amount of contrast in the picture with the Intensity slider (also 1–10). Finally, the Highlight Area slider controls just how bright the brightest areas in the picture are, whether they're just lighter than the rest of the picture or completely blown out to white.

FIGURE 20.9
This filter would look more realistic if all the strokes weren't smudged in the same direction.

Chalk & Charcoal

Charcoal isn't just for barbecues; it's a traditional drawing medium that's often combined with chalk so the artist can produce both dark and light strokes. In Photoshop Elements, the Chalk & Charcoal filter (choose Filter, Sketch, Chalk & Charcoal) combines chalk strokes in the Background color and charcoal strokes in the Foreground color to create an image that can look extremely surreal, depending on your color choices. With the default colors of black and white, however, the filter produces a quite creditable imitation of a drawing made with charcoal and chalk (see Figure 20.10). Using the controls in the dialog, you can control the Chalk Area and the Charcoal Area (both 0–20) and the Stroke Pressure (0–5) to determine how intense the effect is.

Conté Crayon

Often used on canvas to create a preliminary drawing for a painting, Conté sticks or crayons are made from compressed powdered graphite or charcoal, mixed with wax or clay and formed into square sticks. The Conté Crayon filter produces the effect of a crayon on textured paper (see Figure 20.11); choose Filter, Sketch, Conté Crayon to get there. Conté crayons are usually black, dark red, or brown, so if you're looking for a realistic crayon effect, you'll want to use one of these colors as the foreground color and a white, cream, or tan paper color as the background color. The Texture controls will look familiar; they're just like those from the Texturizer filter and several other artistic filters. The dialog also has sliders for Foreground Level and Background Level. Because it doesn't have any controls for stroke length or width, Conté Crayon's results tend to look less believable than those of Chalk & Charcoal; it's more obvious that the picture started as a photograph.

FIGURE 20.10
Not surprisingly, Chalk & Charcoal's results look much like Smudge Stick's, only without the color.

FIGURE 20.11
To me, Conté Crayon looks more like an engraving technique than something you'd do with an actual crayon.

Graphic Pen

Twentieth-century artist Edward Gorey is widely acknowledged to have been one of the all-time masters of pen-and-ink drawing. You can see some of his work on the Web (start with www.lunaea.com/words/gorey/), and I guarantee you'll enjoy it. Now, I've never been able to equal Gorey's work with the Graphic Pen filter (choose Filter, Sketch, Graphic Pen), but I keep trying (see Figure 20.12). Graphic Pen produces a pen-and-ink sketch effect, with no outlining, just shading strokes. You can control the Stroke Length (1–15) and the Light/Dark Balance (0–100), which determines how much of the image is covered with the Foreground and Background colors, with medium settings distributing the colors evenly. You have four choices for Stroke Direction: Horizontal, Left Diagonal, Right Diagonal, and Vertical.

FIGURE 20.12
Here's another filter that leaves our poor flowers nearly unrecognizable; Graphic Pen works best with very high-contrast, low-detail images.

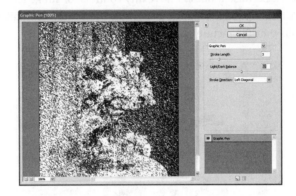

Sumi-e

This traditional Japanese art, literally translated "ink painting," is done with a brush, rice paper, and compressed bamboo charcoal mixed with water to produce black ink. Sumi-e drawings are intended to convey the soul of an object without portraying unnecessary detail. They tend to have a lot of dark areas and soft-edged strokes (see Figure 20.13). Using the Sumi-e filter (choose Filter, Brush Strokes, Sumi-e), you can control the Stroke Width (3–15) and the Stroke Pressure (0 to 15). The Contrast slider (0–40) determines how much the contrast of the original image is bumped up; higher settings increase contrast, and lower ones maintain the existing level of contrast.

FIGURE 20.13
Traditional sumi-e paintings use only black ink, but Photoshop Elements' Sumi-e filter retains much of the picture's color.

More Painterly Effects

Of course, we all know there's more to art than paint and canvas or paper. Sometimes a fun, funky effect is just what an image needs. Other times, you can mix your own special effects by combining more than one filter. The possibilities are endless.

Creating a Neon Effect with Glowing Edges

With this one, we're veering away from traditional art and into the modern world. Whether neon signs constitute art is debatable, but the fact that the Glowing Edges filter (choose Filter, Stylize, Glowing Edges) produces neat effects is not. Glowing Edges combines the Find Edges filter and the Invert command (see Figure 20.14), and it gives you the capability to control the Edge Width (1–14), the Edge Brightness (0–20), and the Smoothness of the edges (1–15). With higher Smoothness settings, the filter locates fewer edges.

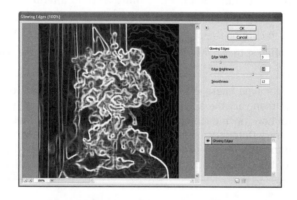

FIGURE 20.14
You can't tell it's a vase of flowers, but it sure looks neat; this filter is more appropriate for a picture of an object whose shape is its most identifiable feature.

Sponging an Image

If you painted a picture with a sponge (in theory, at least), it would look like what you get when you apply the Sponge filter (choose Filter, Artistic, Sponge; see Figure 20.15). The Brush Size slider (1–10) controls how large the theoretical sponge is. The Smoothness slider (1–15) enables you to control the blurriness of the sponge strokes' edges. With the Definition slider, you can make the image darker or closer to the original image; the lowest setting of 1 keeps the colors as is, and the highest setting of 25 darkens them.

FIGURE 20.15
I can definitely
see how this
could happen in
my house with a
sponge and an
empty wall.

Combining Multiple Filters

I've always liked to apply filters on top of filters, but this whole process has gotten so much easier since the introduction of the Filter Gallery that it's hard to know why anyone would stick with just one filter at a time. With an interface much like the Layers palette, the Filter Gallery enables you to stack dozens of filters on top of each other, drag them to change the order in which they're applied, and hide or show specific filters in the list to see just what effect they're having on the whole.

Did you Know?

Another way to combine filters is to apply each filter to a duplicate of the original image layer and then vary the stacking order, opacity, and blending mode of the layers to control how much each one contributes to the overall effect. For example, you could apply Cutout or Underpainting to a bottom layer and then allow the original picture to show on top of it at reduced opacity. This gives you the blocky, primitive look of the filters while retaining some of the image's original detail.

I've put together a few of my favorite combinations for you. Remember, you can download the picture I used (blossom.jpg) from the book's website and try your own combinations. All three of the figures in this section are also in the color section, so you can see for yourself how my experiments worked out.

First, I layered Dark Strokes and Water Paper. The latter, another watercolor-type filter, gave the picture a nice dreamy, smudged quality, and Dark Strokes added some weight in the shadows (see Figure 20.16). I kept Dark Strokes on top of the filter pile because when I put it below Water Paper, it added too much dark, heavy detail to the original photo.

FIGURE 20.16
I think I like this one best of all.

I got a similar but (I think) less attractive result with Poster Edges and Dry Brush. Again, Dry Brush provides the soft color, and Poster Edges provides some depth to the edges of the photo's objects, particularly the round table top (see Figure 20.17). This image is less dreamy and more stylized.

FIGURE 20.17
This reminds me of watercolor-and-ink work I've seen.

Finally, I applied Accented Edges twice with different settings. The first application of Accented Edges, at the bottom of the filter list in the dialog, had high Edge Brightness and Smoothness values. Then I layered another instance of Accented Edges on top of that, with rougher lines and darker edges. The combination results in abstract, flowing colors that still have plenty of edge definition (see Figure 20.18).

Summary

During this hour, you learned about filters that can turn an ordinary photo into a "painted" or "sketched" masterpiece. Photoshop Elements has dozens of filters. By tweaking their settings and combining them in different ways, you can come up with hundreds, or maybe even thousands, of different effects. Several of Photoshop Elements' filters are designed to simulate traditional media, such as watercolors, oil paints, pen and ink, chalk, charcoal, and more. The key to getting good results from the filters you apply is to experiment with them as much as possible so that you know their ins and outs and can use them to best advantage. Some filters require adjusting the image beforehand, and others simply don't look good with certain types of pictures. Trying different filters and settings is useful work and possibly the most fun you'll ever have with a computer.

Q&A

Q. *This stuff is so easy! Who needs brushes and paint? In fact, who needs artists anymore?*

A. Hey, now, slow down a minute. What we're doing with Photoshop Elements' filters is creating *simulated* art that's good enough for everyday. Real artists do a lot more, manipulating color, perspective, and texture in ways that dabblers like me, and maybe you, can only dream of. That said, however, many real artists do use virtual media instead of actual paint, paper, and canvas these days. Their program of choice is actually Corel Painter (www.corel.com); if you think Photoshop Elements does a good job of simulating natural media, wait until you see what Painter can do.

Q. *How many filters can I apply at once using the Filter Gallery?*

A. I have no idea, but let me put it this way: I've never, ever hit the limit, if there is one. Trust me, you won't, either.

Q. *Is there a way to tell ahead of time whether a filter has customizable settings?*

A. Sure. Look at the name of the filter in the Filter menu. If it's followed by an ellipsis (…), it leads to a dialog box. No ellipsis, no dialog box. This goes for all of Photoshop Elements' commands, by the way, not just the filters.

Workshop

If you tried all these art techniques in their real-life forms, you'd have a lot of clean-up to do afterward (and it would cost you a bundle). After you answer these quiz questions, take advantage of Photoshop Elements' nice, clean "art studio" and let some of your favorite artistic filters loose on your photos.

Quiz

1. Which filter can provide texture like that in the Rough Pastels filter for any filter that doesn't have its own texture controls?

    A. Texture Fill

    B. Fibers

    C. Texturizer

    D. Background Texture

2. What does sumi-e mean?

    A. Bamboo painting

    B. Ink painting

    C. Charcoal stick

    D. Black and white

3. What kind of image works best with the Graphic Pen filter?

    A. High-contrast

    B. Low-contrast

    C. Detailed

    D. Grayscale

Quiz Answers

1. **C.** Texture Fill and Fibers erase the image, leaving only texture, and there's no such filter as Background Texture.

2. **B.** The black ink is traditionally made from bamboo charcoal, though.

3. **A.** You want a high-contrast picture without a lot of detail because Graphic Pen's shading is great at conveying shapes but not so great with anything that needs to be outlined to be recognizable.

Activities

1. Find a format portrait in your photo collection; it can be a studio portrait or even just a school picture. Try some different filters on it. Which ones yield the best results? Which ones need to have the picture's saturation, contrast, or brightness adjusted before they work well? And which ones don't work at all?

2. Now do the same thing with a still life. If you don't have a suitable picture, dust off your camera and take one. It can be fruit, your office tchotchkes, or whatever you desire. Now try the same filters you used in the first activity on this picture. Do the same filters work well on this picture?

Creating Art from Scratch

What You'll Learn in This Hour:

▶ Ways to define exactly the color you want
▶ How to draw basic shapes
▶ How to adjust an existing shape
▶ How to draw or paint with the Pencil and Brush tools
▶ How to use the different Eraser tools

Whether it's destined to be combined with one or more photos or to stand on its own, sometimes you just need to draw a picture. Photoshop Elements' drawing tools include both a brush and a pencil, each highly customizable and capable of using any color you can dream up. You also have access to a huge assortment of custom shapes that you can add to your pictures in any size and color. It's all here; let me show you how to use it.

Choosing Colors

The art you create in Photoshop Elements' Editor can be grayscale or even black and white, particularly if it's based on older photos. But in today's world, it's all about the color. Using the right color with your painting and drawing tools can make a tremendous difference in an image, but you have to know how to set that color. Let's take a look at some of the ways Photoshop Elements helps you accomplish this task.

Using the Color Picker

When you're painting, the Brush uses the Foreground color, as does the Pencil tool. The Eraser uses both the Foreground color and the Background color (we get to that shortly). And these colors are always displayed as color swatches in the toolbox (see Figure 21.1). Some tools have their own color swatches in the Options bar; in this case, you can change the color that tool uses next without affecting the Foreground and Background colors that other tools use. You'll even find color swatches right in some dialogs, as you saw in Hour 19, "Using the Improvement Filters," when you learned how to use the Lighting Effects filter; in that dialog, you can click color swatches to specify colors for each light and for the ambient light.

FIGURE 21.1
The Foreground and Background colors are always visible in the toolbox.

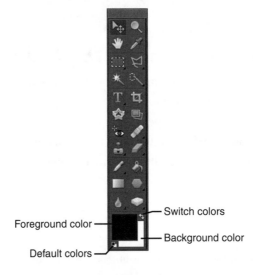

Switch colors

Foreground color —

Background color

Default colors —

In any case, clicking a color swatch opens the color picker. I probably shouldn't say "the" color picker, however, because you do have a choice of which version you want to use: the Adobe color picker or the one that comes with your system software, whether that's Windows or Mac OS. Try both of your options and see which works best for you. I generally prefer the Adobe color picker (see Figure 21.2), but my kids like the system one better (see Figure 21.3). To change which color picker comes up when you click a color swatch, choose Edit, Preferences, General (or press Ctrl+K) and choose an option from the Color Picker pop-up menu at the top of the Preferences dialog; then click OK.

In either color picker, you can choose colors from a color field or enter numeric RGB or HSB values. I like the Adobe color picker better than the Windows one because it enables me to specify colors in hexadecimal code (the color system that HTML web pages use) as well HSB (Hue/Saturation/Brightness) and RGB (Red/Green/Blue). It even has a couple ways to make sure that a color is "web-safe"—in other words, that it's one of the 216 colors that the Mac OS and Windows system palettes share. To display only web colors, check the Only Web Colors box at the bottom of the color picker. Or, if you choose a color from the entire range of colors and then decide it needs to be web-safe, you can click the small color swatch below the web-safe color warning icon (a rainbow-colored cube) to have Photoshop Elements automatically replace the color you picked with the web-safe color that's closest to your selection.

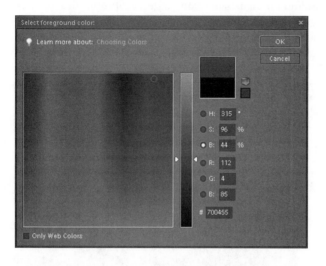

FIGURE 21.2
You can always tell when you're using the Adobe color picker because its window is gray, like the rest of the Photoshop Elements interface.

FIGURE 21.3
If you can't see the right half of the Windows color picker, click the Define Custom Colors button to display it.

> If you need to review the color systems that Photoshop Elements uses, head back to Hour 9, "Printing Your Pictures."

By the Way

The color field and slider work the same way in both the Windows and Adobe color pickers, however. In each case, the slider controls whichever color component you click, whether that's Hue, Saturation, Brightness, Red, Green, or Blue. The color field then displays your options in the other two components for the specified location on the slider. That sounds complicated, I know, but it makes more sense when you start playing around with it. Take a look at Figure 21.4 for an example. Here I've chosen Hue (see the selected radio button next to the H) for the slider, which means that the color field displays all the possible combinations of saturation (intensity) and brightness for the shade shown on the slider. If I switch the slider to B instead, for Brightness, the color field displays all the possible combinations of hue and saturation for the brightness level shown on the slider.

FIGURE 21.4
This green shade is about one-third as saturated as pure green; you can tell that both by the Saturation percentage and by the circle's position one-third of the way from the left side of the color field.

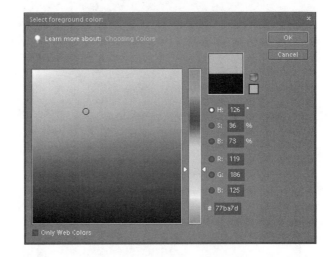

Using the Color Swatches Palette

Maybe you're not the color-mixing type, and you prefer to choose from a predefined set of colors. Photoshop Elements can accommodate this method of working as well, with its Color Swatches palette (choose Window, Color Swatches). This palette, shown in Figure 21.5, comes with seven different preset color collections, listed in the pop-up menu at the top of the palette. Setting the Foreground color is as easy as clicking on a swatch you like; press Alt as you click to specify the Background color.

FIGURE 21.5
Not only can you choose colors from the Color Swatches palette, but you can also save your own favorite colors as swatches.

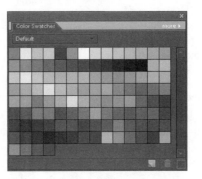

You don't have to stick with the small swatches that are the default setting for the Color Swatches palette. In the palette menu, you'll find options for viewing the swatches as Small Thumbnails, Large Thumbnails, Small List, or Large List. In the List views, each color's name appears next to the swatch.

To add a swatch, click the New Swatch button at the bottom of the palette; it looks just like the Layers palette's New Layer button. If you're using a List view, double-click the swatch's name (Color Swatch, with a number) and enter a new one that makes sense to you. If you want to delete a swatch, just drag it to the Trash icon next to the New Swatch button. When you have a collection of colors you want to use again later, choose Save Swatches from the palette menu, give your swatch collection a name, and then click Save. You can reload that set of color swatches at any time by choosing Load Swatches or Replace Swatches from the palette menu. If you use the Load Swatches command, the new colors are added to the colors already displayed in the Color Swatches palette; with Replace Swatches, only the new colors are displayed.

Other Tips for Selecting Colors

When you're using the Eyedropper tool, the entire image is the equivalent of one big Color Swatches palette. Just click anywhere to choose a Foreground color, or Alt+click to choose a Background color. If you're interested in the numbers behind colors chosen this way, choose Window, Info to display the Info palette (see Figure 21.6). Click the eyedropper next to each color readout to display a different color model in that space. Now, as you move your cursor within the image window, the values for the color immediately underneath it are displayed. You can use this technique to make sure a white background is really white (its RGB values will be 255, 255, 255), among other useful applications.

I'm about to share one of my all-time favorite cool Photoshop Elements tricks with you, so pay attention. You can use the Eyedropper to choose colors from anywhere on your computer screen, not just within the image window. Click in the image window to start, and hold down the mouse button as you move the Eyedropper around the screen. You can pick up colors from your desktop wallpaper, another open image, a different program, and even Photoshop Elements' tabs and tools.

FIGURE 21.6
This pink flower petal contains a lot of red and blue and almost no green—not really surprising.

As you know, you can switch to the default colors of black and white by clicking the Default Colors button on the toolbar. You can also just press D, which is much faster. And you can swap the Foreground and Background colors by clicking the Switch Foreground and Background button—or by pressing X.

Using the Shape Tools

Can't draw a straight line or a round circle? Neither can I. In the Computer Age, we don't need to know how to do those things because Photoshop Elements can do it for us. Our job is to know what we want to draw, how big we want to make it, and where we want to put it; the software does the rest. In this case, the Shape tools do the job. They include the Rectangle, Rounded Rectangle, and Ellipse tools (for drawing squares, circles, rectangles, and ellipses); the Polygon tool (for drawing regular polygons with anywhere from 3 to 100 sides); the Line tool (self-explanatory); and the Custom Shape tool, which can draw any of 568 different built-in shapes, including simple clip-art-type pictures (see Figure 21.7). Finally, you use the Shape Selection tool to select individual shapes and manipulate them.

To draw a shape, you first choose the Shape tool you want to use. With the Custom Shape tool, you then choose a shape from the pop-up menu in the Options bar. Set the other options (color, style, and so on), and then click and drag in the image window (see Figure 21.8). Most people drag downward and to the right so that the starting point becomes the shape's upper-left corner, but you can actually drag in any direction that suits you. No matter which way you drag, the shape will be right-side-up and facing the right way; the only way to make a shape upside-down or backward is to transform it after creating it.

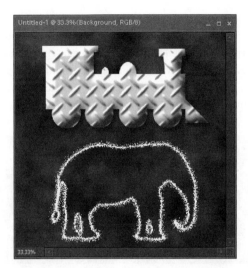

FIGURE 21.7
The train engine and the elephant are just two of the hundreds of shapes the Custom Shape tool can create.

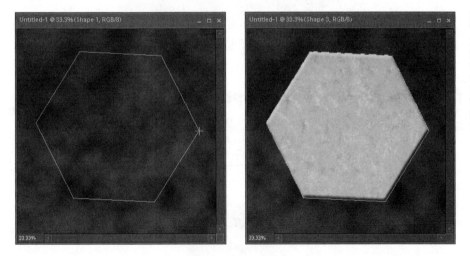

FIGURE 21.8
The shape's outline appears as you draw it; when you release the mouse button, the style is applied to the shape.

By default, each shape is placed on its own layer, which is named Shape and a number. You can change this setting so that you can place more than one shape on a layer, if you want, and you can combine multiple shapes on a layer to create one big shape. Keep reading to learn more about these features.

Changing the Style

Now, when we're talking about shapes, we're not talking about plain white squares and circles. No way—Photoshop Elements' styles are made to be applied to shape layers, meaning that your shapes will never be boring. You don't have to use the Effects menu, either; there's a Style pop-up menu right in the Shape tools' Options bar, next to the color swatch (see Figure 21.9). You can choose a color or a style before you start drawing or after you've completed a shape. Of course, if you prefer to use the Effects palette to apply styles to shapes, you can definitely do that. Click the second button at the top of the palette to see just layer styles.

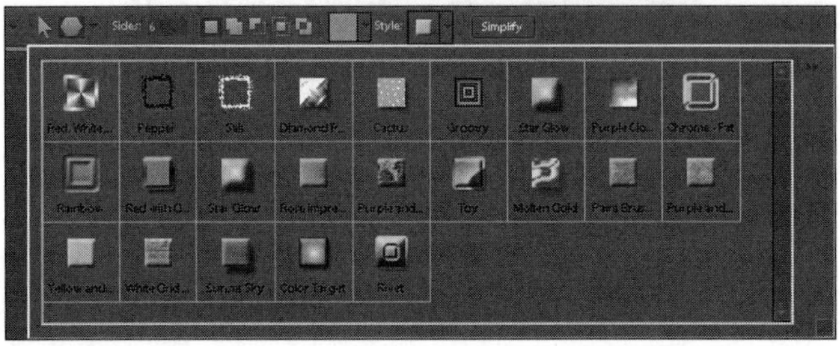

FIGURE 21.9
Click the triangle next to the style swatch to see your style choices; choose from a menu of other style categories by clicking the double arrow.

To apply a style to an existing shape, click the shape's layer in the Layers palette; then choose a style from the pop-up menu in the Options bar or double-click a thumbnail in the Effects palette.

Setting the Geometry Options

Here's another area where the computer's capabilities really outshine people's abilities. When using the Shape tools, you can set options for each kind of shape that control its shape, size, and other attributes (see Figure 21.10). Here's a rundown of what options are available for each Shape tool:

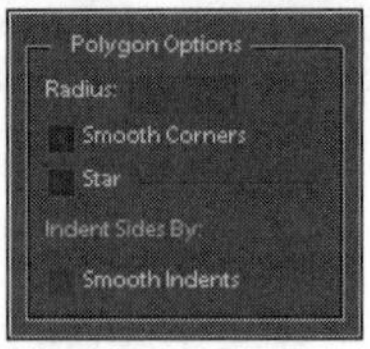

FIGURE 21.10
Click the triangle next to the Shape tool's icon in the Options bar to see its geometry options.

▶ **Rectangle and Rounded Rectangle**—Each shape starts out with the Unconstrained option set, which means you can create it in any size or proportions. Click Square to force the shape's height and width to be the same. To create the shape at a particular size, click Fixed Size and enter the width and height you want to use. If you prefer, you can restrict the proportions by clicking Proportional and entering a ratio in the Width and Height fields (2 and 1, respectively, for a shape that's twice as wide as it is tall, for instance). Check the From Center box if you want to start drawing the shape at its center; this is the best way to center the shape on a particular point in the image. Finally, the Snap to Pixels box forces the shape to align perfectly with the picture's pixels so that it won't be distorted if you're using a low resolution.

▶ **Ellipse**—These options are similar to those for the Rectangle and Rounded Rectangle tools, but instead of Square, you have Circle. There's no Snap to Pixels box because a curved line can't align perfectly with square pixels.

▶ **Polygon**—The first option for a polygon is Radius, where you can enter a specific measurement for the shape's radius (not its diameter). Because the tool creates only regular polygons, there's no option for setting proportions; the ratio for polygons is always 1 to 1. You can check the Smooth Corners box if you want the shape to have rounded corners, such as those on a rounded rectangle. Check the Star box to make a star with the specified number of points instead of a polygon with that number of sides, and then enter a percentage in the Indent Sides By field to determine how large the star's points are compared to its round center. If you want rounded indentations, check the Smooth Indents box (see Figure 21.11).

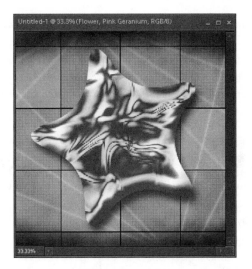

FIGURE 21.11
This star (which uses the Molten Gold style) has both rounded corners and rounded indentations, and its Indent Sides By value is 50%.

▶ **Line**—Lines themselves really don't have any geometry options because their only variables are length, width, and angle. However, you can add arrowheads to your lines by checking the Start box, the End box, or both. The

Width, Length, and Concavity fields control how wide and how long the arrowheads are, and whether their flat ends angle inward or are straight (see Figure 21.12).

FIGURE 21.12
The arrowheads on this line are 500% as wide as the line and 1,000% as long; their Concavity is set to 20%.

▶ **Custom Shape**—The options start with Unconstrained chosen, but you can switch to Defined Proportions (the proportions built into the particular shape you're using) or Defined Size (the built-in size, which might or might not be the size you want). You can choose Fixed Size and then specify Width and Height, and you can choose to draw the shape from the center instead of from its corner.

Combining Shapes to Create Complex Shapes

Ordinarily, each shape you draw appears on its own layer. If you want to combine shapes into more complex shapes, however, you can use buttons on the Options bar to determine exactly how that happens. The first button, Create New Shape Layer, is the default setting and creates a new layer on which you draw your shape; click one of the other buttons to keep drawing on the current shape layer (see Figure 21.13). Add to Shape Area just puts a second shape on the layer; Subtract from Shape Area deletes any overlapping area between the new shape and the old one, keeping the new shape uncolored. Intersect Shape Areas colors only the overlapping area, and Exclude Overlapping Shape Areas colors all the new shape and the old one except the overlapping area.

Subtract from Shape Area
Add to Shape Area ─┐   ┌─ Intersect Shape Areas
Create New Shape Layer ──────┐   ┌────── Exclude Overlapping Shape Areas

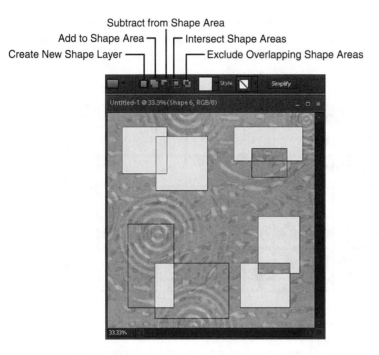

FIGURE 21.13
Clockwise from top left, you see the results of Add to Shape Area, Subtract from Shape Area, Intersect Shape Areas, and Exclude Overlapping Shape Areas.

As you draw additional shapes, you can switch to other Shape tools in the toolbox. Use the Shape Selection tool (accessible via the toolbox or the Options bar) to select and move a single shape when you've got multiple shapes on a layer. You also can combine multiple shapes on the same layer into a single shape; use the Select Shape tool to select the shapes you want to merge, and then click Combine on the Options bar. After you combine shapes, you can no longer select or move the original individual shapes.

Merging shape layers simplifies the shapes, turning them into pixels so that they're no longer editable. You can resize a simplified shape or transform it in other ways, but you're no longer able to combine multiple shapes on a layer or change the fill color using the Options bar.

Watch Out!

Creating a Custom Shape

Drawing a custom shape is just as easy as drawing any other shape. With your image file open in the Editor, choose a shape from the menu in the Options bar, and then choose a color, a style, or both (some styles make use of the shape color; others don't). Click and drag, and you're done.

Photoshop Elements' custom shapes are divided by category into several libraries, accessible via the double arrow at the right side of the shape picker menu. Also in this menu are options to view the shapes with small or large thumbnails (I used large ones in Figure 21.14) or as a list.

The complex layer styles look best on shapes that are silhouettes instead of outlines. Thin lines don't offer enough room for the style to show up; you need large filled areas for that.

Using the Brush Tool

Both Photoshop Elements and traditional Photoshop are considered image editors—programs designed for modifying existing images. But they also have much in common with another category of software, called paint programs. From the earliest days of MacPaint (R.I.P.) to the latest incarnation of Corel Painter, the natural-media king, artists have spent the last quarter-century learning how to let the computer do the messy parts of their jobs for them. For you, that means mastering Photoshop Elements' Brush tool.

The basics of painting with the Brush tool don't need much explanation. First, you choose a color; we talked about several ways to do this at the beginning of this hour. Then you click the Brush tool, make any necessary changes to the settings in the Options bar, and target the layer you want to paint on. You paint with the Brush by clicking and dragging it within the image window. If a selection is active, you can paint only within the selected area.

You can paint on the Background layer or on any regular layer, assuming that it's not locked in the Layers palette. If you try to paint on a type or shape layer, however, Photoshop Elements asks you if it's okay to simplify that layer first. If you don't want to lose the ability to edit that layer, click No and choose another layer on which to paint.

By the Way

Setting Brush Options

Perhaps more than any other tool, the Brush requires you to check its Options bar settings before painting. Don't get me wrong—you *can* start painting right away, but there are so many variables in Brush settings that you're likely to need to undo, change settings, and try again. The Brush does retain the last settings you used with it, except for color, so if you've settled in for a long session and you've got all your settings the way you want them, you're fine to just keep going.

Let's take a look at the Brush's Options bar to see what variables you can change when using this tool (see Figure 21.15). First, you'll need to choose a brush tip from the pop-up menu. You have a choice of many different sizes and shapes, and some are hard-edged while others are soft-edged. If you have trouble distinguishing subtle differences among various tips, click the double arrow and switch to Stroke Thumbnail so that you can see a stroke drawn with each brush tip instead of just its outline. When you find a brush that's the right shape and close to the right size, click it and then adjust the size using the pop-up menu right next to the Brushes menu.

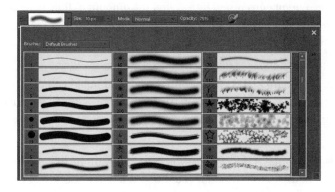

FIGURE 21.15
Photoshop Elements' brushes aren't all boring, round-tipped ones.

To enlarge your brush tip on the fly, press] (the closing square bracket) repeatedly; use [the same way to reduce the brush's size. Make sure you're using Normal Brush Tip cursors so that you can see the brush's size in the image window even when you're not painting with it. To change the type of cursor you see when you're using a painting tool, choose Edit, Preferences, Display & Cursors.

The next section of the Brush's Options bar contains pop-up menus that control blending mode and opacity. Opacity is, of course, the opposite of transparency; with an Opacity setting of 0%, you won't paint anything, and with Opacity set at 50%, you'll be able to see anything below your Brush strokes. The blending mode you choose affects how the new color and the old color blend when you paint over a nontransparent area. In Normal blending mode, the new color simply covers the old color (assuming that you also have the Brush's opacity set at 100%). The other blending modes combine the two colors in different ways, using yet more obscure math that I'm really glad Adobe's programmers know how to do, because I sure don't.

By the Way

I've been promising to explain blending modes "later in the book" for quite some time now, so it gives me great pleasure to confirm that we finally talk about all the different blending modes and how to use them in the next hour—Hour 22, "Making Composite Images."

You click the Airbrush button, which is next on the Options bar, to turn Airbrush mode on or off. When you're working in Airbrush mode, you can control how much paint is applied at any given spot by varying the amount of time you hold down the mouse button as you hover in that spot. Color builds up with repeated strokes over the same area, just as it would with a real-life airbrush (see Figure 21.16).

Finally, the Brush tool has additional options available under the Brush icon on the Options bar (see Figure 21.17). These control what you might call the "physical" attributes of the Brush: how hard it's pressing against the canvas, whether it's hard or soft, what angle it's being held at, and so on. From top to bottom, they're as follows:

▶ **Fade**—This value is the distance you can drag with the Brush until the paint fades to nothing, as it would if you dragged a real brush across a real canvas. Low values make the paint fade out quickly, and higher ones make it fade more slowly. A setting of 0 removes the Fade effect entirely.

▶ **Hue Jitter**—Enter a value here to enable your paint strokes to switch back and forth between the Foreground and Background colors; with higher values, the colors change more often.

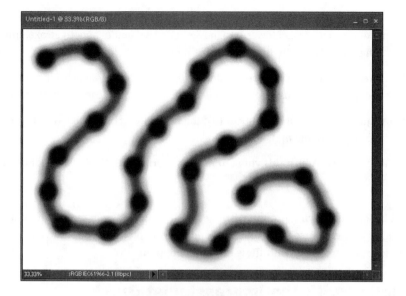

FIGURE 21.16
Each dot along the line is a place where I stopped moving the mouse for a minute to let the paint build up.

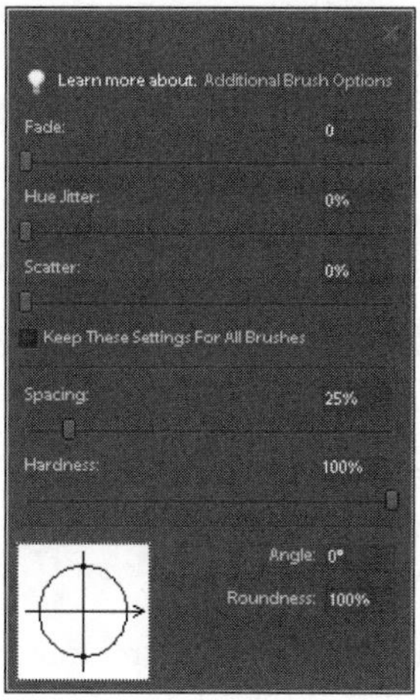

FIGURE 21.17
Who knew there were so many aspects to a simple paintbrush?

▶ **Scatter**—A low value clusters paint marks together along your Brush strokes, with little deviation from the stroke path; higher values allow stray paint marks to appear.

▶ **Keep These Settings for All Brushes**—Check this box to use the current Fade, Hue Jitter, and Scatter settings for all brush tips and disregard the default settings for the selected tip.

▶ **Spacing**—This setting controls the distance between the brush marks that make up each stroke; lower spacing settings give you a smooth stroke, and higher ones make the Brush skip as it paints.

▶ **Hardness**—You can use the Hardness slider to override the default hardness settings for each brush tip; the value is a percentage of the brush diameter.

▶ **Angle**—If the brush is elliptical (see the next setting, Roundness), this control specifies the angle of its long axis.

▶ **Roundness**—Adjust this value to make the brush elliptical instead of perfectly round.

Don't be leery of playing around with the Brush Options; if you're going to paint instead of restrict yourself to retouching and filtering pictures, you'll have much more scope for creativity with these additional options.

Painting with the Impressionist Brush

The name of this tool is a bit misleading because when you "paint" with it, you're not laying down new color. Instead, the Impressionist Brush rearranges the pixels in the existing image to make them look like the brushstrokes in an Impressionist painting (see Figure 21.18). Its Options bar controls are much like those for the regular Brush; instead of an Airbrush button, however, you have a special menu of additional options for the way the Impressionist Brush works:

▶ **Style**—This determines the shape of the brush stroke; the style names are pretty self-explanatory.

▶ **Area**—This value determines how large the brush strokes are. Each stroke is based where your brush goes, but it extends farther than the width of the brush tip, even when Area is set to 0.

▶ **Tolerance**—Change this number to control how close in color adjacent pixels need to be for the Impressionist Brush to affect them. Unless this value is set close to 0, you won't see much change in your image as you paint.

Each stroke with the Impressionist Brush blurs the area under the brush, but it also smudges and swirls it according to the Style you've chosen.

FIGURE 21.18
The left half of this picture has been "Impression-ized"; the right half is the sharp, colorful, and boring original.

Try it Yourself ▼

Create an Impressionist Masterpiece

Even if you think you have no artistic talent whatsoever, you *can* paint an Impressionist work. Start by downloading `iris.jpg` from the book's website at www.informit.com/title/9780672330179 (see Figure 21.19). Open it in the Editor's Full Edit mode, and follow these steps:

1. Switch to the Impressionist Brush and change your brush Size to 10 pixels. Set the Opacity at 75%.

By the Way

If you were using the regular Brush, you'd want to set your Foreground color at this point. With the Impressionist Brush, you don't have to worry about color; the brush uses the image colors, not the Foreground color.

▼

2. In the special Impressionist Brush settings on the Options bar, choose Tight Medium from the Style pop-up menu. Then set Area to 30 pixels and Tolerance to 5.

3. Carefully go over the image with the brush, making short strokes that follow the contours of the image. Drag quickly along each leaf and petal, and go over the street, the flagpole, and the building in the background. Paint over the sky, too, although you won't see much change because it's all the same color.

4. Go back to the Impressionist Brush settings in the Options bar and lower the Tolerance to 0%. Now lightly go back over any areas of the image that didn't get adequately smudged on the previous pass. This is likely to include the street and its yellow lines, as well as some of the leaves (see Figure 21.20).

iris.jpg @ 66.7%(RGB/8)

66.67%

FIGURE 21.20
The vivid colors
of the iris
remain, but its
detail is soft-
ened in the
Impressionist
style.

Using the Pencil Tool

Most of the work done with the Pencil tool comes under the heading of touch-up
rather than creation of original art. The Pencil can't make soft-edged strokes, so any
line you draw with it is solid black, unlike a line you'd draw with a pencil in real
life. But that doesn't mean you won't find plenty of uses for the Pencil here and
there.

Setting Pencil Options

The main difference between the Brush and the Pencil is that the Pencil's tip is
always hard-edged, no matter what it looks like in the Options bar preview. You can
use all the same brush tips that the Brush can use, but the soft-edged ones aren't
soft when used with the Pencil. That said, the tool works the same way the Brush
does: Set the Foreground color, choose a brush tip, and then click and drag in the
image window.

Replacing One Color with Another

The Pencil could well be called a one-trick pony—and this is the trick. When you check the box labeled Auto Erase in the Pencil's Options bar, you make the Pencil into an eraser of sorts. If you click on an area of Foreground color in the image window, the Pencil erases to the Background color. Then if you click in the area of Background color and draw, it uses the Foreground color (see Figure 21.21). Background on Foreground, Foreground on Background. If you click on any other color in the image, the Pencil draws with the Foreground color.

FIGURE 21.21
I created this image without switching colors or using the Eraser; first, I drew the large shape with the Pencil, then I drew on it to produce the Background color, and then I drew in more of the Foreground color in the middle.

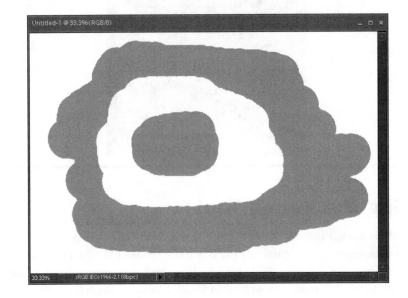

Using the Eraser Tools

Any time you draw, you'll end up erasing at some point. In fact, for artists, erasers aren't just about deleting mistakes; they're used to soften edges and create light in the midst of shadows. Photoshop Elements has a plain old Eraser tool that I suspect you'll find more handy than you ever thought you would. It also has two specialized Eraser tools: the Background Eraser and the Magic Eraser.

Erasing with the Eraser Tool

The Eraser tool operates differently, depending on what kind of layer is active. If you're working on the Background layer, the Eraser erases to the Background color, but if you're working on a regular layer, the Eraser erases to transparency. It can't erase pixels on multiple layers at the same time.

When using the Eraser, the first thing to do is choose a mode in the Options bar. Block mode erases a square whose size is always the same relative to your screen (16 monitor pixels), which means it grows larger as you zoom out of the image and smaller as you zoom in. Brush and Pencil modes enable you to use different brush tips and vary their size, just like the tools they're named after. Pencil mode is always hard-edged, just as with the Pencil tool, but Brush mode can use soft-edged brushes so that the eraser effect fades out at the edges of strokes (see Figure 21.22).

FIGURE 21.22
Using a soft-edged brush tip blurs the edges of the erased area.

Next, if you're using Brush or Pencil mode, you can vary the Size of the Eraser and its Opacity; set the Opacity to 100% to erase things completely, and make the percentage lower to leave traces behind. When your options are set, all you need to do to use the Eraser is click and drag, just as with the Brush or the Pencil.

Erasing with the Magic Eraser

The Magic Eraser is something else again. You can tell it to erase only a specific color or range of colors and ignore anything that's a different color. It works like a combination of using the Magic Wand and pressing Delete, in a single step. And similar to the Magic Wand, it's a tool that's used by clicking, not clicking and dragging, so you can't choose its size.

FIGURE 21.23
This picture
used to include
a rhinoceros,
but I got rid of
him easily with
the Magic
Eraser.

You can set some options for the Magic Eraser, as follows:

▶ **Tolerance**—Like the Magic Wand's Tolerance setting, this value determines
how similar to the pixel you're clicking on the neighboring pixels must be in
order for the Magic Eraser to affect them. With low tolerance settings, you
erase small areas, maybe just a pixel at a time. Higher settings enable you to
erase more at a time because you're allowing the Magic Eraser to overlook
minor color variations in the object you're erasing.

▶ **Anti-alias**—This option smooths the edges of the erased area by only partially erasing pixels at the outer edge of the erased area.

▶ **Contiguous**—Check this box if the image you're working on has other objects
the same color as the one you're erasing. That way, the Magic Eraser removes
only pixels that are adjacent to where you click. If the Contiguous box is
unchecked, the Magic Eraser works on pixels of the appropriate colors
throughout the image.

▶ **All Layers**—This is the exception to the rule I stated earlier, that the Eraser
works on only one layer at a time. With the Magic Eraser, you can choose to
erase pixels from just the current layer or from all layers.

▶ **Opacity**—If you enter a value less than 100%, the Magic Eraser erases areas
only partially, making them partially transparent.

Erasing with the Background Eraser

Similar to the Magic Eraser, the Background Eraser chooses which pixels to erase based on the colors of the pixels over which you drag it. To use it effectively, you need to pay close attention to its cursor, which is a circle surrounding a tiny cross called a hotspot. As you drag the Background Eraser across the picture, it analyzes the pixels directly under the hotspot and erases any pixels it passes over that are close enough to that color. Any pixels of other colors are left alone. You can actually drag the edge of the Background Eraser brush over objects you *don't* want to erase, as long as the hotspot stays clear of them. This enables you to clean up background pixels right next to the foreground object that you want to retain, without affecting the object.

FIGURE 21.24
Here I'm using the Background Eraser to delete the mulch behind the flowers, while leaving the flowers untouched.

Unlike the Magic Eraser, the Background Eraser is a click-and-drag tool, so its Options bar has a Brush pop-up menu in which you can specify the size, softness, and other attributes of the tool's tip. The Brush settings work just like the Brush Options, explained earlier in this chapter.

> The Background Eraser doesn't come with a choice of brush tips in a handy palette, primarily because it's extremely unlikely that you'd want to use anything other than a plain round brush with the Background Eraser.

By the Way

The Background Eraser offers you two more choices about how it works. First, the Limits pop-up menu contains two options: Discontiguous and Contiguous. Discontiguous erases any pixels within the circle that are close enough to the hotspot color, and Contiguous restricts the Background Eraser to erasing areas that both contain the hotspot color and are next to each other. You determine how close to the hotspot color a pixel under the eraser must be for it to be erased by adjusting the Tolerance, which is just like the Tolerance settings for the Magic Wand and the Magic Eraser.

Summary

The next time you get the artistic urge, you'll be fully equipped to act on it using the tools and techniques you learned in this hour. We started with one of the most basic components of art: color. You learned how to choose new colors using the color pickers and the Color Swatches palette, and you saw how the Eyedropper can pick up colors from within the image itself. Then we moved on to drawing basic and custom shapes, combining shapes, and applying style to shape layers. Next we turned to drawing and painting; you learned how to paint with the Brush and the Impressionist Brush, including how you can use different brush tips and customize the brush tip settings to fit your needs. I showed you how to draw with the Pencil tool and how to use it as an eraser, and then we went over the real Eraser tools, including the Eraser, the Magic Eraser, and the Background Eraser.

Q&A

Q. *If I enter the same numeric values in the Adobe color picker and my system color picker, will the resulting colors be the same?*

A. Yes, they will. Numbers are numbers, so the colors won't differ at all.

Q. *What's the difference between combining shapes and merging shape layers?*

A. Combining shapes turns them into bigger, more complex shapes, but it doesn't take away their special editable status. They still reside on shape layers, and you can still move and resize shapes without having to transform them. If you merge shape layers, on the other hand, they turn into regular layers, just as though you'd painted the shapes by hand.

Q. *Can I paint with two colors at once?*

A. Yes, you can. When the Brush is active, click the Brush icon on the Options bar to open the Brush Options menu. Enter a percentage in the Hue Jitter field to determine how often the Brush switches back and forth between the Foreground and Background colors.

Workshop

We covered a lot of ground in this hour, so there are several different activities for you to try. First, do the quiz questions, to make sure you're crystal clear on everything you've learned this hour.

Quiz

1. Pressing X on the keyboard does what?

    A. Deletes the current shape

    B. Inverts the image

    C. Displays the Info palette

    D. Switches the Foreground and Background colors

2. Photoshop Elements can draw polygons with up to _____ sides.

    A. 12

    B. 100

    C. 256

    D. 1,000

3. The Impressionist Brush converts an existing photo into a "painting" done in the style of Monet or Renoir.

    A. True

    B. False

Quiz Answers

1. **D.** Pressing D returns the Foreground and Background colors to their defaults of black and white.

2. **B.** I think if you drew a polygon with 1,000 sides, it would be pretty much indistinguishable from a circle.

3. **A.** Okay, maybe this question isn't quite fair. I didn't actually mention the names of any Impressionist painters in this hour. But if you're not already familiar with the work of these artists, you should be. Spend a few minutes drinking in the beauty at The Impressionist Movement (www.impression-niste.net/impressionism_history.htm). You won't be sorry.

Activities

1. Open the color picker (either the Adobe one or your system one; it doesn't matter which) and enter the following values: Hue 206, Saturation 97, and Brightness 75. What color do you get? It should be a nice dignified blue. Now look at the RGB values for this color. Swap the Red value and the Blue value, and see what color you end up with. It should be a brownish mustard.

2. Draw simple shapes on the same layer, and then combine them so that the final shape forms the first letter of your first name. Then try the same with the first letter of your last name. Yes, I do know that *S* is a lot more challenging than *I*.

3. Switch to the Brush and paint some graffiti in another layer of the same image you created in the previous activity. Use at least three different brush tips and three different sizes.

4. Now switch to the Background Eraser. Merge the Background layer with all your shape layers. Then use the Background Eraser to get rid of all the white around the letters.

HOUR 22

Making Composite Images

What You'll Learn in This Hour:

- ▶ Adjusting scale and lighting in a composite
- ▶ Applying layer styles to image elements
- ▶ Using adjustment layers to fix flaws
- ▶ Working with tool and layer blending modes
- ▶ Applying special effects to image elements
- ▶ Incorporating prebuilt objects from the Content palette

Any time you combine two or more images into a single picture, you're creating a composite image. Composites can be as simple as a corporate logo superimposed over an advertising photo, or as complex as a full-scale photomontage by an artist such as Salvador Dalí. If you've never studied this art form, you'll enjoy the fascinating history of the art of photomontage at the Cut & Paste website (www.cutandpaste.info).

At any rate, creating composite images is more than just a matter of cutting and pasting one picture into another. You have to consider the lighting in each photo, the relative scales of the objects they contain, and ways to enhance the different elements so that they either combine seamlessly or stand on their own as separate parts of a whole, depending on the artistic effect you hope to achieve. We look at all these factors in this hour.

Working with Lighting and Scale

When you're combining images, you need to watch out for two dead giveaways that the images didn't come from the same place originally: their lighting and their relative scale.

If one photo was taken outdoors under harsh sunlight and the other was shot indoors with dim fluorescents, you'll need to do some fancy footwork to make the two blend. The angle of the light can also cause problems because the placement of shadows needs to be consistent throughout the composite for it to be convincing. Try to match lighting as closely as possible when you're choosing pictures for a composite (see Figure 22.1).

FIGURE 22.1
The darker, warmer lighting on the bichon frise at the left side of this composite makes it obvious that she wasn't in the original shot of the greyhound.

Scale is just as much of an issue; unless you're purposely going for a surreal effect, you really need to watch the relative sizes of the objects in your composites to make sure they're convincing. When you're working on a composite, try standing up and looking at the image from more than one angle and distance; this will help you spot elements that just aren't working and figure out what's wrong with them. Watch the positioning of objects that should be at the same level, too; for example, if an elephant is standing next to your cat, their feet should appear to be next to each other. Positioning one of the animals too high or too low destroys the illusion you're trying to create.

Did you Know?

To make sure you can change the size and position of each element without affecting anything else in the image, keep everything on separate layers as you work until you're sure you're done making changes. The fact that pasting automatically creates a new layer in Photoshop Elements makes this about as easy as it could possibly be.

Using Layer Styles to Create Composites

Layer styles, found in the Effects palette (choose Window, Effects), are special effects designed specifically to be applied to individual layers. Each layer style is a combination of color or gradient fills, lighting effects, surface textures, and other individual effects (see Figure 22.2). If you spent a lot of time fiddling with a layer in Full Edit mode, you could reproduce each of these effects yourself—but why bother? I'm all for letting Photoshop Elements do the work, when appropriate.

FIGURE 22.2
Here I selected the green moss around this decorative boulder, copied it to a new layer, and applied a Glass Button layer style to it to turn it into green Jell-O.

You worked with layer styles in Hour 8, "Adding Type," and Hour 21, "Creating Art from Scratch." It's common to jazz up type and shape objects using layer styles, but you can use them on any layer you want. They fall into 13 categories:

- **Bevels**—Sharp or rounded edges of varying widths

- **Complex**—Combinations of several of the other layer styles

- **Drop Shadows**—Soft or hard shadows of any size and color, appearing below the layer and overlapping any layers under it

- **Inner Glows**—A soft glow of any color emanating from the inside edges of an object

- **Outer Glows**—A soft glow of any color coming from the outside of an object

- **Visibility**—Modified opacity so that objects appear translucent or transparent

- **Glass Buttons**—A smooth, shiny, raised surface that appears to be transparent, in a variety of colors

▶ **Image Effects**—Natural and human-made effects such as fog, rain, snow, water reflection, and night vision

▶ **Patterns**—Natural and artificial textures, including fabric, stone, metal, drywall, and more

▶ **Photographic Effects**—Traditional darkroom effects such as sepia and negative

▶ **Wow Chrome**—Chrome effects of varying colors

▶ **Wow Neon**—A bright glow and a curved surface, to simulate neon tubes

▶ **Wow Plastic**—Similar to Glass Buttons, but gives you a less shiny surface

▼

Try It Yourself

Adding Layer Styles

Layer styles are "live," meaning that if you edit a layer's content, its style updates automatically to match the new shape and size of the layer's contents. To apply a style to a layer, follow these steps:

1. Choose Window, Effects to display the Effects palette (see Figure 22.3).

FIGURE 22.3
You can use the palette menu to change the size of the Effects palette's thumbnails.

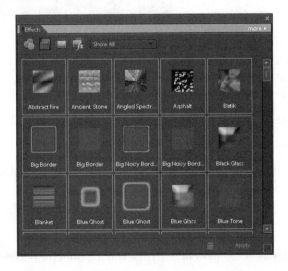

2. Click the Layer Styles button and choose a category of styles from the list.

3. In the Layers palette, click the layer to which you want to apply the style, to confirm that it's active. Make sure that the only things on it are the things that you want the style to affect.

▼

To remove an object from a new layer and place it on its own layer, select it and choose Layer, New Layer via Cut. It's helpful to hide all the other layers while you're working on the selection so that you can see what you're doing.

4. Double-click a style in the Effects palette to apply it to the current layer. An fx icon appears next to the layer's name in the Layers palette to indicate that a layer style has been applied.

Applying a layer style does *not* remove any previously applied styles; Photoshop Elements applies the new style over the old one. If the new style includes any transparency, you'll be able to see part of the old style through it. To remove all the layer styles you've applied to a layer, click the Clear Style button at the bottom of the Effects palette (it looks like a trash can). And, of course, you can remove a layer style that you just applied by clicking the Undo button.

After you've applied a style, or more than one style, you can modify it at any time by activating that layer and choosing Layer, Layer Styles, Style Settings, or double-clicking the fx icon in the Layers palette. The Style Settings dialog enables you to tweak the light angle and other attributes of a style to customize it for your own needs (see Figure 22.4). If your only problem with a style is that it's too big or too small for the objects you've applied it to, activate the layer and choose Layer, Layer Styles, Scale Style; then drag the slider to change the scale of the style relative to the objects on the layer.

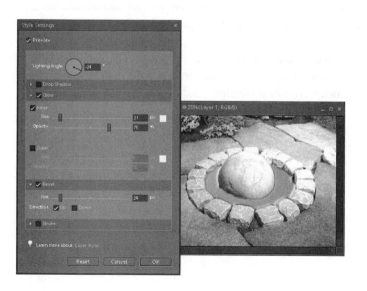

FIGURE 22.4
These are the layer-style settings for the green Jell-O layer shown in Figure 22.2.

Using Adjustment Layers to Fix Image Problems

We talked a lot in previous hours about making backup copies of images before you do anything irrevocable to them. That way, you can always go back to the original version if your edits don't work out the way you envisioned them or if you need to use the same original art in a different way for another project. Adjustment layers provide a different approach to preserving original images by enabling you to adjust color, lighting, and other attributes of a layer or several layers by putting the changes on their own layer.

For example, you could apply the Levels command to a layer, permanently modifying its contents, or you could create a Levels adjustment layer above the layer you want to modify. If you use the adjustment layer, you can change its Levels settings at any time, delete the adjustment layer, or move it to a different position in the Layers palette. You can group the adjustment layer with one or more other layers so that its effects are seen only on those layers. Meanwhile, the original layer stays just as it was, and you can always restore it to its original appearance.

Adding an Adjustment Layer

To add an adjustment layer, click the layer below where you want it to be. Then you have two choices. The quickest way to create the adjustment layer is to click the Create Adjustment Layer button on the Layers palette and choose the type of adjustment you want to apply from the pop-up menu (see Figure 22.5). Using this method, you don't get to specify a name for the layer; it's just named with the type of adjustment and a number, such as Gradient Map 1. If you want to give the layer a particular name when you create it, you need to choose Layer, New Adjustment Layer, and pick the type of adjustment from the submenu. Then you'll see the New Layer dialog (see Figure 22.6), where you can enter a name for the layer, group it with the layer underneath, choose a blending mode, and set its Opacity.

If you use the Layers palette pop-up menu to create an adjustment layer, you can change the new layer's name by double-clicking it in the Layers palette and typing the new name.

FIGURE 22.5
Here I'm adding a Hue/Saturation adjustment layer via the Layers palette.

FIGURE 22.6
The New Layer dialog that you see when adding an adjustment layer is the same one that you see when you add a regular layer.

The types of adjustment layer you can create are the same as many of the commands you used in earlier hours; others are fun effects you'll try out in the next hour. Here's the list:

▶ **Solid Color**—Makes the nontransparent areas of the layer appear to be filled with a solid color that you choose.

▶ **Gradient**—Places a gradient fill of your choice over the nontransparent areas of the layer.

▶ **Pattern**—Covers the nontransparent areas of the image with a pattern of your choice.

▶ **Levels**—Applies the same levels adjustments that we used in Hour 14, "Adjusting Brightness, Contrast, and Color."

▶ **Brightness/Contrast**—The same as the Brightness/Contrast command from Hour 14.

▶ **Hue/Saturation**—Works just like the Hue/Saturation dialog that you learned about in Hour 14.

▶ **Gradient Map:** A neat way to substitute a different new color for each color in an image. We look at this effect in Hour 23, "Going Wild with Your Images."

▶ **Photo Filter**—Subtly modifies the colors of the layers underneath it in the same way a special camera filter would. You have a choice of 20 different filters, including Violet, Sepia, and Underwater.

▶ **Invert**—Reverses all the colors on the layers below; we look at this effect in Hour 23, too.

▶ **Threshold**—Displays all the pixels on the layers below as either pure black or pure white. We try out this one in Hour 23 as well.

▶ **Posterize**—Reduces the colors in the picture to a specified number, for a pop art effect. Hour 23 covers this effect as well.

After you choose the adjustment type from the Layers palette's pop-up menu, or after you click OK in the New Layer dialog if you used the Layers menu command to create the adjustment layer, you'll see a dialog in which you can make whatever settings are appropriate for the type of adjustment you're using. For example, if you create a Levels adjustment layer, you'll see the Levels dialog, just like the one you worked with in Hour 14. Make your changes and click OK. To change the settings later, double-click the adjustment layer icon to reopen the initial dialog. You can't change the type of adjustment this way, however.

> If you want to temporarily hide the effects of an adjustment layer, just hide the layer itself by clicking the eye icon next to its name in the Layers palette.

Each adjustment layer has a built-in mask, whose icon you can see in the Layers palette. The mask controls where the effects of the layer adjustment show up; you can edit it to hide the effect on part of the layer while letting it show through elsewhere. We look at how to do this in the next section.

Editing the Adjustment Layer Mask

By default, a new adjustment layer's mask is all white, meaning that the effect shows through completely in all parts of the layer. If you have a selection active when you create the layer, however, that selection is automatically converted into the adjustment layer's mask. On the mask, the selected area is white (letting the effect show through), the unselected area is black (hiding the effect), and partially selected areas such as feathered edges are gray (partially hiding the effect).

You can edit the mask just as you would edit any grayscale image in Photoshop Elements, and you'll probably find it easier to edit if you can see the mask in the image window instead of working from the small Layers palette icon. To see the mask and the image at the same time, Shift+Alt+click the mask icon. Black areas of the mask are displayed in transparent red (see Figure 22.7); this looks just like the Selection Brush's mask mode (see Hour 7, "Making Selections and Using Layers"). If you'd rather see just the adjustment layer's mask, Alt+click the mask icon in the Layers palette to display the mask in the image window, in grayscale (see Figure 22.8).

FIGURE 22.7
In this view of my decorative boulder, the black areas of the mask show up in the image window as red.

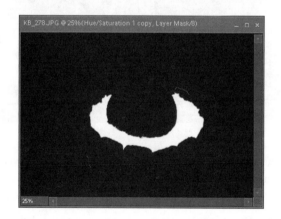

FIGURE 22.8
This view shows only the mask of the Jell-O layer, not the image.

When you click the mask's icon to edit it, Elements changes the Foreground and Background colors to white and black, respectively. You can use any tool to paint the mask, including the Impressionist Brush and the Gradient tool, or you can select areas and fill them or delete them. No matter what technique you use to modify the mask, when you're done, white areas allow the effect to show, black areas hide it, and gray areas make it partially visible.

Add Layer Styles and Adjustment Layers to a Boring Picture

The picture in Figure 22.9 should have been really cool. I was fascinated by the intricate detail of the thistle blossom, but I just couldn't capture all that visual interest in the photo. The flower was green, just like the leaves behind it, so it didn't stand out, and my hand just looks odd there at the side. There has to be a way to salvage this picture, though, so let's take a whack at it. You can download the photo from the book's website at www.informit.com/title/9780672330179 (it's called thistle.jpg) and work along with me.

FIGURE 22.9
This flower is dramatic on its own, but in this picture, it blends into the background.

1. Switch to the Selection Brush tool and use it to select the flower and the leaves that surround this particular blossom. Click along each leaf, and Alt+click in any areas included in the selection that you don't want to be part of it.

2. Choose Layer, New Layer Via Copy to put a copy of the flower on its own layer so that you can apply layer effects to it.

3. With the flower layer still active, double-click any of the Drop Shadow layer styles in the Effects palette to apply it. It doesn't matter which one you use because you'll modify the settings in the next step.

4. Choose Layer, Layer Style, Style Settings. Change the settings to match what you see in Figure 22.10. You're modifying the drop shadow, adding a bevel, and adding a stroke to the flower. Click the color swatch in the Stroke area and set the color to Red **194**, Green **145**, Blue **255** (a thistly sort of purple).

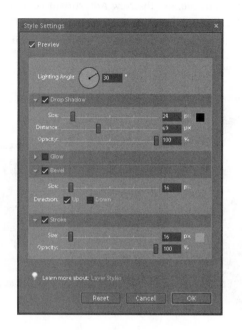

FIGURE 22.10
Here's what
your Style
Settings dialog
should look like.

5. Now click the Background layer in the Layers palette. Using the Selection Brush again, in the same way, select the hand. Don't miss the tiny bits you can see past the leaves!

6. With that selection still active, click the New Adjustment Layer button at the top of the Layers palette and choose Hue/Saturation to create a Hue/Saturation adjustment layer between the Background layer and the flower layer.

7. In the Hue/Saturation dialog, change the settings to Hue **+29**, Saturation **+74**, and Lightness **+26**, and then click OK. Because there was a selection active when you created the layer, it's masked so that the hue/saturation adjustment affects only the hand.

8. Click the Background layer again. Now you'll create a selection that includes everything in the picture *but* the flower and the hand. Start by Ctrl+clicking the flower layer's thumbnail to select just the flower.

9. Then press Shift and Ctrl+click on the Hue/Saturation adjustment layer's mask thumbnail to add the hand to the selection. Invert the selection so that it no longer includes the hand or the flower (choose Select, Inverse).

10. With the selection active, use the New Adjustment Layer button on the Layers palette to add a Posterize adjustment layer between the Background layer and the hue/saturation layer. Set the number of levels to **2** and click OK.

11. You're done! Your layers palette should look like Figure 22.11.

FIGURE 22.11
Your Layers palette should show the Background layer, two adjustment layers, and a regular layer with layer styles applied to it.

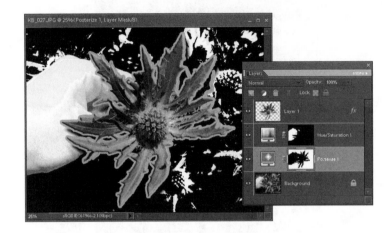

Figure 22.12 shows my version of the modified picture. The best part? The original picture is intact on the Background layer, so if I decide I don't like the way this picture came out after all, I can start over and make a whole new set of changes. Or I can simply change the settings on the adjustment layers and layer styles I applied, for a whole new effect.

FIGURE 22.12
I'm not sure it's art, and I'm also not sure how much I like it, but this version, with two adjustment layers and a few layer styles, definitely showcases the flower. It's in the color section so you can get a better look at it.

Understanding Blending Modes

You've been waiting a long time for this explanation, so let's hope I can make it a good one. Here goes.

Photoshop Elements' blending modes enable you to simulate the real-world phenomenon in which two colors mix to form a new color. In Photoshop Elements, you can go one better than real life because you can control exactly how those colors mix by choosing one of 25 different blending modes. Painting tools have blending modes that determine how the new colors applied by the tools interact with any colors underneath them. Some filters have blending modes; the dialog box that you see when you choose Edit, Fill Selection (remember it from Hour 7?) has a blending mode menu. And, of course, layers have blending modes. If a layer's blending mode is Normal, that layer's contents hide whatever's behind it. But if you choose a different blending mode, the colors on that layer blend with the colors of the layers beneath it.

Blending modes are based on math. Average, for example, looks at each pixel on the layer and the corresponding pixel on the layer below, averages their colors, and displays that color value instead of either of the original colors. When we're working with blending modes, we use the term *blend color* for the new color being applied and *base color* for the original color. Each of the 25 blending modes is shown using a simple graphic so you can see just what's happening. They're in the color section, too, and you'll want to check them out there because it's hard to see the differences in black and white.

▶ Normal is the default mode; the blend color replaces the base color.

▶ Dissolve converts a random number of pixels to the blend color, giving a spatter effect at any point where the blend color is partially transparent.

▶ Darken colors each color channel separately by choosing the darker of the blend color and the base color for each pixel in the channel. This can result in new colors.

▶ Multiply changes the colors by multiplying the base color and the blend color and using the result, which is always darker.

▶ Color Burn increases the contrast of the base color to match the blend color.

▶ Linear Burn decreases the brightness of the base color to match the blend color.

▶ Darker Color chooses the darker of the blend and base colors for each pixel; it doesn't produce new colors as Darken can.

▶ Lighten colors each color channel separately by choosing the lighter of the blend color and the base color for each pixel in the channel. This can result in new colors.

▶ Screen creates a lighter image by multiplying the inverse of the base and blend colors a each pixel.

▶ Color Dodge decreases the contrast of the base color to match the blend color's brightness.

▶ Linear Dodge (Add) increases the brightness of the base color to match the blend color's brightness.

▶ Lighter Color chooses the lighter of the blend and base colors for each pixel; it doesn't produce new colors as Lighten can.

▶ Overlay mixes the base color with the blend color to reflect the brightness or darkness of each pixel in the original image, using the Screen mode to lighten pixels and the Multiply mode to darken them.

▶ Soft Light dodges or burns the base color, depending on whether the blend color is lighter than 50% gray or darker than 50% gray, respectively.

▶ Hard Light multiplies or screens the base color, depending on whether the blend color is lighter than 50% gray or darker than 50% gray, respectively.

▶ Vivid Light darkens or lightens the base color by increasing or decreasing contrast, depending on whether the blend color is lighter than 50% gray or darker than 50% gray, respectively.

▶ Linear Light darkens or lightens the base color by increasing or decreasing brightness, depending on whether the blend color is lighter than 50% gray or darker than 50% gray, respectively (see Figure 22.13).

▶ Pin Light replaces the base color with the blend color where the base color is darker or lighter, depending on whether the blend color is lighter than 50% gray or darker than 50% gray, respectively.

▶ Hard Mix adds the color channel values of the blend color to those of the base color, turning the entire image into primary colors (red, green, blue, cyan, magenta, yellow, black, or white).

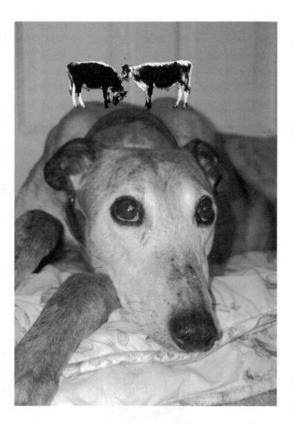

▶ Difference subtracts the blend color from the base color or the base color from the blend color, depending on which is brighter.

▶ Exclusion is similar to Difference but has lower contrast.

▶ Hue uses the brightness and saturation of the base color and the hue of the blend color.

▶ Saturation uses the brightness and hue of the base color and the saturation of the blend color.

▶ Color uses the brightness of the base color and the hue and saturation of the blend color.

▶ Luminosity uses the hue and saturation of the base color and the brightness of the blend color.

Normal

Dissolve

Darken

Multiply

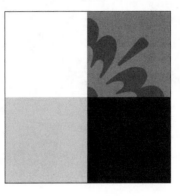

Color Burn

Linear Burn

Darker Color

Lighten

Screen

Color Dodge

Linear Dodge (Add)

Lighter Color

Overlay

Soft Light

Hard Light

Vivid Light

Linear Light

Pin Light

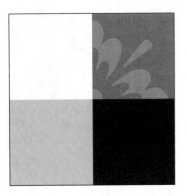

Hard Mix

Difference

Exclusion

Hue

Saturation

Color

Luminosity

Applying Photo Effects and Adding Content

But wait, there's more! That's right, in addition to layer styles, adjustment layers, and blending layers, Photoshop Elements has even more clever photo tricks it can perform. For one thing, you can use the Effects palette to apply 24 different photo effects to your image, in these categories: Faded Photo, Frame, Misc. Effects, Monotone Color, Old Photo, and Vintage Photo. And the Content palette (choose Window, Content) contains hundreds of graphics you can add to your images in these categories: Backgrounds, Frames, Graphics, Shapes, Text, and Themes. You can combine these tricks with all the other techniques you've learned so far to create truly unique images.

You've already worked with the Effects palette to apply filters (in Hours 19, "Using the Improvement Filters," and 20, "Using the Artistic Filters ") and layer styles (earlier in this hour). Now take a look at the photo effects it has to offer. The most important point to remember about these effects is that they're not editable as layer styles are. There are no settings to change; what you see is what you get, and any additional layers that are created in the course of applying the effect are merged so that you can't modify them individually (see Figure 22.14).

FIGURE 22.14
The Pencil Sketch photo effect did wonders for this dark photo.

You can see all the photo effects by clicking the third button at the top of the Effects palette (see Figure 22.15). You apply photo effects the same way you do layer styles, by double-clicking the thumbnail for the effect you want to use. Photoshop Elements duplicates the Background layer and applies the effect to the copy, so you can always delete the duplicate layer if you decide you don't like the effect.

FIGURE 22.15
Most of the thumbnails give a pretty good idea of how the photo effects look when applied to actual images, but some are pretty off, so you'll just have to try them and see what happens.

The Content palette, on the other hand, contains nothing but pictures. Some of them are designed to be dropped into your photos wherever you like, others are frames, and still others are backgrounds or even templates for party invitations or other kinds of documents you might create in Photoshop Elements. You can put a clown hat on Grandpa, stick a flower behind your sister-in-law's ear, and even add old-fashioned photo corners in any of five different colors (see Figure 22.16). To include anything from the Content palette in an image, just drag it to the image window and drop it. Backgrounds and frames are automatically sized and positioned; you can resize and move other objects using the Move tool.

Because there's so much, well, content in the Content palette, you can use the left pop-up menu at the top of the palette to choose how the stuff in the palette is organized—by Type, Activity, Color, Event, Mood, Object, Seasons, Style, Word, or All. After choosing one of these methods, you can choose categories from the right pop-up menu. For example, if you choose Seasons in the left menu, your choices in the right menu are Autumn, Spring, Summer, and Winter (see Figure 22.17).

FIGURE 22.16
Is it a tacky picture?
Absolutely. Did I have a great time making it?
Sure. And would it make a really cute card to send to the dog's owner?
Definitely.

FIGURE 22.17
I particularly like the backgrounds found in the Content palette; they're subtle and attractive.

Summary

We worked with layers and layer styles a lot in this hour, and you learned how to combine layers to create a composite image. You saw how to enhance layers with layer styles, photo effects, adjustment layers, and blending modes so that they stand out or blend in, whichever you prefer. You also learned about how lighting and scale affect the results when you combine images. And you took a look at all the prefab graphics in the Content palette that you can use to customize your pictures in your own way. In the next hour, we look at some more ways to get creative with your pictures.

Q&A

Q. *Can I make my own layer styles?*

A. Not officially, but there's a workaround. If you create a custom style you like, you can copy the style to apply it to other objects by clicking its layer and choosing Layer, Layer Style, Copy Style. To save the style for future use, apply it to a shape layer in an otherwise empty file and save the file with an appropriate name. Any time you need that style, open the document, click the shape layer, copy the style, and go back to the document where you want to use the style. Click the layer you want to apply it to and choose Layer, Layer Style, Paste Style.

Q. *What would happen if I painted on an adjustment layer's mask with colors other than black and white?*

A. Try it—you'll find that you can't. No matter what color you choose before you start editing the mask, you can paint on it only in grayscale.

Q. *Can I apply more than one blending mode at a time?*

A. Not to the same layer, no, but you can duplicate a layer and apply a different blending mode to each copy. This is a great way to get some funky effects. Try combining Dissolve with any other blending mode, for example.

Workshop

This might have been the most experimental hour so far. Photoshop Elements really lends itself to trying new techniques and combining them in different ways. To see how creative you can be with all the tools available to you, take this short quiz and then try the activities.

Quiz

1. Which artist experimented with photomontage?

    A. Renoir

    B. Goya

    C. Dalí

    D. Picasso

2. You can change the adjustment type and settings for an adjustment layer at any time.

> **A.** True
>
> **B.** False

3. Which one of these is *not* a Photoshop Elements blending mode?

> **A.** Screen
>
> **B.** Combine
>
> **C.** Overlay
>
> **D.** Linear Burn

Quiz Answers

1. **C.** You can see an example of his photomontage work (and buy a print of it) at 3D-Dali.com (www.3d-dali.com/Tour/Marilyn.htm).

2. **B.** False. You can always go back and change the settings, but after you've created an adjustment layer of a particular type, it's stuck being that type till the end of time.

3. **B.** It's actually a piece of farm equipment.

Activities

1. Find a picture that needs an adjustment and make a copy of it. In one file, make the adjustment with traditional tools (such as the Hue/Saturation dialog); in the other, make the same fix with an adjustment layer using the same settings. Is there any difference between the two finished files?

2. Locate a picture of yourself and add a type layer with your name. Try different combinations of layer effects and blending modes for the type layer until you get an effect you like.

Going Wild with Your Images

What You'll Learn in This Hour:

▶ How to turn a picture to liquid—or at least dampen it a bit

▶ Ways to twist a picture's colors inside out and backward

▶ Unusual effects to give your pictures a glow and distort their shapes in interesting ways

In this hour, we forget all about practicality and just have fun in the Editor's Full Edit mode—the kind of fun I remember having when I first discovered Photoshop's Distort filters. Photoshop Elements has those same filters (and a bunch that didn't exist back when I learned Photoshop), and I think it's time to give them a workout. None of the effects in this hour will ever appear in a picture on the front page of *The New York Times,* but they should give you some fodder for making your own desktop wallpaper, chat icons, and funny birthday cards. We'll smear pictures around, change their colors, make them glow, and generally mess them up in a bunch of entertaining ways. Let's do it!

Liquifying an Image

The first stop in our Fun Tour of Photoshop Elements is the Liquify filter, which distorts images as though their components had softened in the warm sun and run together. To get there, open the picture you want to liquify and choose Filter, Distort, Liquify. This is another one of those huge dialog boxes with its very own toolbox (see Figure 23.1). To liquify the picture, all you have to do is paint in the image preview, but you have a choice of several tools to do that with; each has a different way of distorting:

FIGURE 23.1
Each tool in the Liquify toolbox has its own unique method of messing up your image.

Warp Tool
Turbulence Tool
Twirl Clockwise Tool
Twirl Counter Clockwise Tool
Pucker Tool
Bloat Tool
Shift Pixels Tool
Reflection Tool
Reconstruct Tool
Zoom Tool
Hand Tool

- ▶ **Warp**—Works like the Smudge tool, enabling you to push pixels around.

- ▶ **Turbulence**—Creates a jittery effect, like a mirage. You can drag the Turbulent Jitter slider in the Tool Options area to the right to increase the amount of turbulence applied with each click or brush stroke.

- ▶ **Twirl Clockwise**—Rotates the image area under the brush clockwise. Click and hold in one spot to keep turning the area.

- ▶ **Twirl Counter Clockwise**—Rotates the image area under the brush counterclockwise. Click and hold in one spot to keep turning the area.

- ▶ **Pucker**—Pulls surrounding pixels toward the brush as you paint.

- ▶ **Bloat**—Pushes surrounding pixels away from the brush as you paint (see Figure 23.2).

- ▶ **Shift Pixels**—Moves pixels to the left of the direction you drag. Press Alt as you drag to move pixels to the right instead.

- ▶ **Reflection**—Copies pixels from one side of your brush stroke to the other.

You can set the Brush Size and Brush Pressure for all these tools in the Tool Options area of the dialog. Higher Brush Pressure settings distort more with each click or brush stroke. The Liquify toolbox also supplies you with a Reconstruct tool; paint with this tool to remove distortion and restore the image to its original appearance. You'll also find the customary Zoom and Hand tools, which work just like their counterparts in Photoshop Elements' regular toolbox so that you can move around in the image preview and see what you're doing.

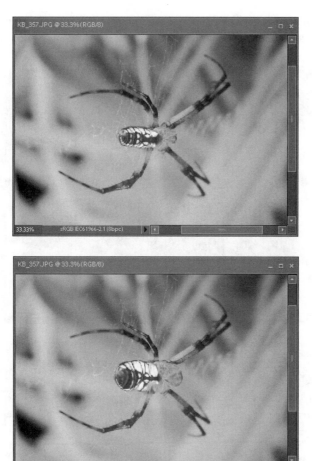

FIGURE 23.2
I wanted to put this spider on the front of a Halloween party invitation, but it just wasn't scary enough, so I used the Bloat tool to bulk it up some.

If you're using a pressure-sensitive graphics tablet, choose Stylus Pressure in the Brush Pressure pop-up menu. And if you've never tried a tablet, I highly recommend it. Think about how much easier it is to sign your name with a pen than it would be to make that signature with the mouse. Now think about how much more free and easy your brush strokes could be with a tablet and stylus. I like the Wacom series of tablets; they're well designed. The Bamboo Fun tablet sells for $99 or less and includes Photoshop Elements in the box—such a deal!

Did you Know?

To paint in a straight line, click and then Shift+click to set the end of the line; this works with the Warp, Shift Pixels, and Reflection tools (see Figure 23.3). If you decide you want to undo everything you've done so far and start over, either click Revert to restore the original picture and reset all the tools to their original settings, or press Alt and click Reset to bring back the picture but leave the tools as they are.

FIGURE 23.3
Using the
Reflection tool, I
created a reflec-
tion of this vin-
tage car in the
parking lot next
to it.

Twisting Colors

Tired of the same old colors—blue sky, green grass, red brick buildings, and black asphalt? I can show you more than one way to fix that problem. Keep reading to learn how to twist the colors in your pictures four different ways, and then how to turn everyday objects into gold, silver, or copper.

Using Gradient Map

When you apply the Gradient Map filter, you get to choose or create a color gradient, with each color shading into the next (see Figure 23.4). Photoshop Elements turns the darkest areas of your image into the color at the extreme left end of that gradient, and does the same with the lightest areas of the image and the extreme right end of the gradient. Everything in between is mapped to its corresponding position on the gradient. So if you used a simple black-to-white gradient, the picture would just be converted to grayscale. If you used a red to white gradient, the picture would be rendered in shades of red, ranging from pure red to palest pink and then white.

FIGURE 23.4
This gradient starts with yellow on the left, shades into purple and then orange in the middle, and then turns blue.

Start by opening an image and choosing Filter, Adjustments, Gradient Map. To change the gradient the filter will use, click the gradient swatch in the Gradient Map dialog to open the Gradient Editor. Pick a gradient from the Presets area or edit one to create your own (see sidebar); the More menu gives you additional gradient collections from which to choose. When you've chosen the gradient you want, click OK; then check the appropriate box if you want to turn on either of the Gradient Options: Dither, which adds random noise to make the gradient look smoother, or Reverse, which swaps the direction of the gradient fill, changing which colors get mapped to black and white in your image. Click OK again to admire your picture in its full glory (see Figure 23.5).

FIGURE 23.5
Remember, you're changing not only the picture's colors, but also its brightness and contrast. Be sure to check out this image in the color section.

Mixing Your Own Gradients

Photoshop Elements' Gradient Editor dialog looks a bit intimidating, but don't let it slow you down. The process of creating a new gradient is really very simple (see Figure 23.6).

First, pick a gradient that's close to what you want. Then you can start changing it.

Want to change an existing color? Click its color stop, the little square handle below the gradient preview bar, and then click the Color swatch in the Stops area to open the color picker and choose a new color. Want to add a new color in its own position? Click beneath the bar to add a new stop; then click the stop to change its color (all new stops start out black).

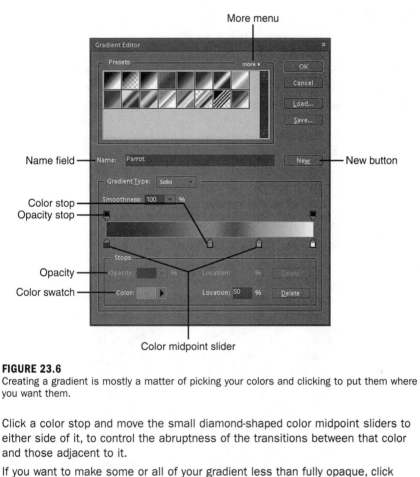

FIGURE 23.6
Creating a gradient is mostly a matter of picking your colors and clicking to put them where you want them.

Click a color stop and move the small diamond-shaped color midpoint sliders to either side of it, to control the abruptness of the transitions between that color and those adjacent to it.

If you want to make some or all of your gradient less than fully opaque, click above the bar to add an opacity stop; then enter an Opacity percentage for it in the Stops area. Click an existing opacity stop to change its Opacity percentage.

And to move either kind of stop, just click and drag it. When you're happy, enter a name for your gradient and click the New button to put it up into the Presets area so you can use it again, and then click OK.

You can also create a gradient map using an adjustment layer instead of a filter; this way, you can change its settings later in the editing process. In the Layers palette, choose Gradient Map from the New Adjustment Layer pop-up menu, and then proceed just as if you were using the filter. To change the settings, double-click the layer's icon in the Layers palette.

Did you Know?

Using Invert

The Invert filter does two things at once. First, it changes each color in an image to its opposite on the color wheel. So red changes to light blue, green changes to pink, and so on. The filter also inverts the brightness of each pixel in the picture so that shadows become highlights and vice versa. To apply the Invert filter, choose Filter, Adjustments, Invert (see Figure 23.7).

FIGURE 23.7
These red roses turned a lovely cyan color when I inverted the image.

You might think that you could scan a color negative and then apply Invert to the image to make a positive. Unfortunately, you'd be wrong because color print film is tinted orange. If you do invert a negative, however, you can work with the Adjust Color commands in the Enhance menu to restore a natural color balance.

Posterizing Colors

Posterizing is another fun effect that I like to combine with Invert. It enables you to dramatically reduce the number of colors in the picture, to achieve a pop art feel. Choose Filter, Adjustments, Posterize to get started (see Figure 23.8). The only choice you have to make for the Posterize filter is how many color levels you want to use in the resulting picture. The number you choose determines how many levels are used in each color channel, so multiply that number by three (for the red, green, and blue channels) to determine how many colors the image will contain overall.

FIGURE 23.8
The inverted roses look even cooler when they're posterized.

> You can also apply the Posterize filter via an adjustment layer so that you can change the settings at any time.

By the Way

Adjusting the Threshold

If the Posterize filter leaves in too many colors for you, you need the Threshold filter. This command converts the image into all black and white pixels. Choose Filter, Adjustments, Threshold, or create a new Threshold adjustment layer. In the Threshold dialog box, first click the Preview box and then drag the slider to determine the point at which black changes into white (see Figure 23.9).

FIGURE 23.9
After using the Threshold command, I used the Hue/Saturation command to change the black to pink; and then I filled the entire image with a light blue using the Darken blending mode in the Fill Layer dialog and applied a burlap texture. Check it out in the color section.

After you've turned your picture into black and white, however, it doesn't have to stay that way. You can substitute any two colors for black and white, or leave the white and just change the black to a color. To do that, choose Enhance, Adjust Color, Adjust Hue/Saturation, and check the Colorize box. Drag the Lightness slider to the right so that you can see the color in the formerly black areas, and then drag the Hue slider till you get a color you like.

You can also use the Threshold command to find the darkest and lightest areas of your image. Drag the slider all the way to the right and then back to the left again until you see white; that white is the lightest part of the image. Do the same in reverse—drag the slider all the way left and then slowly right—to find the darkest point in the picture. You can use this information in many ways; for example, the darkest and lightest areas of the image are the best spots to click with the eyedropper when you're using the Remove Color Cast command because they're the closest to pure black and white.

Using Weird Effects

I think you're going to enjoy these next effects. These tend to produce pictures that look, well, downright odd in some way. But you never know what might inspire you to produce something truly unique; give these filters a try and add them to your repertoire. Maybe someday one of these will be a part of your masterwork.

> Several of these filters are available in the Filter Gallery, which you might recall makes it very easy to compare their effects with those of other filters and offers a nice, large preview area. You can also use the Filter Gallery to apply more than one filter or more than one instance of the same filter at the same time.

Neon Glow

Using three different colors, this filter adds an eerie glow to the picture. All right, technically it doesn't have to be eerie, but it usually ends up that way. When you apply Neon Glow, Photoshop Elements blurs the picture a bit, turns the highlights into the Foreground color, turns the shadows into the Background color, and adds the glow color, which you choose in the Neon Glow dialog, to the shadows, edging into the midtones. The higher you set the Glow Size, the more glow color is added to the image; you have a second slider to control Glow Brightness (see Figure 23.10). Choose Filter, Artistic, Neon Glow to get there.

FIGURE 23.10
Is it a radioactive toddler? Or simply one whose mother has gone way too far with Photoshop Elements? You decide.

Plastic Wrap

Ever wanted to wrap a picture in plastic wrap, just to see how it looked? Me neither. Nonetheless, you can simulate this effect using the Plastic Wrap filter. The effect actually looks sort of like a shiny embossing method; choose Filter, Artistic, Plastic Wrap to try it out (see Figure 23.11). You can use three sliders to fine-tune the effect:

► **Highlight Strength**—Controls the height of the embossing effect.

► **Detail**—Determines how closely the plastic follows the apparent contours of the objects in the picture. I say "apparent" because Photoshop Elements interprets a patterned area as a bumpy surface. This explains why there are so many more wrinkles in the plastic covering the tiger cat in Figure 23.11 than in that covering the black-and-white cat.

► **Smoothness**—Sets the gloss level for the surface of the plastic.

FIGURE 23.11
These cats should keep very well in the refrigerator.

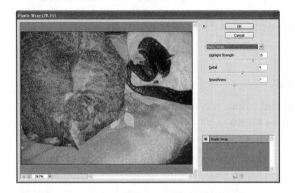

Diffuse Glow

This filter yields an effect much like that of Neon Glow, but with just one glow color. That's the Background color, and it's applied to the image's highlight areas. Because it adds only one color to the picture, this filter is slightly less likely than Neon Glow to take the picture entirely out of this world; just make sure your Background color is set to a nice, friendly color before invoking the filter, and you should be fine. Choose Filter, Distort, Diffuse Glow, then adjust the filter's three sliders (see Figure 23.12):

► **Clear Amount**—Enables the glow color to emanate from the entire layer or selection. Turn it all the way down to make the entire image glow and all the way up to make the whole thing clear, with just a few glowing spots.

► **Glow Amount**—Controls the size of each glowing area.

► **Graininess**—Adds noise to the glowing areas.

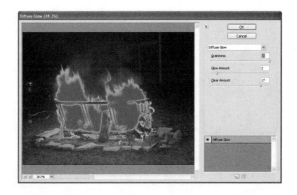

FIGURE 23.12
I used a blue glow to turn these flames blue instead of yellow.

Ocean Ripple

The Ocean Ripple filter (choose Filter, Distort, Ocean Ripple) is supposed to make it look as though the picture is underwater. I think it actually looks more like an Impressionist painting (hmmmm…), but it's definitely funky, whatever you think it resembles (see Figure 23.13). You have two sliders to control the effect: Ripple Size and Ripple Magnitude. The former controls the size of the ripples themselves, and the latter determines how many ripples are placed in the picture.

FIGURE 23.13
Is the picture underwater? Is it a reflection? What's your take on Ocean Ripple?

Wave

If you're serious about watery effects, Wave should satisfy you (choose Filter, Distort, Wave). Wave offers a lot of settings to fiddle with, and the preview area in its dialog box is tiny, so you can easily spend an entire afternoon going back and forth between the image and the Wave dialog box, undoing and redoing to get the effect just right (see Figure 23.14). Waves are much like Ocean Ripples, only larger, and you can determine how many points they originate from. Here are the controls that the Wave filter offers:

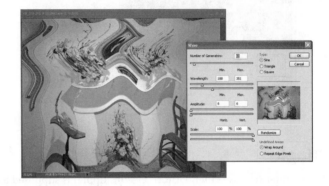

▶ First, you can choose a wave type in the Type area: Sine (curved), Triangle, or Square.

▶ Drag the slider to set a value for Number of Generators.

▶ Adjust the minimum and maximum Wavelength sliders to set the relative distance from one wave to the next and determine how much that distance varies. If both sliders are set to the same number, the waves will be evenly spaced.

▶ Do the same with the minimum and maximum Amplitude sliders to set the relative wave height.

▶ Drag the horizontal and vertical Scale sliders to set the actual height and width of the waves.

▶ Choose Wrap Around or Repeat Edge Pixels to determine how the image's edges are handled. Wrap Around uses pixels from the opposite side of the picture to fill in any gaps along the edge, and Repeat Edge Pixels just stretches the pixels along the edges of the image to fill in gaps.

Click Randomize to insert a random group of settings generated by Photoshop Elements. Keep clicking until you like what you see.

Solarize

Everyone knows that you shouldn't expose undeveloped film to regular light, or you'll destroy the image. But what a lot of people *don't* know is that, actually, if you allow in some light at just the right second during the developing process, you can create a cool effect that combines a negative and a positive image (see Figure 23.15, both here and in the color section). This filter doesn't have any dialog box; it's executed as soon as you choose the command, and you don't get to set any options.

The Solarize filter (choose Filter, Stylize, Solarize) generally produces a somewhat dark image, so you'll probably want to brighten the picture either before or after you apply the filter. Try it both ways to see which works better for the particular image you're editing.

FIGURE 23.15
This picture started out with yellow flowers, but Solarize made them blue. When I lightened the picture, the colors turned very intense.

Summary

The effects you learned about in this hour are unconventional, but they can potentially turn a picture into something really special. And I still haven't shown you all the filters Photoshop Elements has to offer; you'll just have to check out the rest for yourself. Meanwhile, however, you learned how to use Liquify, Gradient Map, Invert, Posterize, Threshold, Neon Glow, Plastic Wrap, Diffuse Glow, Ocean Ripple, Wave, and Solarize.

Q&A

Q. *Why does the Liquify effect look so familiar? I've seen it before, but I can't remember where.*

A. As it happens, the artist I mentioned in the last hour, Salvador Dalí, was known for painting "soft" objects that drooped all over the place. His most famous painting is *The Persistence of Memory,* featuring liquefied clocks (see www.artchive.com/artchive/d/dali/persistence.jpg).

Q. *Can I use Threshold to convert a picture to red and green, or blue and orange, instead of black and white?*

A. No, but you can replace black and white with other colors after applying the Threshold filter. You've learned several ways to accomplish this: using Hue/Saturation, selecting and filling an area, and using the Replace Color command.

Q. *I can't seem to get anywhere with the Wave filter settings. There are just too many sliders, and I don't know what to do with them all.*

A. If you can't settle on numbers that you like for the Wave filter, click Randomize to generate a random group of settings. Keep clicking until you come up with something you like. As you try different combinations, try to pay attention to how the different numbers affect the results.

Workshop

We're almost done! You've accomplished so much, and I hope you're enjoying learning about Photoshop Elements as much as I'm enjoying showing it to you.

Quiz

1. Which two filters have a similar effect?

   A. Solarize

   B. Posterize

   C. Invert

   D. Threshold

2. Setting the number of Levels in the Posterize dialog to 3 results in _____ total colors in the image.

   A. 3

   B. 6

   C. 9

   D. 36

Quiz Answers

1. **A and C.** Solarize inverts some of the colors in the image, and Invert does the same to the entire image.

2. **C.** Each of the color channels (red, green, and blue) will have three levels, resulting in a total of nine colors in the Posterized picture.

Activity

Pick one of the filters you saw used in this hour and choose an image to use it on. First, apply the filter to the original image; then go back and process the picture in different ways before you apply the filter. Try lightening it, darkening it, increasing the contrast, increasing the saturation, and anything else you can think of.

Creating Photo Projects

What You'll Learn in This Hour:

▶ Creating professionally printed books and calendars from your photos

▶ Designing print-at-home projects such as scrapbook pages and CD covers

▶ Ordering prints and flipbooks from within Photoshop Elements

You can work with a photo for only so long before you really need to *do* something with it. Whether that's simply printing it or something as ambitious as featuring it in a hardbound book of your favorite photos, Photoshop Elements has a way for you to get the job done. All these tasks appear in the Create tab of both the Editor and the Organizer, and they all come with step-by-step instructions that you won't have any trouble following. So instead of repeating those instructions here, I'd like to just show you what several of the Create projects look like. By the end of this hour, you should be mightily inspired to start creating your own photo projects.

Books

Professionally printed photo books have become incredibly popular in the last few years. They make wonderful gifts, and I know a professional photographer who uses books he orders from Shutterfly.com as his actual portfolios. We owe it all to the marked improvement in the quality of on-demand digital printing in recent years.

Photoshop Elements' books can range from 20 to 80 pages and can use any of 45 different predesigned templates. To start creating a book in Photoshop Elements, first start up the Organizer and choose the photos you want to feature in the book. Then click the Photo Book button on the Create tab in either the Editor or the Organizer. (If you're starting out in the Editor, make sure you're looking at the Projects side of the Create tab.) After you choose a cover photo and a template (see Figure 24.1), you can check Auto-Fill with

Project Bin Photos and click Done; Photoshop Elements creates the book for you (see Figure 24.2). Or, if you prefer, you can choose a layout for each page and place the photos yourself.

When you click the Order button, Photoshop Elements turns the book's pages into a PDF and connects you to the Kodak EasyShare Gallery website. At this point, you choose a cover material (leather, linen, or the like) and fill in your ordering information. The books start at about $30 and go up as you add more pages or use more expensive cover materials.

Calendars

As with photo books, calendars featuring your own photos are a fabulous gift. You know the recipient can always use a calendar, right? And if you buy one for your home office, it can be a tax-deductible business expense! How can you go wrong?

You can use as many photos as you like. Select your photos in the Organizer and click Photo Calendar in the Create tab. From here, this procedure is a bit different from the one for creating a book. Instead of choosing your design in Photoshop Elements, you're started right off at the Kodak site, with your selected photos uploaded right after you log in so that you can create the design there on the website (see Figure 24.3). Again, you need to choose a template, and you have the option of choosing a layout for each month and specifying the photos that go in it, or letting Photoshop Elements fill in the pages automatically. When all the pages are complete, you can preview the calendar (see Figure 24.4) and then order it; the books cost $20 apiece.

FIGURE 24.3
You start your calendar order by choosing a template.

FIGURE 24.4
When the calendar is complete, you can preview all the pages before ordering; if you want, you can go back and make changes.

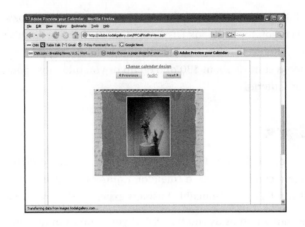

Photo Collages

I have no idea why Adobe didn't just call this project Scrapbook Pages, because that's clearly what it was designed to produce. Regardless, you start by choosing your photos in the Organizer and clicking the Photo Collage button on the Create tab. You're presented with three choices of paper size (8.5" × 11", 12" × 12", or 10.25" × 9") and the same selection of templates that you can use for photo books (see Figure 24.5). Here, however, you have to choose a layout; Photoshop Elements won't choose one for you. When that's done, you can have the photos dropped into place automatically or you can place them yourself, and you can choose whether to include captions. When you click Done, your page is created (see Figure 24.6).

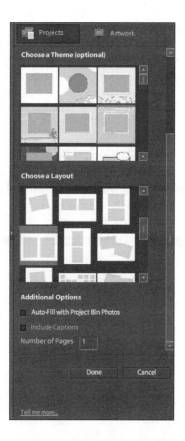

FIGURE 24.5
The layouts vary from single-photo pages to those with photos piled all over the place.

FIGURE 24.6
The page is complete and ready to print.

Prints and Stamps

Most of us spend a lot of time emailing photos and viewing pictures on the Web. But the traditional photo print is by no means dead. And did you know you can order custom stamps with your own photos on them? And use them on real letters as real postage?

Ordering prints works just the way it would on any website. You select your photos in the Organizer and choose More Options, Order Prints in the Create tab. You're taken to a login page for Kodak EasyShare Gallery, then a page where you can choose sizes and quantities (see Figure 24.7). After that, all you have to do is specify names and addresses for the prints' delivery and give your credit card info.

FIGURE 24.7
The order form indicates the sizes at which you'll be able to print each photo.

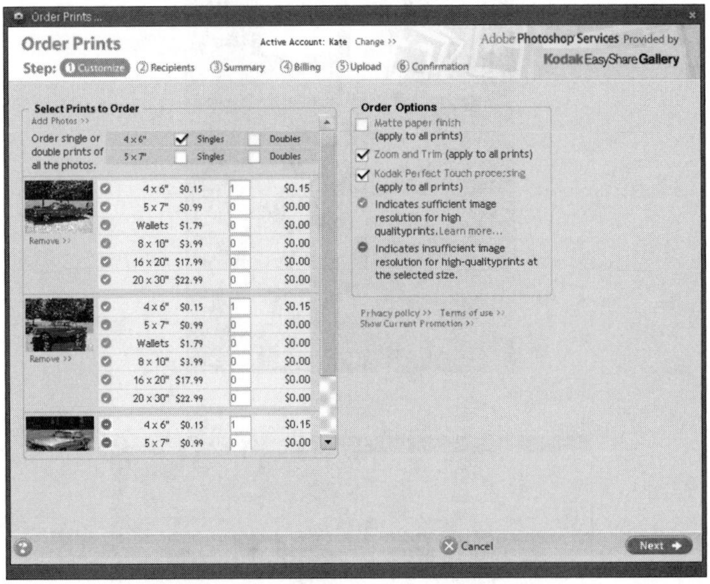

Ordering stamps is almost as simple. First you select your pictures in the Organizer; then you choose More Options, PhotoStamps. Photoshop Elements uploads your photos to the Stamps.com website, and you choose which one you want to turn into a stamp (see Figure 24.8). Then you have the opportunity to rotate the picture, if needed, add a custom border, and choose the denomination (see Figure 24.9). After that, the only thing left to do is give your shipping and payment information.

FIGURE 24.8
You can upload more than one photo at a time, but you can use only one image per stamp.

FIGURE 24.9
Custom borders come in several categories.

Disc Jackets and Labels

The mix tape has gone the way of the dinosaur, but not so the mix CD. And if you're going to the trouble of creating a mix CD, why not jazz it up with a custom label and jacket? These are both print-your-own projects; for the labels, you also need the right media: pre-scored sticky CD labels. You can get these at any office supply store from companies such as Avery.

▼   **Try it Yourself**

Create a CD Jacket

The steps for creating a CD jacket and a DVD jacket are the same. For this project, let's make a jacket for a new mix CD I'm putting together in iTunes. Follow these steps:

1. Begin by choosing photos in the Organizer and clicking the More Options menu. Choose CD Jacket, DVD Jacket, or CD/DVD Label—in this case, we're creating a CD jacket.

2. Choose an appropriate theme and a layout, and click Done. Photoshop Elements drops your photos into the layout.

3. Rearrange the photos, if you want, by dragging and dropping them into different slots using the Move tool.

4. To change a photo's size, position within its frame, or angle, double-click it (see Figure 24.10).

FIGURE 24.10
Here I'm rotating the larger photo slightly so it will be straight.

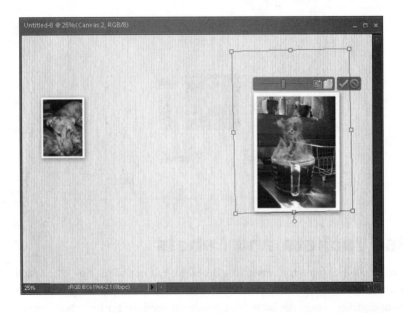

Oddly, the templates don't include any text, so you need to add your own titles and credits to the jacket yourself using the Type tool. If you need to review how to do that, turn back to Hour 8, "Adding Type."

▲

Cards

You have two choices when it comes to cards; you can design and print your own, or you can use your photos to design a professionally printed card and order as many as you need.

The first option requires you to select a photo in the Organizer and choose More Options, Greeting Card in the Create tab. Again, you get to choose a theme and a layout. After you do so, Photoshop Elements drops your photo or photos into a 5" × 7" document that you're free to embellish as you'd like before printing. You'll probably want to add text, and you can edit the picture in any other way you like (see Figure 24.11).

FIGURE 24.11
The flamingos on my banner photo go perfectly with the card's beach theme.

Then you'll need to print the card, and here's where things get a bit tricky. The image is only the front of the card, so if you want to make a folding card, you need to position the image correctly on the printed page (off to one end), and then fold it and trim it, with no markings on the page to guide you. I'm sure you'll be able to manage, but it's a bit surprising that Adobe doesn't offer more assistance.

If you need a pile of cards for the holidays, you probably won't want to print, trim, and fold them all yourself. Not to worry—the Kodak EasyShare Gallery site can also turn your photo into as many cards as you need. Select the perfect photo in the Organizer, and then choose More Options, Order Kodak Photo Greeting Cards in the Create tab. You're whisked away to the Kodak site, where you log in, click to start uploading your photos, and begin designing your cards (see Figure 24.12).

FIGURE 24.12
My card uses
the Blue Paper
template.

After choosing a template, you can add text to accompany the photo. You don't get to choose the color or font, however. When you're done, all you have to do is enter your shipping and payment info to order your cards. They run about $17 for 20 cards—not a bad deal at all.

Summary

This last hour showed you some of the ways you can make use of all the great photos you've been taking, especially now that you know how to make them even greater. If you need to go back and review anything in previous hours (such as the printing information in Hour 9), go right ahead. You've got all the time in the world.

Q&A

Q. *Do I need special paper to print all these projects?*

A. You don't *need* it, but it's a good idea to get some. You can use coated photo paper to make your photos look stunning, or you can try different "fancy" papers to see which ones take the ink best.

Q. *Some of these projects are bigger than a sheet of letter-size paper. How am I supposed to print those?*

A. Well, the printer you have now might not be able to. In that case, you'll probably want to get these projects printed at Kinko's or your favorite local print shop. You can order large prints online for lower prices, too. Or you can buy a new printer; HP has models selling for less than $200 that can handle 11" × 17" paper.

Workshop

Just a couple more questions to keep you on your toes....

Quiz

1. Which of the following isn't a photo project found on the Create tab?

    A. CD labels

    B. Recipe cards

    C. Greeting cards

    D. Calendars

2. What famous photography company is responsible for printing the photo projects that you don't print yourself?

    A. Fuji

    B. Canon

    C. Kodak

    D. Olympus

Quiz Answers

1. B. But now that you're an expert at Photoshop Elements, I have no doubt that you can design and print your own recipe cards.

2. C. Kodak has been in the photography business since 1880.

Activities

Guess what? This hour has no activities. You're done with the book, and you're on your own. Explore, experiment, and always remember to have fun!

Index

roundness, 402

scatter, 401

spacing, 402

tips, 399-400

brushes. *See also* Brush tool

Color Replacement, 30,
251-252

Healing

bleeding edges, 232

painting over areas, 289

removing dust &
scratches, 231-232

Impressionist, 402-404

Quick Selection, 27, 116

Selection Brush tool,
117-118

Spot Healing

removing dust &
scratches, 232

tears/folds, 293

tips, 399-400

Bubble Jet Set website, 163

built-in presets, 42

Burn tool, 30, 287-289

burning black and white photos,
287-289

C

calendars, creating, 457

cameras

connecting, 65

raw file format, 48

transferring photos from, 63

card readers, 66-68

USB cables, 65-66

canvas

extension colors, 75

size

choosing, 40

modifying, 73-75

Canvas Size dialog box, 74

card readers, importing photos,
66-68

cards, creating, 463-464

casts (color), 305-307

CD jackets/labels, creating,
461-462

cell phones

compatibility, 64

transferring photos from,
63-66

CF (CompactFlash) cards, 66

Chalk & Charcoal filter, 378

chalk effect, 378

Change Text Orientation button
(Options bar), 141

charcoal effect, 378

Choose Contact Source dialog
box, 172

choosing

canvas

extension color, 75

size, 40

colors, 103

Color Picker, 387-390

Color Swatches palette,
390-391

Eyedropper tool, 391

file formats, 50-51

fonts, 138-139

paper, 156

photos

Photo Browser, 20

selection tools, 27

printers, 151

color laser, 153-154

dye sublimation, 153

inkjet, 152

Quick Fixes, 97

Selection tools, 132

Clone Stamp tool, 30

backgrounds, creating, 315

painting over areas, 289

removing small objects,
223-225

tears/folds, 293

clouds, 350

Clouds filter, 350

CMYK (cyan, magenta, yellow, and
black), 149

cnet.com website, 151

collages, creating, 458

color

average, 344

blend colors, 425

brightness, 104

canvas extension colors, 75

casts, 245

choosing, 103

Color Picker, 387-390

Color Swatches palette,
390-391

Eyedropper tool, 391

CMYK, 149

color systems, 149-151

converting to black and white,
248

fixing

Auto Color Correction, 242

casts, 305-307

Color Curves tool, 255

Color Variations, 243-244,
262

Guided Edit mode, 7,
272-274

Hue/Saturation dialog box,
246-248

photos, 104-105

Remove Color Cast, 245

selective adjustments,
307-308

shadows/highlights, 309

skin tone, 256-257

Smart Fix, 99

gamuts, 149

hand-coloring black and white
photos, 315-316

HSB, 150

hue, 103

intensity, 311-312

management, enabling,
155-156

posterizing, 444

problems, 304

472

creating

How can we make this index more useful? Email us at indexes@samspublishing.com

COLOR GALLERY

FIGURE 6.6
Hour 6, page 105

FIGURE 8.8
Hour 8, page 142

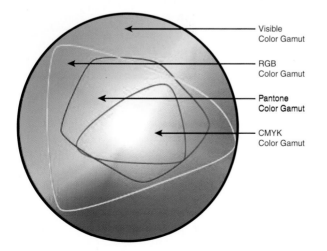

Visible
Color Gamut

RGB
Color Gamut

Pantone
Color Gamut

CMYK
Color Gamut

FIGURE 9.1
Hour 9, page 150

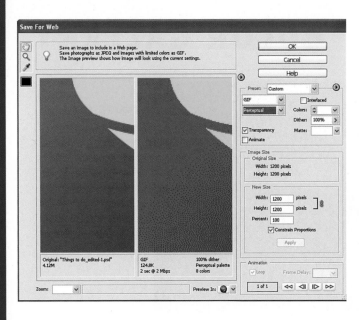

FIGURE 10.2

Hour 10, page 167

FIGURE 13.7

Hour 13, page 227

FIGURE 14.1
Hour 14, page 240

FIGURE 14.2
Hour 14, page 241

FIGURE 14.3
Hour 14, page 242

FIGURE 14.4
Hour 14, page 243

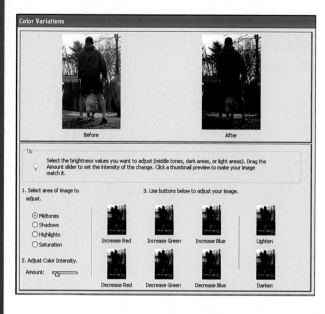

FIGURE 14.5

Hour 14, page 244

FIGURE 14.9

Hour 14, page 249

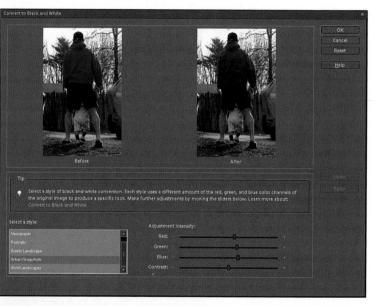

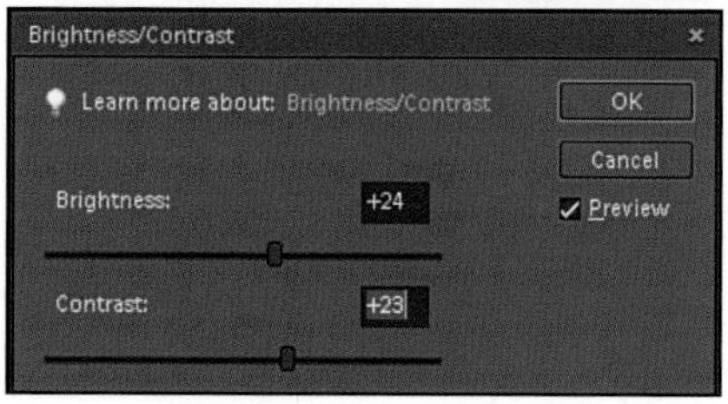

FIGURE 14.17

Hour 14, page 257

FIGURE 14.24
Hour 14, page 263

FIGURE 17.1
Hour 17, page 305

FIGURE 17.15
Hour 17, page 316

FIGURE 20.1
Hour 20, page 372

FIGURE 20.16
Hour 20, page 383

FIGURE 20.17
Hour 20, page 383

FIGURE 20.18
Hour 20, page 384

Normal

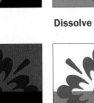

Dissolve

Darken

Multiply

Color Burn

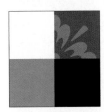

Linear Burn

Darker Color

Lighten

Screen

Color Dodge

Linear Dodge (Add)

Lighter Color

Overlay

Soft Light

Hard Light

Vivid Light

Linear Light

Pin Light

Hard Mix

Difference

Exclusion

Hue

Saturation

Color

Luminosity